T0208500

Recasting Egalitarianism

The Real Utopias Project

Series editor: Erik Olin Wright

The Real Utopias Project embraces a tension between dreams and practice. It is founded on the belief that what is pragmatically possible is not fixed independently of our imaginations, but is itself shaped by our visions. The fulfillment of such a belief involves 'real utopias': utopian ideals that are grounded in the real potentials for redesigning social institutions.

In its attempt at sustaining and deepening serious discussion of radical alternatives to existing social practices, the Real Utopias Project examines various basic institutions – property rights and the market, secondary associations, the family, the welfare state, among others – and focuses on specific proposals for their fundamental redesign. The books in the series are the result of workshop conferences, at which groups of scholars are invited to respond to provocative manuscripts.

Recasting Egalitarianism

New Rules for Communities, States and Markets

The Real Utopias Project
Volume III

◆

SAMUEL BOWLES and HERBERT GINTIS

with contributions by
Harry Brighouse, Michael Carter, Steven Durlauf,
Paula England, David Gordon, Daniel Hausman, Karla
Hoff, Andrew Levine, Elaine McCrate, Karl Ove Moene,
Elinor Ostrom, Ugo Pagano, John E. Roemer, Peter Skott,
Michael Wallerstein, Erik Olin Wright

Edited and introduced by Erik Olin Wright

VERSO
London • New York

First published by Verso 1998
© the collection Verso 1998
© individual contributions the authors 1998
All rights reserved

Verso
UK: 6 Meard Street, London W1F 0EG
USA: 20 Jay Street, Suite 1010, Brooklyn, NY 11201

Verso is the imprint of New Left Books

ISBN 978-1-85984-255-3

British Library Cataloguing in Publication Data
A catalogue record for this book is available from the British Library

Library of Congress Cataloging-in-Publication Data
Bowles, Samuel.
    Recasting egalitarianism : new rules for
communities, states and markets / Samuel Bowles and
Herbert Gintis.
        p.   cm. — (Real Utopias Project ; v. 3)
    ISBN 1–85984–863–X (cloth). — ISBN 1–85984–255–0 (pbk.)
    1. Income distribution.   2. Equality.
3. Competition.   4. Markets.   I. Gintis, Herbert.
II. Title.   III. Series: Real Utopias Project (Series)
; v. 3.
HB523.B69   1998
339.2 — dc21   98–35498
                                                              CIP

Typeset by SetSystems Ltd, Saffron Waldon

Contents

Acknowledgements

We would like to thank gratefully the John D. and Catherine T. MacArthur Foundation for their very generous support in initially funding the Real Utopias Project conference on which this book is based and subsequently funding part of the production costs of the book itself. We would also like to thank the University of Wisconsin Alumni Research Foundation and the Anonymous Fund for providing funding for the conference. The staff of the A. E. Havens Center provided invaluable help in arranging the logistics of the conference and much of the administrative coordination for the preparation of the book.

Earlier versions of a number of papers included in this volume were previously published in a special issue of *Politics & Society*, copyright Sage Publications, Inc., December 1996, vol. 24, number 4, and are reproduced here with permission. They are:

Samuel Bowles and Herbert Gintis, 'Efficient Redistribution: New Rules for Markets, States and Communities', pp. 307–42.

Daniel Hausman, 'Problems with Supply-side Egalitarianism', pp. 343–52.

Erik Olin Wright, 'Equality, Community and "Efficient Redistribution"', pp. 353–68.

Karl Ove Moene and Michael Wallerstein, 'Redistribution of Assets versus Redistribution of Income', pp. 369–82.

John E. Roemer, 'Efficient Redistribution: Comment', pp. 383–90.

Steven Durlauf, 'Associational Redistribution: A Defense', pp. 391–410.

Karla Hoff, 'Market Failures and Distribution of Wealth: A Perspective from the Economics of Information', pp. 411–32.

David M. Gordon, 'Conflict and Cooperation: An Empirical Glimpse of the Imperatives of Efficiency and Redistribution', pp. 433–56.

Harry Brighouse, 'Egalitarian Liberals and School Choice', pp. 457–86.

We dedicate these pages to the memory of our friend and colleague, David Gordon, 1944–1996.

Preface
The Real Utopias Project
Erik Olin Wright

'Real Utopia' seems like a contradiction in terms. Utopias are fantasies, morally inspired designs for social life unconstrained by realistic considerations of human psychology and social feasibility. Realists eschew such fantasies. What is needed are hard-nosed proposals for pragmatically improving our institutions. Instead of indulging in utopian dreams we must accommodate to practical realities.

The Real Utopias Project embraces this tension between dreams and practice. It is founded on the belief that what is pragmatically possible is not fixed independently of our imaginations, but is itself shaped by our visions. Self-fulfilling prophecies are powerful forces in history, and while it may be Polyannish to say 'where there is a will there is a way', it is certainly true that without 'will' many 'ways' become impossible. Nurturing clear-sighted understandings of what it would take to create social institutions free of oppression is part of creating a political will for radical social changes to reduce oppression. A vital belief in a utopian destination may be necessary to motivate people to leave on the journey from the status quo in the first place, even though the actual destination may fall short of the utopian ideal. Yet, vague utopian fantasies may lead us astray, encouraging us to embark on trips that have no real destinations at all, or worse still, which lead us over some unforeseen abyss. Along with 'where there is a will there is a way', the human struggle for emancipation confronts 'the road to hell is paved with good intentions'. What we need, then, are 'real utopias': utopian ideals that are grounded in the real potentials of humanity, utopian destinations that have pragmatically accessible waystations, utopian designs of institutions that can inform our practical tasks of muddling through in a world of imperfect conditions for social change. These are the goals of the Real Utopias Project.

The Real Utopias Project is an attempt at sustaining and deepening serious discussion of radical alternatives to existing institutions. The objective is to focus on specific proposals for the fundamental redesign of basic social institutions rather than on either vague, abstract formulations of grand designs, or on small reforms of existing practices. In practical terms, the Real Utopias Project consists of a series of workshop conferences, each revolving around a manuscript that lays out the basic outlines of a radical institutional proposal. The essays presented at these conferences are then revised for the books in the Real Utopias Project.

Introduction
Erik Olin Wright

The market – defined roughly as uncoerced exchanges between people of goods and services – is one of the many possible ways of organizing the allocation of things people want in a society and coordinating the complex decisions and practices that constitute an economy. No one believes that markets should be the only way goods and services are distributed. Even the most ardent free-market libertarian believes in the necessity of some taxation for supporting the 'night watchman state' and the appropriateness of parents coercing their children to perform household chores. And, equally, virtually no one today believes that a complex economy can function without some presence of markets. No serious thinker on the left still upholds the vision of comprehensive centralized planning as a viable institutional design to replace capitalism. The issue, then, is how market exchanges are to be articulated with other institutional mechanisms, not whether an economically developed society can work effectively with only markets or with no markets.

While there may be near universal acknowledgment of the need for markets, the right and left remain divided in their basic belief about how markets and nonmarket institutions should be linked to advance certain core values. The right is highly skeptical of nonmarket institutions of economic regulation and allocation, and while acknowledging their necessity, has wanted to hedge them in, restrict them to the minimal possible domains out of fear that nonmarket mechanisms are like Frankenstein – once created they tend to run amok and be uncontrollable. Accordingly the right sees the alleged virtues of the market – especially enhanced individual freedom and economic efficiency – as constantly threatened by the excessive encroachments of the state. The left, in contrast, has generally been skeptical of the moral and economic virtues of markets, and while acknowledging the practical necessity of markets, wants to hem them in within effective political and normative limits on the grounds that markets are corrosive of other values and will constantly generate pressures to expand. The danger that such interference by the democratic affirmative state will become oppressive is seen as much less serious than the danger of weakly regulated markets generating socially explosive inequalities, perpetuating oppressive conditions of daily life for many, and fostering a moral callousness that is profoundly destructive of basic human values.

At the moment, the right-wing perspective on markets is certainly dominant ideologically. Many on the left have significantly softened their traditional hostility to market institutions, acknowledging that strong market mechanisms are important for certain kinds of efficiency considerations and that excessive restrictions on voluntary exchanges can produce all sorts of undesirable consequences. While many people may continue to worry about the consequences of unfettered markets, there is much less confidence on the left today about how to properly design such fetters so as to reap the virtues of markets while avoiding their negative consequences.

This volume in the *Real Utopias Project* intervenes on this ideological terrain. In their provocative proposal for what they call 'efficient redistribution', Samuel Bowles and Herbert Gintis argue that if institutions are properly designed, markets can actually enhance the achievement of certain core values on the left, especially equality, while at the same time preserving (and maybe even enhancing) various forms of efficiency. With such 'new rules for markets, states and communities', they argue, left-wing consequences can be built into institutions traditionally defended by the right. This proposal is more than a reluctant acknowledgment that for pragmatic reasons the left has to tolerate certain aspects of market relations; it is a left-wing affirmation of the positive virtues of markets under suitably designed rules of the game.

At the core of this proposal is a simple idea. The twin goals of enhanced and sustainable equality – a value stressed by the left – and economic efficiency – a value emphasized by the right – can both be met if the basic assets which underlie various kinds of transactions are redistributed in a particular way. Specifically, Bowles and Gintis argue that equality and efficiency can both be advanced if assets are broadly redistributed from principals to agents. Here is the basic argument:

One of the commonly alleged virtues of markets is that markets hold people who make consequential decisions accountable for their actions. This personal accountability is responsible for much of the vaunted efficiency of markets, for it creates incentive structures in which people have an interest in avoiding waste and in correcting mistakes when they occur. Much of what are called 'market failures' in the standard economics literature can be considered situations in which such accountability breaks down. Above all, when there is a conflict of interest between 'principals' and 'agents' it can often happen that agents can make consequential decisions which are deficient from the point of view of principals, but the principal has no effective way of holding the agent accountable, at least not without expending considerable resources in monitoring and sanctioning the actions of the agent.

Bowles and Gintis propose that if the assets used in economic transactions are properly distributed, then many of these accountability-linked market failures can be avoided. Specifically, if assets are redistributed from principals to agents so that the agents directly experience the consequences of their actions, then such efficiency-enhancing accountability will be strengthened. Such redistribution will also further the goals of the left by generating a much more egalitarian distribution of all sorts of valuable assets in the population. The results will be what might be termed a radically egalitarian market economy in which the affirmative state plays a significant role in maintaining the egalitarian character of the asset distributions, but the actual use of those assets takes place within relatively unfettered market relations.

The opening essay in this volume of the *Real Utopias Project* lays out the underlying logic of this proposal in some detail. This is followed by a series of chapters which respond to various aspects of the model. Some of these essays are highly critical of the proposal on both normative and institutional grounds. Other contributors agree broadly with the idea of an asset redistributive market economy and explore various additional ramifications of the Bowles and Gintis proposal. Some of the contributions revolve around philosophical issues about the nature of the proposals. Others deal with hard-core economics questions about the details of the model and its elaboration. And still others focus more on empirical matters linked to the problem of assets, equality and efficiency. Taken together, this collection provides a context for a serious discussion of the problem of designing economic institutions in ways which capture the virtues of markets while neutralizing at least some of their destructive consequences.

PART I

A Proposal for Egalitarian Markets

Efficient Redistribution:
New Rules for Markets, States and Communities
Samuel Bowles and Herbert Gintis*

1. Introduction

Socialism, radical democracy, social democracy, and other egalitarian movements have flourished where they successfully crafted the demands of distributive justice into an economic strategy capable of addressing the problem of scarcity and thereby promising to improve living standards on the average. Land redistribution, social insurance, egalitarian wage policies, central planning, and human investment expenditures have all been attractive when they promised to link the redistribution of economic reward to enhancing the performance of the economic system as a whole.

For this reason economic analysis has always been central to the construction of more democratic and egalitarian alternatives to capitalism as well as egalitarian reforms of capitalism itself. Keynesian economics, for example, supported state regulation of the macroeconomy and was also provided a rationale for income redistribution to the less well-off who, by spending a larger portion of their incomes, could be relied upon to generate higher levels of demand for consumer

* Thanks to Pranab Bardhan, Robert Brenner, Albert Breton, G. A. Cohen, Steven Durlauf, Mehrene Larudee, Nancy Folbre, David Lewis, Karla Hoff, Paul Malherbe, John Roemer, Michele Salvati, Peter Skott, Philippe Van Parijs, Elisabeth Wood, Erik Wright, and members of the Political Economy Workshop at the University of Massachusetts for their valuable contributions to this paper. We would like to thank the MacArthur foundation for financial support. The ideas presented here are in part the result of literally hundreds of conversations (some of them extending over years) with grassroots political activists, trade unionists, policy makers, and elected officials attempting to forge a new egalitarian policy paradigm; we are indebted to them.

goods and thereby sustain higher levels of employment. Similarly, the model of general competitive equilibrium was deployed by market socialists, from Oskar Lange to John Roemer, to demonstrate the possibility and advantages of planning in a socialist economy.

But today both Keynesianism and planning lack credibility, and it appears that the left has run out of economic models.[1] Even among egalitarians, the conviction is widespread that while some combination of social democracy, market socialism and workplace democracy would be preferable on democratic or egalitarian grounds, only capitalism has a workable answer to the problem of scarcity. Economic theory has proven, one hears, that any but cosmetic modifications of capitalism in the direction of equality and democratic control will exact a heavy toll of reduced economic performance. Yet economic theory suggests no such thing. On the contrary, there are compelling economic arguments and ample empirical support for the proposition that there exist changes in the rules of the economic game which can foster both greater economic equality and improved economic performance. Indeed, as we will see, inequality is often an impediment to productivity.

Following an overview of our major propositions in the next section, we will take up the empirical evidence suggesting the possibility of a productivity-enhancing egalitarianism and the related evidence suggesting the obsolescence of older egalitarian models. We then address the peculiar capacities and disabilities of the institutional forms – markets, states and communities – upon which an egalitarian strategy must necessarily rely. We draw on this discussion to present a model of the relationship between the distribution of assets and the level of output in an economy, pointing to the contradictory effects of egalitarianism on productivity. We then present four concrete cases of egalitarian asset redistributions that support higher levels of economic performance. In our two penultimate sections we turn to the major problems intrinsic to our strategy of asset-based redistribution in a competitive economy and suggest how these drawbacks might be attenuated.

2. An Overview

Inequality fosters conflicts ranging from lack of trust in exchange relationships and incentive problems in the workplace to class conflict and ethnic clashes. To influence the outcomes of these conflicts, individuals and groups invest resources that otherwise might have been productively used. Also, high levels of conflict and the lack of agreed-upon rules of division with broad legitimacy often preclude solutions to the coordination failures that beset sophisticated economic systems. 'Coordination failures' occur when the independent actions of agents lead to outcomes less desirable than could have been achieved in the presence of coordinated action – examples are environmental pollution, unemployment, traffic jams, and the common inability of employers and workers to adopt potentially beneficial changes in work rules and technology. Since in highly unequal societies states often cannot or have little incentive to solve coordination failures, the result is not only the proliferation of market failures in the private economy, but a reduced capacity to attenuate these failures through public policy.

Economic performance depends on what may be termed the *structure of economic governance*: the rules of ownership, forms of competition, norms, and conventions that regulate the incentives and constraints faced by economic actors, and hence that determine the nature of coordination failures and their feasible solutions. Ideally, a structure of governance is a means of avoiding or attenuating coordination failures, but there is nothing in the process determining the evolution of governance structures that insures this result. Governance structures may endure because they are favored by powerful groups for whom they secure a large slice of a given pie, not because these structures foster the growth of the pie itself.

The relationship between inequality and economic performance is thus mediated by the structure of economic governance. Governance structures critically influence both the level of productivity and the degree of inequality in the economy. Correspondingly, the feasibility of distinct forms of governance is itself strongly influenced by the degree of inequality, and in particular by the nature and distribution of property rights. We will define a change in governance structures as *productivity enhancing* if the gainers could compensate the losers, except that the implied compensation need not be implementable under the informational conditions and other incentive problems in the economy. The proposals developed in this paper are then based on our first major claim: *inequality impedes economic performance by obstructing the evolution of productivity enhancing governance structures.* We offer three arguments in support of this position.

First, institutional structures supporting high levels of inequality are often costly to maintain. Solving economic problems requires a state empowered to intervene effectively in the economy. But an activist state is capable of using its power not only to improve economic efficiency, but also to redistribute income in response to populist pressures. For this reason economic elites may prefer a weak state in an inefficient economy to a strong state in an efficient economy. Moreover, states in highly unequal societies are often obliged to commit a large fraction of the economy's productive potential to enforcing the rules of the game from which the inequalities flow.

The private sector also incurs costs in enforcing inequality, in such forms as high levels of expenditure on work supervision and security personnel. Indeed, one might count high levels of unemployment itself as one of the enforcement costs of inequality, to the extent that the threat of job loss contributes to employers' labor discipline strategies: in less conflictual conditions, unutilized labor might be allocated to productive activities.[2] Moreover, in highly inegalitarian societies the insecurity of property rights is often widespread, militating against long-term investments by the rich and the poor alike.

A second reason for a positive relationship between efficiency and equality is that more equal societies may be capable of supporting levels of cooperation and trust unavailable in more economically divided societies. Yet both cooperation and trust are essential to economic performance, particularly where information relevant to exchanges is incomplete and unequally distributed in the population. Of course trust and cooperation do not appear in conventional economic theory. A time-honored prejudice among economists holds that there are two possible relationships among economic actors – unfettered competition or hierarchical command. Yet these do not exhaust the range of economic relationships essential to high levels of economic performance. In any economy, a third type of relationship is ubiquitous and essential: long-term agreements over the creation and sharing of the results of cooperative efforts.[3] Kenneth Arrow (1971, p. 22) writes:

> It is useful for individuals to have some trust in each other's word. In the absence of trust it would be very costly to arrange for alternative sanctions and guarantees, and many opportunities for mutually beneficial cooperation would have to be foregone ... norms of social behavior, including ethical and moral codes [may be] ... reactions of society to compensate for market failures.

In addition to the invisible hand of competition and the fist of command, a well-governed society must also rely on the handshake of trust.

One of the possible productivity effects of greater equality thus may operate through the political and cultural consequences of redistribution. A well-run welfare state or a relatively equal distribution of property holdings may foster the social solidarity necessary to support cooperation and trust. These and related sentiments frequently provide the basis for low-cost solutions to coordination failures.[4] By providing the cultural and political preconditions for bargained solutions with sufficient legitimacy to require little enforcement, egalitarian distributions of assets and income may contribute to the solution of complex problems that would otherwise be highly costly to solve.[5]

A third source of equality-productivity complementarity concerns the inefficient incentive structures that arise in economies with highly unequal asset distributions.[6] An example may make this clear. Consider a single owner of a machine who hires a single worker to operate the machine. The worker has little reason to supply a high level of effort, since the owner is the residual claimant on the income associated with the asset and hence receives the profit from the worker's labor. Thus without costly monitoring, productivity in the firm will suffer. But monitoring uses up resources that could have otherwise been productively employed. A rental contract in which the worker rents the machine from the owner for a fixed sum and becomes residual claimant on the entire income stream of the firm would of course avoid this particular incentive problem.[7] But this solution to the effort incentive difficulty simply displaces the conflict of interest to the issue of the treatment of the machine – in this case the firm's capital stock itself. For the worker would then be residual claimant on the income produced by the machine, but not on the value of the machine itself, and hence would have little incentive to maintain the asset.

The generic problem here is that behaviors critical to high levels of productivity – hard work, maintenance of productive equipment, risk-taking and the like – are difficult to monitor and hence cannot be fully specified in any contract enforceable at low cost. As a result, key economic actors, workers and managers, for example, cannot capture the productivity effects of their actions, as they would if, for instance, they were the residual claimants on the resulting income stream and asset value.

The result of these incentive problems is that a highly concentrated distribution of capital is often inefficient: there may exist a more egalitarian distribution, in which the worker becomes the owner of the firm's capital goods which, by more effectively addressing the incentive, monitoring, and maintenance problems involved, allows general improvements in well-being (including possible compensation for the former owner).[8]

This being the case, one might wonder why the redistribution does not come about spontaneously, for if worker ownership of the firm avoids incentive problems and supervision costs, it might be thought that the firm will be worth more to the worker than to the employer, so the worker would profit by borrowing to purchase the firm's capital stock. But an asset-poor worker cannot borrow large sums at the going rate of interest, so cannot purchase the firm's capital stock. Furthermore, the worker would be unlikely to agree to assume the risk of concentrated ownership of a risky asset, even if it could be financed. For this reason inefficient distributions of property rights may prove immune to disruption through private contracting despite the existence of other more efficient distributions.[9] More technically, inefficient property right distributions may be sustained in a competitive equilibrium.

Modern economies, of course, cannot avoid such incentive problems by implementing the simple property ownership structures appropriate to an idealized Robinson Crusoe world of individual production. The economies of scale that characterize all contemporary economies make team production ubiquitous. Thus free-riding and related agency problems will arise under any conceivable set of property distributions and institutional arrangements. None the less, structures of economic governance will differ markedly in the costliness of the incentive problems to which they give rise.

It will be clear from the above that devising governance structures capable of supporting both equality and higher living standards requires a fundamental rethinking of relationships between markets, states, and communities. The necessary reconstruction of political economy must therefore confront three widespread prejudices common among social scientists and political actors alike.

The first is that competitive markets determine prices that measure the real scarcity of goods and for this reason allocate resources efficiently. For the most part they do not; as we will see, the considerable contribution of markets to effective economic governance lies elsewhere.

The second prejudice, particularly widespread among egalitarians, is that in a suitably democratic society government intervention can efficiently supplant the private provision of goods and services where market failures occur. But state failures in the production and delivery of goods and services are as ubiquitous as market failures. As in the

Figure 1:   Alternative Approaches to Economic Policy

State \ Economy	No Market Failures	Market Failures
No State Failures	Both *laissez-faire* and planning can support optimal allocations	Keynesian and other state interventions can support optimal allocations
State Failures	*Laissez-faire* with minimal state can support optimal allocations	market/state/community complementarity can support second-best optima

case of markets, the distinctive capacities of the state in the process of economic governance are frequently overlooked by the advocates of interventionist policies.

The third prejudice, common across much of the political spectrum, is to see communities as archaic rather than modern institutions and to suppose that whatever social value communities have, their contribution to contemporary economic governance is minimal. By a 'community' we mean a group of individuals whose interactions are long-term, frequent, and personal. Families, residential neighborhoods and workplaces are communities in this sense. Moreover, while community governance structures cannot be subsumed under the rubrics of state and market, their viability critically depends on the structure of states and markets, and in particular on the nature and distribution of property rights implied by the structure of markets and states.[10]

In sum, the prejudices of conservative policy stem from its recognition of weaknesses in the state but not in the market as governance structures. This selective treatment leads to the view that the state is an arena of wasteful rent-seeking, while the market economy is efficient, a view from which exclusive reliance upon the market ineluctably follows. Advocates of egalitarian economic policy, by contrast, while treating the market system as riddled with coordination failures, have often failed to recognize the limitations of the state as a governance structure, and hence have treated the state as an effective instrument for the implementation of economic objectives. Both strands of political economy have overlooked the critical role of communities as governance structures.

These alternatives are summarized in figure 1. The optimism of post-Second World War Keynesian policies, and that of the neo-liberal policies that supplanted them, can be seen to flow from the choice of assumptions concerning the location of coordination failures (the lower-left to upper-right diagonal in figure 1). Our approach recognizes coordination failures in both state and market, and achieves only those (generally Pareto-inferior) allocations compatible with feasible incentive structures. Figure 1 also includes a fourth policy approach (the upper left corner) that does not recognize coordination problems in either economy or state. This position is taken both by some traditional neoclassical economics and its socialist adversaries, and implies that in the absence of market failures such as externalities, increasing returns to scale, and cyclical volatility, both *laissez-faire* and central planning can support optimal allocations.

Our reconstruction of egalitarian political economy begins by recognizing that markets, states, and communities, each with its characteristic capabilities and deficiencies, will necessarily play a complementary role in any governance structure worthy of support. A key to such a reconstruction is the recognition that the nature and distribution of property rights critically affects the workings of all three. This view reflects what may be termed the new economics of property, a distinguishing characteristic of which is the representation of ownership not simply as a claim on the residual income deriving from an asset, but the right of control of access to the asset and disposition over its use.

This view motivates our second major claim: *where hard work, innovation, maintenance of an asset and other behaviors essential to high levels of economic performance cannot be specified in costlessly enforceable contracts, the assignment of control rights and residual claimancy status influences the kinds of exchanges that are possible and the costs carrying out these exchanges.*

This second claim directly supports our third: *Some distributions of property rights are more efficient than others; in particular there exists an implementable class of distributions that are both more egalitarian and more efficient than the concentrations of asset holding observed in most capitalist economies.*[11]

The most important implication of the above is that egalitarian strategies should abandon what has hitherto been an exaggerated emphasis on overriding market outcomes through tax and transfer policies designed to attenuate the consequences of concentrated ownership. Given the high and apparently rising levels of inequality generated by the private sectors of the advanced economies in recent years, a redistribution of income of suitable magnitude to achieve even minimally acceptable levels of equality will incur prohibitive political and economic costs. The logic of this conundrum is inescapable. If the current degree of asset inequality is taken as given, market determined rewards will be correspondingly unequal, so the egalitarian project becomes one of superseding market outcomes and thereby undermining the beneficial disciplining effects of market competition.

A more promising approach is to identify those aspects of the concentrated ownership of assets that give rise to perverse incentives and costly enforcement strategies and then to devise asset redistributions that can attenuate the resulting coordination failures without introducing their own costly incentive problems. In contrast to income-based egalitarian strategies which are at best productivity-neutral, asset-based egalitarianism can in principle be productivity enhancing. This is true both because it can implement more efficient distributions of residual claimancy and control rights and because redistributing assets addresses a major cause of unequal incomes and thus gives greater scope for markets and other forms of competitive discipline.

3. Is Equality Passé?

Our confidence that such productivity enhancing asset redistributions can be effected may seem out of step with the pervasive contemporary skepticism concerning the viability of egalitarian alternatives. But the intellectual foundations of 'equality pessimism', as this frame of mind might be called, have been badly shaken. Recent research has both questioned the presumption that economic performance is best promoted by *laissez-faire* policies and cast doubt upon the existence of the fabled efficiency-equity trade-off, which asserts that the pursuit of egalitarian objectives necessarily impairs economic performance.

A comparison of the economic performance among nations supports no such presumption and reveals no such trade-off. Countries experiencing rapid productivity growth from the 1960s to the 1990s, including China, Japan, Singapore and South Korea, exhibit a degree of economic equality and a level of state involvement in economic decision-making considerably greater than in the relatively *laissez-faire* industrialized countries which, in the same time period, have experienced weak productivity growth and increases in economic inequality. The contrast with the relatively stagnant and highly unequal Latin American economies is even more stark. Systematic analysis of aggregate data on the level of income equality and rates of investment and productivity growth across nations fail to find evidence that equality impedes macro-economic performance. Our anal-

Figure 2:　Inequality and Productivity Growth 1979–1992

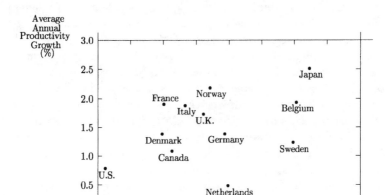

Average Annual Productivity Growth (%)

Degree of Equality: Ratio of income shares, bottom 20% to top 20%

In this figure, productivity growth is defined as an average annual rate of growth of gross domestic product per employed person, 1979–92 (US Bureau of Labor Statistics 1994). Data on income distribution is from the World Bank's World Development Report (various years). We have restricted our analysis to countries present in both the Bureau of Labor Statistics and the World Bank data sets.

Ideally one would use a measure of total factor productivity growth, but these measures are not available. Output per hour of labor input is generally available only for the manufacturing sector, which constitutes a small fraction of most economies. The data are from the comparative productivity growth data set of the US Bureau of Labor Statistics. The choice of dates also conveniently allows an assessment of the period of conservative economic hegemony in the US and the UK. (President Carter appointed Paul Volcker to head the US Federal Reserve System in 1979 and rapidly accelerated the deregulation process in the previous year.) Annual hours worked per employed person varies considerably among these countries (2034 in Japan and 1415 in Norway, for example), and productivity growth will be understated in those countries that experienced a reduction in hours over this period.

The simple correlation between our measure of equality and the rate of productivity growth is 0.32. However a regression of productivity growth on inequality (both singly and along with the initial productivity levels of each country converted to a common unit of account using purchasing power parities) indicates that the relationship is not statistically significant, though the positive covariance of equality and productivity remains even when accounting for initial productivity levels.

ysis of income equality and productivity growth appears in figure 2. Other studies support these conclusions.[12]

However, cross national comparisons of inequality and macroeconomic performance are of limited use in assessing the effects of policies to reduce inequality on economic performance. We are interested not

Figure 3: Post-war Growth in Long-term Perspective

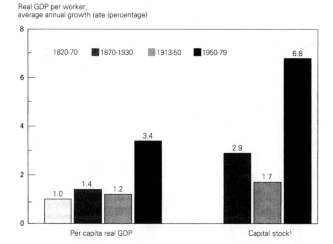

Real GDP per worker,
average annual growth rate (percentage)

Sources: see text. Capital stock is tangible, reproducible, non-residential fixed capital stock.

in the *correlates of equality* but in the *effects of egalitarian policies*. The fact that more equal countries have more rapid rates of economic growth could well be accounted for by a statistical association between measures of equality and unmeasured causes of economic growth. Determining the effects of a decision to redistribute land, or to raise the minimum wage requires the study of the evolution of policies and their outcomes over time.

Thus a better indicator of a positive relationship between egalitarian institutions and policies on the one hand and economic performance on the other is the fact that the advanced capitalist countries, taken as a whole, have grown faster under the aegis of the post-Second World War welfare state than in any other period for which the relevant data exist. In historical retrospect, the epoch of the ascendant welfare state and social democracy was capitalism's golden age. This relationship is exhibited in figure 3.[13]

We do not conclude that equality *per se* promotes high levels of economic performance. But a more modest inference seems inescapable: under favorable institutional circumstances egalitarian outcomes are not incompatible with the rapid growth of productivity and other valued macroeconomic outcomes.

'Equality pessimism' thus finds little support in the empirical record of macroeconomic performance. Rather the sense that egalitarian projects may now be unfeasible appears to derive more from the demise of a particular model of redistribution and from the way in which global competition is said to constrain the autonomy of nation states in their pursuit of egalitarian objectives.

The optimism of the golden age of egalitarian economic policy, roughly the first three decades following the Second World War, was fostered by the Keynesian belief that the expansion of publicly funded social services and transfers, as well as wage increases in the private sector, would promote full employment and economic growth. This belief served to minimize political opposition to egalitarian redistribution by promising 'soft redistribution': even the wealthy would benefit from policies to stabilize and expand aggregate demand and to provide adequate schooling and medical care for the work force.

Underlying this faith was a macroeconomic model that could be termed 'national Keynesianism'. The first of its three main tenets was that the level of output in a national economy is limited by the level of aggregate demand for goods and services. The second tenet equated aggregate demand to the home market. The third held that more egalitarian distributions of income support higher levels of aggregate demand. Egalitarian redistribution was thus doubly blessed: it promised 'soft redistribution', addressing the needs of the less well-off, while promoting the general interest of abundance for all.

The evidence does not support the third, and most critical, of these tenets, however, and the second tenet, upon which the third is based, is also flawed. An econometric study by Bowles and Boyer (1995) of the US, France, the UK, Japan, and Germany over the post-war period shows that increased wages are likely to lead to a decline, not an increase, in aggregate demand and that this is particularly the case the more open the economy is to exports and imports.[14] Also, even in the cases where Bowles and Boyer found that increasing the real wage would expand aggregate demand, the estimated effect is small, and is insufficient to support a positive relationship between the real wage and the rate of investment.[15] Thus even if a wage increase were to expand employment in the short run, it seems likely that it would diminish private investment, thus jeopardizing the long-run viability of this particular egalitarian strategy. The estimated effects of increased unemployment benefits and other income redistributive measures on aggregate demand and investment are no more promising.

Smaller and more internationally open economies are unlikely to be exceptions to these findings. Thus there is some doubt concerning the relevance, even in the heyday of social democracy, of a Keynesian wage-led growth regime. The positive macroeconomic effects of social democratic policies may be more plausibly attributed to such productivity-enhancing policies as unifying wage structures across industries and active labor market policies.[16] The first tenet is not wrong: demand constraints continue to limit output and employment. But the global integration of national economies has rendered the level of output in each country increasingly sensitive to world-wide demand conditions and to the competitive position of each economy and less dependent on the domestic distribution of income.

As a result, attention has shifted from the demand-enhancing effect of high wages and social expenditures to the effect of wages and other redistributive policies on costs and on productivity. Many economists and others have argued that the policies once thought to induce a virtuous cycle of redistribution and growth are in fact a prescription for economic decline and long-term reduction in living standards. The post-golden age appeared to promise at best hard redistribution.

With the analytical underpinnings of soft redistribution thus shaken, and the political viability of hard redistribution doubted, the egalitarian project has stalled. The reorientation of economic policy to supply-side rather than demand-side problems appears to have entailed a corresponding shift from egalitarian redistribution to its converse: policies promoting greater inequality, justified by the promise of long-run trickle-down effects. The new emphasis on long-term productivity growth is entirely welcome; and arguments for greater emphasis on other supply-side issues are compelling. But we have shown that the abandonment of the egalitarian project is a *non sequitur*. Rather than a simple correspondence between demand-side economics and egalitarian policy on the one hand and supply-side economics and trickle-down policy on the other, there is a complex array of choices. Perhaps surprisingly, the Keynesian focus on demand does not favor egalitarian policies. As we have observed, in a world of globally integrated national economies, aggregate demand may be fostered by a redistribution from wages to profits, rather than by the reverse. Analogously, the focus on supply-side problems does not entail trickle-down policies: egalitarian redistributive policies can be productivity enhancing. The expanded menu of choices is presented in figure 4.

A further implication of the globalization of production is that it may be very costly to redistribute against the owners of factors of production that are globally mobile, notably capital. The point is easily exaggerated, and often is by opponents of redistribution. The process of investment is still primarily national: the vast majority of

Figure 4:   Economic Diagnosis and Distributional Outcomes

		Distributional Aspect of Policy	
		Egalitarian	*Trickle-down*
Diagnosis of the Problem	*Demand Side*	Left Keynesianism	Low Wage Export Led Growth
	Supply Side	Productivity Enhancing Redistributions	IMF 'Structural Adjustment' Policy

investment in every country is of domestic origin. Moreover most international movements of direct investment are among high-wage countries, not from these countries to the low-wage economies.[17]

But any sharp reduction in the after-tax rate of profit expected by wealth holders in any particular country may provoke responses capable of devastating an egalitarian program. The mobility of goods and finance thus does not preclude egalitarian policies, but it does substantially raise the political and economic costs of policies that are purely redistributive. Without growth in productivity, substantial increases in the well-being of the less well-off cannot be implemented without these disruptive declines in the profit rate.

4. Conflict and Coordination

We stress productivity growth as a welfare measure because the long-run gains in living standards obtainable through redistribution are limited by the size of the pie, while the benefits of productivity growth, including increased leisure, are cumulative.[18] For this reason if one considers a sufficiently long time-horizon, redistributions that are productivity reducing are difficult to support, even if one's sole concern were the well-being of the less well-off: after some years, they would have had a higher living standard under the less egalitarian status quo.[19]

A single minded desire to redivide the pie has sometimes diverted egalitarians from the task of producing a better pie. More precisely, the characteristic leftist focus on the conflictual aspect of social interactions has obscured its coordination aspect. Interactions typically exhibit both aspects, but we can define polar cases. A pure conflict interaction between two people is one in which all possible outcomes can be ranked as better for one and worse for the other.

Figure 5:   Productivity-Enhancing Redistributions

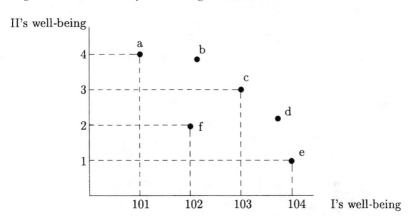

Zero-sum games are an example. Conversely, a pure coordination problem is one in which all feasible outcomes can be ranked such that if one outcome is better than another for one of the actors the same will be true for the other actor.[20]

The exploitation of one person by another may be a pure conflict, while a traffic jam may be more nearly a pure coordination problem. The difference is illustrated in figure 5, which presents a measure of well-being for two individuals (it does not matter what it is, income, 'utility' or whatever), with each dot the result of a particular outcome of their interaction. Which outcome occurs depends both on the economic institutions regulating their interaction, and on the actions taken by each. Person I is evidently advantaged as all of I's outcomes (102, 103, etc.) are far better than any of II's (2, 3, etc.). If the possible outcomes included only points *a* through to *e*, it would be a pure conflict game; if only *f* and one of *b* through to *d* were possible it would be a pure coordination game. If point *f* obtains under existing institutions, and if *b*, *c*, and *d* are the other technically feasible outcomes, getting to any of them may be considered to be more important than the which of them one obtains: solving the coordination aspect of the problem may be more important than resolving the conflict aspect. Point *f* indicates what we have called a coordination failure: at least one point superior to *f* for both people is possible, but is not obtained due to the lack of coordinated action of the two.

The logic of productivity-enhancing redistributions is that moves from *f* to *b* are possible, and that movements in a similar direction in the figure ('soft redistribution') may be a more promising strategy than movements to the northwest ('hard redistribution') even if the claims of justice would support the latter.[21]

If mutually beneficial solutions to coordination failures exist, it may be asked why they are not adopted. Why, that is, are coordination failures so common? The answer, we think, is that privileged groups often prefer the economic institutions resulting in f to an alternative set of institutions that has as possible outcomes all the other points, the reason being a fear that among these, point a will be chosen.

A generalization of this example is as follows. The holders of concentrated wealth often find themselves in opposition to effecting the changes in the rules of the game necessary to solve coordination failures. Coordination failures arise because people cannot make binding agreements among themselves. Solving coordination failures therefore frequently involves introducing institutions for the enforcement of collective decisions. But the only broadly legitimate way to make these decisions is by majority rule, and institutions created to solve one problem are readily deployed for other ends. Thus, where the wealthy exercise sufficient power, the result may be the failure to adopt a superior institutional structure capable of averting coordination problems by facilitating collectively binding agreements.[22]

To analyze how governance structures can impede desirable solutions to coordination failures, we will use a concrete example to which figure 5 applies. Person I, let us say, is the owner of a firm, and II is one of a team of 100 identical workers. The two actors each decide whether to select one of two production inputs: the worker may apply high or low effort to the job, and the owner may or may not devote resources to modernizing the firm's capital stock. Let us assume, realistically, we believe, that these decisions are not easy to reverse: the investment, once committed is costly to redeploy, and the workers' agreement to new work rules, once conceded, is difficult to withdraw. When they each select Low, the result is indicated by point f in figure 5: each worker gets 2, the owner gets 102 and the total income (value added) of the firm (counting all 100 workers) is 302. They could do better, but the problem is that each could also do worse; this is the challenge facing the governance structure.

If both select High, the combination of effective labor in a modernized plant yields any of points b, c, or d, depending on how the gains are shared. Assume the outcome is c, each worker gets 3 and the owner gets 103; the value added of the firm is then 403. However, in many situations each will prefer to select Low while the other selects High; the worker would prefer less intense work in a

Figure 6:   Investment and Productivity as a Prisoner's Dilemma

		Employer Investment Level	
		High	*Low*
Employee Support for Productivity Development	*High*	I's second best (103) II's second best (3) (point **c**)	I's best (104) II's worst (1) (point **e**)
	Low	I's worst (101) II's best (4) (point **a**)	I's third best (102) II's third best (2) (point **f**)

Note: Points *a*, *c*, *e*, and *f* refer to Figure 5. Points *b* and *d* have been eliminated by the bargain struck over the gains to cooperation (see text).

more modern plant (point *a*), while the capitalist would prefer to meet his output and cost targets through speedup or cost-cutting change in work rules than through a long-term commitment of capital expenditure (point *e*). The worst outcome for each is to select High while the other selects Low. A high level of investment when workers give a low level of support to productivity-enhancing practices will lock the employer into an unprofitable operation. Similarly, for the worker: supporting productivity enhancing practices while the employer invests little will lead to both exhaustion and job terminations.

The above strategies and outcomes are summarized in figure 6, from which it can be seen that the employer-employee relationship in production is a prisoners' dilemma: the dominant strategy for each, that which it is rational for each to follow regardless of what the other does, is to select Low, leading to the third best outcome for both.[23]

The dismal third-best result occurs because the interaction is non-cooperative in the sense that binding agreements between the two cannot be made. In the absence of such agreements, the more desirable outcome (High, High) is not an equilibrium: if by chance it occurred, each would have the incentive to defect to the Low option. Hence the high productivity outcome cannot be sustained in this governance structure.

How might the collectively rational joint high levels of both investment and work be secured? The two (for simplicity regarding the worker as a single actor) could agree to select High. Arriving at and enforcing an agreement of this kind would present serious obstacles under existing institutional conditions. Workers, for example, would require access to the firm's financial records, as well as a way of sanctioning the owners should they fail to comply. Owners likewise would require a low cost and effective way of monitoring the work activities of the work force. But monitoring is often exceptionally costly, if not impossible, given the nature of the work process, and the difficulties are exacerbated by the unwillingness of workers to cooperate in such monitoring activities since the employer is the residual claimant on the resulting income and hence the sole beneficiary of the effectiveness of the monitor and of the workers' efforts.

Less obvious difficulties arise. Workers may bargain collectively with the employer, perhaps offering to monitor their own work activities in return for investment guarantees and open books. Mutually beneficial agreements might be struck on these terms allowing the preferable outcomes b, c, or d. But which one? The answer will depend on the bargaining power of the two parties, and this, in turn, would depend on the consequences for each of failing to come to an agreement, or the so-called fallback outcome point f.

In a bargaining situation, then, both persons have an incentive to avoid any move that worsens their fallback position. Thus the employer would want to avoid any type of fixed investments that cannot be relatively easily redeployed elsewhere, including, importantly, investments in the worker's own job skills. Workers, for their part, would want to avoid any simplification of the work process which would facilitate their own replacement. Thus both workers and employers will direct their efforts towards activities that increase their expected share of the firm's net revenue. These activities may be very costly; they need not contribute to productivity, and typically they do not.[24]

To the waste associated with the bargaining process must be added the likelihood that in many cases no agreed-upon rule for sharing the benefits of cooperation will be adopted, therefore no agreement will be struck, and the productivity gains will be foregone. Or perhaps an agreement will be secured only after costly strikes or lockouts.[25]

Often no agreement will be struck at all, and the employer will simply offer the worker a wage high enough to make the job worth keeping, and then threaten to fire any worker who does not work sufficiently hard. But such threats are ineffective unless the employer devises a system of surveillance of the labor process, deploying surveillance equipment and supervisory personnel around the workplace for this purpose. In actual capitalist economies, these monitoring costs constitute a considerable fraction of the cost of employing labor.[26]

No particular importance should be attributed to the specific coordination failure we have chosen for purposes of illustration. A similar situation with analogous results could describe the worker's decision as to how much learning of firm-specific skills to undertake and the employer's decision as to how much employment security to grant workers. For example, see Pagano (this volume) and Levine and Parkin (1993). Firm-specific skills contribute to productivity, but they are useless to a terminated worker, and hence there is little reason to acquire them in the absence of a job guarantee.

The example can be no more than a metaphor for the far more complex coordination failures resulting from the non-cooperative nature of the microeconomic interactions which determine the level of productivity and its growth. But the model is not misleading in its major conclusion: namely, that overcoming coordination failures often requires agreements which are difficult to secure and costly to enforce given the governance structures that are feasible when property rights are highly concentrated.

5. The Institutions of Economic Governance

What new configurations of state, communities, and markets would be permitted by a more egalitarian distribution of residual claimancy and control rights? Among these would any be productivity enhancing? The answers, we will see, depend on the types of information available to some people and not to others, the way in which information can be acquired, hidden and shared, and the way in which governance institutions and property rights distributions alter the information structures and types of conflict of interest typical of social interactions.

For two reasons, the analysis of differential access to information should be central to any attempt to answer the above questions. The first is obvious: as a factual matter, much information is 'asymmetric' in the sense that different pieces of information are private to different agents. Individuals generally have better knowledge concerning their own preferences, needs, and wants, their personal skills and productive capacities, as well as their past, present, and intended future actions, than do outsiders. Moreover, the costs of information transmission from one person to another may be very high, as in the case of specialized technical information, craft, skills, or personal tastes.

Even where the transmission costs are potentially low, people typically have an interest in misrepresentation – in not revealing a serious medical condition while applying for insurance, for example, or in exaggerating the difficulty of a task in response to a job supervisor's inquiry.

The second reason is less obvious. If everyone knew the same things, institutions might not matter from an allocational standpoint. If no one had privileged access to information, efficient coordinations would be possible under a variety of governance structures and property rights configurations, including markets with private property and central planning with property owned in common. We may summarize this point more formally. With symmetric information, private contracting and the state are allocationally equivalent in the following sense: any Pareto-efficient allocation feasible under given preferences and technologies can be implemented either directly by the state or as a result of some initial distribution of assets followed by private contracting.[27]

This equivalence result does not require that economies of scale be absent or that markets be competitive; the key result is that as long as whatever is known is known by all (symmetric information) all mutually beneficial trades will be made. The result is true even when the technical assumptions required to demonstrate the Pareto-optimality of competitive equilibrium fail to obtain, that is, in the presence of spillover effects such as pollution. The assumption of symmetric information is key to this result because contracts enforceable at low cost are typically unavailable if they require access to information known to one but not to other parties to the exchange, and in the absence of these contracts it will not be the case that all beneficial trades will be made. Similar problems arise when information is common to all parties but is not legally admissible (i.e., cannot be used in a court of law).

The importance of allocational inefficiencies occasioned by contractual problems stemming from the private (or legally non-admissible) nature of information depends in part on the extent to which the interests of the exchanging parties differ. Where conflicts of interest are attenuated (or absent, as in pure coordination interactions) the prospect of mutual gain through cooperation is often sufficient to induce the emergence of rules and conventions supporting an efficient solution. By contrast, coordination problems with a large element of conflict – prisoners' dilemmas with large rewards for unilateral defection and little advantage of mutual cooperation over mutual defection, for example – present far greater challenges to a governance structure.[28]

An adequate evaluation of the state, markets and other systems of private contracting must thus address how each deals with asymmetric information, or with the distribution of property rights, or with both. The two cannot be easily separated: once one admits the importance of information asymmetries, the distribution of property rights makes a difference not only for the distribution of output, but also in its efficient production. We have already seen this in the prisoners' dilemma example above, where an efficient solution of the coordination problem is precluded by some property rights distributions. We can now generalize the point. The effects of information asymmetries on efficiency depend on the distribution of property rights: coordination failures arise when the distribution of both private information and property rights is such that agents' interests are in conflict and their noncontractible actions affect one another's well-being.

It follows that the coordination failures that arise in these cases may be attenuated by property rights systems that accomplish one or more of the following *desiderata*: they more closely align rights of control and residual claimancy so that individuals own the results of their actions, they reduce the conflict of interest among affected parties, or they reduce the extent or importance of private information. Our task in this section is to examine the unique capacities of markets, governments and communities that might be germane to a redesign and redistribution of property rights capable of serving these ends.

Markets have two major attractive properties. The first concerns one of the above *desiderata*, that of reducing the importance of private information: market competition is a means of inducing agents to make public the economically relevant private information they hold. In centralized non-market systems, producers typically have an incentive to understate their productive capacities in order to secure a lower production quota. Consumers similarly have an incentive to overstate their needs hoping to establish a superior claim on goods and services. By contrast, misrepresenting capacities or wants in a market economy is costly and rarely beneficial. It is often said that in markets people vote with their dollars. The implication is not that markets are democratic, but that it is costly to express a preference in a competitive market system. Indeed, the only way to register a preference in a market is to make a purchase, and the price at which one is willing to purchase a good conveys what would otherwise be private information, namely that the good is worth at least as much as the price paid.

Similarly it is often rewarding to reveal a productive capacity, and costly to misrepresent the true costs of production. In a competitive market equilibrium, profit-maximizing producers will make goods available at their private marginal cost of production, thereby revealing an important and otherwise private piece of information. Those who might be said to be misrepresenting their productive capacities by offering goods at prices not equal to their true cost of production will make lower profits.[29]

Thus where key aspects of production and demand are subject to private information, markets are often superior to other governance structures.[30] But as we will see private information combined with highly concentrated assets also generates market failures in the provision of credit and insurance, the management of firms, the conduct of work, the process of innovation, and the maintenance of assets.

Second, where residual claimancy and control rights are closely aligned (our first *desideratum*), market competition provides a decentralized and relatively incorruptible disciplining mechanism that punishes the inept and rewards high performers. Markets, it is said, impose hard budget constraints on actors, but they do this only when decision-makers own the results of their decisions. However property rights assignments that are efficient in this sense often do not obtain in highly unequal societies; as a result, the disciplining process is often poorly targeted.

The comparative advantage of the state is in the production of rules: the state alone has the power to make and enforce compliance with the rules of the game that govern the interaction of private agents. The state does not have particular advantages in the production and distribution of most goods and services. Where individuals face prisoners' dilemma-like situations or other coordination problems in which the autonomous pursuit of individual objectives leads to an undesirable outcome, the state can provide or compel the coordination necessary to avert this outcome. Services that governments can perform well that communities and markets cannot include the definition, assignment, and enforcement of property rights, the provision of public goods, the regulation of environmental and other external or 'spillover' effects, the regulation of natural monopolies, the provision of some forms of insurance, and macroeconomic regulation. Less obvious cases include what is termed equilibrium selection where multiple equilibria exist – for example a high-wage

and a low-wage growth path may both be feasible and state intervention may determine which occurs (we provide an example concerning
wealth redistribution in our concluding essay).

The state addresses prisoners' dilemmas in a manner diametrically
opposed to that of markets. Competitive markets hinder the formation
of cartels and other forms of collusion by providing incentives for
defection, while the state can induce cooperation by preventing
defection. Since both defection and cooperation are desirable under
different circumstances, markets and states serve complementary roles
in solving coordination problems. The state prevents defection by
compelling participation in exchanges that would not be voluntarily
chosen by economic agents acting singly, for example, cooperating in
a prisoner's dilemma situation. This capacity to force compliance can
contribute to the solution of coordination problems even where
individuals have information that is private and therefore inaccessible
to the state.

An example involving the availability of insurance illustrates this
principle. Before they have learned the capacities, health status, and
the special risks they face as individuals, all members of a population
might prefer to purchase insurance. But after they have learned their
own special position, those with a low probability of collecting on the
insurance will not be willing to purchase it, as they would be
subsidizing those with a high probability of collecting. Thus the low-
risk people would drop out of the market, and the price of the
insurance would be too high for the high-risk people. Since before
obtaining specific knowledge of their own risk position, all would
have been willing to purchase the insurance, and since it is unavailable
on the market, there is a clear market failure. By providing the
insurance and compelling all agents to pay for it, the state overcomes
this market failure.[31]

This reasoning extends to several important areas of social policy.
Consider, for instance, health insurance. Suppose that everyone would
be willing to purchase insurance covering a particular illness, if people
did not know their personal likelihood of contracting the illness. But
once people do learn how likely they are to contract the illness, and if
coverage for this illness is optional, the healthy will not purchase the
insurance. To cover the costs of claims with fewer subscribers, insurers
will raise rates, with the eventual result that those prone to the illness
will not be able to afford the insurance. Universal coverage, compelling all to subscribe and extending benefits to all, solves this problem.
This insurance can be supplied by the state, or the state can merely
compel all citizens to subscribe to such insurance privately. Since it is

costly to enforce private subscription to insurance, and virtually impossible in the case of people who cannot afford the price of insurance, in this case state supply of insurance would be a superior alternative.

For another example, consider unemployment insurance. Suppose everyone would be willing to purchase a certain level of insurance covering the costs associated with losing their job through no fault of their own – e.g., through a macroeconomic downturn causing layoffs and bankruptcies. Once all individuals acquire knowledge of the likelihood of job loss in their particular cases, and if unemployment insurance is optional, those with job security will not purchase the insurance, premiums will rise and those with insecure jobs will not be able to purchase unemployment insurance. Again, universal coverage, which can only be effected by the state compelling all to subscribe and extending benefits to all, solves this problem.

The state, however, has several fundamental weaknesses as a governance structure. The first is its lack of access to private information held by producers and consumers. The second is the mirror image of the first: the lack of access by voters and citizens (assuming a democratic polity) to the private information held by those who operate within the state, and hence the difficulty in rendering the state's actions democratically accountable. The third is the weakness of voting as a decision rule. Because there is no consistent democratic way to aggregate individual preferences into consistent social choice criteria, the results of majority rule and other voting mechanisms depend critically on who controls the voting agenda. Moreover, unlike markets, voting schemes have difficulty representing the intensity of preferences for different goods or social outcomes. Finally, where government intervention suppresses market outcomes, economic actors privileged by the intervention earn rents – incomes above their next best alternative. Thus groups will engage in 'rent-seeking behavior', attempting to influence it to intervene on their behalf rather than for another group or the public at large, thereby wasting resources and distorting policy outcomes.

These weaknesses are virtually inescapable, by the very nature of the state and the character of democratic processes. To compel while preventing exit requires that the state be universal and unchallenged in some spheres. This universality of the state prevents its being rendered accountable by subjecting the state to the competitive delivery of its 'services'. Moreover, the inability of voting schemes to aggregate preferences in a consistent manner requires that non-electoral ways of influencing collective decision making – including interest group activities – must be available as correctives. But rent-seeking activity directed towards these non-electoral processes is difficult to regulate. Of course states can be rendered more accountable by fostering competition among local governments and public agencies, by carefully monitoring the actions of state officials, by subjecting elected and administrative positions within the state to well designed incentives, and by limiting the state's actions to those which cannot be regulated in a more accountable manner by some other governance structure.[32]

It may seem that we are exaggerating the disabilities of the state as a governance structure. But in fact we are merely applying to the state the same reasoning that is commonly used to demonstrate the existence of coordination failures in markets. We regard elected officials, voters, state administrators, and the private individuals with whom they interact as acting strategically in pursuit of their own ends, subject to whatever incentive and monitoring systems they face. Our point is not that officials are selfish but that whether selfish or not, their individual objectives need to be taken into account. In this framework one cannot advocate a state policy without specifying its implementation; i.e., giving reasons why all of the individuals involved will take the actions required for the goals of the policy to be achieved.

A convenient way to check that a policy meets this test is to ask if its objectives are realized as a Nash equilibrium, given the constraints, incentives, and other instruments used to implement the policy. A Nash equilibrium is a set of strategies, one for each agent, such that no agent has an incentive to choose a different strategy, given the strategies followed by the other agents. Successful implementation in this framework will of course be promoted by choosing government personnel with such competencies and commitments that their personal goals align well with the public purposes they are called upon to fulfill. But it equally includes a structure of incentives – rewards, penalties, and forms of accountability – ensuring that government personnel find it in their interest to behave as prescribed by the policy.

We turn now to a third governance structure, distinct from and complementary to both state and market – the community.[33]

The special and common character of the community as a governance structure derives from the fact that its members share a common set of norms and are in frequent and close face-to-face interaction. What makes a group of people a community is not the degree of affection or altruism amongst them (community members may be envious and spiteful) but rather the commitments, incentives and constraints governing their behavior.

Communities may solve coordination problems where other governance structures would fail. Examples of the success of communities as governance structures include cooperative governance of irrigation systems and other common property resources, mutual credit associations, and worker owned and managed enterprises.[34] Communities structure social interactions by applying rewards and punishments to members according to their conformity with or deviation from community norms. Further, a community can monitor the behavior of its members in a manner rendering them accountable for their actions. In this respect communities contrast with other governance structures, for communities more effectively foster and utilize the incentives that people have traditionally deployed to regulate their common activity: trust, solidarity, reciprocity, reputation, personal pride, respect, vengeance, and retribution, among others.

Three aspects of communities account for their unique capacities as governance structures. First, in a community the probability that members who interact today will interact in the future is high, and thus there is a strong incentive to act in collectively rational ways now in order to avoid retaliation in the future.[35] Consider a case in which interactions are such that the benefits to each member depend on the actions taken by each, and that any action once taken is known to the other party but is not admissible as evidence in court and therefore cannot be used as the basis for contracting for the actions of the other prior to the interaction. An example would be a two person prisoners' dilemma in which the action taken by one's partner was known *ex post*, but was not judicially verifiable. In this case neither private contracting nor state regulation would address the underlying coordination problem. But the threat of retaliation on the next and successive rounds of the game will effectively deter defection if each expect the interaction to continue over a long period as will typically be the case in communities.[36]

Third, communities share norms that allow members to coordinate their behavior and thereby settle on efficient interactions. For example, where property rights cannot be well defined, costly contestation can be avoided by the prevalence of other legitimate norms of division, such as 'first come first served' or 'finders keepers' or equal shares. The point is not that communities foster norms that appeal to a sense of fairness, but that agreed-upon norms often allow cooperation to take place by deterring costly conflicts. 'Last come, first served' would do equally well for this purpose.[37]

Thus, over some range of governance problems, communities contribute to all three *desiderata* outlined above: aligning control and residual claimancy through retaliation for socially destructive actions in repeated interactions, making information less private by providing incentives to establish reputations through consistent behavior, and reducing the degree of conflict of interest over non-contractible aspects of exchange through the provision of division rules and other norms capable of working even when property rights are not well defined. These reasons may help explain why communities, long dismissed by social scientists and all but utopian leftists as anachronistic remnants of an earlier era, have not been supplanted by markets and the state.

Community governance structures are not, however, substitutes for markets and the state, since the very factors accounting for the unique capacities of communities to solve difficult coordination problems also account for their weaknesses. Notably, the necessarily small scope of community governance structures required to support frequent encounters among members and low mutual monitoring costs prohibits them from coordinating interactions on a national, much less global, scale.[38] Moreover, the high cost of exit and durability of social interactions essential to the workings of communities may militate against innovation.

The ability of communities to address coordination problems depends on the types of property rights in force and their distribution among the population. Where community members are not residual claimants on the results of their actions there may be little incentive to engage in the forms of sanctioning and reputation building we have stressed. Were property rights assignments to make some members vastly more wealthy than others, shared norms of division may be difficult to maintain, and threats of retaliation against non-cooperative actions may lack effectiveness or credibility. For similar reasons, the distinctive capacities of communities are likely to be undermined where the costs of exit are very asymmetrical, for instance when some members have attractive outside options and others do not. In short, the effectiveness of communities depends on the assignment of property rights.

In this respect communities are not unlike markets. The allocational efficiency advantage of the decentralization of control rights (either the extensive use of market or community-based governance systems) lies in the placing of decision making in the hands of those who have information which others lack. For this to be beneficial, the holders of private information must have residual claimancy rights on the results of their actions. On efficiency grounds, decentralization to individuals through use of markets is favored over decentralization to communities where contracts are relatively complete and enforceable at low cost and hence where interests may conflict without generating coordination failures. Decentralization to communities is favored where complete contracting is precluded but where low levels of conflict of interest within the community and other aspects of community structure facilitate the transmission of private information among community members.

6. Risk-taking, Project Quality, and Labor Incentives

There is no reason of course to think that the nature and ownership of existing property rights is such as to make either markets or communities maximally effective in solving coordination failures. The state, markets, and communities that make up the governance structure of capitalist societies sustain coordination failures, some of which, we will argue, could be attenuated through a redistribution of ownership and control from current owners to the less wealthy. However, egalitarian asset redistribution may also reduce productivity. Before turning to concrete cases of productivity enhancing redistributions, then, we will use a simple model to outline the complex and partially contradictory consequences of asset redistribution. We will see that there is indeed an analogue to the efficiency equality frontier, a locus of feasible levels of wealth equality and output, but that for plausible values of the parameters of the model the relationship between the two may be complementary rather than contradictory over some range of wealth distributions.

The intuitions motivating our model are now familiar. Output depends on such intangibles as decision-makers' choice of levels of risk, the quality and intensity of workers' labor effort, and the process of project design and innovation. Information concerning these productivity enhancing intangibles is for the most part private, and hence not subject to contract. Where this is the case, as we have seen, a decentralization of residual claimancy and control to the private holders of information may be productivity enhancing. Thus asset redistribution may attenuate coordination failures due to private information by more closely aligning residual claimancy rights with *de facto* control over actions governed by private information, or less technically, by making actors liable for the consequences of their actions.

We will focus on three aspects of the relationship between asset distribution and productivity. First, the wealthy are likely to be risk-neutral and hence to manage projects so as to implement an (approximately) socially optimal level of risk-taking.[39] By contrast, less wealthy individuals will be risk-averse and will implement socially suboptimal levels of risk-taking. Second, the non-wealthy will be unable to implement projects, or will implement fewer, a result of which will be that 'good' projects which are the private information of the non-wealthy will not be implemented, while 'less good' projects of the wealthy will be implemented. Third, where wealth constraints force some to seek employment on the projects of others, the labor incentive problems arising from the fact that workers are not residual claimants on the income stream resulting from their labor will lead to monitoring and other costs not required when self-employment is possible.

Consider an economy composed of n individuals, some of whom are wealthy and some of whom are not. Income may be generated by implementing a 'project' that yields a base income y plus additional returns to the project. Projects are chosen from a list of projects known only to each person, each project costing $1 to implement. Projects once implemented may be managed with varying degrees of risk, selected by the owner of the project, as a result of which the project fails (and yields just y) with probability f. Every person will work a given amount of time and experience a given disutility of labor (though on the above reasoning the amount of quality and intensity of work done will vary according to the labor contract). If hired labor is used, the returns are a fraction β times the returns to the project when the work is done by the residual claimant, where $1 - \beta$ reflects the monitoring costs associated with the wage contract. Each project requires just one person to work it. No income can be generated without a project, that is without investing $1.

The return on each project depends on the level of risk assumed, with riskier projects (if they do not fail) yielding higher returns. Suppose the return to a successful project varies linearly with the risk undertaken, so that a person who implements a project, providing the necessary investment and labor, receives a net return of $y + rf$ if the project succeeds, and y if it fails. Thus the expected return $\hat{y}$ from the project is just the weighted sum of the 'failure' and 'success' pay-offs:

$$\hat{y} = fy + (1 - f)(y + rf)$$

Figure 7:   The Risk and Expected Return to a Project

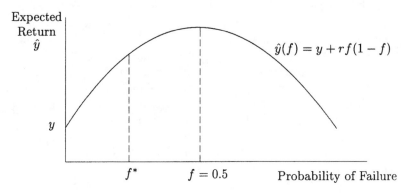

which, letting F = (1 − f)f, can be rewritten

$$\hat{y}(f) = y + Fr.$$

This relationship is illustrated in figure 7.

If this project is implemented by a wealthy and hence risk-neutral person, the chosen level of risk is simply that which maximizes expected income, on the margin balancing the contribution of greater risk to the returns of the project should it succeed against the greater probability that the project will fail. This optimizing process determines that for the wealthy person $f = 0.5$ which, when substituted into the above equation, yields

$$\hat{y} = y + 0.25r.$$

Thus if the sum of all assets is n (just enough to employ everyone) and a single person owns all of these and has n equally good projects to implement, there will be 1 self-employment contract and $n − 1$ wage labor contracts. Thus total expected output is

$$Y = (y + 0.25r)(1 + (n − 1)\beta).$$

Now let f^* be the level of risk chosen by a non-wealthy person who has just enough wealth to initiate a project, and let $F^* = f^*(1 − f^*)$. Because $f^* < 0.5$, $F^* < 0.25$. Suppose wealth is distributed so that m non-wealthy people are just able to fund their own projects (the remainder of the wealth is in the hands of a single person, who employs the remainder of the population $(n - m - 1)$ on wage contracts). Our measure of asset inequality is thus m, ranging from perfect equality $(m = n - 1)$ to perfect inequality $(m = 0)$. Then we can write the expected output–equality trade-off as follows:

$$Y = Y(m, r, \beta, .5 - f^*)$$

where m measures the level of equality and the remaining three arguments measure the return to risk-taking, the monitoring cost of wage labor contracts and the extent to which the risk-aversion of the non-wealthy depress risk-taking below its socially optimal level. Using the above results we see that total expected income is the sum of expected returns on three types of projects: the single project owned and operated by the wealthy individual, the $n - m - 1$ projects employing wage labor, owned by the wealthy person, and the remaining m self-employment projects of the non-wealthy:

$$Y = (y + 0.25r) + (n - m - 1)\beta(y + 0.25r) + m(y + F^*r).$$

The effect of redistribution (increasing m) on total expected income (the 'slope' of the output–equality trade-off locus) is thus

$$\frac{dY}{dm} = y(1 - \beta) + (F^* - 0.25\beta)r,$$

where the first term is the positive effect of greater equality on base-level incomes from improved labor incentives and the second term incorporates the loss in expected income occasioned by reduced risk-taking by the non-wealthy. The level of expected output and the degree of equality clearly may co-vary positively or inversely. The sign of the trade-off depends, as expected, on the strength of the labor incentive effect relative to the extent of risk-aversion among the non-wealthy and the return to risk-taking. If, for example $y = 1$, $\beta = 0.7$, $r = 2$ and $f^* = 0.4$ (so that $F^* = 0.24$), $dY/dm = 0.43$ indicating a positive contribution of asset redistribution to output.

Now suppose that the quality of projects varies. Everyone's 'best' project has the return structure rf and everyone's q^{th} project has returns of $r(q)f$ with $r' < 0$. As above there are n units of capital, m of which are owned by the non-wealthy and $n - m$ of which are owned by a single wealthy person. More equality entails fewer projects undertaken by the wealthy person, so the average quality of the project adopted by the wealthy person, $\tilde{r}$, increases with the level of equality, m. Writing $\tilde{r} = \tilde{r}(m)$ with $\tilde{r}' > 0$, we can now express total expected income

$$Y = (y + 0.25\tilde{r}(m))(1 + (n - m - 1)\beta) + m(y + F^*r),$$

and the effect of egalitarian redistribution on total expected income is:

$$\frac{dY}{dm} = y(1 - \beta) + r(F^* - 0.25\beta\tilde{r}(m)) + 0.25\tilde{r}'(m)(1 + (n - m - 1)\beta),$$

where the first and second terms are interpreted as above, and the third represents the gain in the average quality of the projects undertaken associated with more people having sufficient wealth to undertake their best project (or more precisely the rich person investing in fewer of his not so good projects and hence raising his average returns).

It is reasonable that projects will vary in the degree of disadvantage of the labor contract as opposed to self-ownership. Some may be characterized by production processes in which the cost of effective monitoring is very high, or conversely perhaps negligible so that piece rate contracts can be used. Distributing wealth from a single large owner to other members of the population will thus induce changes in β. We can model these changes by assuming that the wealthy person abandons first the projects that are least advantageously exploited using wage labor, and that the non-wealthy first take up projects for which self-employment is most advantageous. For this reason β will rise with m: the greater the level of equality in the distribution of assets, the less the relative advantage (on average) of self-employment contracts. In the example below we assume that when wealth is equally held, we have $\beta = 1$; i.e., the advantages of residual claimant status by workers in self-employment are matched by fully offsetting disadvantages.

Figure 8 illustrates an output–equality locus for some representative parameter values (labeled 'Benchmark').[40] For levels of inequality such that fewer than half the population can undertake their own projects, egalitarian redistribution increases expected income; more egalitarian distributions of wealth confront an equality–output trade-off. It is clear from the equation above that asset redistribution is likely to be productivity-enhancing when the costs of labor contracting are high (β is low), the risk-aversion of the non-wealthy is limited ($0.25 - F^*$ is small), and when the gradient of project quality is steep

Figure 8:   The Expected Output–Equality Trade-off

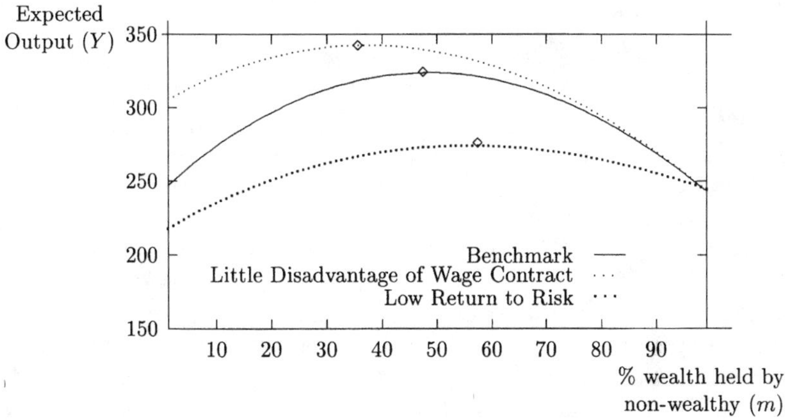

Note: Graphing details in Note 40.

(i.e., when $\bar{r}'$ is large). The magnitude of returns to risk-taking may affect the benefits and cost of redistribution positively or negatively, depending on the above parameters. In figure 8 we compare the benchmark locus with two others. The first is based on a lesser disadvantage of the wage labor over the self-employment contract. Not surprisingly, output is higher in this case, and the maximum output occurs at a more unequal distribution of assets, with a more pronounced trade-off between output and equality. The second, a lower return to risk-taking compensated by an upward shift in the risk-free base income of projects, yields an output maximum at a greater level of equality, reflecting the concomitant reduction in the output losses induced by the socially sub-optimal risk-taking by the asset-poor.

The centrality of the parameter β in the above analysis suggests that the possibility of productivity-enhancing redistribution depends critically on the ability of a relocation of residual claimancy to alter the costs of contract enforcement. Let us then turn to a concrete case of exchange involving noncontractible intangibles critical to productivity: employee ownership of firms.

7. Wealth Redistribution and Worker-owned Firms

To show that an egalitarian redistribution of assets may support a superior governance structure, we will identify the conditions under which a relocation of residual claimancy and control rights of the firm from a capitalist owner to the firm's worker-members will improve productivity. Moreover, we will explain why such transfers will not occur spontaneously in a market economy. The upshot is that despite the advantages of this form of governance in addressing problems of labor discipline and incentives, the limited wealth of most workers will impede the expansion of worker ownership.

Consider first the capitalist firm, where the profit of the owner depends upon the level of effort workers devote to their assigned tasks. The two ingredients of a coordination failure, a conflict of interest and asymmetric information, are present in this interaction. We assume work effort is private information, in the sense that a worker's level of effort is known by the worker and perhaps by some co-workers, but not by the employer. For this reason, a worker's promise to work hard is legally unenforceable.

Where work effort cannot be contracted for, it must be elicited through the adoption of a costly enforcement strategy. Thus the employer uses monitoring of the workers and the threat of dismissal to ensure the delivery of any particular level of effort per hour of labor time supplied.[41] The effectiveness of the threat of non-renewal depends on the wage, since the larger the difference between the worker's current position and the worker's expected next-best alternative, the greater the cost of job loss. The employer thus selects the wage and the level of monitoring by maximizing profits subject to the worker's reaction function, in equilibrium balancing the labor disciplining effects of the higher wage against the cost of the higher wage payments.[42] It is not difficult to show that the resulting equilibrium is inefficient, in that both employer and worker would prefer some combination of more work and more pay; but given the property rights defining the capitalist firm there is no way that the necessary trades can be made.[43] The reasoning is as follows. Because the owner has varied the wage to maximize profits, the owner is indifferent to small changes in the wage in the neighborhood of the profit maximum (but prefers increases in work effort). Because the worker has varied the level of effort to maximize the present value of utility (trading off increased disutility of labor against increased probability of retaining the job), the worker is indifferent to small changes in the level of effort in the neighborhood of the equilibrium, but prefers wage increases. Thus there must be some wage increase and effort level increase that is preferable to both parties over the competitive equilibrium.

Consider another firm, owned by its workers and governed by their elected representatives. We assume that workers direct the managers of the democratic firm to select investments, systems of work monitoring, and other policy options to maximize the workers' welfare. The workers' incomes then consist of their share of the revenues of the firm net of monitoring, materials and other non-labor costs. While we may expect the capitalist and the democratic firms to differ in many respects, our argument is facilitated by assuming that the two firms employ identical workers, produce with identical technologies, and that both use the threat of termination as a means of labor discipline.[44]

Because workers own the assets with which they work, the conflict of interest between the owner and the workers concerning the choice of an investment policy, a conflict discussed in section 4, has disappeared. Workers' interests are now to save and to invest in a way that protects or enhances the value of their asset. Critics often claim that cooperatives will under-invest, myopically preferring to devote the income of the firm to current consumption.[45] This view may be correct where workers do not individually own the assets of the enterprise, but where workers hold shares that are sold upon leaving the firm, this anti-investment incentive does not exist. Individually owned worker cooperatives may indeed have too little capital, but this, we will see, is because workers are poor, not because they have shortsighted objectives.

Not surprisingly, the main advantages of the worker-owned firm are most evident in the regulation of the labor process. We will offer two reasons why the democratic firm will be more efficient than the capitalist firm, in the technical sense that the democratic firm uses less of at least one input to produce the same output.

First, because workers are residual claimants on the income of the democratic firm owners, they receive all returns that flow from their choice of effort levels. If the work team is sufficiently large one might think that the worker would have no less incentive to slack on the job in the democratic firm than in the capitalist firm, since individual workers receive only a small portion of whatever gains accrue to the firm because of their individual efforts. But this view is mistaken. Workers frequently have access at low cost to information concerning the work activities of fellow workers, and in the democratic firm each worker as a residual claimant on the income of the firm has an interest in the effort levels of other workers. The residual claimancy status of workers thus alters the information structure of the interaction of participants in the production process by providing a motive for mutual monitoring. The democratic firm could thus deploy a considerably more effective monitoring structure at less cost than the capitalist firm.[46] For this reason it is easier for worker-owners to secure among themselves a binding agreement concerning the quality and quantity of work than it is for capitalist employers to secure such an agreement from non-owning workers.

The second reason for the technical efficiency of the democratic firm is that the profit-maximizing labor-discipline system adopted by the capitalist firm is typically inefficient in that it uses too many monitoring resources and not enough wage incentives. The reason is that the capitalist firm faces two prices in selecting its enforcement structure. One, the price of monitoring may (at least under ideal competitive conditions) correctly measure a social marginal cost, for the use of monitoring equipment or personnel employs resources with valued alternative uses and hence has a social opportunity cost. The TV cameras and the supervisors could be used to produce output instead of insuring compliance. The payment of a higher wage, by contrast, is simply redistributive, akin to a transfer rather than to a claim on resources. Using the firm's revenues in this way does not use up any societal resource; as a transfer, the wage corresponds to no social opportunity cost, though it is of course a private cost to the employer. Not surprisingly then, the capitalist firm uses too little wage incentive and too much monitoring relative to an efficient alternative. To workers, of course, the wage is a payment to themselves and is hence not a cost but a benefit. So in the democratic firm where they design the system regulating the labor process they would not replicate the inefficient choice of the capitalist.

An analogy may make this reasoning clear. Imagine a trucking company choosing between a shorter route over a toll road and a somewhat longer route without tolls. The two prices in question are the operating cost of the truck and the tolls. The trucking company would rationally treat these two costs as equivalent, perhaps avoiding use of the shorter but costlier toll road. But the toll does not represent a social cost, while the operating costs of the truck (wear and tear, fuel, the driver's time and effort) do. The choice of the longer toll-free route, like the capitalist's choice of lower wages and more intense monitoring is cost minimizing but inefficient.

Though few firms exist with the democratic structure we have assumed, a good number of more or less close approximations exist, and many have been studied extensively in recent years. Studies tend to show that these firms have higher productivity than their capitalist counterparts.[47]

In a competitive economy one might expect the ownership of assets (and hence residual claimancy) to accrue to those who can use the assets most efficiently, since if workers can make better use of productive assets than capitalist owners, the relevant assets will *ceteris paribus* be worth more to them. Hence one might wonder why they do not purchase the assets and thus acquire the associated control and residual claimancy rights. The result would be to attenuate the coordination failure associated with ownership by non-workers.

But lenders face the same problems of asymmetric information that confront employers: potential borrowers have private information concerning the quality of their projects and how they intend to operate them (including the choice of risk levels). Thus credit markets exhibit the same enforcement problems as labor markets, since it is normally impossible for a lender to specify contractually the probability of loan repayment. It follows that lenders will adopt strategies designed to attenuate the conflict of interest between the two sides of the credit market, often requiring borrowers to invest equity in their projects. But equity requirements typically prevent workers from borrowing sufficient funds or impose prohibitive costs on such transactions. Even when this is not the case, asset-poor workers are typically risk-averse, and risk-averse persons do not choose to concentrate their wealth in a single asset.[48]

Thus even when more efficient in regulating work than their capitalist counterparts, worker-owned firms none the less operate at a competitive disadvantage and hence do not flourish in a capitalist economy, since wealth constraints inhibit the formation and lower the profitability of such firms. This credit market disability of worker-owned firms obviously has greater force the larger and more transaction specific is the firm's capital requirement.

8. Efficient Redistributions

We now consider three additional cases of productivity enhancing asset-based redistribution. First, in residential communities – neighborhoods, apartment complexes, or housing projects – the relationship between tenants and landlords is often analogous to that between workers and employers in that private information is held by tenants and wealth differences impose an inefficient outcome – the agent who is most capable of maintaining and improving the value of the asset (the tenant) has only a limited incentive to do so. As in the previous case the inefficiency arises because a conflict of interest exists concerning a set of actions known to only one of the parties to the exchange. The interests of the two diverge because the tenants' care of the property and its physical and social environment enhances the value of the property, an asset in which the tenant has no rights. The tenants' physical care of the property, attention to the appearance of the neighborhood, and participation in educational, recreational, crime prevention and other collective activities to improve the social environment of the community, while beneficial to the tenant, are also time consuming. Moreover much of the benefit of these activities, when they occur, redounds to the owner of the asset, whose property values rise and fall with the physical and social quality of the neighborhood.

As in the case of the work process, the tenants rather than the landlord are best situated to undertake these amenity producing and wealth-enhancing activities. A comment from a neighbor concerning a loud party or a neighbor's watchful eye on the street cannot be replaced by the landlord's direct monitoring or police supervision, except at prohibitive cost. Of course tenants do undertake some of these activities, even without ownership of the asset whose value is thereby enhanced, but their status as nonowners considerably reduces their incentive to do so.

The landlord faces difficulties in attempting to harness the capacity of tenant care to improve property values. The reason is that the landlord's ability contractually to induce the tenants to undertake the relevant activities is restricted because knowledge concerning the tenant's action is asymmetrically held – shared perhaps among other tenants but not readily available to the landlord and even if known often not legally admissible. The result is an inefficiently low level of community amenities and an inefficiently high rate of physical depreciation of the housing stock. Thus there exists an alternative exchange in which the tenant provides more care and the landlord receives less rent and in which both tenant and landlord are better off. This alternative, while technically feasible, is not implementable under the stated property rights, however.

If residential tenancy is inefficient for reasons analogous to the inefficiency of the capitalist firm, it follows that the housing assets are worth more to the tenants than to the landlords. Literally, the benefits they would derive from owning these assets exceed the net income that the landlord can extract in rents. Why, then, do tenants simply not buy out their landlords? Some may not expect to settle in a place for long enough to justify the transaction costs of owning the property. But many simply lack the wealth to make the purchase. Residential tenancy, like the capitalist ownership of firms, is a market failure exacerbated by an unequal distribution of wealth.

Residential ownership might take a variety of forms, ranging from single unit ownership, perhaps in condominiums with a democratic governance structure regulating common spaces, to housing cooperatives with ownership shares along the lines of the worker-owned firm. Asset transfers to foster this kind of ownership might take the form of subsidized purchase options in publicly held housing units and subsidized private construction of low cost housing.[49]

Our next two cases similarly concern a misalignment of residual claimancy and control, but with a different twist. The problem in the case of tenants and workers is that beneficial actions are often not rewarded through full claims on the consequences of hard work or care of the residential property. The problem in our next two cases – schooling and parental care of children – might better be understood as establishing liabilities for damages in cases where agents fail to act beneficially towards principals. As in the case of workers and tenants, the problems illustrated by both of our next cases arise because existing property rights fail to align residual claimancy and control, the assignment of liability and benefits merely being the negative and positive side of residual claimancy over one's own actions.

It is widely agreed that the costs of schooling should be substantially subsidized, that the content of schooling should be socially regulated, at least to the extent of establishing minimal standards in key areas of competency, and that schooling should be so structured as to avoid reproducing racial, class and other inequalities, and to offer equal educational opportunities to all.

Parents and children of course regard the school at least in part as any consumer would regard the deliverer of a valuable service, for instance a hospital or a restaurant. The consumer's interest is that the school offer a service addressed as nearly as possible to the needs or wants of the child (we will elide the not small problem of possible differences in interest between the parents and the child). Given the considerable size of the educational sector in most economies, a failure to serve the consumer's interest here must be considered to be a substantial shortcoming of the economy not dissimilar in principle or in magnitude from an agricultural sector that regularly produces poor tasting food. Thus an adequate governance structure for the educational system ideally balances the various social interests and the consumers' interests in a broadly acceptable manner.

The effective implementation of the consumer's interest in any educational governance structure poses problems of incentives and accountability not dissimilar from those already confronted. Consider the relationship between the parents and the school leadership. The parents and children in this case are in a situation analogous to the employer or the landlord, since they are dealing with another person whose actions are of great importance to them but which they cannot observe or control.[50] As in the earlier cases, the presence of private information and a conflict of interest support inefficient outcomes, given that the *de facto* property rights entail a separation between control and residual claimancy. The parents (and their children) are the residual claimants (the child is educated well or not); but the control rights are being exercised by teachers and the school head who hold private information concerning their own actions. For at least three reasons, the parents and children cannot secure any enforceable agreement with the leadership of the school: the parents are unlikely to agree among themselves, the school leadership has little incentive to enter into such an agreement with parents, and if they could agree, parents would have neither the information nor the judicial means to enforcement.

Can the parents not exercise control through the electoral process given that the school board is democratically accountable? In a limited way, they can. But the expression of the parents' and children's interests in schooling is confined largely to the use of democratic voice in periodic elections, the results of which will be determined by voter preferences on issues among which schooling may be relatively unimportant. Unless the school system is substantially failing a significant majority of parents and voters, and in a way that admits a readily available remedy, a democratic voice is not likely to offer an effective avenue for the expression of the consumer's interest.

The opportunity for accountability through exit is generally ineffective, either because there is no choice of which school a student attends, or if there is there is little penalty to the school leadership if students move elsewhere. Under these circumstances, parental voice in direct interventions at the school or its advisory bodies is likely to be ineffective as well. This governance structure seems designed to mute the consumers' interest.

Yet opportunities for exit could both directly empower parents and would also make parental voice more effective. This is particularly true if exit imposed costs on the school leadership so that they would more nearly be residual claimants on the results of their actions. An example would be a variant on the voucher proposal: parents would annually be issued vouchers of no direct monetary value to them but that when given to a school attended by the child, would represent a claim by the school for appropriations from state revenue. In the absence of private contributions to school finance, this is equivalent to saying that school budgets are proportional to the number of students enrolled, and students are free to move. Vouchers would be acceptable at any institution certified as adequate by the Department of Education. The funding of schools through vouchers would give the leadership a powerful incentive to attend to the parents' and students' interest, as long as the value of the voucher to the school exceeded the cost of accommodating an additional child (which could easily be insured, as average costs of schooling decline with enrolments, at least over a wide range).

Though most voucher plans currently under discussion have paid scant attention to egalitarian and pluralistic objectives, this is more a commentary on the conservative origins of these proposals than its intrinsic logic. The scope for egalitarianism and pluralism is considerable, provided that the level of voucher funding be sufficient to cover the costs of quality education, and that schools accredited to receive vouchers be prohibited from charging parents additional tuition fees. Whatever legal requirements concerning the integration of the school population and the pluralism of its curriculum obtaining prior to the adoption of vouchers could easily be maintained or strengthened. Further, decentralized incentives for racial, class, gender, and other integration of schools could also be written into the system by making the value of the voucher to the school depend on the demographic and economic characteristics of the family perhaps in relationship to that of the current composition of the school enrollment. For example, a voucher presented by a low income student to a school of predominantly high income children could be worth more, thus giving the school an incentive to accommodate, even recruit these students. The converse, and analogous principles concerning race could also be applied. Implementing these provisions would not require that the government have information not already available to it.[51]

The voucher proposal highlights the important distinction between the public or private funding and regulation of schools on the one hand and their status as private or public bodies on the other. If funding were entirely public and egalitarian and if regulation of schools were adequate, the objections to private provision of schooling would be attenuated, and the benefits of competition might be enhanced.[52]

Of course an increase in the degree of mobility of students may promote socially wasteful forms of competition among schools. Among these, grade inflation and standards erosion might be particularly damaging, as they would reduce the information value of the resulting credentials. For this reason any program for enhanced competition among schools should include strengthened national certification of competencies. Adopting some variant of the above proposals would most likely increase the regulatory activities of the state in education and reduce the extent of private as opposed to tax-based finance, while decreasing the state's production activities. The proposals would thus take better advantage of the state's unique advantages as a structure of governance.

Lastly, consider the case of property rights concerning children, and in particular the assignment of obligations to provide for their care. The common *de facto* assignment of these obligations to mothers rather than to fathers implies that marital separation generates a substantial increase in income inequality even if the mother and father have equal incomes.[53] As a result, a reassignment of property rights over the incomes of the two parents could significantly alter the level of inequality.

Aside from hardships occasioned by the existing arrangements, the distribution of implied property rights is inefficient for the same reason that tenancy and wage labor are inefficient: it separates residual claimancy from control. By shielding fathers from liability for their actions, *de facto* property rights concerning children provide a distorted structure of incentives for the mother and father in matters concerning the decision to have children, the care of children, and the amount of attention given to maintaining the relationship. The father has the *de facto* right not to provide financial or other care for his children should he choose not to continue a relationship with their mother, and he does not bear all the costs resulting from his action, displacing these costs to others (to the children, the mother, other members of the community). The father, in other words, is not a residual claimant on the net benefits and costs arising from his activities, just as workers in the capitalist firm do not own the results of their work (or lack thereof), and the tenant does not enjoy the full benefit resulting from his activities in improving the residential property. The solution here, as before, is to align residual claimancy and control more closely. But in this case the requirement may be better expressed by saying that the father should be made liable for the costs that his lack of attention might inflict on others.

The underlying problem is not that information is private. Indeed, the actors' actions could be fully known without altering the structure of the interaction. The problem rather is that because information on one's spouse's actions in a couple may not be admissible in court (the actions are observable but not verifiable), it would be pointless to contract for a level of care. Similar problems, we will see, confront any attempt to specify contractually the consequences of breakup.

The unequal distribution of costs upon separation being well known, it might be asked why women do not simply contract for a level of child support should the relationship end? As in the case of the capitalist owner seeking to contract for labor intensity or the landlord seeking to contract for care of the property, the answer is simply that such contracts are most often unenforceable. But unlike the two previous cases, where the problem of unenforcibility arises due to the intangible and complex nature of the service to be performed, here it arises because the absent parent may be impossible to locate, or without funds, or (in the contrary case) in a position to deploy superior legal resources.

But unlike individual parents the state, precisely by virtue of its comparative advantage in low-cost enforcement of universal rules, could enforce contracts of this nature. The state could in this case make and enforce new rules of the game. In particular, children can be assigned limited property rights in the income streams of their parents. The state could establish standard levels of child support corresponding to this property right, perhaps a given amount plus a fraction of the parent's reported taxable income, for children of various ages. This amount could then be transferred directly to children, through the parent currently caring for them. Assessing and collecting these charges could be effected by the revenue collection system.[54] Not all cases of neglected child support would thereby be addressed, but the vast majority may well be.[55]

Figure 9 summarizes the common logic behind these four cases. In each case there is a principal-agent problem flowing from the fact that important aspects of the agent's behavior are not subject to contractual enforcement. And in each of the cases, a transfer of property rights, residual claimancy, and control can, under the appropriate conditions, increase the efficiency of the system in an egalitarian fashion.

Figure 9: Redistributing Property Rights to Align Residual
Claimancy and Control of Non-Contractible Actions

Agent (A)	Agent's non-con-tractible action	Principal (P)	Problem	Solution
Worker	Quality and level of work effort	Employer and owner of work-related asset	P is residual claimant on A's actions	Transfer ownership of work-related asset to worker
Residential Tenant	Provision of community amenities and care of residential asset	Owner of residential asset	P is residual claimant on changes in asset value caused by A's actions	Transfer ownership of residential asset to tenant
School Manager	Quality of educational services	Student, and family as student's representative	A controls the relevant asset but P is resid-ual claimant on quality of services	Transfer school choice to student/family, so school is residual claimant over its actions
Father	Child support and care of the relationship with the mother	Child, and mother as child's representative	A controls level of care but P is liable for the costs of A's actions	Enforce default liabilities for child care, assigning residual claimancy to the father

9. Implementation: Insurance and Innovation

We have proposed four redistributions of property rights designed to align control of non-contractible actions more closely with residual claimancy over the results of these actions. We shall deal here with what we consider the possible shortcomings of these proposals. We could produce a long list of concerns that are simply not addressed by an asset-based redistribution strategy, but since our policy proposals do not interfere with the implementation of solutions to such concerns by other means, they pose no problem for our approach. Perhaps of greater interest, then, are the potential difficulties intrinsic to our approach as a general strategy.

First, and perhaps most serious, is the potential of asset-based redistribution, if widely implemented, to reduce the level of risk-taking and hence the pace of economic innovation, with the result of lowering long-term productivity growth. This difficulty is unavoid-able, for it is based on an aspect of the strategy that is key to its success. Unlike tax- and transfer-based approaches to redistribution our approach distributes not only claims on income but rights of control over productive assets as well. Indeed it is by unifying claims on income with control rights that the asset-based approach promises to attenuate the incentive problems that arise when actors are not the residual claimants on the income streams which their actions affect. But by redistributing control as well as income, the strategy places decision making power in the hands of less wealthy actors, who are likely to be more averse than the wealthy to taking risks and more conservative in evaluating potential innovations.[56]

Second, our proposed redistributions of property rights are egalitarian only in the sense that it shifts ownership of assets to the less wealthy. But since the value of these assets are subject to the vagaries of the market, and since the advantages of ownership of productive assets may be greater for those with more adequate initial resources, these redistributions may tend to increase the degree of inequality among the less wealthy.[57] This difficulty is also unavoidable, since it could not be eliminated completely without undermining the incentives that render asset-based redistribution productivity enhancing: if winners are not allowed to win and losers are not allowed to lose, then the relocation of property rights will undermine economic efficiency. Moreover, a redistribution of productive assets will not address the low incomes and wealth of individuals who are incapable of or choose not to supply high levels of effort in utilizing productive assets.

A third problem intrinsic to our proposal is that its reliance on competition may have unwanted cultural effects. The culture of a people is affected by its economic institutions, and the heavy reliance on competition in our model may foster a culture of self-interest, invidious distinction, individualism and materialism, by comparison to the cultural traits that would flourish in a society in which cooperation is favored over competition.

Consider first the possibility that asset redistribution to the less wealthy will reduce the level of risk-taking and hence the pace of economic innovation. This possibility flows from the fact that individual risk-aversion tends to decline with increasing wealth; i.e., the lower their wealth, and the larger a particular asset is as a fraction of their wealth, the less willing they are to expose their assets to the risk of loss. Thus by redistributing assets to the less wealthy, our proposal would have the effect of lowering the amount of risk taken in the economy as a whole. While this might be a desirable side-effect with respect to speculative risk-taking, it would not be with respect to technical change and product innovation.

The magnitude of the problem can be overstated; indeed, because asset inequality also limits the pace of innovation, an egalitarian redistribution might promote greater innovation. First, where access to education and other forms of human capital is highly unequal, and where the content of education for the vast majority is oriented towards accommodation to the bureaucratic organization of production characteristic of private economies with high levels of asset concentration, a large fraction of the population is deprived of the cognitive skills and personal capacities to innovate. Second, where wealth is highly unequal, the fraction of the population with the material resources to innovate is highly circumscribed. As we saw in our analysis of the output–equality trade-off in section 6, good projects may not be implemented when their value is based on private information held by the less wealthy. Finally, where most people are not residual claimants on the results of their productive activities, they have little incentive, individually or together, to seek new ways to solve production problems.

However, the tendency for egalitarian asset redistribution to reduce risk-taking is likely to be prominent in such areas as small businesses and democratic firms, especially when the capital requirements of production are high and the nature of the capital goods is specific to the particular enterprise and hence not salvagable should the project fail. Yet as we have suggested, asset-poor workers would be unlikely to want membership in such enterprises, as the level of risk exposure to which they would be subjected would be prohibitive. Thus the types of asset redistribution that would most depress innovation are unlikely to arise as long as workers' ownership is not mandated universally by *fiat*.

Indeed, barring a redistribution to achieve asset equality, the risk-aversion of the asset-poor will leave ample room for innovative private entrepreneurship based on personal or venture capital. If, after asset redistribution, these owners remain sufficiently wealthy, they could diversify their portfolios to spread the risk over many independent investments, and could thus behave in a virtually risk-neutral and hence socially optimal manner. Yet the innovation promoted by such firms would be readily emulated by worker-owned firms, under the pain of loss of market position. Finally, much product and technical innovation takes place in non-market institutions, including academic and research settings, that would continue and could be expanded as a means of increasing the pace of innovation.

Even with these provisos, however, the problem remains. We suggest two forms of state intervention that would increase risk-taking by the less wealthy, and thereby expand the scope of productivity enhancing asset-based redistribution. In both cases the state would offer insurance contracts designed to promote risk-taking without adversely affecting other productivity relevant incentives. Both could be self-financing in the sense that the expected revenues equal the expected costs. Both also draw on the state's particular advantage as a governance structure – its capacity to make and enforce the rules of the game – in this case to insure universal compliance.

We explain the impact of these forms of insurance using the following model of individual income, which we consider a plausible representation of the interaction of wealth, individual choices concerning risk exposure, and unavoidable risk exposure. Suppose a person's income has three parts: a fixed income y, a variable income that cannot be controlled by the person, and an investment income with risky return $r(f)$, where f is the risk associated with the investment, and is chosen by the person. We term the risk associated with the investment income 'controllable', as the level of exposure to this risk is chosen; other sources of income variation are termed 'exogenous risk'. We assume the expected return to the investment is an increasing function of the risk taken, at least up to a certain point (as in our previous treatment of risky investment in section 5). As before, we assume the degree of risk-aversion in the economy decreases with wealth. This means that for wealthier persons (in this case, for those with higher fixed incomes y, which can be considered an annual risk-free return to wealth) the risk premium needed to induce the person to accept a given risky investment is relatively low.

We can show (Bardhan, Bowles and Gintis, 1999) that those with higher wealth choose higher levels of controllable risk, so increasing the wealth of the less wealthy will promote higher levels of risk-taking. This assertion is intuitively plausible, and we have used it in developing our model in section 5. We also find that a decrease in the level of unavoidable risk exposure increases the level of controllable risk assumed by the person. A reduction in the volatility of the business cycle or the variability of prices of inputs, for example, would induce people to select higher levels of risk in the design of their projects. Universal and adequate health insurance has the same effects. We conclude that egalitarian asset-based redistribution, coupled with insurance against forms of uncertainty that cannot be controlled by the person – policies valued on egalitarian and personal security grounds – promote innovation.

The design of the appropriate insurance instruments, however, must balance the objective of reducing risk exposure against that of maintaining productivity-enhancing incentives. Consider again unemployment insurance. Workers lose jobs for two quite different reasons:

their employer may cut back employment for reasons unrelated to actions taken by the worker, and the worker's job may be terminated as the result of actions taken by the worker. An insurance policy consistent with the above principle would insure the worker against the first but not against the second eventuality. For instance, unemployment insurance with a very high replacement rate (unemployment benefits approximating income on the job) may induce the worker to be relatively unconcerned about job loss. But suppose the value of the benefit (the replacement rate or the duration of benefits) is designed to vary inversely with the business cycle, generous benefits being granted during recessions but not during expansions. Insurance would then be extended predominantly to those who lose their jobs for reasons outside their control, with limited payments only going to those whose own actions are implicated in their joblessness.

A high level of well-designed unemployment insurance could thus support higher levels of risk-taking in two senses: by directly protecting workers against risk, and its indirect effect in attenuating variations in aggregate demand, and hence dampening the volatility of the business cycle and reducing the extent of risk. Similar beneficial effects would be fostered by tying unemployment benefits to other observable variables indicative of exogenous risk, such as world prices, bankruptcy rates in an industry, and the pattern of technical change. We conclude that even without insuring people against the risks they may choose to take, higher levels of insurance against exogenous risk could promote innovation, simply by reducing the level of overall risk exposure.

But can insurance be provided against exogenous risk without reducing incentives for productivity? A worker-owned firm may make losses, for example, because of an exogenous increase in the real cost of borrowing, or because it failed to adopt an effective system of mutual monitoring. Is it possible to insure against the first without also insuring against the second? The answer is yes: insuring people against exogenous risk will, under plausible conditions, lead them to assume more controllable risk without altering other incentives. It follows that asset-based redistribution, coupled with insurance against forms of exogenous risk that is compatible with the incentives of agents to exploit their investments efficiently and does not reduce the level of innovation.

The problem is to provide such insurance in a manner that does not reward people for reducing their productive activity. Clearly insuring people against bankruptcy in general does not meet this criterion, since this would induce people to be indifferent to avoidable risks. However there are many risks that firms face that can be assessed independently from the discretionary actions of individual firms that can be the subject of social insurance. Suppose, for instance, that the probability of failure of a firm can be written as $\phi(f, e, x)$, where f is the level of project risk chosen by the work team, as described above, e is the effort of the firm members, and x are environmental factors not controlled by the firm. We assume ϕ is an increasing function of f and x, and a decreasing function of e. Suppose the state supplies insurance against failure, but it observes only the outcome (success or bankruptcy) and the level of x. Then the state could offer insurance $\gamma(x)$ that is increasing in x. For instance, the state may observe the average failure rate and profit rate in the industry, and reimburse firms that fail when these indicators of adversity are high, but not when these indicators are low. Similarly insurance can help firms recover from short-term economic down-turns, adverse movements in the terms of trade, consumer demand, or the price of production inputs. By thus dampening the uncontrollable aspects of asset risk, people can be induced to increase their risk level, and hence their level of innovation, in areas under their discretionary control. These examples of well designed insurance are not simply hypothetical. In the United States unemployment benefits are typically extended during periods of prolonged unemployment. In India crop insurance is sometimes based not on one's own crop, but on the average yields in neighboring areas (Dandekar 1985). Both insurance designs implement the *desideratum* that people should be shielded from exogenous risk, but not from controllable risk.

The effects of the insurance contracts proposed above would be a favorable shift in the output–equality trade-off defined in section 6, as can be seen in figure 10 over. There we reproduce the $Y(m, \ldots)$ function from figure 8 as well as the same output-equality function embodying the effects of insurance in inducing higher levels of risk-taking by the non-wealthy.[58] As is clear, the provision of insurance both shifts the function upwards and displaces it to the right, increasing the scope for output-enhancing asset redistribution (the level of equality that maximizes total income is greater with the insurance, indicated by the diamond-marker in the figure).

Figure 10:   Insurance Improves the Output–Equality Trade-off

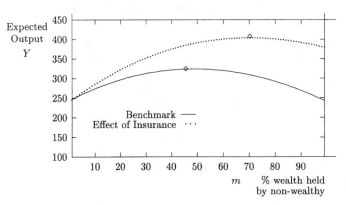

Note: See Note 58.

10. Implementation: Equality and Culture

Our second problem, the possibility that a redistribution of assets to the less wealthy might not be egalitarian, has a ring of paradox about it. Indeed, were there a simple correspondence between asset holdings and income this problem could not arise. But in a world of asymmetric information and incomplete contracts no such correspondence can be assumed. In this context our asset-based redistribution strategy may induce increased inequality among the less wealthy, arising either because the vicissitudes of the market inevitably create winners and losers, or because some individuals and groups cannot or prefer not to participate in the control of productive assets.

It might be suggested that any such inequalities that arise be corrected by other, traditional forms of redistribution, such as progressive income or estate taxation. But were this our only response asset-based redistribution, however attractive otherwise, could not be described as 'egalitarian'. We therefore address strategies that contribute to solving this problem that themselves draw upon the logic of asset-based redistribution.

In fact, the insurance policies we have advocated to promote risk-taking are effective means of increasing the egalitarian impact of asset-based redistribution. Many of the causes of low income are closely correlated with the observable and exogenous variations in the economy, personal health, and other determinants of well-being for which incentive-compatible insurance policies can be designed. To the extent that the less wealthy are risk-averse, they would welcome forms of insurance that reduce the expected fluctuations in the value of their assets. Such forms of insurance would also reduce the degree of inequality among less wealthy asset owners, and hence contribute to the solution of this problem.

With assets more equally distributed among the population, estate taxation may also be a considerably more potent instrument of intergenerational redistribution than it is with a highly unequal wealth distribution. For where wealth is highly unequally distributed, the rich have critical positions in the economy that they can deploy to ensure the transfer of their capital across generations. Where wealth is more equally distributed, however, no asset holder has a significant degree of economic power, and while the collective gains associated with rent-seeking behavior to subvert redistributive taxation may be undiminished, these gains are less concentrated, and hence provide more limited incentives and opportunities for rent-seeking efforts. Perhaps more important, with a more egalitarian distribution of wealth, intergenerational redistribution becomes a form of social insurance to which most relatively modest wealth holders might readily assent, prior to the unfolding of their own individual histories of success or failure.

To address the problem of poverty among groups unable or unwilling to hold assets in a productivity-enhancing manner we return to our notion of governance structures and incentive-compatible interventions. We make two proposals, one concerning the distribution of claims on income and the other the provision of services to persons with lower income. The logic of our proposals is that the state has unique and decisive advantages in the former and few in the latter.

Bad luck, as we have seen, is a contributor to poverty. So are good works. People engaged in the unpaid work of raising children, caring for home-ridden relatives, and performing community volunteer work typically have reduced access to income as a result of the services they perform. Some of this work has non-monetary rewards, but much of it remains unrewarded. The result is a standard market failure, in which the beneficial effects of one person's actions are enjoyed by others without full compensation to the actor. The uncompensated status of what Folbre (1994) calls 'caring labor' biases individual decisions against performing this type of service and in favor of entering the market for paying jobs, thus exacerbating the problem of unemployment. There are thus strong *prima facie* efficiency grounds for subsidizing caring labor and for supporting the institutions that promote it.[59]

We propose that all individuals be given a basic income grant, provisional on performing some useful but unpaid social service, such as the unpaid rearing of children or the care of those confined to their homes.[60] The grants would be financed by the state, but distributed by non-profit organizations, thereby strengthening the role of the community in economic governance. Only those constitutionally incapable of providing useful social functions would be exempt from this requirement, and the determination of what sorts of activities are socially useful would be determined by the non-profit organizations themselves.

Which caring institutions should be supported? We propose that every taxpayer have the right to transfer a certain fixed sum directly to non-profit organizations, subject to the proviso that the groups be appropriately accredited (for instance by the state or designated professional bodies). This sum would then be deducted from the taxpayers' obligation to the government.[61] The result of this decision mechanism is that community groups and other non-profit organizations would compete for grants, thus giving performance incentives to these groups, and individuals could formulate their own concepts of socially useful service, without having to conform to anything but a minimal uniform state-enforced norm. Non-profit organizations would also have an incentive to participate in the monitoring of groups with which they compete, thereby rectifying a major shortcoming of state provision, in the absence of competition among state agencies.

Our second proposal concerns the provision of services. Except in areas such as insurance, where the unique advantages of state supply of services are compelling, the role of the state should be in financing and regulating the delivery of services, not the provisioning of services itself. The most incentive-compatible alternative to service delivery by the state is a combination of public funding and private (or possibly private and public) competitive provision along the lines of the Canadian health care system. The replacement of publicly owned rental housing for low income residents by public subsidies, to reduce the cost of acquiring private ownership of residences, is a typical case in which the redistribution of assets could be both productivity enhancing and targeted to raise economic well-being among the poor. In other areas, eligible recipients of such services as mental health, family counseling, home care for the sick and elderly, and dependency treatment, could be given vouchers that could be redeemed by any accredited private agency supplying these services, in the same way as food stamps, rent subsidies, and income supplements are provided under the current system in the United States. Individuals not competent to choose would, of course, be exempted from this system. This system, if well designed, could make the supply of services responsive to the needs of the recipients, much as in the case of school vouchers, and also give the recipients the dignity that comes from the right to choose.

The third intrinsic difficulty posed by our proposal concerns the evolution of culture. An economic system in which competitive markets and competition for public monies occupy an important place constitutes a distinct cultural environment, one that may favor the replication of some behaviors and cultural traits over others. Many of the traits plausibly favored by competition are widely considered to be socially valuable – personal responsibility, and an ethic of entrepreneurship for example – while others are not.

There is little doubt but that a society with no other societal interaction other than competitive exchange and in which rewards went to people who conform most rigorously to the archetypal *homo economicus* would induce others to adopt similar values and behaviors, thus promoting a set of widely deplored cultural values.[62] But we have not suggested that society be reduced to competitive exchange or advocated a reduced presence of the state or of communities.

In a heterogeneous governance system, we would expect the social pressures that individuals face in competitive market relations to be complemented by the potentially cooperative relations they face within communities and workplaces, and by the ethic of human rights, party competition, and social purpose fostered by a liberal democratic political environment, particularly one whose public life was enhanced by the flourishing of non-profit organizations that might be expected under the tax credit system we propose.

Many egalitarians will applaud the promotion of community and state values, but consider the values fostered by competition, the market, and private property to be at best a necessary evil. We think this is incorrect. Developing the capacity to compete through the instrumental choice of strategies in competition with others doing the same is as much a part of personal development as is developing a capacity to cooperate, share and submit to legitimate authority. Indeed, competing is a common strategy for the assertion of one's individuality and the expression of one's creativity.

Finally, we cannot assess the culture engendered by our nexus of economic governance structures in the abstract, but must compare it with other suggested alternatives. Excluding utopian communitarian proposals, an obvious alternative to asset-based redistribution would be the restriction of competition and markets in favor of an enhanced role for central planning and hierarchical command relations, subjected to democratic accountability. It would be hard to argue that the cultural values promoted by such institutions would compare favorably to those suggested by our proposal. Evidence on the complex questions concerning the cultural consequences of alternative economic arrangements is hard to come by, but the reasoning of those who have studied the question with care is suggestive. Putnam (1993) concludes from his study of networks of civic engagement in Italy that 'A vertical network, no matter how dense and no matter how important to its participants, cannot sustain trust and cooperation'. Similarly, Kohn's comparative study of work organization (Kohn et al., 1990) supports a causal link between bureaucratic structures and the evolution of authoritarian personality traits. These studies are hardly decisive, but they serve as a reminder that the cultural consequences of the alternatives to competition may be far from attractive.

11. Conclusion

The four egalitarian reallocations of property rights we have discussed – worker-ownership, home ownership, children's rights and educational vouchers – illustrate a general point: property rights allocations affect both equity and efficiency. There is no reason to expect that an observed distribution of property rights is economically efficient, since those who might make the socially most valuable use of a bundle of property rights often lack the wealth to acquire the rights. Indeed, precisely because the less wealthy are differentially excluded from obtaining property rights in productive assets, it is likely that existing distributions of rights are excessively unequal from a purely efficiency standpoint.

Our analysis also illustrates a second general point: where people with differing objectives interact, resolving differences through compromise or permitting a third party (such as the state) to determine a uniform outcome is often inferior to restructuring the incentives facing the interacting parties and then allowing each to choose his or her preferred alternative. Markets and communities, in different but complementary ways, are thus necessary elements of any economically efficient nexus of governance structures.

Figure 11: Interventions for Redistribution

		Redistribution of Market Determined Income Flows	
		High	*Low*
Redistribution of Assets	*High*	Market Socialism Central Planning	Asset-Based Redistribution
	Low	Social Democracy Developmental State	Laissez-Faire Capitalism

The resulting economic policy paradigm, which we have termed 'asset-based redistribution' might be described as 'competition on a level playing field'. In this paradigm the role of the state is to implement outcomes not directly, by *fiat*, but by establishing the property rights and rules of competition, as well as other rules that determine the outcomes of social interactions. This conception is a redefinition of the state's role in governance as compared with traditional notions of the interventionist state, but not necessarily a reduction in its presence in economic affairs. While the state's role in production would be minimal, the scope of its activities in redefining and reassigning rights of residual claimancy and control, in its credentialing role in an educational voucher system, or in implementing children's rights, and in providing insurance, would be considerable. Moreover, the state would have an ongoing role in redistribution, though less in overriding market outcomes than in the continuing redistribution of property rights to overcome the disequalizing consequences of luck, increasing returns to scale, differences in individual abilities, and other forces contributing to uneven development.

A comparison may illuminate differences between our and alternative approaches. A fundamental difference among paradigms is the importance each gives to the redistribution of assets on the one hand and redistribution of the income or other benefits resulting from assets, on the other. Four possible approaches are illustrated in figure 11. Market socialism and central planning involve high levels of asset redistribution as well as state determination of at least some of the key prices in the economy and a centralized claim on a substantial fraction of the income flows received by productive units. In this they contrast with *laissez-faire* capitalism, which accepts no such interference with market outcomes. Social democracy and the developmental state (by the latter we mean the forms of state intervention undertaken by many Asian economies, such as South Korea and Japan) involve extensive intervention on the level of price determination (incomes policies, price supports, tariffs and quotas), but relatively little interference with the distribution of property titles. Asset-based redistribution is the polar opposite of this pattern, reallocating residual claimancy and control rights among private owners, but not directly intervening in the market determination of prices, except where market externalities (e.g., environmental effects) indicate a divergence of market prices from social costs.

There are two economic advantages of asset-based redistribution. First, it is productivity enhancing because of its positive incentive effects in exchanges involving goods and services for which contracts enforceable at low cost cannot be written (this includes labor effort, information, and the intangibles determining the productivity in the production process). These advantages are diminished in the market socialist model (by the commitment to public rather than private ownership of property) and the social democratic model (by concentration of private property rights, depriving workers and others of the positive incentives of residual claimancy). Second, because asset-based redistribution achieves egalitarian outcomes through asset transfers, it can use markets to discipline economic actors without thereby enforcing a high level of inequality in economic outcomes. For the same reason it avoids the productivity-dampening incentives that accompany income redistribution through taxes and transfers. While asset redistributions involve some incentive distortion – there would be opportunities for wasteful rent-seeking in the provision of subsidized credit to worker-owned firms, for example – we believe that the support of productivity-enhancing forms of egalitarian ownership could accomplish considerable redistribution at an acceptable cost.

But are not such proposals utopian in the face of the globalization of production and the heightened competition among producers facing radically differing wage structures? While global competition challenges many conventional redistributive policies, it does not preclude a recasting of the egalitarian project along the lines we have suggested. An economically viable egalitarianism would rely substantially on the kinds of productivity enhancing asset-based redistributions that simultaneously promote equality and strengthen the economy's competitive position. The chief impediments to egalitarianism in the globally integrated economy may not be a dearth of economically viable programs, but rather a surfeit of political obstacles. There are three reasons for this.

First, as we have seen, by enhancing the degree of competition in most markets, international integration reduces the effectiveness of demand expansion policies that once helped secure the support of disparate elements in the egalitarian coalitions that promoted redistributional policies during the post-Second World War golden age. Second, the contemporary more globally competitive situation has heightened a divergence of interest between public sector and private sector workers, between the employed and the unemployed, among workers, farmers and those in the informal sector, and between these and other groups whose unified endorsement of egalitarian policies was often critical to their success. Owners of firms in consumer goods industries, for example, may be less likely to join workers in support of wage increases and other domestic demand-enhancing policies and look instead to the world market. Producers – employers and workers – in sectors exposed to competition may find alliances difficult to build with those in protected sectors, and particularly with those in public employment.[63]

Finally, to the extent that new policies require asset-based redistributions, they are likely to incur strong opposition by an anti-egalitarian coalition that in many countries can readily unify under the banner of the defense of the existing distribution and definition of property rights.

On the other hand, a broader dispersion of asset holdings in the population and the close association of property holdings with both residence and workplace entailed by the asset-based redistribution strategy would reduce the global mobility of capital and thereby might relax one of the major constraints on egalitarian policy.

Notes

1. This is not to say that leftist economists have run out of models or have abandoned the construction of alternatives to capitalism, as a reading of Bardhan and Roemer (1992), Roemer (1996) and van Parijs (1995), will indicate.

2. In the United States in 1987, for example, the above categories of 'guard labor' constituted over a quarter of the labor force, and the rate of growth of guard labor substantially outstripped the rate of growth of the labor force in the previous two decades (Bowles et al., 1990).

3. A tripartite division of governance structures has been proposed by a number of authors. Ouchi (1980) refers to these as markets, bureaucracies and clans, while Ostrom (1990) analyses centralized, market decentralized and decentralized mutual enforcement systems of governance.

4. A critical example of a coordination failure of this type are strikes. It is perhaps not surprising that in the more advanced welfare states and more egalitarian capitalist economies, Sweden, Netherlands, Denmark and Germany, for example, the fraction of workdays lost to strikes in the period 1955–89 averaged less than a third of the level

in countries with less well-developed welfare states, the United States, Canada, Australia and Italy (US Bureau of Labor Statistics, 1990).

5. Bardhan (1993), Boyce (1988), and Bardhan, Bowles and Gintis (1999) argue that the many commons-type coordination failures are easier to solve where inequality among participants is limited. Singleton and Taylor (1992) argue that the inability to solve coordination failures often stems from the lack of community, defined as a set of people with shared beliefs, stable membership, and ongoing, relatively unmediated interaction: 'The more a group resembles a community, the lower are the transactions costs which it must meet in order to solve a given collective action problem' (p. 319). Putnam (1993) finds that horizontal networks of civic engagement support forms of cooperation that enhance economic performance while vertical (hierarchical) networks do not.

6. For some recent treatments of the relationship between property rights and efficiency, see Dasgupta and Ray, 1986, Grossman and Hart 1986, Milgrom 1988, Moene 1989, Stiglitz 1989, Hart and Moore 1990, Eaton and White 1991, Aghion and Bolton 1992, Moene 1992, Manning 1992, Hoff and Lyon 1995, Hoff 1994, Newman 1994, Banerjee and Newman 1994, Aghion and Bolton 1997, Mookherjee 1997, and Bardhan, Bowles and Gintis 1999.

7. The 'residual claimant' owns whatever remains (the residual) after all fixed claims (in this case the rent paid to the owner) are settled.

8. For examples of wealth inequality inducing economic inefficiency, see Eswaran and Kotwal (1989), Stiglitz (1988), Bowles and Gintis (1993b), and for an overview, see Bardhan, Bowles and Gintis (1999). Several mechanisms of this type have been analysed. First, low wealth producers tend to be highly risk-averse, leading them to hold low productivity, but highly liquid capital (Rosenzweig and Wolpin 1993, Nerlove and Soedjiana 1996, Hoff 1996a). Second, credit limitations faced by non-wealthy producers lead to inefficient production. Several plausible models illustrating this behavior (Loury 1981, Stiglitz 1974, Gintis 1989, Stiglitz 1989, Banerjee and Newman 1993, Rosenzweig and Wolpin 1993, Galor and Zeira 1993, Bowles and Gintis 1994, Barham, Broadway, Marchand and Pestieau 1995, Hoff and Lyon 1995, Hoff 1996b, Legros and Newman 1996, Aghion and Bolton 1997, Bénabou 1996, Piketty 1997), and several empirical studies have found it operative (Laffon and Matoussi 1995, Carter and Mesbah 1993, Barham, Boucher and Carter 1996, Carter and Barham 1996, Sial and Carter 1996, Rosenzweig and Wolpin 1993, Rosenzweig and Binswanger 1993, Laffont and Matoussi 1995). Finally low wealth depresses labor market opportunities (Bardhan 1984).

9. For a review of the literature on this topic, see Bardhan, Bowles and Gintis (1999).

10. This point is developed in Bowles and Gintis (1998a) and Bowles and Gintis (1998b).

11. We do not specify the metric in which these distributions are measured, for nothing in the following pages hinges on our use of any particular measure of wealth, income, or other attributes of concern to egalitarians.

12. Bowles et al. (1990) also find a negative association between income inequality and both the long term rate of growth of output per employed person and the investment share of output in ten advanced capitalist economies. Persson and Tabellini (1996), for instance, find that inequality and growth in gross domestic product are negatively correlated in a cross section of 67 nations as well as in long time series for nine advanced capitalist nations. Similarly Alesina and Rodrik (1994) find that a measure of asset (land) inequality is inversely associated with economic growth in a sample of 39 countries. Glyn (1995) surveys the impact of the 1980s shift in economic policy in most of the advanced capitalist nations towards less egalitarian objectives. See also Chang (1994).

13. These data are from Glyn, Hughes, Lipietz and Singh (1990), based on Maddison (1982).

14. A redistribution from profits to wages has predictably positive effects on the

demand for consumer goods, but it is offset by the negative impact of wage increases on demand for investment goods and net exports.

15. Gordon's (1995) study of the US comes to similar conclusions.

16. This argument has been compellingly made by Moene and Wallerstein (1993); see also their contribution to this volume.

17. See Koechlin (1992).

18. Productivity growth means an increase in output per unit of a composite of inputs in which both the measure of inputs and outputs takes account of environmental effects. As defined, productivity growth is both conceptually and practically distinct from other criteria such as income growth or 'competitiveness'. Further, policies designed to reduce working time would be consistent with the objective of productivity growth, but not with the objective of output growth.

19. For example, suppose the bottom half of the income distribution receives 25 per cent of total income. Equalizing income would on the average double the income of members of the bottom half of the distribution. Continuous productivity growth at a rate of 2.5 per cent per year for 27 years could also double the income of each member of the bottom half of the distribution, with no change in the degree of inequality. Of course economic welfare may depend on one's relative economic position in addition to one's absolute. To the extent that this is true, sustained productivity growth overestimates welfare growth for the less well-off. However, economic welfare may also depend on one's expected future absolute economic position relative to one's current position, in which case sustained productivity growth underestimates welfare growth for all persons.

20. We define a pure conflict situation as one in which all feasible outcomes are Pareto-optimal, and a pure coordination situation as one in which there is only one Pareto-optimal outcome and given any two distinct feasible outcomes, one is Pareto-preferred to the other.

21. This example should not be taken literally, of course. There will necessarily be losers in any major change in property rights or other aspects of the institutions that coordinate economic activity. The fundamental point is not that all changes should be strictly Pareto-improving (no losers) but egalitarian redistributions should be productivity enhancing.

22. An example is the initial opposition by US business to Keynesian economic policy and its preference for minimalist regulation of the macroeconomy by means of monetary policy. To many, macroeconomic instability was the lesser evil if the alternative was a carte blanche for the state.

23. This model borrows from Bowles, Gordon and Weisskopf (1992). Employer employee relationships have been modeled extensively as prisoners' dilemmas, starting with Leibenstein (1982), and including Solow (1990).

24. Johansen (1979) first elaborated this argument. It has been convincingly applied by Moene (1989).

25. Elster (1989) has argued that the failure to solve coordination failures typically arises from the lack of an agreed-upon principle for the division of the benefits of cooperation.

26. Estimates vary, of course, but monitoring expenses appear to be about a fifth of the cost of labor in the US. The resources devoted to monitoring the labor process are of roughly the same magnitude as those devoted to producing the capital goods with which workers are employed. See David Gordon (this volume).

27. This fact was first brought out in the so-called 'socialism debate' in the 1930s, between the market socialist Oskar Lange and the *laissez-faire* proponent Friedrich Hayek, for the case of perfectly competitive markets (Lange and Taylor, 1938). The analysis was extended by Coase (1960) to the case of market failures. The central point here is that when there are market failures, bargaining among agents can correct the market solution, and under conditions of symmetric information bargaining will be efficient. See Farrell (1987) for an analysis of the Coase Theorem and its limits.

28. Wade (1987), for example, studied coordination problems in South Indian

villages and found that an important correlate of a village's capacity to solve prisoners' dilemma-type coordination failures was the extent to which the mutual cooperation solution improved on the mutual defect outcome.

29. The observation that market competition makes producers more accountable by increasing the information concerning production that is available to non-producers (including individual consumers, community planning boards, and state regulators) should be contrasted with the assertion that market competition promotes allocational efficiency by 'getting the prices right'. The role of markets in promoting allocational efficiency has been seriously overrated, in our opinion. By contrast, the role of markets in promoting the accountability of producers has been seriously underrated. In effect, market competition turns production into a prisoners' dilemma in which producers have a common interest in hiding their conditions of production (e.g., by overstating their costs, overstating their effort levels, and understating their opportunities for innovation), while each individual producer has an incentive to 'defect' by undercutting its rivals, thereby revealing its true production conditions. Markets induce socially beneficial defection in this case.

30. This is a statement about the relative merits of imperfect forms of governance, not about the optimality of markets. The claim that competitive markets support Pareto-optimal outcomes plays little role in current debates about alternative forms of governance and is true only under implausibly stringent conditions.

31. This point is developed in Bardhan, Bowles and Gintis (1999). For a simple example, suppose n entrepreneurs have investments that cost k in initial capital costs. To the outside world these projects are indistinguishable, with a probability p of succeeding, in which case the firm would gross π, and a probability of $(1 - p)$ of failing, in which case the firm's revenue is zero. Then these investments should be undertaken if their expected return $p\pi$ is greater than their cost $k(1 + \varrho)$ where ϱ is the interest rate which we assume is equal to the social opportunity cost of capital.

If the entrepreneurs are risk-averse, they may not undertake the projects unless they can obtain insurance against failure. If investments are identical, it is clear that the entrepreneurs will be able to obtain fair and full insurance through the market (abstracting from the transactions cost involved in writing the contracts), since an insurance company will agree to pay the entrepreneur $k(1 + \varrho)$ if the project fails, and receive from the entrepreneur $(1 - p)k(1 + \varrho)/p$ if the project succeeds (the expected value of this policy to the insurance company is zero). In this case the entrepreneur receives $\pi - (1 - p)k(1 + \varrho)/p - k(1 + \varrho) = \pi - k(1 + \varrho)/p > 0$ in case of success, and zero in case of failure, which is also acceptable to the entrepreneur.

However, suppose the investments are not identical, and the entrepreneurs must make the investment of k to start the business before applying for insurance, but by investing they learn more about the probability of success. Again for simplicity, assume that half the entrepreneurs find that their investment will surely succeed, and the other half find that they will surely fail. In that case the fortunate entrepreneurs will not buy insurance at all, and the unfortunate ones will be unable to purchase insurance, since the insurance company knows that only a failing business will seek insurance. Since we can expect all the entrepreneurs to understand this situation prior to their decision to invest the k, we conclude that they will not invest, and the socially beneficial projects will not be undertaken.

32. See Przeworski (1996), Schmitter (1995), Cohen and Rodgers (1995), and Wittman (1989) for suggestions along these lines.

33. We analyze communities as governance structures in greater detail in Bowles and Gintis (1997) and Bowles and Gintis (1998b).

34. See, for example, Ostrom (1990), Thomas and Logan (1982), Craig and Pencavel (1995), Greenberg (1986), Hossain (1988), Frolich, Godard, Oppenheimer and Starke (1997), Verba, Schlozman and Brady (1995), and Sampson, Raudenbush and Earls (1997).

35. This follows directly from repeated game theory, which shows that cooperative behavior can be sustained when actors have long time horizons relative to the time

between interactions, a condition that is ensured by a sufficiently high frequency of interaction. See Bowles and Gintis (1998b).

36. Models illustrating this point are developed in Bowles and Gintis (1998b) and Bowles and Gintis (1997).

37. It may also be observed that norms effective in reducing costly contestation may induce waste in seeking to satisfy the norm. Any division rule based on first arrivals for example is bound to lead to waste in competition to be first, as was pointed out by Sugden (1989).

38. For example, Greif (1994) argues that the eventual superiority of the Genoese over the North African Maghribi traders in the early development of Mediterranean trade stemmed from the scale limitations of the locally very effective community-based enforcement strategies of the Maghribi traders.

39. Risk-neutral actors are indifferent between a gamble and a sure thing if their expected value is the same. Thus risk-neutral actors choose risk levels that maximize the expected value of the outcome irrespective of the dispersion of the distribution of outcomes around its expected value. We assume that a large society in which the endogenously determined stochastic elements in the returns to projects are substantially uncoordinated across projects can provide insurance against these risks to its members.

40. Figure 8 was drawn using a $\tilde{r}(m) = r - cm/(n - 1)$, so $\tilde{r}(m)$ falls from r to $r - c$ as m increases from 0 to $n - 1$. Similarly, we have defined

$$\beta(m) = \beta + \frac{(1 - \beta)m}{(n - 1)}$$

so $\beta(m)$ rises from β to 1 as m increases from 0 to $n - 1$. The 'benchmark' values of the variables are $\beta = 0.4$, $r = 20$, $c = 2$, $y = 1$, and $F^* = 0.07$. The 'steep' value of β is 0.5, and the 'low' value of r is 10 (we also shifted the latter curve upward by 75 for easier comparison purposes).

41. The employer may also use the promise of promotion and other incentives, but adding these to our model would not change the argument.

42. The contingent renewal model of the employment relationship is developed in Gintis (1976), Shapiro and Stiglitz (1984), Bowles (1985), Gintis and Ishikawa (1987) and Bowles and Gintis (1993a). We may briefly describe such a model as follows. Firm profits are an increasing function of worker effort e. The employer has an imperfect measure of worker effort, and dismisses a worker who is caught shirking. The probability of dismissal is thus a decreasing function $p(e, m)$ of the level of effort e chosen by the worker and depends on the level m of monitoring chosen by the firm. The worker has utility function $u(w, e)$ that is increasing in the wage w and decreasing in effort e. The worker chooses e to maximize the discounted present value v of the job. If the discount rate is ϱ and the worker's fallback position upon losing the job is z, the worker's objective function can be written as

$$\max_e v = \frac{u(w, e) - \varrho z}{p(e, m) + \varrho} + z.$$

The quantity $(u(w,e) - \varrho z)/(p(e) + \varrho) = v - z$ is thus the rent the worker enjoys from the relationship, the threat of withdrawal of which induces a high level of effort. The firm then chooses the wage w and the level of monitoring m to maximize effort per dollar $e/(w + m)$.

43. We demonstrate this in Bowles and Gintis (1993a).

44. We have in mind something of the type that, according to Craig and Pencavel (1995), is approximated in practice by the ownership structure of a large number of worker-owned plywood mills in the Northwest of the United States; see also Dow (1986) and Fehr (1993). Like the passive owner, the team uses contingent renewal to motivate member effort. Team members who are terminated must sell their share of

the asset without penalty other than the loss of the enforcement rent $v - z$ (we are using the notation developed in note 42 on this page).

The decision facing the active ownership firm (abstracting from the problem of the optimal number of members), is to select a level of monitoring m to maximize members' present value v of tenure. Each member receives an income from the team equal to $q(\sum_i e_i)/n - m$, where $q(\cdot)$ is revenue as a function of total team effort. Thus the net payment taking account of the member's forgone interest income, ρk_0 on each member's capital contribution k_0, is $w = q(\sum_i e_i)/n - m - \rho k_0$. Thus the team must select m according to

$$v = \max_m \frac{u(w, e) - \rho z}{\rho + p(e, m)} + z.$$

Given that each worker's best response function is still of the form $e = e(w, m)$, we interpret the problem as follows: the team collectively selects a level of monitoring and agrees to pay the residual income of the organization to members as a salary equal to w plus the forgone return on assets ρk_0. Each team member j then selects e_j to maximize v_j.

45. See Ward (1958), Vanek (1970), Domar (1966), Meade (1972), Furubotn and Pejovich (1974), and Jensen and Meckling (1979). For an insightful review of this literature, see Bonin and Putterman (1987).

46. Mutual monitoring is not without cost, of course, as it may require a coordinator and may be time consuming in cases where verification of insufficient work by a team member is contested. Where work is highly dispersed, as is sometimes the case in agricultural production, mutual monitoring may be ineffective as workers will lack good information on the work activities of their teammates. For a model of mutual monitoring, see Weissing and Ostrom (1991) and Bardhan, Bowles and Gintis (1999).

47. Levine and Tyson (1990), for instance, surveyed fourteen studies of worker cooperatives and found positive effects on productivity in thirteen of them, with no negative effects in any. Weitzman and Kruse (1990) surveyed 16 econometric studies of the effects of profit sharing on productivity and found that of the total of 226 estimated regression coefficients for variables measuring profit sharing 94 per cent were positive and 60 per cent were twice or more than their standard errors, while no negative coefficient estimates were statistically significant by this standard. For related studies supporting this research, see Cable and FitzRoy (1980), Ben-Ner (1988), and Conte and Svejnar (1990). Worker participation in decision making and residual claimancy status appear to be complementary in that their joint effects exceed the additive effects of each separate factor.

48. Indeed, the capital stock per worker required to operate most firms is considerably in excess of the total assets of most working families. In the US, for example, the value of the capital goods used in production per worker employed averages just under $100,000, while the average net assets of the least wealthy 80 per cent of families, including car and home ownership, is $64,000. So most working families, even if they sold their house and car could not finance the capital goods to employ even a single family member.

49. A general subsidy of home ownership, by contrast, serves no productivity-enhancing purpose as most home owners have sufficient wealth to avoid the market failures associated with tenancy.

50. By contrast the leadership has every reason to pay careful attention to the directives of the local board, for this is the source of the school funding, including the leadership's salary, tenure, and perks.

51. For an expanded analysis of school choice as part of an educational governance structure, see Gintis (1995) and Jencks (1992).

52. If it were deemed desirable to have schools remain part of the state sector on grounds of greater democratic control of educational content and the social relations of schools, the use of vouchers could be restricted to public schools. The important

point is that free entry and the competitive delivery of educational services be part of the educational governance structure.

53. In a society composed of an equal number of adult men and women and children in which women receive incomes two thirds that of men and couples pool and share income, there is no income inequality if all are in couples (one child per couple). Yet the Gini coefficient of income inequality would be a substantial 0.27 if all the couples separated and women were responsible for the support of the children, assuming no other changes in the data. This is a greater amount of inequality than is generated by unequal ownership of capital, assuming that the richest five per cent of income earners own all the capital.

54. The standard child-support levels (similar to standard charges for medical procedures in many insurance systems) could be the 'default' amounts to be paid. These default amounts could be altered by the courts, or under some conditions, by mutual agreement of the parents.

55. We do not consider reassigning enforceable property rights concerning children to be a retreat from a general social responsibility for the care of children. Rather it is a social strengthening of the family as a support system for financing and caring for children. Where parents cannot provide adequate financing, or where provisioning children's education, health care, recreation and other needs are most effectively provided by the public sector, public provisioning remains appropriate.

56. See Bardhan, Bowles and Gintis (1999), section 4.

57. Moene (1992) argues convincingly that land redistribution may have these disequalizing consequences.

58. The model underlying figure 10 is described in Note 40. The 'Benchmark' curve describes the wealth inequality versus expected output relationship for $F^* = 0.07$, corresponding to a choice of failure rate $f = 0.076$. The effect of insurance is to increase F^* to $F^* = 0.10$, corresponding to a failure rate $f = 0.112$.

59. Of course 'caring labor', like worker effort, managerial effort, borrower prudence, and other actions that are difficult to monitor and hence cannot be effectively specified by contract, should be rewarded in a manner most likely to induce recipients to develop 'caring skills' and to elicit a high level of recipient effort. This could entail performance-contingent subsidies rather than flat grants.

60. This idea is inspired by the basic income grant proposal of van Parijs and Van Der Veen (1986), though the conditionality of the grant derives from the related proposal of Atkinson (1995).

61. Schmitter (1992) has developed a related proposal designed to support secondary institutions promoting civic engagement.

62. For a critical evaluation of the effects of markets as cultural environments, see Bowles (1998a, b).

63. Trade liberalization might enhance the viability of egalitarian coalitions in other respects. Gerschenkron (1944) argues that conflicts over tariff policies obstructed a potentially egalitarian farmer-worker alliance in pre-First World War Germany, for example. A general argument might be made that tariff and other policies that politicize the relative prices of commodities tend to favor within-industry alliances seeking to gain income by altering relative goods prices, rather than cross-industry coalitions seeking to alter income distribution directly. The latter type of coalition may be more viable as a vehicle for egalitarian policy.

References

Aghion, Philippe and Patrick Bolton, 'An Incomplete Contracts Approach to Financial Contracting', *Review of Economic Studies*, 59 (1992), pp. 473–94.

——, 'A Theory of Trickle-down Growth and Development', *Review of Economic Studies*, 64, 2 (April 1997), pp. 151–72.

Alesina, Alberto and Dani Rodrik, 'Distributive Politics and Economic Growth', *Quarterly Journal of Economics*, 109 (1994), pp. 465–90.

Arrow, Kenneth J., 'Political and Economic Evaluation of Social Effects and Externalities', in M. D. Intriligator (ed.), *Frontiers of Quantitative Economics* (Amsterdam: North Holland, 1971).

Atkinson, Anthony, *Public Economics in Action: The Basic Income/Flat Tax Proposal*, Lindahl Lectures Series, (Oxford: Oxford University Press, 1995).

Banerjee, Abhijit and Andrew Newman, 'Occupational Choice and the Process of Development', *Journal of Political Economy*, 101, 2 (April 1993), pp. 274–98.

——, 'Poverty, Incentives, and Development', *American Economic Association Papers and Proceedings* (May 1994), pp. 211–15.

Bardhan, Pranab, *Land, Labor and Rural Poverty: Essays in Development Economics*, (New York: Columbia University Press, 1984).

——, 'Analytics of the Institutions of Informal Cooperation in Rural Development', *World Development*, 21, 4 (1993), pp. 633–9.

——, and John Roemer, 'Market Socialism: A Case for Rejuvenation', *Journal of Economic Perspectives*, 6, 3 (Summer 1992), pp. 101–16.

——, Samuel Bowles, and Herbert Gintis, 'Wealth Inequality, Credit Constraints, and Economic Performance', in Anthony Atkinson and François Bourguignon (eds.), *Handbook of Income Distribution* (North Holland, 1999).

Barham, Bradford, Steve Boucher, and Michael Carter, 'Credit Constraints, Credit Unions, and Small-Scale Producers in Guatemala', *World Development*, 24, 5 (1996), pp. 792-805.

Barham, Vicky, Robin Boadway, Maurice Marchand, and Pierre Pestieau, 'Education and the Poverty Trap', *European Economic Review*, 39, 7 (August 1995), pp. 1257–75.

Ben-Ner, Avner, 'Comparative Empirical Observations on Worker-Owned and Capitalist Firms', *International Journal of Industrial Organization*, 6 (1988), pp. 7–31.

Bénabou, Roland, 'Inequality and Growth', NBER Macroeconomics Annual, (March 1996).

Bonin, John P. and Louis Putterman, *Economics of Cooperation and the Labor-Managed Economy*, (New York: Harwood, 1987).

Bowles, Samuel, 'The Production Process in a Competitive Economy: Walrasian, Neo-Hobbesian, and Marxian Models', *American Economic Review*, 75, 1 (March 1985), pp. 16–36.

——, 'Mandeville's Mistake: The Evolution of Norms in Competitive Environments', University of Massachusetts Discussion Paper (1998a).

——, 'Endogenous Preferences: The Cultural Consequences of Markets and Other Economic Institutions', *Journal of Economic Literature*, 36 (March 1998b).

——, and Herbert Gintis, 'The Democratic Firm: An Agency-Theoretic Evaluation', in Samuel Bowles, Herbert Gintis, and Bo Gustafsson (eds.), *Democracy and Markets: Participation, Accountability, and Efficiency*, (Cambridge: Cambridge University Press, 1993a).

——, and Herbert Gintis, 'The Revenge of Homo Economicus: Contested Exchange and the Revival of Political Economy', *Journal of Economic Perspectives*, (Winter 1993b).

——, and Herbert Gintis, 'Credit Market Imperfections and the Incidence of Worker-Owned Firms', *Metroeconomica*, 45, 3 (October 1994), pp. 209–23.

——, and Herbert Gintis, 'Optimal Parochialism: The Dynamics of Trust and Exclusion in Communities', (University of Massachusetts Working Paper, June 1997).

——, and Herbert Gintis, 'How Communities Govern: The Structural Basis of Prosocial Norms', in Louis Putterman and Avner Ben-Ner (eds.), *Economics, Values and Organizations* (New York: Cambridge University Press, 1998a).

——, and Herbert Gintis, 'The Moral Economy of Community: Structured Populations and the Evolution of Prosocial Norms', *Evolution & Human Behavior*, 19 (January 1998b), pp. 3–25.

——, and Robert Boyer, 'Wages Aggregate Demand and Employment in an Open Economy: A Theoretical and Empirical Investigation', in Gerald Epstein and Herbert Gintis (eds.), *Macroeconomic Policy After the Conservative Era: Research on Investment Savings and Finance*, (Cambridge: Cambridge University Press, 1995).

——, David M. Gordon, Thomas E. Weisskopf, *After the Waste Land: A Democratic Alternative for the Year 2000*, (New York: Armonk, NY: M.E. Sharpe, 1990).

——, David M. Gordon, Thomas E. Weisskopf, 'We Need Handshakes and Arm-Twisting to Mobilize our Recovery', *Challenge*, (March–April 1992), pp. 48–54.

Boyce, James, 'Technological and Institutional Alternatives in Asian Rice Irrigation', *Economic and Political Weekly*, (March 26, 1988).

Cable, John and Felix Fitzroy, 'Co-operation and Productivity: Some Evidence from West German Experience', *Economic Analysis and Worker's Management*, 14 (1980), pp. 163–80.

Carter, Michael R. and Bradford Barham, 'Level Playing Fields and *Laissez-Faire*: Post-Liberal Development Strategies in Inegalitarian Agrarian Economies', *World Development*, 24, 7 (1996), pp. 1133–50.

——, and Dina Mesbah, 'Can Land Market Reform Mitigate the Exclusionary Aspects of Rapid Agro-Export Growth?', *World Development*, (July 1993).

Chang, Roberto, 'Income Inequality and Economic Growth: Evidence and Recent Theories', *Economic Review* (July–August 1994), pp. 1–10. Federal Reserve Bank of Atlanta.

Coase, Ronald H., 'The Problem of Social Cost', *Journal of Law and Economics*, 3 (October 1960), pp. 1–44.

Cohen, Joshua and Joel Rogers, *Associations and Democracy*, (London: Verso, 1995).

Conte, Michael A. and Jan Svejnar, 'The Performance Effects of Employee Ownership Plans', in Alan Blinder (ed.), *Paying for Productivity: A Look at the Evidence*, (Washington: Brookings Institution, 1990), pp. 143–72.

Craig, Ben and John Pencavel, 'Participation and Productivity: A Comparison of Worker Cooperatives and Conventional Firms in the Plywood Industry', *Brookings Papers: Microeconomics*, (1995), pp. 121–60.

Dandekar, V.M., 'Crop Insurance in India: A Review 1976–1984–5', *Economic and Political Weekly*, 20, 25 (1985), A46–A59.

Dasgupta, Partha and Debraj Ray, 'Inequality as a Determinant of Malnutrition and Unemployment: Theory', *Economic Journal*, 96 (December 1986), pp. 1011–34.

Domar, Evsey, 'The Soviet Collective Farm as a Producer Cooperative', *American Economic Review*, 56 (September 1966), pp. 743–57.

Dow, Gregory, 'Control Rights, Competitive Markets, and the Labor Management Debate', *Journal of Comparative Economics*, 10, 1 (1986), pp. 48–61.

Eaton, B. Curtis and William D. White, 'The Distribution of Wealth and the Efficiency of Institutions', *Economic Inquiry*, 39, 2 (April 1991), pp. 336–50.

Elster, Jon, *The Cement of Society*, (Cambridge: Cambridge University Press, 1989).

Eswaran, Mukesh and Ashok Kotwal, 'Credit and Agrarian Class Structure', in Pranab Bardhan (ed.), *The Economic Theory of Agrarian Institutions*, (Oxford: Oxford University Press, 1989).

Farrell, Joseph, 'Information and the Coase Theorem', *Journal of Economic Perspectives*, 1, 2 (Fall 1987), pp. 112–29.

Fehr, Ernst, 'The Simple Analytics of a Membership Market in a Labor-Managed Economy', in Samuel Bowles, Herbert Gintis, and Bo Gustafsson (eds.), *Democracy and Markets: Participation, Accountability and Efficiency*, (Cambridge: Cambridge University Press, 1993), pp. 260–76.

Folbre, Nancy, *Who Pays for the Kids? Gender and the Structures of Constraint*, (London: Routledge, 1994).

Frohlich, Norman, John Godard, Joe Oppenheimer, and Frederick Starke,

'Employee vs. Conventionally Owned and Controlled Firms: an Experimental Analysis', (University of Maryland, November 1997).

Furubotn, Eirik G. and Svetozar Pejovich, *The Economics of Property Rights*, (Cambridge MA: Ballinger, 1974).

Galor, Oded and Joseph Zeira, 'Income Distribution and Macroeconomics', *Review of Economic Studies*, 60, 1 (1993), pp. 35–52.

Gerschenkron, Alexander, *Bread and Democracy in Germany*, (Berkeley: University of California Press, 1944).

Gintis, Herbert, 'The Nature of the Labor Exchange and the Theory of Capitalist Production', *Review of Radical Political Economics*, 8, 2 (Summer 1976), pp. 36–54.

——, 'Financial Markets and the Political Structure of the Enterprise', *Journal of Economic Behavior and Organization*, 1 (1989), pp. 311–22.

——, 'The Political Economy of School Choice', *Teachers College Record*, 96, 3 (Spring 1995).

——, and Tsuneo Ishikawa, 'Wages, Work Discipline, and Unemployment', *Journal of Japanese and International Economies*, 1 (1987), pp. 195–228.

Glyn, Andrew, 'Stability, Egalitarianism and Dynamism: An Overview of the Advanced Capitalist Countries in the 1980's', in Gerald Epstein and Herbert Gintis (eds.), *Macroeconomic Policy After the Conservative Era: Research on Investment Savings and Finance*, (Cambridge: Cambridge University Press, 1995).

——, and Alan Hughes, Alain Lipietz, and Ajit Singh, 'The Rise and Fall of the Golden Age', in Stephen Marglin and Juliet B. Schor (eds.), *The Golden Age of Capitalism; Reinterpreting the Postwar Experience*, (Oxford: Clarendon Press, 1990), pp. 39–125.

Gordon, David M., 'Growth, Distribution and the Rules of the Game: Left Structuralist Macro Foundations for a Democratic Economic Policy', in Gerald Epstein and Herbert Gintis (eds.), *Macroeconomic Policy After the Conservative Era: Research on Investment Savings and Finance*, (Cambridge: Cambridge University Press, 1995).

Greenberg, Edward, *Workplace Democracy: The Political Effects of Participation*, (Ithaca: Cornell University Press, 1986).

Greif, Avner, 'Cultural Beliefs and the Organization of Society: An Historical and Theoretical Reflection on Collectivist and Individualist Societies', *Journal of Political Economy*, (October 1994).

Grossman, Sanford J. and Oliver D. Hart, 'The Costs and Benefits of Ownership: A Theory of Vertical and Lateral Integration', *Journal of Political Economy*, 94, 4 (August 1986), pp. 691–719.

Hart, Oliver and John Moore, 'Property Rights and the Nature of the Firm', *Journal of Political Economy*, 98, 6 (December 1990), pp. 1119–58.

Hoff, Karla, 'The Second Theorem of the Second Best', *Journal of Public Economics*, 25 (1994), pp. 223–42.

——, 'Comment on 'Political Economy of Alleviating Poverty: Theory and Institutions', by Timothy Besley', *Annual World Bank Conference on Development Economics*, (1996), pp. 139–44.

——, 'Market Failures and the Distribution of Wealth: A Perspective from the Economics of Information', *Politics & Society*, 24, 4 (December 1996), pp. 411–32.

——, and Andrew B. Lyon, 'Non-Leaky Buckets: Optimal Redistributive Taxation and Agency Costs', *Journal of Public Economics*, 26 (1995), pp. 365–90.

Hossain, M., 'Credit for Alleviation of Rural Poverty: the Grameen Bank in Bangladesh', *International Food Policy Research Institute Report*, 65 (1988).

Jencks, Christopher, *Rethinking Social Policy: Race, Poverty and the Underclass*, (Cambridge: Harvard University Press, 1992).

Jensen, Michael C. and William H. Meckling, 'Rights and Production Functions: An Application to Labor-Managed Firms and Codetermination', *Journal of Business*, 52 (1979), pp. 469–506.

Johansen, Leif, 'The Bargaining Society and the Inefficiency of Bargaining', *Kyklos*, 32, 3 (1979), pp. 497–522.

Koechlin, Timothy, 'The Determinants of the Location of USA Direct Foreign Investment', *International Review of Applied Economics*, 6, 2 (1992), pp. 203–16.

Kohn, Melvin et al., 'Position in the Class Structure and Psychological Functioning in the US, Japan, and Poland', *American Journal of Sociology*, 95, 4 (January 1990), pp. 964–1008.

Laffont, Jean Jacques and Mohammed Salah Matoussi, 'Moral Hazard, Financial Constraints, and Share Cropping in El Oulja', *Review of Economic Studies*, 62 (1995), pp. 381–99.

Lange, Oskar and F.M. Taylor, *On the Economic Theory of Socialism*, (Minneapolis: University of Minnesota Press, 1938).

Legros, Patrick and Andrew F. Newman, 'Wealth Effects, Distribution, and the Theory of Organization', *Journal of Economic Theory* (August 1996).

Leibenstein, Harvy, 'The Prisoner's Dilemma in the Invisible Hand: An Analysis of Intrafirm Productivity', *American Economic Review*, 72, 2 (May 1982), pp. 92–7.

Levine, David and Richard Parkin, 'Work Organization Employment Security and Macroeconomic Stability', *Journal of Economic Behavior and Organization*, (1993).

Levine, David I. and Laura d'Andrea Tyson, 'Participation Productivity and the Firm's Environment', in Alan Blinder (ed.), *Paying for Productivity: A Look at the Evidence*, (Washington DC: Brookings Institution, 1990), pp. 183–244.

Loury, Glen, 'Intergenerational Transfers and the Distribution of Earnings', *Econometrica*, 49 (1981), pp. 843–67.

Maddison, Angus, *Phases of Capitalist Development*, (Oxford: Oxford University Press, 1982).

Manning, Alan, 'Imperfect Labour Markets, the Stock Market, and the Inefficiency of Capitalism', *Oxford Economic Papers*, 44 (1992), pp. 257–71.

Meade, James E., 'The Adjustment Processes of Labour Co-operatives with Constant Returns to Scale and Perfect Competition', *Economic Journal*, 82 (1972), pp. 402–28.

Milgrom, Paul R., 'Employment Contracts, Influence Activities, and Efficient Organization Design', *Journal of Political Economy*, 96, 1 (1988), pp. 42–60.

Moene, Karl Ove, 'Strong Unions or Worker Control', in Jon Elster and Karl Ove Moene (eds.), *Alternatives to Capitalism*, (Cambridge: Cambridge University Press, 1989).

——, 'Poverty and Land Ownership', *American Economic Review*, 81, 1 (March 1992), pp. 52–64.

——, and Michael Wallerstein, 'Egalitarian Wage Policies', (University of Oslo, July 1993).

——, and Michael Wallerstein, 'Solidaristic Wage Bargaining', *Nordic Journal of Political Economy*, 22 (1995), pp. 79–94.

Mookherjee, Dilip, 'Informational Rents and Property Rights in Land', in John Roemer (ed.), *Property Rights, Incentives, and Welfare*, (London: MacMillan, 1997).

Nerlove, Marc and Tjeppy D. Soedjiana, 'Slamerans and Sheep: Savings and Small Ruminants in Semi-Subsistence Agriculture in Indonesia', (Department of Agriculture and Resource Economics, University of Maryland, 1996).

Newman, Andrew, 'The Capital Market Inequality and the Employment Relation', (Columbia University, 1994).

Ostrom, Elinor, *Governing the Commons: The Evolution of Institutions for Collective Action*, (Cambridge: Cambridge University Press, 1990).

Ouchi, William, 'Markets Bureaucracies and Clans', *Administrative Sciences Quarterly*, 25 (March 1980), pp. 129–41.

Persson, Torsten and Guido Tabellini, 'Is Inequality Harmful for Growth? Theory and Evidence', *American Economic Review*, 48 (1996), pp. 600–621.

Piketty, Thomas, 'The Dynamics of the Wealth Distribution and the Interest Rate with Credit Rationing', *Review of Economic Studies*, 64, 2 (April 1997), pp. 173–89.

Przeworski, Adam, 'On the Design of the State: A Principal-Agent Perspective',

(Presentation at the Workshop on Economic Transformation and the Reform of the State, National Research Council, November 8–9, 1996).

Putnam, Robert, *Making Democracy Work: Civic Traditions in Modern Italy*, (Princeton: Princeton University Press, 1993).

Roemer, John, *Equal Shares: Making Market Socialism Work*, (London: Verso, 1996).

Rosenzweig, Mark and Hans P. Binswanger, 'Wealth, Weather Risk and the Composition and Profitability of Agricultural Investments', *Econmic Journal*, 103 (January 1993), pp. 56–78.

Rosenzweig, Mark R. and Kenneth I. Wolpin, 'Credit Market Constraints, Consumption Smoothing, and the Accumulation of Durable Production Assets in Low-Income Countries: Investment in Bullocks in India', *Journal of Political Economy*, 101, 2 (1993), pp. 223–44.

Sampson, Robert J., Stephen W. Raudenbush, and Felton Earls, 'Neighborhoods and Violent Crime: A Multilevel Study of Collective Efficacy', *Science*, 277 (15 August 1997), pp. 918–24.

Schmitter, Philippe, 'The Irony of Modern Democracy and Efforts to Improve Its Practice', *Politics and Society*, 20, 4 (December 1992), pp. 507–12.

——, 'Commentario', in Fundacao Alexandre Gusmao (ed.), *O Brasil e as tendencias economicas e politicas contemporaneas* (Brasialia: Fundacao Alexandre Gusmao, 1995).

Shapiro, Carl and Joseph Stiglitz, 'Unemployment as a Worker Discipline Device', *American Economic Review*, 74, 3 (June 1984), pp. 433–44.

Sial, Maqbool and Michael Carter, 'Financial Market Efficiency in an Agrarian Economy: Microeconometric Analysis of the Pakistani Punjab', *Journal of Development Studies*, 32, 2 (June 1996), pp. 771–98.

Singleton, Sara and Michael Taylor, 'Common Property Collective Action and Community', *Journal of Theoretical Politics*, 4, 3 (1992), pp. 309–24.

Solow, Robert, *The Labor Market as a Social Institution*, (Cambridge: Basil Blackwell, 1990).

Stiglitz, Joseph, 'Incentives and Risk Sharing in Sharecropping', *Review of Economic Studies*, 41, 2 (April 1974), pp. 219–55.

——, 'Why Financial Structure Matters', *Journal of Economic Perspectives*, 2, 4 (Fall 1988), pp. 121–26.

——, 'Rational Peasants, Efficient Institutions, and a Theory or Rural Organization', in Pranab Bardhan (ed.), *The Economic Theory of Agrarian Institutions*, (Oxford: Oxford University Press, 1989), pp. 10–29.

Sugden, Robert, 'Spontaneous Order', *Journal of Economic Perspectives*, 3, 4 (Fall 1989), pp. 85–97.

Thomas, Henk and Chris Logan, *Mondragon: An Economic Analysis*, (London: George Allen and Unwin, 1982).

US Bureau of Labor Statistics, *Industrial Disputes Workers Involved and Worktime Lost 15 Countries 1955–1989*, (Washington, DC: Office of Productivity and Technology, November 1990).

——, *Comparative Real Gross Domestic Product per Capita and per Employed Person, Fourteen Countries 1975–1992*, (Washington, DC: Office of Productivity and Technology, March 1994).

van Parijs, Philippe, *Real Freedom for All: What (if anything) can justify capitalism?*, (Cambridge: Cambridge University Press, 1995).

——, and Robert Van Der Veen, 'A Capitalist Road to Communism', *Theory and Society*, 15 (1986), pp. 635–55.

Vanek, Jaroslav, *The General Theory of the Labor-Managed Market*, (Ithaca: Cornell University Press, 1970).

Verba, Sidney, Kay Lehman Schlozman, and Henry Brady, *Voice and Equality: Civic Voluntarism in American Politics* (Cambridge, MA: Harvard University Press, 1995).

Wade, Robert, *Village Republics: Economic Conditions for Collective Action in South India*, (Cambridge: Cambridge University Press, 1987).

Ward, Benjamin, 'The Firm in Illyria: Market Syndicalism', *American Economic Review*, 48 (December 1958), pp. 566–89.

Weissing, Franz and Elinor Ostrom, 'Irrigation Institutions and the Games Irrigators Play: Rule Enforcement without Guards', in Reinhard Selten (ed.), *Game Equilibrium Models II: Methods Morals and Markets*, (Berlin: Springer-Verlag, 1991), pp. 188–262.

Weitzman, Martin and Douglas Kruse, 'Profit Sharing and Productivity', in Alan Blinder (ed.), *Paying for Productivity: A Look at the Evidence* (Washington, DC: Brookings Institution, 1990) pp. 95–142.

Wittman, Donald, 'Why Democracies Produce Efficient Results', *Journal of Political Economy*, 97, 6 (1989), pp. 1395–1424.

PART II

General Assessments of the Proposal

2

Problems with Supply-side Egalitarianism

Daniel M. Hausman

Samuel Bowles and Herbert Gintis want to redirect egalitarianism away from redistribution of income and toward redistribution of assets, particularly productive assets. Their main reason, apart from the fact that income redistribution is so obviously dead in the political waters, is that income redistribution lowers productivity and competitiveness, while asset redistribution raises these, and in the long run the welfare of the worst-off depends more on increasing productivity than it does on distribution. Compound interest is a wonderful thing. Young workers in an inegalitarian society growing at 5 per cent a year making half the wages of those in an egalitarian society growing at 0.5 per cent a year will catch up in 16 years, and by the time of their retirement, will have four times the income. Bowles and Gintis argue that such mathematics, which has long been an argument for inegalitarian trickle-down policies, in fact supports egalitarian asset redistributions.

The trick for egalitarians who do not want to shoot themselves in the foot and who also seek political success, is to espouse egalitarian reforms that will increase productivity. If egalitarian reforms increased productivity sufficiently, they could be painless. Those who suffer initially from the redistribution would be better off in the long run. More modestly and more realistically, most people would gain enough that the political opposition could be overcome. More plausibly still, one might argue that even if the productivity enhancements due to well-conceived asset egalitarianism do little to weaken political opposition to redistribution, they are essential to long-run feasibility: unless a policy leads to sustained growth, it cannot endure long. Feasibility requires physical productivity and hence economic growth, *not* the possibility that gainers could compensate losers, which is how 'productivity enhancement' is defined by Bowles and Gintis.

It is obvious that badly conceived and implemented income-redistribution programs lower productivity, but so do poorly conceived and implemented asset-redistribution policies. It is not at all obvious that well-designed programs of income redistribution impede productivity. An impressionistic comparison of policies and growth rates over the past two generations suggests just the opposite. There is little solid evidence one way or another and no good reason why egalitarians should drop their support for income-redistributive programs in favor of programs to redistribute assets. If Bowles and Gintis are right that their policies would enhance productivity and lessen inequality, egalitarians should find them attractive and should *widen* their program to include *both* income and asset redistribution.

Are Bowles and Gintis right? Would their programs lessen inequality and increase productivity? Although I am a philosopher and not a social scientist, let me register some qualms. Bowles and Gintis sketch four asset redistributions, which I shall discuss in a different order than theirs.

First, Bowles and Gintis urge a change in housing policy. Rather than building public housing or providing rent subsidies, the government should subsidize home ownership. Since home owners have better incentives to maintain their housing and police their neighborhoods, such a policy will lead to more efficient maintenance and surveillance. This seems, at first glance, sensible enough and politically feasible to boot. But egalitarians might reasonably complain that the policy is only weakly egalitarian. Since those who are currently renting their homes or apartments are, on average, poor, giving them (mortgaged) titles to their homes would increase equality. But so would giving them an equivalent amount of cash. What is redistributive about the home ownership *per se*? I can see only two answers. The first is essentially paternalistic: the redistribution can be designed so that the mortgaged titles cannot be easily converted into immediate consumption, so the redistribution will not be undone by the imprudence of the poor. Second, homes should be worth more to owner-occupants than to landlords, because owner-occupants face lower costs in maintaining their homes and neighborhoods. So a redistribution of titles rather than cash provides a greater egalitarian effect. I doubt whether either of these reasons would make this reform especially attractive to egalitarians.

The efficiency claims are also questionable, because Bowles and Gintis do not carefully consider the alternatives. Other things being equal, home owners have, perhaps, the strongest *motivation* to maintain their homes and neighborhoods. But unlike landlords, they may spend little time thinking about maintenance and neighborhood concerns. Since they are more numerous than landlords and each has a smaller stake, they may face more serious collective action problems. They may also be less competent and less well informed concerning maintenance and community problems than their landlords. The do-it-yourself plumbing in my home does not compare favorably to the minimally competent work done by the superintendent in the New York apartment building I used to live in, and I suspect that the plumbers I call to repair the damage I've done rip me off. What about alternatives such as subsidizing small-scale rental housing, in which resident owner-landlords maintain their property and neighborhoods, screen their tenants, and exert informal social control over deviant tenant behavior? Would such a policy be less egalitarian or less efficient?

Second, Bowles and Gintis argue that the inequalities created by divorce should be remedied by assigning to children rights to a portion of their parents' income. Such a proposal is designed to address inequalities that have often been overlooked by traditional egalitarians, who have been more concerned with inequalities among classes than with inequalities between the sexes or between adults and children. It is not clear whether such a policy would be appreciably more egalitarian than effective enforcement of existing child-support laws. (Indeed it is unclear how this proposal differs from effective enforcement of existing child-support laws.) Since husband and wife are typically of the same social class, this proposal does not address class inequalities. It seems to me that egalitarians should support something like this proposal, but the proposal is not distinctively egalitarian, and there are plenty of reasons for non-egalitarians to support it, too.

Third, Bowles and Gintis argue for a system of educational vouchers. Their efficiency arguments are exactly those of conservatives. Anyone who has experienced frustrations with public schools can sympathize with their case. If schools had to compete for children, incentives would be very different. Furthermore, there is a strong and specifically egalitarian case for vouchers. If the rules of the game were properly designed, a voucher system could bring about desegregation and equalization of school funding peacefully. Vouchers could even partly overcome the differentiation of schools by social class. Vouchers could thus constitute a radically egalitarian reform, and at the same time could make a major contribution to productivity by increasing the efficiency of the use of educational resources and by improving the level of education of our semi-literate population.

Any voucher system has, however, major risks; and the attenuation of local democratic control (such as it may be) should give one pause. My principal qualm is that the consequences of voucher systems depend on the details of their design, and those details will be determined by those who write and implement the legislation. If egalitarians were to join conservatives in supporting a voucher system, what sort of voucher system would we actually get? I'm not optimistic. One might respond (as Samuel Bowles did) that the consequences of every proposal depend on the details of the implementation, and that this objection thus applies equally to all reforms. But the consequences of proposals are not equally sensitive to design details. The egalitarian consequences of vouchers require incentives (or sanctions) to encourage diversity, and they require that schools not be allowed to charge parents any fees in addition to the vouchers. The first of these runs into parental opposition to diversity. Currently only the accidents of school-district boundaries and the mandates of court rulings overcome this opposition. The ban on additional fees collides both with the desires of the relatively affluent to secure advantages for their children and with a deeply entrenched ideology of individual freedom. Conservatives will say, 'Why shouldn't parents be allowed to provide more resources for their children if they want to?' 'If we don't allow parents to supplement vouchers, they will enroll their children in exclusive after-school programs anyway.' Will egalitarians be able to respond persuasively to these arguments?

Finally we come to what is Bowles' and Gintis' main asset-redistributive egalitarian reform: the transfer of productive assets to workers. Since wealth depends so significantly on ownership of productive assets, this reform would necessarily be part of a massive transfer of wealth and as such would obviously lessen inequalities, even if inequalities among workers in different enterprises remain. Bowles and Gintis argue that this radical reform would enhance productivity, but they recognize that it has the potential to do just the opposite. Given their lesser wealth, workers are in general more risk averse. Since the wealth of workers who own their own firms will be concentrated in a single asset, they will be especially unwilling to take risks. Furthermore, if the structure of worker-ownership is not carefully devised, there can be perverse incentives to avoid increasing employment so as not to share the profits. On the other hand, costs of surveillance and enforcement of work effort will be lower, and one will be able to draw more effectively on the projects and innovations conceived by those who are not wealthy. With institutional reforms to ameliorate difficulties arising from risk aversion and the unwilling-ness of banks to provide credit, worker-owned firms will, Bowles and Gintis argue, be more efficient.

The propagation of worker cooperatives seems desirable on many grounds, and its contribution to economic growth is a slender reed for supply-siders to rely on. The argument for the efficiency of worker-owned firms is speculative and inconclusive. Although there is some empirical evidence supporting Bowles' and Gintis' claim (Craig and Pencavel 1992), there is not much. If one studies a very successful cooperative,[1] such as the Mondragon cooperative in Spain, one finds no spectacular caches of hidden productivity. Mondragon has been a splendid success, and it has in particular provided much improved job security and social services for its members. Salary differentials have also been much smaller than in capitalist firms. But there are thousands of capitalist firms that have grown more rapidly. Why? Credit limitations were a problem during the early years, but during the last two decades the Mondragon cooperatives have had more investment funds than they have known what to do with. Risk aversion is a more plausible explanation. Indeed the fact that so few of the new investments undertaken by Mondragon have failed – which is cited as a proud achievement – shows that the cooperative has avoided risky investments. Bowles and Gintis argue that such risk aversion could be mitigated by a complicated scheme to provide contingent insurance against bankruptcy. But Mondragon is big enough that it has been able to self-insure against investment failures. It is dubious that any feasible system of state insurance would have changed things appreciably. The problem is that insurance won't give workers in an unsuccessful venture a new successful enterprise. Workers are not just investing capital. Even a return of the full value of the investment would leave them without work and drastically worse off, and that much insurance would severely diminish incentives to invest prudently. It is not obvious that the factors that limit the growth of worker-managed firms can be overcome.

Conversely, it is not obvious that there are large benefits to be gained from mutual monitoring and worker initiatives in cooperatives. Workers in capitalist firms (particularly small firms) may form close bonds with each other and even with owners, and in many cases they carry out the same monitoring and innovating that Bowles and Gintis argue contribute so much to the greater productivity of worker-managed firms. Without full authority and rights to the full residual earnings of the firm, the incentives for workers to control the workplace efficiently will be smaller, and distrust of owners and management lessens these incentives further. How much more efficiently will worker-owners monitor individual effort? In a 100-person firm, an individual worker's share of the profits will be 1 per cent. How much of an incentive is that? Isn't there an efficiency case to be made for shared residual claimancy between workers and owners of capital?

Just as there is no compelling evidence for the productivity losses of well-designed income-redistribution policies, so there is no compelling evidence for the productive benefits of asset redistributions. Bowles and Gintis have not demonstrated that worshippers of productivity should be egalitarians.

If Bowles and Gintis were to accept this conclusion, I doubt that their commitment to egalitarianism would be shaken. Although the reasons for their egalitarianism are not evident in this essay, one can judge from their other work that their espousal of asset redistribution does not derive from a commitment to economic growth, nor from a belief that economic growth is the best means to improve the lives of the worst-off. What one instead finds in this essay is an attempt to sell egalitarian policies to devotees of efficiency who have a soft spot for those on the bottom.

I've argued that the sales pitch isn't credible. It is also dangerous, because it obscures the grounds for egalitarianism and thereby undermines the real case for egalitarian policies. If one is mainly concerned about the incomes of the worst-off, then the case for egalitarianism turns on whether egalitarian policies will increase income over the next couple of decades. (Beyond that time period the uncertainties are usually too great to permit comparisons.) If one wants the worst-off to have sustainable higher incomes, then one should be an egalitarian if, and only if, egalitarian policies in fact achieve this. This sort of egalitarianism depends on the answers to technical questions in the theory of economic growth. If egalitarian policies are in the medium run worse for the worst-off, those concerned about the incomes of the worst-off should not be egalitarians.

I doubt that many egalitarians would be happy with the argument. Most would certainly hesitate before instituting egalitarian policies, if it could be shown that such policies clearly led to lower incomes for the worst-off, but most would not wait to espouse egalitarian reforms until there is good evidence concerning their consequences for the incomes of the worst-off. For income may not reflect well-being, and a concern for the well-being of those on the bottom is not the sole motivation for egalitarianism. Indeed for many egalitarians, it is not even the main concern. *One* reason why one might favor egalitarian policies would be that one is concerned with the well-being of the worst-off, just as one reason for concern with the well-being of those who are worst off is a prior commitment to egalitarianism. But egalitarianism and a concern for those on the bottom are distinct positions,[2] and there are reasons to pursue egalitarian policies that are independent of any concern with the worst-off.

Why should anybody be concerned about equality? What's good about lessening inequality? Bowles and Gintis never say, and the reasons why people should support egalitarian policies may be easily overlooked altogether in Bowles' and Gintis' concern with productivity.

Some people support egalitarian policies because they believe that such policies increase the well-being of the worst-off. This may be a good reason, particularly if one does not identify well-being with income. There are other reasons, too. Utilitarians have argued for lessening inequalities because of diminishing marginal utility: since transferring $100 from a rich person to a poor person increases the happiness of the poor person more than it diminishes the happiness of the rich person, equalizing wealth tends to increase total happiness.[3] Democrats may support egalitarian policies as a precondition for effective democracy. These concerned with liberty may oppose inequality as a threat to effective liberty.

There are thus a variety of reasons why equality is valuable as a means to other ends. But one might wonder whether egalitarianism is a sensible *ideal*.[4] Could equality be of value apart from its consequences for liberty, democracy, productivity, total welfare, or the welfare of the worst-off? David Miller presents the basic puzzle as follows:

> Why should *equality* be thought desirable? Equality after all means a levelling of differences; it means a smoothing down of irregularities or idiosyncrasies. Although I may from an aesthetic motive desire to trim my rose bushes to an equal height or polish my wine glasses to an equal shine, to treat people in such a way would be at best perverse and at worst immoral. The pursuit of equality seems to be impaled on a fork: either the ultimate end of the pursuit is not equality at all but some other value or values which have become confused in the popular mind with equality, or our societies are aiming at a goal that cursory inspection revealed to be quite monstrous.[5]

In response Miller points out that even if economic equality, like negative liberty, has mainly an instrumental value, it may also have an intrinsic connection to some of the goals it serves, just as negative liberty has an intrinsic connection to autonomy. Miller lists four different ends that equality, including economic equality, may serve, and to which equality has an intrinsic connection.

First, *equality is sometimes required in order to be fair*. If there are benefits or burdens to distribute, then, other things being equal, it is unfair to distribute them unequally. In the absence of good moral reasons for an unequal distribution, fairness requires equality. This is the reason for egalitarianism that is most closely tied to a concern for the welfare of the worst-off. It is also the reason that is least closely connected to the Marxian tradition. The weight and reach of concerns about fairness are controversial. I suspect that the only basis for extreme proposals to equalize opportunity for welfare (Arneson 1989) is the view that any differences in outcomes that are not the responsibility of the agents involved are unfair.

Second, equality is a good thing, because *some measure of equality is necessary for self-respect*. Except when they have behaved stupidly or immorally, individuals should be able to say, 'I am as good as anybody else; I may not be as clever or hard-working as you are, but I am as good as you are'.[6] The great inequalities that characterize the United States today make it very difficult for individuals at the bottom to maintain their self-respect. The homeless are not only impoverished and uprooted, but they are also often regarded with suspicion, fear and contempt by the more fortunate. This concern with self-respect is associated with the concerns for creative self-realization that Marx expresses so vividly in his 1844 manuscripts.

Third, equality is a good thing, because *equal treatment implements the duty to show equal respect*. The notion of equal respect is arguably the fundamental notion of morality. Views that morality requires recognizing and respecting individual rights or that morality requires treating the interests of individuals equally can be regarded as interpretations of the notion that there is a duty to show equal respect (Dworkin 1977, Kymlicka 1990). Equality is linked to a particular interpretation of equal respect. 'While [people] differ profoundly as individuals in capacity and character, they are equally entitled as human beings to consideration and respect'.[7] The issue is not how well those who are at the bottom are able to maintain their self-respect, but how they are *treated*. Showing equal respect implies recognizing that all people without severe mental and emotional handicaps have capacities to deliberate for themselves, to engage in relationships and activities that are intrinsically valuable, and to develop skills and traits that are admirable.[8] Large economic inequalities are inconsistent with the social acknowledgment that everyone has such capacities, and they violate the duty to show equal respect. The commodification of human relationships jeopardizes equal respect in so far as it leads to a view of human beings 'merely as means'[9] – as things (hopefully soon to be replaced by less troublesome robots) whose services can be bought and sold.

Equality is also necessary for 'fraternity'. There should be some measure of solidarity among the inhabitants of a nation, and indeed among all human beings; and there should be no systematic barriers to social intercourse. Inequalities are objectionable in part because they place barriers to friendship, community, and love. 'What is repulsive . . . is that some classes should be excluded from the heritage of civilization which others enjoy, and that the fact of human fellowship, which is ultimate and profound, should be obscured by economic contrasts, which are trivial and superficial.'[10] Fraternity and solidarity are again values that have been prominent in the socialist tradition.

Equality is thus not only a means to unrelated goals. Severe inequalities degrade those on the bottom. This degradation violates the duty to show equal respect. It damages self-respect. It destroys fraternity. It is unfair. Equality is of intrinsic moral importance because of its links to fairness, self-respect, equal respect, and fraternity. True egalitarians, who are committed to equality as an ideal rather than merely as a means to unrelated goals, need to consider whether policy proposals such as those made by Bowles and Gintis serve fairness, self-respect, equal respect and fraternity.

The egalitarian case is independent of the productivity case and indeed the level of income is not of ultimate concern to egalitarians. The level of income (as opposed to its distribution) is important only when it is so low as to threaten self-respect and the possibility of fraternity. The distribution of income, in contrast, is of general moral importance to egalitarians because of its link to all the underlying values. In a society like the United States, in which so much consumption goes to creating barriers to fraternity and to undermining the bases of self-respect, egalitarians should not be greatly concerned about increasing productivity (except in so far as the increased output makes its way to relieve the absolute poverty of those in poor nations). The misery of those who are poorest in the United States could be alleviated without any economic growth, and (or so I would conjecture) will not be greatly alleviated by economic growth. The misery of the poor in the United States results as much from relative deprivation with its attendant insecurities and disorders as from absolute need. There is wealth enough in the United States to create a heaven on earth here, if only people could individually and jointly determine how to employ that wealth to shape rich and fulfilling lives. Economic growth may contribute to well-being, but focusing on productivity or growth dodges the real problems. (This is of course not the case for the majority of people who do not live in rich nations.)

Bowles and Gintis are, I think, so busy making a pitch for egalitarian policies to soft-hearted efficiency worshippers that they risk inviting their readers to forget what egalitarianism is all about. It is not about Nintendo games in every home and more trips to the Mall. It is about self-respect, fairness, equal respect and fraternity. I am not sure to what extent Bowles' and Gintis' policy proposals serve these fundamental goals or to what extent they should be supported by egalitarians. The case needs to be made. Showing that well-designed asset redistribution will not greatly diminish productivity establishes the feasibility of the proposals and may help to limit opposition to them. It is thus a worthy (though very difficult) task to undertake, provided that the asset redistributions serve egalitarian ends. But in investigating implications of asset redistributions for productivity, one should not forget what the point of the redistribution is.

The fundamental mistake of those who think mainly of productivity is not, as Bowles and Gintis hint, that they fail to appreciate the role of government and community in economic growth. The fundamental mistake is that they fail to ask what economic growth is *for*, and they surrender all thought of questioning, let alone controlling, the future that markets dictate to us. Even if Bowles and Gintis are right that those concerned with efficiency should support egalitarian policies, egalitarians – whether they call for redistribution of income or of assets – should keep their distance from supply-side economics.

Notes

1. These remarks on the Mondragon cooperative are based on Whyte and Whyte (1991).

2. Even if the distribution of income were unaffected, much higher incomes for the worst-off might satisfy those concerned with the well-being of those on the bottom.

3. For a classic presentation of this argument, see Lerner (1944).

4. The ensuing discussion of egalitarianism as an ideal draws on chapter 10 of Hausman and McPherson (1996).
5. Miller (1982), p. 73.
6. Davies (1963), p. 45, quoted in Benn (1967) p. 69.
7. Tawney (1931), p. 34.
8. Miller (1982), p. 81.
9. Kant (1785), chapter 2.
10. Tawney (1931), p. 139.

References

Arneson, Richard, 'Equality and Equal Opportunities for Welfare', *Philosophical Studies*, 56 (1989), pp. 77–93.

Benn, Stanley, 'Egalitarianism and the Equal Consideration of Interests', in J. Roland Pennock and John W. Chapman (eds.), *Equality* (New York: Atherton Press, 1967), pp. 61–78.

Bowles, Samuel and Herbert Gintis, 'Efficient Redistribution: New Rules for Markets, States and Communities', *Recasting Egalitarianism*, (London: Verso, 1998).

Craig, Ben and John Pencavel, 'The Behavior of Worker Cooperatives: The Plywood Companies of the Pacific Northwest' *American Economic Review*, 82 (1992), pp. 1083–1105.

Davies, J.C., *Human Nature in Politics* (New York, 1963).

Dworkin, Ronald, *Taking Rights Seriously* (Cambridge: Harvard University Press, 1977).

Hausman, Daniel and Michael McPherson, *Economic Analysis and Moral Philosophy* (Cambridge: Cambridge University Press, 1996).

Kant, Immanuel, *Groundwork of The Metaphysics of Morals*, 1785. H. Paton (Tr.), (New York: Harper & Row, 1948).

Kymlicka, Will, *Contemporary Political Political Philosophy: An Introduction* (New York: Oxford University Press, 1990).

Lerner, Abba, *The Economics of Control* (London, Macmillan, 1944).

Miller, David, 'Arguments for Equality'. *Midwest Studies in Philosophy*, 7 (1982), pp. 73–88.

Tawney, R.H., *Equality* (New York: Harcourt, Brace and Co., 1931).

Whyte, William and Kathleen Whyte, *Making Mondragon: The Growth and Dynamics of the Worker Cooperative Complex*, 2nd ed. (Ithaca: Cornell University Press, 1991).

3

Equality, Community, and 'Efficient Redistribution'
Erik Olin Wright

In their essay, 'Efficient Redistribution', Bowles and Gintis challenge the frequently held view that there is a necessary trade-off between the values of equality and efficiency. They argue that the extent to which these two values are compatible or contradictory depends not upon the *level* of equality achieved in a society, but upon the specific mechanisms used to generate greater equality.[1] More specifically, they argue that in a variety of contexts, when greater economic equality is achieved by redistributions of assets rather than outcomes (thus allowing the competition and voluntary exchanges of the market to remain in place), increasing equality is likely to foster, rather than undermine, greater efficiency. These arguments are elaborated for three main cases: a redistribution of assets in enterprises to the employees increases efficiency by reducing monitoring costs and improving incentives to work hard; in schooling, a redistribution of assets in the form of a radically egalitarian system of vouchers makes schools more accountable to parents and thus likely to more efficiently meet educational needs; and a redistribution of public housing assets by giving residents ownership rights in their housing will lead to improved maintenance of the housing stock.[2] In each case, a move towards a more egalitarian distribution of assets not only generates more equality of welfare for people, but, by enhancing productivity, actually increases the pie as well.

I will not take issue with the general claim Bowles and Gintis elaborate. I agree with them that redistributing assets is, for many desirable components of human welfare, a plausible way of improving equality in the distribution of that welfare, and further that this can be done in ways which are at least compatible with efficiency and perhaps even increase efficiency. I do, however, want to explore three potential problems with the broad approach to equality which they support:

1. Redistribution of capital assets in the form suggested by Bowles and Gintis may not generate sufficient improvement in equality of material conditions of life within the general population to satisfy left-wing egalitarian values.
2. Redistribution of outcomes also need not be a threat to efficiency. Given the claim that the redistribution of capital assets may not decrease inequality in the society as a whole very much, a radical egalitarian program, therefore, probably needs to combine asset and outcome redistributions.
3. Both asset and outcome redistributions politically depend upon a strong sense of community in the population within which redistribution of either sort is to take place. If asset or outcome redistributions are to be sustainable, therefore, they need to strengthen rather than weaken community. In these terms, some of the asset redistributions proposed by Bowles and Gintis may be vulnerable because of adverse effects on community.

In discussing these problems, I will assume that the specific models advanced by Bowles and Gintis are presented in the spirit of proposals for a thoroughgoing institutional redesign of society. In places, this seems to be what they are suggesting. Worker-owned cooperatives, for example, are not simply being held up as one among a variety of desirable ways of organizing firms in an egalitarian manner, but as the most promising way of organizing the core of the entire economy. In other places, the proposals are presented in more tentative ways as partial components of a still unspecified broader project of institutional change.[3] The concerns I will discuss below mainly concern the more ambitious form of these proposals in which the specific models of asset-based redistribution are treated as the foundations for broad societal design.

1. How Much Equality Will Be Generated by Redistributing Capital Assets to Employees?

With respect to the distribution of income, Bowles and Gintis draw a sharp contrast between two kinds of proposals: the first, characteristic of the social-democratic welfare state, leaves the distribution of capital assets untouched and redistributes the income generated through market transactions; the second redistributes the capital assets and leaves relatively untouched the income people acquire through the use of those assets. Their specific proposal for accomplishing this asset redistribution involves turning the employees of capitalist firms into owners of those firms. In effect, capitalist corporations are turned into worker-cooperatives. By making workers the residual claimants on the profits of the firm, the argument goes, their incentives to work hard will increase and the costs of monitoring and social control within the firm will decline.[4]

In and of themselves, worker-cooperatives may be a good thing, and compared to capitalist corporations, they certainly represent a move in an egalitarian direction. Nevertheless, for several reasons it seems unlikely that they would dramatically reduce societal inequalities in the distribution of income in a market society. First, a great deal of income inequality, including some of the most vicious forms of that inequality, is generated in the labor market and is not directly linked to ownership of capital assets. Even if capital assets were equally distributed to all citizens, there would still be many quite poor people and some extremely rich ones. John Roemer estimates that a completely egalitarian distribution of capital assets in the United States in the 1980s would have at most generated an income dividend of something around $1000–$1500 per year for every adult.[5] This is not a trivial amount of redistribution to the poorest end of the income distribution, but it would still leave many people quite poor and others very rich. While the Bowles and Gintis proposal to equalize educational assets through a radical voucher system might somewhat mitigate such inequalities, it is not plausible in a developed capitalist economy that without substantial income taxes used to redistribute labor market earnings, the inegalitarian effects of competitive labor markets would be dramatically attenuated.

Second, this redistribution mechanism does not provide capital assets to anyone not employed in a profit-making private enterprise. In the United States this would mean that only about 50 per cent of the adult population would be in a position to receive capital assets; the roughly 11 per cent who are employed in the public sector and in the non-profit organization sector, the 4 per cent who are unemployed, and the 33 per cent who are not in the paid labor force at all, would be excluded from the asset-redistribution scheme.[6] Since the latter group includes among the poorest people in the income distribution, a redistribution of corporate assets exclusively to employees would not improve their standing in the income distribution at all.

Third, firms differ enormously in their capital-intensiveness. Any scheme for asset redistribution that merely equalizes asset ownership within firms inherently means that employees in some firms will have vastly more assets than employees in other firms. While this would still be a meaningful improvement in the society's wealth distribution relative to that generated by conventional capitalist ownership, nevertheless it still constitutes a great deal of inequality.[7]

Of course, it could be the case that while a great deal of inequality in assets and material conditions of life remains in an economy of worker-cooperatives, this continuing level of inequality might be morally acceptable. If one believed, for example, that the only morally offensive property of inequality centered around domination – the ways in which inequalities of assets place some people under the control of others – then redistributing capital assets within workplaces, by creating the conditions for workplace democracy, would be at the heart of the egalitarian project. However, most egalitarians are morally concerned in one way or another about the material welfare of people, and it is hard to see what moral theory would provide a defense for the level of redistribution created by worker-cooperatives that would not also justify much more radical redistributions. Defenders of egalitarianism have proposed a variety of ways of understanding what is the ethical core of their egalitarian values: equality of welfare, equality of opportunity, equality of resources, equality of opportunity for welfare.[8] None of these moral foundations is satisfied in an economy of worker-owned firms, unless worker-cooperatives are combined with considerable redistribution of income as well.

The fact that a worker-cooperative economy may not by itself generate morally acceptable levels of equality does not indict the more general idea of the desirability of redistributing capital assets; it merely questions the limited form of this redistribution proposed in the Bowles and Gintis model. An alternative form of such redistribution has been elaborated in some detail by John Roemer (1994). Instead of simply redistributing capital assets to the employees of a given firm, those assets are redistributed to the entire adult population on a per capita basis. Roemer develops an interesting model of how such an egalitarian distribution can be roughly sustained and how it can be organized in such a way that market institutions remain relatively vigorous. This is not the place to review Roemer's specific arguments. The relevant point is that one can have a radically egalitarian distribution of capital assets along with effective markets without restricting the form of that redistribution to worker-owned cooperatives.

One reply to a proposal like Roemer's is that while this more radical redistribution may be more egalitarian than that generated by the Bowles and Gintis model, it will not have the efficiency-enhancing effects of worker-owned firms, and indeed may have serious efficiency-dampening effects. By distributing assets so widely, it could be argued, the incentives for monitoring managerial behavior go down and the incentives for workers to exert themselves decline as well. A dispersed egalitarian asset distribution, therefore, will face the same kinds of monitoring costs of workers that characterize normal capitalist enterprises, and will also face incentive failures for management. As a result, the move from within-firm asset redistribution to across-firm asset redistribution will encounter the vaunted equality-efficiency trade-off, and by virtue of this will ultimately produce inferior welfare effects. Under these conditions, the best we can hope for is equality within firms. Any broader redistribution of assets, however morally desirable it might seem, will not be sustainable because of serious incentive failures.

These are familiar criticisms of various forms of socialism. They are derived from a model of human motivation and interaction within which the only motives are pure individual self-interest. If workers are equal owners of the firm within which they work, the argument goes, they will have strong incentives to monitor each other as well as the managers they hire because they are the residual claimants to the profits of the firm. In contrast, if they are equal owners of the wealth of the entire society, then there is no longer a direct connection between the profitability of their own firm and their own welfare, and thus the incentive for cheap monitoring (of both their own behavior and that of the managers of the firm) declines.

If human agents in fact had such an impoverished set of motives, then it might be the case that worker-owned cooperatives would be the most egalitarian form of asset distribution achievable. However, even in capitalist societies, with their intense pressures of competition and individualism, motivations are much more complex. As Michael Burawoy (1978, 1985) has demonstrated in his research on why workers work so hard, work is, to a variable extent, regulated by various kinds of norms which create a sense of obligation and responsibility on the part of both workers and bosses. The expression 'a fair day's work for a fair day's pay', is not just an ideological smokescreen for exploitation; it reflects a set of norms about the terms for sustainable cooperation between conflictual actors.[9] Such norms, of course, do not fall from heaven, nor are they maintained simply by some kind of diffuse cultural inertia. Norms are reproduced or undermined by sets of practices in the workplace which continually validate or contradict them. 'A fair day's work for a fair day's pay' is sustained by the on-going practices of workers and managers, in which responsible performance of work is rewarded by fair treatment.[10]

The implication of this elementary excursus into the sociology of work is that monitoring costs in the workplace – and, more broadly, the conditions for sustaining high productivity – depend in part on the normative structure of work and the material conditions which sustain or undermine a given normative order. In what Burawoy calls a 'hegemonic factory regime', relatively high levels of loyalty and commitment of workers to a firm can be created by guarantees of job security and prospects for wage increases linked to aggregate productivity increases. In the framework proposed by Bowles and Gintis, high job security and wage increases linked to aggregate (rather than individual) rises in productivity should underwrite relatively high levels of shirking: the harder it is to fire an individual worker, the less the worker has to worry about the 'costs of job loss'. Exactly the opposite often occurs. Why? Because the longer time horizons of the worker and the sense of job security creates a sense of common fate with the fate of the firm, and the sense of fair treatment validates a norm of worker-obligations.

None of this implies that a democratic, worker-owned firm does not create a set of material conditions in which high levels of cooperation and hard work are generated. Bowles' and Gintis' arguments that worker-owned firms have governance structures which create productivity-enhancing incentives are persuasive. The point, however, is that even where workers are not the residual claimants of the profits of their own firm, such cooperation and commitment can still be forthcoming. It is thus plausible that a democratic market-socialist economy in which firms were publicly owned – either via a Roemer-type equal distribution of shares or through more conventional forms of public ownership – can potentially sustain the required incentives and norms to achieve the efficiency-gains described in the Bowles and Gintis model. The difference is that this would occur with a much more egalitarian distribution of capital assets in the population as a whole than is possible if the employees, and only the employees, own all of the assets of the firm in which they work.

2. Redistribution of Outcomes and Efficiency

If Roemer's estimates of the impact on per capita income of an equal distribution of capital assets is even roughly correct, then it will be impossible to move significantly towards egalitarian ideals without substantial redistributions of income itself. The data Bowles and Gintis present at the beginning of their paper indicate that even under capitalist conditions significant amounts of income redistribution are quite compatible with high rates of productivity increase. As they write in commenting on figure 2 in their paper, 'countries with more equal distributions of income appear to perform, if anything, better on standard macroeconomic measures'. With the exception of Japan, to a significant extent these more egalitarian countries have less income-inequality because of redistributive taxation and spending policies or collective actions directed explicitly at muting wage dispersion in the labor market. And, even including the Japanese case, none of the more egalitarian countries have achieved their relatively equal income distributions because of egalitarian distributions of capital assets. Ironically perhaps, the data Bowles and Gintis themselves present suggest that significant amounts of income (as opposed to asset) redistribution can occur without apparently threatening efficiency.

Bowles and Gintis are quite pessimistic about the continuing possibility of generating equality through redistribution of income itself: 'Given the high and apparently rising levels of inequality generated by the private sectors of the advanced economies in recent years, a redistribution of income of suitable magnitude to achieve even minimally acceptable levels of equality will incur prohibitive political and economic costs'. The issue of political costs is not especially compelling in a comparison between their proposals for massive asset redistribution and proposals for tax-and-transfer income redistribution, since their proposal to redistribute capital assets to employees would almost certainly encounter even more intense political resistance than social democratic policies of income transfers. Bowles and Gintis may, however, be correct that the economic costs of income redistribution have become prohibitive. If, as some people have argued, the correlation between income equality and macroeconomic performance is largely the result of successful Keynesian demand-side policies of the welfare state in the post-Second World War period, and if the capacity of states to pursue Keynesian demand-side strategies has dramatically declined with the heightened international integration of national economies and the ease of global movement of capital, then the link between income-equality and productivity growth displayed in their figure 2 would also decline. If this diagnosis is correct, and if my arguments about the limited impact on economic inequality of within-firm asset-redistribution proposals are also correct, then the prospects for significant moves towards a society with relatively egalitarian distributions of the material conditions of life are dismal indeed.

It is not at all obvious, however, that on strictly economic grounds a significant redistribution of income consistent with increasing productivity is unfeasible. The positive correlation between redistributively-generated income equality and productivity may not primarily work through Keynesian macroeconomic demand policies. As Bowles and Gintis themselves observe, relatively egalitarian income distributions may, in many instances, be part of a politically negotiated package of affirmative state interventions which include such things as active labor market policies, supportive state policies for strong unions, and productivist industrial policy, along with more straightforward redistributive welfare state programs. This array of state policies which are collectively productivity-enhancing may be unsustainable without the egalitarian income-distribution component.

Furthermore, there may be direct productivity-enhancing effects of the taxation and income support policies that are at the core of the egalitarian redistributive policies of the more social democratic welfare states. On the tax side, up to a point as marginal taxes rise, people may increase rather than decrease their labor supply in an effort to achieve or maintain a particular target standard of living. The frequent observation that in order to compensate for falling real wages since the early 1970s, American households have dramatically increased labor supply (mainly via increasing labor-force participation of married women, especially mothers), suggests more generally that labor supply (and labor effort) may increase to compensate for lower levels of take-home pay due to tax increases. Of course, confiscatory marginal tax rates would act as a disincentive to work, but the increases in marginal tax rates required to underwrite significant income redistribution fall far short of this and thus might create incentives for many people to increase rather than decrease labor effort.

On the redistribution side of the equation, the greater income security and job security that accompany redistributive welfare state policies may stretch people's time horizons and increase their broad sense of social commitment and reciprocity. The level of effort people are willing to expend out of a sense of obligation rather than simply in response to immediate incentives may be higher in societies within which there is a generalized expectation that individual welfare is a collective concern. Of course there are obviously cases where income redistribution reduces labor effort. High unemployment insurance undoubtedly makes it easier for people to wait for the right job, and in some instances may even lead people to opportunistically use unemployment payments as a basis for an extended paid vacation.[11] But this is only one kind of effect. The normative effect of higher security may do more to increase productivity than the opportunistic use of income support reduces it.

The relationship between redistribution of income and productivity is thus complex, with some effects tending to enhance efficiency and others to depress it. Some of these effects work through the subjectivities of actors, others work through macroeconomic conditions. Some of these effects may be quite sensitive to the details of redistributive programs, others may be largely a consequence of the resulting income distribution itself. It could well be the case, for example, that the specific institutional form of tax-and-transfer policies in the post-Second World War period, in either the social-democratic model or the more miserly liberal-democratic welfare state, has become a drain on productivity, whereas more radical redistributive models, such as the proposal to establish universal basic income grants, might, to use Philippe van Parijs' words (1990), constitute 'a second marriage of justice and efficiency'. At this point I do not believe that we know enough about the complex effects of income distributions, or about the broader contexts in which these effects are generated, to specify the relative magnitudes of the productivity-enhancing and depressing effects. Thus, the severity of the economic limits on direct income redistribution is open to a great deal of debate. What is fairly clear, however, is that the level of equality of material conditions of life that radical egalitarians value requires a serious redistribution of market-generated income, and that a significant level of such redistribution is probably consistent with satisfactory levels of efficiency.

3. Community and Equality

Any kind of significant redistribution under democratic conditions, whether of assets or of income itself, requires a sense of community, a belief by people that they share a common fate and to a significant extent value each other's welfare.[12] Sustainable egalitarian redistributions are implausible in a population of purely selfish individualists. This is true for two distinct reasons.

First, if actors mobilize politically only under the narrowest conceptions of material self-interest it is unlikely that a durable coalition for significant redistribution would be sustainable. Of course, it is theoretically possible that a population of rational egoists might still vote for massive redistribution of either assets or income if a majority would have their material conditions of life improved by such redistribution. But we know that democratic institutions do not work this way, at least in capitalist democracies. Because political mobilization is costly, because in most political systems affluent people have higher voting rates than poor people, and because a significant number of people from any class are likely to be mobilized politically on the basis of non-class issues, a stable democratic coalition for redistribution must include a substantial number of people who will not immediately benefit from such redistribution. In the absence of a broad sense of community within the polity, such coalitions are likely to be relatively fragile.

Second, in a political setting of rampant selfishness and atomism, tax evasion is likely to be high. Cooperation with redistribution is not simply a collective matter of voting for parties with strong egalitarian commitments. It is also a question of individual compliance with the redistributive regime. Such compliance revolves around two issues: tax cheating and legal tax avoidance. Tax cheating is a chronic problem in liberal societies because the state's ability to appropriate taxes depends upon what Margaret Levi (1991) aptly calls the 'quasi-voluntary' payment of taxes by taxpayers. Compliance with tax authorities should be understood neither as purely voluntary nor as purely coerced. Most people voluntarily pay their taxes on the condition that they believe most other people pay their taxes. Most taxpayers do not want to be free-riders, but neither do they want to be suckers. While coercion is needed to raise the compliance rate among the unconditional defectors, the costs of monitoring would be prohibitively high if most tax payers only paid their taxes out of fear. A sense of community is one of the ingredients which underwrites the feeling of obligation to pay taxes. A failure of community also underwrites the willingness of wealthy individuals to emigrate to avoid taxes. This poses a particularly acute problem today in the European community where geographical mobility across tax jurisdictions has increased so dramatically. But even if individuals do not emigrate, they can choose to invest their wealth in low-tax areas and engage in other strategic acts to avoid taxes.

The Bowles and Gintis proposal for asset redistribution, just as much as a more conventional income transfer program, requires high levels of taxation. In one way or another the state has to underwrite the acquisition of capital assets by workers who lack collateral to buy those assets using normal, unsubsidized credit markets. High levels of tax evasion would thus constrain both kinds of redistribution.

The existence of a strong sense of community within a polity is not a given; it is produced through a wide range of social practices. Furthermore, once achieved, a sense of community does not continue simply through an alchemy of cultural inertia. Arguably, one of the central reasons why political support for redistribution has declined in recent years, even in the social democratic welfare states, is a decline in the required sense of community as social differentiation of various forms has increased. The problem of sustaining a sense of community is also one of the reasons many people on the left fear the long-term impact of European integration. The sense of solidarity between the people in the wealthier regions of the European Community and those in the poorer periphery is relatively weak, thus making high levels of European-wide redistribution unlikely, even if the European parliament had the power to enact such redistribution. What is more, the ease of mobility of both wealthy individuals and their capital across national borders makes it harder to raise taxes for within-country redistribution. European integration thus risks eroding the social conditions for sustainable redistributive policies of any sort.

The Bowles and Gintis proposal for asset redistribution, like any project of egalitarian redistribution, requires a strong sense of community for its implementation and reproduction. Unlike more social-democratic proposals, however, certain features of the Bowles and Gintis model may have the unintended effect of themselves systematically eroding community. The crux of the Bowles and Gintis proposal for firms and education is to place everyone on as equal a footing as possible in competitive markets, and then let markets flourish with minimal constraint. All that is wrong with existing markets, in this view, is that because of unjust distributions of assets (or more broadly 'opportunity') they generate unjust, inegalitarian outcomes. If the injustice of those outcomes is neutralized by giving everyone equal opportunity to compete, then markets become virtuous, effective devices for insuring accountability and efficiency. In the case of firms, asset redistribution entails turning capitalist firms into workers cooperatives. In the case of public education, asset redistribution entails giving students vouchers and creating a vigorous market in educational services.

Markets may have certain virtues, but as Cohen (1994) has argued, in general they are the enemy of community. Markets encourage people to think of their own welfare rather than that of others. Competition may encourage excellence, but it does so by reinforcing values of self-interest and greed, and spurring people on through fear. More generally, as Fred Hirsch (1976) has argued, capitalism 'depletes' the moral conditions which make market exchange stable: 'This legacy [social morality needed for capitalism] has diminished with time and with the corrosive contract of the active capitalist values. . . . As individual behavior has been increasingly directed to individual advantage, habits and instincts based on communal attitudes and objectives have lost out. The weakening of traditional social values has made predominantly capitalist economies more difficult to manage.' Of course, there are counter-tendencies as well. As Albert Hirschman has argued, in addition to eroding social morality, it is also true that 'the constant practice of commercial transactions generates feelings of trust, empathy for others and similar *doux* feelings.' Whether the socially corrosive effects will be stronger or weaker than the cohesion-enhancing effects, Hirschman believes, is a contingent matter. In any case, because the Bowles and Gintis model encourages a deepening of market relations in social life, it risks undermining the sense of community which is essential for any significant redistribution, including their own, to be sustainable.

How specifically are the Bowles and Gintis proposals for schools and firms likely to affect the sense of community? The schooling example is likely to have several consequences adverse to community. First, the voucher system being proposed makes it especially easy for parents to change schools if they are dissatisfied for some reason. Exit rather than voice would become the dominant mode of affecting school policy.[13] Education would become commodified, and parents would become experts in comparison-shopping for educational services. Second, because of parental shopping, school administrators will be under considerable pressure to compete with other schools for students. Instead of seeing education of children as a common mission requiring exchange of ideas and best practices across schools, schools will feel threat from other schools. Advertising will become a core preoccupation of schools, and as in most commodified advertising, the goal will be to seduce rather than inform. Third, there will be a strong tendency for schools to become more internally homogeneous under conditions of universal vouchers than in egalitarian public schooling, unless there were very strong mechanisms in place to counter the tendency for self-selection into homogeneous schools.[14] Indeed, this is one of the arguments in favor of vouchers: each particularistic identity-group in society can, if they choose, set up their own schools and withdraw from the broader community. This would apply to ethnic identities, religious identities, political identities, and so on. A broad sense of community is thus threatened by universal egalitarian vouchers both because it reinforces more particularistic identities around schooling, and because it encourages atomized exit rather than voice.

The proposal for worker-owned firms poses similar problems, although perhaps somewhat less poignantly since the existing structure is already so competitive and atomized. Class-wide solidarity within the working class has always been difficult to achieve and sustain, but turning workers into owners, directly competing with each other as members of firms and not simply as individuals in the labor market, is likely to make such solidarity even more fragile. Workers in successful firms will feel little desire to create infrastructure to help struggling firms. What is more, as in the school voucher case, worker's cooperatives are likely to recruit members at least partially on the basis of shared identities, and thus cooperatives are likely to become rather homogeneous. Because these worker-owned firms compete fiercely with each other, this relative uniformity of identity will be reinforced as antagonism to other identities. The combination of organizing workers into self-interested groups competing with other self-interested groups of workers, and overlaying these groups with relatively homogeneous cultural identities, is likely to make any sense of broad community and class solidarity even more difficult to achieve than under capitalism. The reproduction of an egalitarian regime of asset redistribution, however, requires, if anything, a strengthening of community within the working class.

Even the housing asset redistribution, which is arguably the least controversial aspect of the Bowles and Gintis proposal, poses certain risks to a sense of community. Gosta Esping-Anderson (1985), in a comparative study of the fates of the Swedish and Danish social democratic parties in the post-Second World War period, argues that the Danish party's housing policy – which encouraged home ownership rather than subsidized public housing as in Sweden – had the unintended effect of creating a constituency of voters who, once they owned their own homes, no longer felt much ongoing loyalty to the social democratic party. The decomposition of the electoral base of Danish social democracy compared to Sweden, according to Esping-Anderson, was to a significant extent the result of a successful commodification and privatization of the housing market in Denmark. Of course, this may have gone along with an improvement in the efficiency of the repair and maintenance of the housing stock in Denmark – an issue not addressed by Esping-Anderson – but it did not foster the kind of community-consciousness needed to sustain social democratic politics.

Now, one can imagine various amendments to the basic scheme of school vouchers and worker-owned firms that would counter some of these community-eroding effects. For example, Bowles and Gintis propose that schools could be given incentives to increase diversity by having the value of a voucher dependent upon the extent to which adding a given student moves the school towards some standard of diversity. A school with mainly children of rich parents would get much higher funds for adding a poor student than for adding another rich student. One could extend this reasoning to other forms of diversity, although extending the criteria for differential value of vouchers to more cultural dimensions would run more deeply against the grain of the rationale of vouchers, since one of the justifications of the system is to render schools more in line with the cultural preferences of parents. The constraints on curriculum imposed on schools by the state licensing authority as a condition for receiving vouchers could also be relatively tight (rather than lax) in order to foster more commonality among students across schools. Similar constraints on the internal practices (including recruitment) of worker-owned firms could be instituted. Still, unless such amendments effectively neutralized the commodification of schools and the intensified competition among workers, then the community-eroding effects of marketized schooling and worker-owned firms are potentially a serious threat to the sustainability of a redistributive politics.

It is impossible to predict whether or not these community-eroding effects constitute fatal flaws in the Bowles and Gintis model. I do not think that our social science knowledge of how norms are formed and transformed, or of how solidarities are created or fractured, is fine-grained enough for us to assess the magnitude of these effects. It is certainly possible, for example, that the egalitarian redistributive effects of a radical voucher system could be huge and the community-eroding effects weak. And while it may be the case that a democratically invigorated, egalitarian public school system would strengthen community relative to a voucher system, it might in other respects prove less efficient. These criticisms, therefore, indicate points of vulnerability in the proposals offered by Bowles and Gintis rather than decisive grounds for rejecting those proposals.

4. Conclusion

One of the core insights of the Bowles and Gintis proposal is that there are a variety of institutional designs which can potentially further radical egalitarian values. The simplest design is redistributing income. Bowles and Gintis argue convincingly that redistributing assets is an alternative that may accomplish the goals of simple redistribution even more effectively. As a general proposition this seems quite sound. Indeed, in one sense of the expression 'equality of assets', socialism and democracy are both egalitarian projects of asset redistribution.

What I have questioned is the specific proposals advanced by Bowles and Gintis for combining an egalitarian project of asset redistribution with a strengthening of markets as a way of regulating human interaction and choice. I have raised three main criticisms: first, that an employee-centered system of redistribution of capital assets combined with market competition is unlikely to generate sufficient levels of income equality from the vantage point of radical egalitarianism; second, that a significant level of direct redistribution of income (rather than simply assets) is at least compatible with fairly high levels of productivity and may even enhance productivity; and third, that a form of equality which intensifies the market by bringing more spheres of life under its sway and making the average person more deeply involved in market competition will undercut community. This does not imply that a complex, industrial society within which individual autonomy and choice are values can function effectively without markets. But it does mean that a political project of egalitarian reform needs to be as concerned with constraining the cultural and political effects of the market as with enabling everyone to participate in it on an equal basis.

Notes

1. Strictly speaking one should speak of reductions in *in*equality rather than increases in equality, since 'equality' literally designates the end point of a range of possible distributions. Nevertheless, I will treat equality itself as occurring in varying degrees – one can have more or less equality of material conditions within a population.

2. Bowles and Gintis offer a fourth example of a 'redistribution' of assets in which children are given property rights in the incomes of their parents. This is supposed to improve the 'efficiency' of child support for kids in the face of divorces. Unlike the other two cases, this use of the expression 'redistribution of assets' seems mainly a semantic trick. Current child-support laws, if fully enforced, would also provide for

adequate support for kids. I do not see what is gained by redescribing a child's right to adequate financial support from parents as a child's ownership of an asset.

3. For example, Bowles and Gintis write: 'To show that an egalitarian redistribution of assets *may* support a superior governance structure, we will show that *under some conditions* a relocation of ownership and residual claimancy of the firm from a capitalist to the firm's worker-members will improve productivity' (italics added). It is much less controversial to claim that under some conditions an egalitarian redistribution of assets may be superior to an inegalitarian one than to argue that such redistributions can be at the center of an egalitarian project.

4. Bowles and Gintis also propose a range of interesting devices for dealing with various problems workers might face in such a situation – like risk-aversion because of overly concentrated asset portfolios, or difficulties in obtaining credit. These are important kinds of institutional details for the design of an economy made up largely of worker-cooperatives since they will affect the long term stability and growth of the system, but they do not touch on the basic issue of how much equality will be generated by this form of asset redistribution.

5. It should be noted that Roemer's proposal for asset redistribution is more radical than Bowles and Gintis in so far as capital assets are redistributed equally to all adult citizens, not simply employees. (Roemer, 1994, p. 141)

6. These figures actually overstate the number of people who would actually receive profit-generating assets since official census data only distinguish non-profit membership organizations from private firms, but does not distinguish non-profit private firms from profit-making private firms. Thus, employees in a non-profit hospital or a non-profit private university would be treated as employees in private firms in the census.

7. Depending upon the details of the mechanism by which assets are redistributed to employees, it could be the case that workers in capital-intensive firms would not be particularly better off than workers in labor-intensive firms. For example, if workers acquire their assets through borrowing subsidized by the state, the degree of subsidy and interest rates could possibly be adjusted in ways which reduce the effects of differential capital intensity. Without some kind of strong provision, however, within-firm redistributions would leave massive between-firm inequalities in per capita wealth intact.

8. In my judgment the most morally compelling concept of equality is, roughly, the view that to the greatest extent possible burdens and rewards should be equally borne by all, or, equivalently, that everyone should have equal opportunity for well-being. This concept corresponds closely to the view advocated by G.A. Cohen (1994, 1995).

9. For an extended discussion of the implications of 'a fair day's work for a fair day's pay' for Bowles' and Gintis' model, see Burawoy and Wright (1990), reprinted as chapter 4 in Wright (1994).

10. The central mechanism at work here is that where this norm is operative, workers monitor each other's behavior fairly intensively, thus considerably saving monitoring costs for employers. Workers impose sanctions on shirking because a shirking worker is not 'pulling his or her own weight' in the collective effort of providing a fair day's work.

11. A case could be made that, under conditions of advanced capitalism, these labor-reducing effects might be socially desirable, at least if one believes that an increase in lifetime 'leisure' would be a good thing. While such redistribution would not be productivity-enhancing in the sense of increasing the amount of output per unit input, it might still be net welfare-enhancing.

12. I am using the term 'community' as a normative term in the sense proposed by G.A. Cohen (1994). As he writes: 'I mean, here, by "community", the anti-market principle according to which I serve you, not because of what I can get out of doing so, but because you need my service. That is anti-market because the market motivates productive contribution, not on the basis of commitment to one's fellow human beings and a desire to serve them while being served by them, but on the basis of impersonal cash reward.' A loving family is a strong form of 'community' in this sense, but any

social unit within which other-regardingness is an effective value would constitute a community. This idea of community is very close to 'solidarity' as this concept has been elaborated by Jon Elster (1985) in terms of 'conditional altruism'. For a discussion of how this sense of community bears on the politics of egalitarian justice, see Van Parijs (1993). This usage differs from the purely institutional definition adopted by Bowles and Gintis.

13. Anecdotally, when I lived in Berkeley, California, for a year in the late 1980s, I was struck by how much time and energy people devoted to 'shopping' for schooling. Instead of being actively involved in Parent-Teachers Associations, parents were mainly concerned with finding the best school on the market. I was also impressed with how much anxiety this caused for many parents who were never certain that they had made the right decision.

14. The appropriate comparison, of course, is not between the existing highly inegalitarian public school system in the United States today and a model of egalitarian vouchers, but between an egalitarian public school system and a voucher system. It may well be the case that the Bowles and Gintis egalitarian vouchers would produce more diversity in many schools than exists in some US cities today, but less diversity than in a properly reconstructed egalitarian public school system.

References

Burawoy, Michael, *Manufacturing Consent*, (Chicago: University of Chicago Press, 1978).

——, *The Politics of Production*, (London: Verso, 1985).

——, and Erik Olin Wright, 1992, 'Coercion and Consent in Contested Exchange', *Politics & Society*, June 1990.

Cohen, G. A. 'Back to Socialist Basics', *New Left Review*, 207 (1994).

——, *Self-Ownership, Freedom and Equality*, (Cambridge: Cambridge University Press, 1995).

Elster, Jon, *Making Sense of Marx*, (Cambridge: Cambridge University Press, 1985).

Esping-Anderson, Gosta, *Politics Against Markets*, (Princeton: Princeton University Press, 1985).

Hirsch, Fred, *Social Limits to Growth*, (Cambridge: Harvard University Press, 1976).

Hirschman, Albert I., 'Rival Interpretations of Market Society: Ccivilizing, Destructive or Feeble?', *Journal of Economic Literature*, vol. XX (December 1982), pp. 1463–484.

Levi, Margaret, *Of Revenue and Rule*, (Cambridge: Cambridge University Press, 1991).

Van Parijs, Philippe, 1990, 'The Second Marriage of Justice and Efficiency', in Van Parijs (ed.), *Arguing for Basic Income*, (London: Verso, 1992), pp. 215–40.

——, 'Rawlsians, Christians and Patriots: Maximin Justice and Individual Ethics'. *European Journal of Philosophy*, 1, pp. 309–42.

Wright, Erik Olin, *Interrogating Inequality*, (London: Verso, 1994)

Which Norms? How Much Gain?
Two Reasons to Limit Markets
Elaine McCrate

Bowles and Gintis establish several criteria for a progressive economic and social blueprint. Toward the general goals of equality and efficiency, they assess markets, states and communities with respect to the capacity of each for generating appropriate incentives.

Bowles and Gintis evaluate each of these institutions, or governance structures, with respect to the specific criteria of enforcing discipline or rules.[1] For example, markets do a good job of compelling discipline when agents experience the consequences of their own actions. However, when information about behavior is private and asset ownership is concentrated, markets engender serious coordination problems. The state may have an advantage in enforcing rules to overcome these difficulties. Communities also sometimes perform well in enforcing rules (norms), most notably in situations where the state has limited access to information.

However, Bowles' and Gintis' criteria for the evaluation of institutions and the enforcement of discipline and rules/norms are clearly not the only criteria one might wish to invoke. At least two others seem crucial to me.

The first of these is the *production* of norms. Bowles' and Gintis' emphasis on the enforcement of norms and other rules sidesteps the question of whether our communities have norms that advocates of efficiency or equality would care to enforce in the first place. When new norms are called for – for example, when the existing ones militate against cooperation in production, or when they are racist, sexist or homophobic – how do we get new ones?[2]

My second additional criterion is the problem of unintended effects – in this context, due to unlimited appreciation. Bowles and Gintis are concerned with the incentives of individual asset owners to preserve the asset – and properly so. But are there no acceptable restrictions on asset appreciation? At least in the housing market, I think some limits are necessary to preserve affordable housing for future generations, and to avoid inegalitarian redistributions.

A. The Production of Norms

In families, schools, neighborhoods and workplaces, undesirable norms abound. In schools, for example, the sexual harassment of girls as young as ten years old by boys is widespread, but until quite recently it was not considered a serious problem.[3] Gay and lesbian adolescents are often treated cruelly by students and teachers alike.

Bowles and Gintis propose free school choice, through vouchers to be redeemed at any minimally competent school. What will this wider marketplace in education do to change norms?

Bowles and Gintis are likely to argue that people will more effectively demand different norms in a marketplace where they can simply walk away from the ones they don't like. And indeed markets have often facilitated salutary changes in norms – for example, the contemporary women's liberation movement probably would not have had such breadth and depth were it not for the massive entry of white women into the labor force. Markets have swept aside many other traditional forms of domination and the norms that went with them.

But markets are as likely to undermine good norms as bad ones – for example, in the destruction of many effective traditional local norms for managing commonly pooled resources. Furthermore, it is not always true that the victims of bad norms can walk away from the source – for example, norms upholding sexual harassment and abuse in communities and families may mean that a school-age daughter who complains to her parents of sexual harassment at school is not taken seriously.

So markets are not going to do a very consistent job of changing norms on their own. Something else is needed. And in the history of a democratic society, that something else is often public debate and deliberation.[4] As Albert Hirschman pointed out a long time ago, markets aren't very good at promoting this – when problems are left behind by exit, voice solves far fewer of them.[5] (There is an important exception which I will take up momentarily.) And therefore the preservation of spaces where this deliberation can take place ought to be of the highest priority. Unlike Bowles and Gintis, I value the local school board for exactly this reason. Its functions ought to be broader than the certification of minimally competent schools. It also ought to be a place where concerned students, parents, teachers and citizens can come forward and debate critical issues, such as the removal of *Heather Has Two Mommies* from the library shelves.[6]

Curiously absent from Bowles' and Gintis' discussion of schooling is the inculcation of democratic values or norms, a topic they have pursued extensively elsewhere.[7] By democratic norms, I am not referring to superficial issues like dress codes or conventions. I am referring to democratic habits of mind. For educator Deborah Meier, students adequately educated for democratic life routinely ask, 'how do we know what we know?', 'who's speaking?', 'what causes what?', and 'who cares?'[8] Asking and seeking to answer these questions are the very intellectual skills which are compromised by the rote education provided to most working-class children.[9]

Under Bowles' and Gintis' proposed system, probably the best that can be hoped for with completely transportable vouchers is that parents who have strong *ex ante* preferences for democratic schooling will demand, and get it, in the educational marketplace. Other parents who are extremely alienated and suspicious may not. Melvin Kohn's work shows that working-class parents often favor a rule-oriented education for their children, which enforces submission to authority.[10] Schools in affluent communities often do not do much better at inculcating democratic habits of mind; often they simply imprint a habit of privilege for those fortunate enough to be attending them. Thus parents themselves may reproduce the kinds of educational class distinctions in a school choice system which they already support in a neighborhood school system. Again, this could change if there were a place to talk about educational priorities.

However, none of this is to say that there is no role for choice in schools. Deborah Meier see choice in public education as the only practical vehicle for cultivating and diffusing educational innovations. Teachers and parents must develop the sense of investment in the school which only comes with choosing freely what kind of school to affiliate with. But Meier makes it clear that it is not market discipline that makes choice work. She points out that innovation is the exception rather than the rule in private schools, and that many ineffective ones remain afloat.

It is rather the collaboration and mutual respect among students, parents, staff, faculty and community in Meier's own Central Park East schools that accounts for their success. The Central Park East schools are part of a choice system in Harlem's District IV which started in the 1970s. District IV permitted teachers to set up smaller schools within large school buildings to experiment with their own ideas. Within ten years, over fifty schools (the largest of them with about 300 students) emerged in two dozen buildings. Parents got more involved, teacher morale improved, and students learned much more. The costs were less than one additional teacher per new school.

Harlem District IV's choice plan was successful because much of the decision-making devolved to those with the greatest stake in the school (a point Bowles and Gintis will have no argument with), not because competition winnowed out the failures (on which I expect we disagree). This argument is strengthened by similar success stories in educational experiments which do not involve choice at all (although they are not inimical to it). For example, the Accelerated School Project helps poor students catch up with the mainstream by addressing governance issues within the school.[11] Instead of school administration and teachers working at cross purposes, excluding parents and the community, the project establishes collaborative decision-making and implementation in all aspects of the school – curriculum, instruction and school organization. As in East Harlem, parents and teachers were much more involved and enthusiastic, and students improved very quickly. No new major funding was required.

Precisely because choice, along with smaller size and collegiate organization, stimulates commitment, the Central Park East schools have had some of the very difficult discussions about norms that all schools need to have. The schools were able to respond immediately and flexibly to such racially charged events as the assault of the Central Park jogger and the Rodney King riots, and their own internal racial conflicts. Class schedules were sometimes changed to accommodate the necessary discussions with students. Teachers and parents addressed the issues in advisory board meetings. Because teachers, parents and students shared a commitment to the school, they all learned something about navigating the difficult waters of racial conflict, without tearing the school apart.[12]

So choice can facilitate commitment and democratic discussion within schools – an important exception to the general rule that voice and exit don't mix. But what about the larger society which must finance the schools? If we do not retain some forms of public accountability and some sense of a common future, how are we to persuade the millions of citizens who have no children in the schools to continue to pay educational taxes? Already newspapers are burgeoning with letters to the editor from older people whose children are long gone from the public schools, from people with children in private schools, and from people who expect to have no children – all wondering why they should pay to educate other people's children. Without their support, how do Bowles and Gintis expect to pay for school vouchers? Will the public really come back just because schools are run more efficiently?

One cannot easily escape the conclusion that the schools need deliberative bodies and public accountability to nurture the commitment of the taxpaying public. We need choice, but we need it within a public school system. (This is also Meier's position.) A choice scheme will provide more educational variety. It will create space for pathbreaking innovations. But no school receiving public funds should be exempt from debate over its practices. Schools which flagrantly violate democratic values, for example by teaching extreme racial or religious intolerance, should even be considered for decertification. This requires that public schools of choice operate under the jurisdiction of a public body, such as a board.

Good sense, justice and intellectual integrity will not always prevail at the school board. Also, it is certainly true that a wider role for the board opens the possibility of public sector opportunism (for example, consider the numerous cities in which boards have administered the schools as big patronage systems). But I can think of no other way to raise important public issues at all without public deliberative bodies. The authority of boards can be limited to restrict public sector rent-seeking. Boards should be required to allocate funds roughly in proportion to enrollment and to permit schools to make their own budgetary decisions thereafter, subject only to the requirement that the books balance each period.[13] Schools ordinarily should have authority to make their own personnel decisions, subject to some independent professional review. But boards ought to have some authority to communicate and enforce expectations about critical social issues. I don't know how exactly to draw the line between decentralization and appropriate public authority, but we have one advantage in that school boards are so localized in the United States; this structure ought to make it easier to pursue local needs.

Although I have discussed the production of norms with respect to education, it is equally important with respect to workplaces, neighborhoods, and families. The norm of racial segregation in neighborhoods has been extraordinarily impervious to other improvements in the welfare of African Americans in the late 1960s and early 1970s.[14] How can we challenge these norms?

B. Unintended Effects

Let me preface this section by observing that the left is used to thinking about the consequences of its agenda on a relatively small scale. But Bowles and Gintis are offering a society-wide blueprint for change, not the occasional, usually local, largely isolated interventions that comprise most left activity today. It's important to consider the side-effects of Bowles' and Gintis' proposals on the scale they envision.

In this context consider the US housing market. In the US in the 1970s and 1980s, the housing crisis resulted from soaring housing prices fueled by speculative pressures. Giving mortgages to the vast numbers of low- and moderate-income people who now cannot afford to buy homes could exacerbate the problem of the speculative market through elevated (owner-occupied) housing demand. This is in part because housing supply is quite inelastic in the short run. More importantly, housing supply departs from the textbook model through rigidities associated with residential segregation by class and race. Especially when there has been discrimination, excess demand in housing markets has historically fueled extraordinary increases in housing prices for the disadvantaged group.

Think of discrimination as a bottleneck, slowing down the flow of black families into white neighborhoods. For example, among blacks migrating to northern cities during the world wars, the demand for and supply of housing were on different sides of the bottleneck, corresponding to different 'sides of the tracks'. Housing prices shot up in the desirable neighborhoods, and crashed in the dilapidated ones.[15] Today if low-income blacks are given mortgages, most will not want to use them to buy homes in the slums, again putting supply of and demand for housing in different places. Housing prices in different areas will follow familiar patterns, and there will be perverse transfers of wealth among homeowners.

This is hardly an argument against providing mortgages for low-income people. But asset redistribution in the housing market could easily misfire unless accompanied by other initiatives, most importantly, reducing racial barriers and taking housing off the speculative market through provisions for limited appreciation.

Many local community land trusts have been working for a long time to do both of these. These nonprofit organizations acquire land through purchase or donation with the intention of retaining title in perpetuity. They offer lifetime or longterm leases on land, exclusively for people who will be using the land themselves, for residential (or sometimes commercial, agricultural or aesthetic) purposes. Leaseholders may own homes and other buildings on the land they have leased.

When a property owner in a community land trust wishes to sell her home, she has equity in any improvements she has made, but her gains from purely speculative increases in value, or from increases in value due to community efforts, are strictly limited. (As examples of the latter type of increase, consider the improvement of public schools and neighborhood character.) Thus she is permitted to sell her home for no more than x per cent of what she paid for it, in excess of private improvements.

The land trust has the first option to buy the house. Ordinarily it purchases the house and resells it to another leaseholder, on the same terms as before. Thus housing is permanently taken off the speculative market. In addition, land trusts often develop packages of attractive terms for buyers, pool volunteer labor to help with construction, or help with the cost of maintenance. The land trust makes homeownership possible for people who otherwise could not afford it, and in turn requires that this affordability be preserved for future generations.[16]

Community land trusts are the product of a deliberate search for different property forms by activists starting in the 1970s. They are a good example of the 'social republican' property form discussed by Roemer elsewhere in this volume. At least since the Supreme Court upheld zoning restrictions in 1926, no one has had the right to do absolutely anything she wishes with her real property. Antidiscrimination laws in the 1960s further muddied the distinction between public and private. The community land trust is another step in this direction, recognizing that there are both legitimate private interests and legitimate public interests in property, and trying to strike a balance between them. The specific social republican features of the land trust are limited appreciation, and the requirement that the member make personal use of the land.

Land trusts are pioneering novel governance structures as well as property forms. They have given a great deal of thought to the design of effective new governance structures. (They sometimes refer to themselves as 'the third sector', in contrast to the public and private for-profit sectors.) For example, they explicitly address the oppositional incentives of low-income owners and nonowners through the composition of their boards. A land trust board has equal representation of member-owners on the one hand (who might be tempted to subvert the limited appreciation agreement they originally benefited from), and renters on the other, the latter to represent the interests of future owners. (The boards also include representatives of other community housing groups.) The boards discuss and act on local housing priorities.

Bowles and Gintis argue that expanded home ownership will create the correct incentive structure for property maintenance and neighborhood enhancement, by placing ownership in the hands of those who live with the consequences of maintenance (or disinvestment). How does a land trust preserve incentives to maintain property when selling prices are capped? If for example, appreciation is limited to 25 per cent for land-trust members but market prices increase by more than 25 per cent, the members could sell their property for the maximum permitted price even though they may have allowed the structure to deteriorate.

Many land trusts have flexible selling price formulas to internalize the external benefits of neighborhood amenities, by making appreciation a function of the average selling price in the neighborhood, and to deal with other problems attendant upon rapid appreciation. Land trusts have boards which can discuss the trade-off between incentives and affordability, and handle them locally. The boards are also a place to air problems of discrimination, a process which otherwise goes on invisibly (unless a housing audit team makes a call). And because the boards typically include members of other community housing organizations, racial discrimination has been a central concern of many community land trusts.

C. Conclusion

Bowles and Gintis take issue with the left's emphasis on redistribution through taxes and income transfers, and instead they argue for a more appropriate combination of these and asset redistributions. Essentially their strategy is (1) give people a stake in the maintenance or productivity of critical assets, (2) let markets perform their disciplinary function, then (3) mitigate the effects of bad luck by establishing a system of insurance and a basic income grant (the latter conditional only upon performing some socially useful unpaid service).

But the problems I anticipate simply cannot be addressed by mitigating the effects of markets; we need careful interventions in markets themselves. None of the governance structures Bowles and Gintis describe or that humans invent will ever be perfect, and we need to anticipate the problems resulting from market activity as much as those attendant upon state authority. There are sometimes real trade-offs between market incentives and social goals. Projects can often be designed to maintain incentives to a degree even without allowing unlimited gains. In the future, I hope Bowles and Gintis and all the rest of us will consider the hard questions of where to draw the barriers between markets and other governance structures, and what kinds of new governance structures are needed.

Notes

1. They also consider the ability of governance structures to elicit information.

2. This oversight characterizes much of current economic work on norms, which in prisoner's dilemma situations, mostly explores the demand for and enforcement of norms, rather than their evolution. See Nancy Brooks, 'The Effects of Community Characteristics on Community Social Behavior', (PhD dissertation, University of Pennsylvania, May 1995), for a useful summary and an exception.

3. American Association of University Women Educational Foundation, 'Hostile Hallways: The AAUW Survey on Sexual Harassment in America's Schools' (Washington, DC, 1993).

4. For an excellent recent example, see William Lee, Miller, *Arguing About Slavery: The Great Battle in the United States Congress* (New York: Alfred A. Knopf, 1996).

5. Hirschman, Albert, *Exit, Voice and Loyalty: Responses to Decline in Firms, Organizations and States* (Cambridge: Harvard University Press, 1970).

6. Leslea Newman, *Heather Has Two Mommies* (Boston: Alyson Wonderland, 1989) is a children's book about lesbian parenting which several school boards have debated in the past few years.

7. Bowles and Gintis, *Schooling in Capitalist America* (New York: Basic Books, 1976). In this book, just about everyone had a hand in reproducing antidemocratic norms: school boards (which became captive to bureaucratic interests in the progressive era), parents and teachers.

8. Deborah Meier, *The Power of Their Ideas: Lessons for America from a Small School in Harlem* (Boston: Beacon Press, 1995), p. 50.

9. For example, see the results of classroom observations in Martin Carnoy and Henry Levin, *Schooling and Work in the Democratic State* (Stanford: Stanford University Press, 1985).

10. Melvin Kohn, *Class and Conformity: A Study in Values* (Homewood, Illinois: Dorsey Press, 1969).

11. Henry M. Levin, 'New Schools for the Disadvantaged', *Teachers Education Quarterly*, vol. 14 no. 4 (1987), pp. 60–83.

12. This discussion is based on Meier, *The Power of Their Ideas: Lessons for America from a Small School in Harlem* (Boston: Beacon Press, 1995).

13. Actually, Bowles and Gintis propose a more complicated funding scheme, to reflect the proportion of more educationally needy students, and to establish affirmative action incentives. I largely agree.

14. Racial discrimination has been extensively documented both in the real estate and credit markets, both through regression methods and housing audits. See Bradbury, Katharine L., Karl E. Case and Constance R. Dunham, 'Geographic Patterns of Mortgage Lending in Boston, 1982–87', *New England Economic Review*, (September–October 1989) pp. 3–30; Fix and Struyk (eds.), *Clear and Convincing Evidence: Measurement of Discrimination in America* (Washington, DC: Urban Institute Press, 1993); Douglas Massey and Nancy Denton, *American Apartheid: Segregation and the Making of the Underclass* (Cambridge, MA: Harvard University Press, 1993).

15. For an excellent description of this process in Chicago, see Arnold Hirsch, *Making the Second Ghetto: Race and Housing in Chicago, 1940–1960* (Cambridge: Cambridge University Press, 1983).

16. This discussion is taken from Institute for Community Economics, *The Community Land Trust Handbook* (Emmaus, Pennsylvania: Rodale Press, 1982).

5

Norms and Efficiency

Elinor Ostrom*

Samuel Bowles and Herbert Gintis in their excellent paper, 'Efficient Redistribution: New Rules for Markets, States, and Communities' (1995), address the theme of 'Real Utopias' by outlining a general strategy to increase the egalitarian structure of society through redistributing assets rather than income. Their general argument is that many processes related to providing and producing goods (including private goods, common-pool resources, toll goods, and public goods) can be more egalitarian and efficient through changes in the forms of ownership and control. Bowles and Gintis point to the centrality of coordination failures where all participants in ongoing situations could be made better off if they agreed to coordinate their activities rather than acting independently. Without governance structures that help solve coordination failures, mutually advantageous opportunities are lost. This leads to lower overall productivity and adversely impacts on those with the fewest assets. Bowles and Gintis identify three governance structures that help solve coordination failures: market, community, and state. They provide an initial sketch of the complementary strengths of these forms of governance. The broad sweep of their argument is consistent with my own theoretical and empirical work.[1]

In our empirical studies of farmer-owned irrigation systems in Nepal, for example, we find that farmer-owned systems are able to achieve higher levels of agricultural productivity and more equitable distribution of water (and therefore of income to the farmer) than government-owned systems serving similar sized irrigation systems in similar ecological terrain.[2] In a recent study of irrigation systems in

*The author is appreciative of the support extended to the Workshop in Political Theory and Policy Analysis by the Ford Foundation (Grant no. 950–1160) to support our research on Community Management.

113

Taiwan, considered by many to be among the most efficient systems in the world, Lam (1996) points to the combined incentive systems of small-scale, farmer-owned irrigation associations working in concert with parastatal water districts that operate and maintain large-scale public works. In this system, the farmer-owned systems are as important as the larger, parastatal enterprises in achieving productive and equitable outcomes.

In our earlier studies of urban service delivery, we consistently found that smaller-scale, community-controlled police departments were able to provide a higher level of direct response services to matched neighborhoods than those served by large-scale, center-city police departments.[3] At the metropolitan level, we found that complex, mixed systems composed of some very large public or private producers of indirect services (such as crime lab, training, and dispatching) combined with large numbers of community-controlled police producers of direct services (such as patrol, immediate response, and traffic control) were more effective than consolidated systems (Parks and Ostrom, 1981). The purpose of this volume, however, is not only to provide supplementary empirical evidence in support of Bowles' and Gintis' general thesis but also to extend their theoretical analysis and potentially challenge some of their arguments. There are two topics that I wish to address: 1. the issue of monitoring and sanctioning as these support mutually productive agreements about contracts individuals have *ex post* incentives not to perform; 2. the idea of a community as a form of governance.

1. Monitoring and Sanctioning in Potential Dilemma Situations

Many of the situations Bowles and Gintis discuss are potential social dilemma situations. A social dilemma exists whenever the immediate pay-offs to participants from choosing an opportunistic action in a transaction are sufficiently great that at least some (or all) participants choose opportunistically, thereby yielding an equilibrium where feasible, higher joint pay-offs are not achieved. When the probability of others choosing opportunistically (e.g., cheating, stealing, and not keeping promises) is high, many potentially productive transactions are not initiated. Unresolved social dilemmas produce lower overall net benefits for those involved. When described formally, the prisoner's dilemma is a classic form of a social dilemma familiar to most social scientists.

It is frequently assumed that the only deterrent to adopting opportunistic behavior is the imposition of sanctions by monitors external to those who are participants. Whenever the expected value of cheating is greater than the expected value of noncheating, one would then have to invest in severe sanctions (and assume that juries and/or judges will actually impose them) and/or in high levels of monitoring so that the frequency of detection is substantial. Franz Weissing and I have analyzed several much more complex games, involving temptations to steal water from a community-owned irrigation system and the costs and rewards of monitoring (Weissing and Ostrom, 1991, 1993). In irrigation games where opportunistic behavior is deterred by the probability of detection and sanctioning, the rate of stealing is never equal to zero in an equilibrium. The rate of stealing rises with increases in the cost of monitoring and increases in the size of the group affected. It is negatively affected by increases in the rewards offered to monitors and a decrease in the relative cost of detection and the probability of being detected. Consequently, the higher the potential benefit to a participant of acting opportunistically, the higher the costs that must be invested in monitoring and/or sanctioning. In a setting where individuals do not learn internal norms that reduce the rates of opportunistic behavior, the costs of monitoring and sanctioning can be high enough that many highly productive transactions are never undertaken.

A major objective of classical political economy according to Sen (1977) was to show that the market as a governance institution could perform optimally when all transactors had hedonistic, short-term preferences and did not share norms such as those involved in keeping promises. To accomplish this theoretical objective, it was necessary to assume a set of individuals with hedonistic, short-term preferences. That set of assumptions, which has proved so powerful in conducting analysis of market behavior, has come to be accepted by many political economists as the model of rational choice. It is thereby presumed to be rational to lie, cheat, and steal, but not rational to feel guilty if one lies, cheats, or steals.[4] The same set of assumptions is now routinely used to analyze all choice behavior. In 'no norm' situations, the costs of monitoring and sanctioning can be sufficiently high that many productive activities are not even contemplated and trust can be destroyed (Frey, 1993).

In societies where individuals acquire personal or social norms, however, individuals can agree upon and fulfill long-term contracts that are not dependent entirely on the investments made in costly monitoring and sanctions. Crawford and Ostrom (1995) define norms as a shared belief that actions in specific kinds of situations must, must not, or may be done. In using the concept of a norm in formal theory, one needs to include a parameter that increases or decreases the value of a pay-off derived from an action–outcome sequence. Individuals who feel a high cost of guilt when they do not keep a promise face a different pay-off matrix than individuals whose utility is derived only from external costs and benefits. Crawford and Ostrom introduce a syntax and a mode of formal representation to expand our capabilities of dealing with modeling individual behavior in potential social dilemma situations. The introduction of shared norms is not, of course, sufficient to eliminate all opportunistic behavior. Unless internal norms to keep promises generate internal costs that are higher than the expected value of cheating, it is still impossible to get cheating down to zero. Productive regimes tend to rely both on social norms and on monitoring and sanctioning. Individuals who share strong norms, however, are able to use economic resources to generate more benefits than individuals who do not share strong norms. If norms are an important way for humans to achieve higher productivity, it is necessary to begin addressing how norms are transmitted from one generation to the next.

2. Communities

Communities affect the costs of monitoring and sanctioning in four ways – only three of which are discussed by Bowles and Gintis. According to Bowles and Gintis, communities are important because:

1. Individuals in a community tend to share norms of behavior that can include the value of hard work, the extension of reciprocity to others, and keeping promises, that enable individuals to solve some coordination failures that would not otherwise be solved. By creating a smaller group who interact with one another repeatedly, a strictly prudential calculus leads individuals to develop a reputation for keeping promises and thus being good partners with whom to undertake coordinated ventures, since monitoring and enforcement costs will be less. Thus, many mutually productive activities can be undertaken that would not have been possible without the presence of individuals in a community setting.

2. Individuals in a community can monitor each other's conformance to shared understanding and/or specific contracts or covenants made at a lower cost than individuals who are not from the same

community. The costs of monitoring are lower within a community since individuals interact in a variety of activities on a face-to-face basis and easily and accurately learn about the past behavior of other specific individuals in keeping past agreements.

3. Sanctioning nonconformance to agreements to switch from independent to coordinated action can be less expensive in a community. Sanctioning is less costly since formal punishments will need to be applied less frequently and lower-cost sanctions – sometimes in the form of simple avoidance of contact – are available to participants.

I agree with all of the above. In regard to monitoring and sanctioning, Bowles and Gintis do not focus on the importance of communities in teaching shared norms of behavior that are essential for arguments (1) through (3). Also, they do not focus on the importance of communities in teaching other skills essential for the success of self-governing enterprises and in the provision and production of local public goods and common-pool resources.

Let me first turn to the role of communities in providing an environment where productive norms can be transmitted from one generation to another. The origin of individual preferences is not often considered when using economic models. And, for analyzing the exchange of private goods (as classically defined) in perfectly competitive markets, the origin of preferences is not important. When one is interested, however, in the design of 'real utopias', shared beliefs about the dos and don'ts of behaving in relationship to other individuals are essential. After several centuries of analysis trying to focus on external institutions that will 'get the incentives' right, we have to recognize that every institutional arrangement – including worker-owned firms, farmer-owned irrigation systems, voucher systems for education, etc. – can be shown to fail to perform under circumstances that may occur quite frequently. The rate of institutional failure can be reduced by teaching individuals how to modify their own preferences for short-term pleasures by choosing internalized norms that restrict the opportunistic behavior that they would otherwise adopt.

Teaching others moral behavior is itself a social dilemma when the teachers have little long-term incentives to undertake this time-consuming and costly activity. Families tend to be an appropriate institutional arrangement for the transmission of shared norms, as well as many other social and economic skills, as part of the day-to-day life of being in a family. In an era when parents would be dependent upon their children for old-age care, parents have a very strong incentive to imbue responsibility and other virtues in their children. Thus, while the costs of moral training were high, the long-term costs of not bringing up children to keep promises, to work hard, and to care for those around them were extremely high and felt strongly by the family itself (Oberschall, 1993). And, if the training were successful, families would be the recipient of much of the trusting and responsible behavior both in the short-run as children were growing up in the household (and could do considerable damage to common property if they were not responsible) and over the length of the lifetime of the parent.

Parent–child relationships are fundamentally asymmetric in structure. The investment of parents in their child's practical and moral education can be negated by children who do not reciprocate when parents are old and need care. Families that reside in a community for a long time, where children also reside in the same community, are aided in this task both during the years when children are still dependent and need further investment and when the time comes for parents to be cared for by their children. If children play with neighbors who have also made a similar investment in rearing children, children learn a consistent set of norms from their play activities as from their parents. The higher the number of different settings in which the child engages and obtains a similar image of the kind of behavior expected, the lower the cost for parents of teaching, monitoring, and re-enforcing these shared norms. Parents who find themselves in a rapidly changing neighborhood where others do not share similar views about the importance of shared norms, initially bear a much higher cost than those in an effective community. Further, the likelihood that children will reciprocate when the time comes for them to take care of their parents is much higher if the children are part of a smaller community with shared norms about the importance of caring for older parents.

A major reason to support their proposal to transfer housing projects from government ownership to tenant ownership is that the population of such units will tend to be relatively stable and agree upon norms. Thus, the resources expended on governance (including monitoring and sanctions) will be less and the probability of better performance will be higher. Another reason to support this proposal is that individuals who live in a self-governing housing project will learn new skills that are important for them as individuals and for the creation of productive economies and policies.

Individuals who must make decisions that affect themselves and their neighbors in settings where the information they need to make effective choices is available to them and the results of their choices are made known to them through experience, learn governance and management skills. Governance is no longer something that is done in a capital city by other types of individuals. Governance is what the owners of a housing project or the citizens of a small rural or urban community learn. One essential skill relates to learning how to craft rules that change the incentives of participants while keeping monitoring and sanctioning costs low. The production of local public goods – safety in the neighborhood – is also accomplished more by those living in a neighborhood than by a police force that may come from other neighborhoods and understand very little about the problems faced by residents. These contributions of communities were not taken into account when efforts to undertake massive consolidation of local communities were accomplished during this past century[5]. It would not be difficult for Samuel Bowles and Herbert Gintis, however, to incorporate these aspects of how communities contribute to the dynamic stability and growth of societies and polities in their essay.

Notes

1. See E. Ostrom, Schroeder and Wynne (1993) where we address the problem of unsustainable investments in infrastructure using an approach that is similar in regard to identifying underlying strategic problems and the set of counteracting institutions that can be used to cope with these problems. See also E. Ostrom, Gardner and Walker (1994).

2. Benjamin et al. (1994); E. Ostrom, Lam and Lee (1994); Lam (1998); E. Ostrom (1996).

3. See for example, E. Ostrom and Parks (1973); E. Ostrom and Whitaker (1973); and E. Ostrom, Parks and Whitaker (1978).

4. The assumption of narrow, hedonistic calculation being central to decisions is consistent with this hypothetical question-and-answer situation described by Sen (1977, p. 332).

'Where is the railway station?' he asks me. 'There,' I say, pointing at the post office, 'and would you please post this letter for me on the way?' 'Yes,' he says, determined to open the envelope and check whether it contains something valuable.

5. See V. Ostrom, Bish and E. Ostrom (1988); and E. Ostrom (1993).

References

Benjamin, Paul, Wai Fung Lam, Elinor Ostrom, and Ganesh Shivakoti, *Institutions, Incentives, and Irrigation in Nepal*, (Decentralization: Finance & Management Project Report, Burlington, VT: Associates in Rural Development, 1994).

Bowles, Samuel, and Herbert Gintis, 'Efficient Redistribution: New Rules for Markets, States, and Communities', Working paper (Amherst: University of Massachusetts, Department of Economics, 1995).

Crawford, Sue E.S., and Elinor Ostrom, 'A Grammar of Institutions', *American Political Science Review*, 89, 3 (September 1995), pp. 582–600.

Frey, Bruno S., 'Does Monitoring Increase Work Effort? The Rivalry with Trust and Loyalty', *Economic Inquiry*, 31, 4 (October 1993), pp. 663–70.

Lam, Wai Fung, 'Institutional Design of Public Agencies and Coproduction: A Study of Irrigation Associations in Taiwan', *World Development*, 24, 6 (1996).

——, *Governing Irrigation Systems in Nepal: Institutions, Infrastructure, and Collective Action*, (Oakland, CA: Institute for Contemporary Studies Press, 1998).

Oberschall, Anthony, 'Rules, Norms, Morality: Their Emergence and Enforcement', Working paper (Chapel Hill: University of North Carolina, Department of Sociology, 1993).

Ostrom, Elinor, 'A Communitarian Approach to Local Governance', *National Civic Review*, 82, 3 (August 1993), pp. 226–33.

——, 'Incentives, Rules of the Game, and Development', in *Proceedings of the Annual World Bank Conference on Development Economics 1995*, (Washington, DC: The World Bank, 1996).

——, Roy Gardner and James Walker, *Rules, Games, and Common-Pool Resources*, (Ann Arbor: University of Michigan Press, 1994).

——, Wai Fung Lam and Myungsuk Lee, 'The Performance of Self-Governing Irrigation Systems in Nepal', *Human Systems Management*, 13, 3 (1994), pp. 197–207.

——, and Roger B. Parks, 'Suburban Police Departments: Too Many and Too Small?', in *The Urbanization of the Suburbs*, Louis H. Masotti and Jeffrey K. Hadden (eds.), Urban Affairs Annual Reviews, vol. 7 (Beverly Hills, CA: Sage, 1973), pp. 367–402.

——, Roger B. Parks and Gordon P. Whitaker, *Patterns of Metropolitan Policing*, (Cambridge, MA: Ballinger, 1978).

——, Larry Schroeder and Susan Wynne, *Institutional Incentives and Sustainable Development: Infrastructure Policies in Perspective*, (Boulder, CO: Westview Press, 1993).

——, and Gordon P. Whitaker, 'Does Local Community Control of Police Make a Difference? Some Preliminary Findings', *American Journal of Political Science*, 17, 1 (February 1973), pp. 48–76.

Ostrom, Vincent, *The Meaning of American Federalism: Constituting a Self-Governing Society*, (San Francisco, CA: Institute for Contemporary Studies Press, 1991).

——, Robert Bish and Elinor Ostrom, *Local Government in the United States*, (San Francisco, CA: Institute for Contemporary Studies Press, 1988).

Parks, Roger B., and Elinor Ostrom, 'Complex Models of Urban Service Systems', in *Urban Policy Analysis: Directions for Future Research*, Terry N. Clark (ed.), Urban Affairs Annual Reviews, vol. 21 (Beverly Hills, CA: Sage, 1981), pp. 171–99.

Sen, Amartya K., 'Rational Fools: A Critique of the Behavioral Foundations of Economic Theory', *Philosophy & Public Affairs*, 6, 4 (Summer 1997), pp. 317–44.

Weissing, Franz J., and Elinor Ostrom, 'Irrigation Institutions and the Games Irrigators Play: Rule Enforcement without Guards', in *Game Equilibrium Models II: Methods, Morals, and Markets*, Reinhard Selten (ed.) (Berlin: Springer-Verlag, 1991), pp. 188–262.

Weissing, Franz J., and Elinor Ostrom, 'Irrigation Institutions and the Games Irrigators Play: Rule Enforcement on Government- and Farmer-Managed Systems', in *Games in Hierarchies and Networks: Analytical and Empirical Approaches to the Study of Governance Institutions*, Fritz W. Scharpf (ed.), (Frankfurt am Main: Campus Verlag; Boulder, CO: Westview Press, 1993), pp. 387–428.

6

Efficiency Politics
Andrew Levine*

From a political point of view, Samuel Bowles' and Herbert Gintis' proposals for 'efficient asset redistributions' represent an effort to revive left politics at a time when the left is everywhere in eclipse. From the purview of contemporary economic theory, their proposals exemplify work in an emerging paradigm that, in contrast to the old neo-classical orthodoxy, takes seriously such phenomena as incomplete and asymmetrical information, incomplete markets, and imperfect competition. On the old assumptions, the allocation of resources and therefore equity considerations were demonstrably independent of efficiency concerns. The new paradigm, in contrast, supports models which imply that, in many circumstances, the efficiency of outcomes depends, in part, on the distribution of assets among economic agents.

In their effort to revive leftwing thinking about questions of institutional design, Bowles and Gintis advance proposals that promote policies associated historically with the pro-capitalist, pro-market right. I would nevertheless urge those of us who, like myself, find more traditional leftwing ideas still timely to resist the temptation to find their proposed reforms guilty by association.[1] I would suggest too that we not fault Bowles and Gintis for the modesty of their plans in comparison with the sweeping social transformations envisioned by the historical Left. In the present conjuncture, any and all attempts at reviving leftwing politics are welcome. The issue is whether Bowles' and Gintis' proposals really would have this effect. In the remarks that follow, I will voice some doubts in this regard.

Bowles and Gintis claim that, in at least four important areas of social life – schooling, housing, childrearing and manufacturing – it

* I am grateful to Erik Wright for his comments on an earlier draft of this essay, and to Daniel Hausman for discussions of the issues in contention here.

would be efficiency-enhancing to redistribute (private) property rights in a more egalitarian direction. The general idea is that market failures and information asymmetries work against the beneficial incentive effects of private ownership and markets, and that these defects can be rectified by the asset redistributions they propose. There is no way to evaluate this claim in general. Within the new economic paradigm, it is well established that 'excessive' inequalities can be detrimental to efficient resource allocations. But there are also countervailing considerations – above all, the fact that the asset-rich are more likely than the asset-poor to assume the risks necessary for optimal economic performance. There is no way in general to say where the efficiency advantages lie. Therefore, in order to assess Bowles' and Gintis' claims properly, we would need to know more than they tell us about exactly what they have in mind. Indeed, more information is needed before we can even be confident that Bowles' and Gintis' proposals can be implemented in genuinely egalitarian ways. Even the most ostensibly egalitarian of their reforms – their advocacy of workers' ownership of firms – may not have the consequences they suppose. Since asset-poor workers lack personal resources to invest in enterprises, workers would have to borrow extensively in order to become worker-owners. Thus workers' ownership could generate personal debts that would offset the equalizing consequences of redistributing ownership rights in the way that Bowles and Gintis suggest.[2] It should be possible to solve this problem by ongoing state subsidies or massive lump-sum transfers – though, from an efficiency standpoint, the cure might then be worse than the disease.[3] In any case, until Bowles and Gintis tell us more about their institutional designs, the worry remains that their plans, if implemented, might actually exacerbate wealth inequalities. Then they would be of little or no use in implementing leftwing ideals.

For the sake of argument, however, let us concede that the asset redistributions Bowles and Gintis envision can be satisfactorily fleshed out and implemented, and that they really will do what the authors claim. Then there are still issues to be raised about the respects in which the 'efficiency' advantages of their proposals cohere with the political commitments that motivate them. Efficiency is an important topic in its own right, and a convenient focus for discussing some of the political implications of Bowles' and Gintis' reforms. I will therefore venture some observations about their use of the idea, before going on to reflect on school vouchers and, briefly, on their other proposals. I will argue that Bowles' and Gintis' plans for the design of social institutions reflect an imprecision and a narrowness of vision that leftwing intellectuals ought to resist. As an outsider to the economics profession, it is tempting to attribute these shortcomings to a certain *déformation professionelle*. But my aim here is not so much to quarrel with economists' uses of 'efficiency', as to question the political implications of according this value as much weight as Bowles and Gintis evidently do.

Efficiency: What and Why

For economists who came of age during the Great Depression and their students, unemployment was the major practical and theoretical concern. Nowadays, efficiency has taken its place. This change appears to have come about largely in consequence of the comparatively high rates of employment in developed capitalist countries in the past half-century, and the slow (but not catastrophic) economic decline of the past two and a half decades. The stagnation and eventual implosion of the planned economies of 'actually existing socialism' is also an important cause of this shift of focus, especially for economists on the left. By all accounts, the inefficiencies pandemic in the erstwhile 'socialist' regimes helped bring them down. They also helped bring down some traditional Left sureties about the economic superiority of central planning and public ownership.[4] But for all the apparent relevance of efficiency concerns, it is hard, at least for strangers to the economics profession, to understand why economists today focus so doggedly on a structural property of economic systems that represents real world concerns in only the most indirect and attenuated fashion.

This last comment pertains to efficiency in its more technical sense(s). 'Efficiency' invokes a cluster of non-technical ideas – delivering the goods, avoiding waste (of time, effort and resources), running smoothly, and so on. Sometimes too, the term is used loosely as a synonym for 'productivity'. But in more theoretical contexts, the reigning idea is Pareto-optimality. An allocation of resources is efficient if it is Pareto-optimal – that is, if any change would make someone worse off (holding technologies, preferences and the (initial) distribution of resources constant). It is far from obvious that this structural property of resource allocations gives theoretical expression to the variety of meanings that attach to 'efficiency' in less technical contexts. Nor should we assume that Pareto-optimality is automatically a good thing. The most vile situations can be Pareto-optimal if a change would make someone worse off. It is not even clear that a state of affairs that is Pareto-optimal is better normatively than a

Pareto sub-optimal state of affairs when everything else about the two situations is normatively equivalent. To draw this conclusion, one would have to suppose that the advancement of individual well-being is overwhelmingly important, that well-being is identical with preference satisfaction, and that preferences are beyond rational criticism.[5] In any event, Bowles' and Gintis' proposals for efficient asset redistributions mainly involve informal, not technical, understandings of 'efficiency'. As we shall see, they use 'efficiency' as a place-holder term for almost anything they think worthwhile that is not itself a matter of justice or equality.[6] I mention Pareto-optimality here because I suspect that one reason why efficiency matters as much as it does to Bowles and Gintis, and to economists generally, is that they unwittingly equivocate between the term's technical and informal senses. The technical understanding of the idea lends an appearance of rigor to otherwise indeterminate speculations; in turn, the meanings that informally attach to the idea lend an air of normative relevance to economic analyses that revolve around Pareto-optimality. In any case, my contention is that efficiency, even in its informal senses, is of less importance from a leftwing perspective than Bowles and Gintis suppose, and that their inordinate focus on efficiency sometimes leads them astray. Again, this is not to say that the efficiencies Bowles and Gintis impute to the reforms they envision do not matter. Quite the contrary. So long as scarcity exists, so long as we cannot have everything we want without expending effort we do not want to expend, it is important not to waste effort or time or resources generally. This is plainly the idea that underlies 'efficiency' on virtually all of Bowles' and Gintis' (implicit) construals of the term, and this is why their various efficiencies matter. But it is one thing to matter and something else to be of paramount importance in the design of fundamental economic, social and political institutions.

It is instructive to compare Bowles' and Gintis' emphasis on efficiency with John Roemer's ostensibly similar emphasis in *A Future for Socialism*, the focus of volume 2 of *The Real Utopias Project*.[7] Roemer accords efficiency pride of place in designing economic institutions. But his rationale for doing so applies mainly to socialist societies, not to the capitalist economy Bowles and Gintis evidently have in mind. Roemer never quite says why he thinks efficiency matters. But the outlines of his position are clear enough. The general idea is that an economic order that promotes egalitarian outcomes denies itself the support that comes from individuals' beliefs that they can somehow become egregiously rich. This problem is exacerbated when, as is inevitable under socialism, the hand of public policy is evident to everyone. Then the economy must work well in order to survive. A socialist economy that does not 'deliver the goods' satisfactorily will be unable to sustain the support of those who live under it. It will therefore collapse, as the Soviet Union eventually did, or else survive by coercion, as did the Soviet Union for many years.[8] Roemer conjectures that a sustainable socialism, true to the emancipatory objectives of the socialist tradition, must do at least as well as the best capitalist economies. Under socialism, efficiency must therefore be a paramount concern.

Now it is impossible to speculate confidently about the economic order Bowles and Gintis imagine; it is much too under-specified. Let us assume, however, that, it would be somewhat more egalitarian than existing capitalisms, and therefore that the (illusory) prospect of striking it rich would be somewhat less effective in sustaining a sense of *de facto* legitimacy in Bowles' and Gintis' capitalism than it is in actually existing capitalisms. Even so, unless the institutions Bowles and Gintis imagine require constant and visible meddling with market forces – and there is no indication whatsoever that they do – a Bowles and Gintis economy would face no devastating 'legitimation crisis' of the kind that a socialist economy would inevitably confront. People tend to regard the 'invisible hand' of the market as if it were an (unalterable) force of nature. The impersonal, structural constraints individuals would probably confront in the economy Bowles and Gintis imagine would therefore seem more legitimate in the face of poor economic performance than the 'visible' governmental interventions endemic to socialism, including market socialism.[9] Thus we can expect that there will be widespread support for the political economic system in place, no matter how poorly it performs for most people, even when the regime cannot rely substantially on individuals' dreams of personal enrichment to diffuse dissent. Ironically, efficiency matters more in Roemer's 'real utopia' than in Bowles' and Gintis', precisely because Roemer's vision is more radical than theirs. His program would undermine the illusion that market-driven outcomes are 'natural' and therefore legitimate to a far greater extent than theirs would.

Bowles' and Gintis' efficiencies still matter, of course; just as efficiencies matter in existing capitalism. But the fate of their egalitarian project (assuming, again, that the institutions they envision really can be implemented in an equality-enhancing way) would not depend, as in Roemer's case, upon the efficiency of the institutions they propose. Efficiency, in Bowles' and Gintis' many senses is an important consideration in the design of economic institutions. But it is hardly a condition for the possibility of moving society in a more progressive direction.

Left Capitalism

Is there any harm, though, in according efficiency as much attention as Bowles and Gintis do? Again, this question is best addressed on a case by case basis. Before turning to an actual case, however, it will be useful to invoke an appropriate frame of reference.

I will not dwell on Marxist accounts of the divergence between capitalist development and the human interests that motivate it,[10] nor on other traditional anti-capitalist themes. Bowles and Gintis appear to believe that alternatives to capitalism are either unfeasible or undesirable or both. I disagree. But it is not necessary to argue against capitalism generally to fault the politics implicit in Bowles' and Gintis' institutional designs. My complaint about their proposals pertains even within a broadly capitalist framework. Left capitalists seek means to mitigate the problems *laissez-faire* capitalism generates. At most, Bowles and Gintis address only one of these problems, economic inequality. I will suggest that there are other problems that their proposals may actually make worse.

First, though, in order to supply the rudiments of a context for the discussion that will follow, I would urge that the reader bear in mind several of the lines of argument that, in the past, Bowles and Gintis, along with other radical political economists, forced upon our attention: in particular, the importance of a strong labor movement in taming capitalist markets, and the critique of consumer society that was so important several decades ago in the rise of the New Left. The issues raised recently by Juliet Schor about leisure-consumption trade-offs in the American economy exemplify the former kind of consideration.[11] Schor investigates the factors that cause Americans to labor for so many hours in the paid economy in comparison with workers in other developed capitalist countries. She argues that Americans could work less and live better, without breaking away from capitalism altogether. Thus, in her view, American capitalism is worse than need be, and it is the configuration of class forces in American society, especially the sorry state of the labor movement, that explains this unfortunate state of affairs. This point is relevant to the political bearing of Bowles' and Gintis' proposed reforms. I will return to it in the course of discussing their plans for school vouchers. With regard to consumerism and its shortcomings, it should suffice to recall the once familiar truism: that owning more things does not always make life better. Even in this period of capitalist triumphalism, it is plain that it is only with respect to providing more things for people to own that contemporary capitalism does a good job of 'delivering the goods'. Its record with respect to social consumption, environmental protection and education is uneven; and its performance overall, on any plausible reckoning, is miserable to poor. Existing capitalism's record with respect to those things that, by all accounts, make life worth living – meaningful work, for example, and affective community – is, if anything, even worse.

The left capitalist frame of reference implicit in these considerations and others that could be adduced in a similar spirit should be borne in mind as we reflect on Bowles' and Gintis' proposals. Schemes for designing economic institutions must be assessed in their own right. But in so far as the point is to revive left theory and practice – and that plainly is one of the motivations behind Bowles' and Gintis' proposals – we must also consider their institutional reforms in the light of the political *tendencies* they represent.

School Vouchers

Bowles' and Gintis' case for vouchers rests on the supposed advantages of more exit opportunities for parents in the schooling of their children. What has this to do with efficiency?[12] In this case, there are no 'goods' to be 'delivered', unless we are meant to think of 'human capital' as a good. 'Efficiency' here seems to mean nothing more than 'working well'. Of course, as in any attempt at predicting the consequences of institutional arrangements by reflecting on incentive structures and 'deducing' their consequences, the soundness of Bowles' and Gintis' conclusions depends on what else is going on in the world (inasmuch as the *ceteris absentibus* condition that implicitly accompanies all such speculations can never be satisfied) and on whether they have indeed focused on the most salient aspects of the situation and drawn the right inferences. If they have, school vouchers would improve schooling. Needless to say, this conclusion has nothing to do with Pareto-optimality[13] nor, with one possible exception, with less technical senses of 'efficiency' that bear some connection to Pareto-optimality.[14] All that their arguments for the 'efficiency' advantages of school vouchers amount to, then, is the claim that vouchers would produce better outcomes than imaginable alternatives, where 'better' is understood in a non-equity sense.

Is this a defensible claim? The answer depends on the relative merits of exit and voice and of decentralization and bureaucratic administration in the provision of educational services. I will not address these issues here. But I would point out that what we think about the efficiency advantages of school vouchers depends, in part, on *whom* we think vouchers are supposed to help. When 'efficiency' means Pareto-optimality or some less technical approximation of that idea, the answer is clear – efficient resource allocations help at least some individuals while harming no one. Unanimity, so conceived, is integral to Paretian evaluations of social and economic phenomena.[15] What Bowles and Gintis mainly argue, however, is that vouchers would make schools work better for just one group, the parents of school children. Parents would have a more significant role in shaping their children's education than they would if states provided schooling directly, and if children were assigned to schools administratively, according to their place of residency or on some other likely basis. Except by insisting on publicly enforceable educational standards, Bowles and Gintis do not take the interests of schoolchildren themselves into account, in so far as their interests differ from the interests of their parents.[16] Nor do they take the interests of education providers into account; a very serious lapse to which I shall presently return. They do worry about the need to train citizens for their role(s) in the emerging world economy, and argue that the reforms they propose can help in this regard. In fact, it is mainly through this prism that Bowles and Gintis take the public's interest in schooling into account. Thus they effectively dismiss the influential and compelling (small-r) republican case for public schools, according to which an important aim of schooling is to train democratic citizens, a task public schools are particularly well-suited to perform.

The general idea is that schools that are deliberately non-sectarian and in which children interact on terms of equality – irrespective of class, race and religion – are good inculcators of democratic values. Of course, in practice, many existing public schools fail miserably at this task, for much the same reason that they perform poorly in general – lack of adequate funding, residential segregation, and the background of public neglect and general social disintegration in which they operate. Remedies are urgently needed. But it hardly follows from the fact that existing public schools fall short of realizing the expectations we have for them that the very idea of public schooling as such is seriously impugned. In Bowles' and Gintis' scheme, the inculcation of democratic values through schooling could only be achieved through extensive state regulation. States would somehow have to force private schools, otherwise driven by market imperatives, to do what public schools would do automatically in a fiscally and socially healthier and more egalitarian society. Indeed, without extensive state regulation, public interests would not register at all in a regime of privatized educational provision; only parents' interests would. Therefore, unless parents' interests in shaping their children's futures coincide reliably with all other relevant interests – an extremely unlikely proposition – the 'efficiency' Bowles and Gintis expect to obtain from school vouchers would be a dubious achievement; an efficiency for some but not for all, and not even for everyone whose interests one would expect proponents of a left capitalist agenda to privilege.

Right-wing advocates of school voucher plans are motivated, in part, by the conviction that private enterprises and private service-providers always or nearly always do better at their appointed tasks than public enterprises or public service-providers. For many on the right, this is an article of faith, an element of a larger pro-market theology. These right-wingers seldom make a secret of their political agenda: they want to crush public sector trade unions, especially teachers' unions, and believe that they have a better chance of doing so if education is privately, not publicly, provided. For them, school vouchers are both an end and a means. Obviously, Bowles and Gintis defend vouchers for other reasons altogether. Their arguments appeal to facts about information asymmetries and their implications for monitoring school performance, not to the desirability of *laissez-faire* capitalism. But by focusing, as they do, on parents' interests only, Bowles' and Gintis' arguments effectively reinforce the anti-labor, pro-*laissez-faire* agenda of rightwing advocates of school vouchers. I would venture that the *déformation professionelle* I remarked upon at the outset partly explains this ironic convergence of views.

Institutional changes, even when they are very well thought out and carefully specified, have unintended consequences. The likelihood of unintended consequences upsetting prior expectations is especially acute when, as in Bowles' and Gintis' speculations, what is mainly taken into account are those features of institutions that are of theoretical interest – in this case, to economists working in the emerging, information-centered paradigm. Then, as in any kind of modeling exercise, whatever is not part of the model or, more generally, whatever is not of particular theoretical interest is effectively relegated to the category of 'noise'. This, I fear, is what has happened to workers' rights and democratic aspirations in Bowles' and Gintis' proposals for school vouchers. Theoretical exigencies

oblige them to focus on monitoring problems. Schoolchildren themselves are unable to perform monitoring functions satisfactorily. In
any case, they are only the 'products' of the schooling industry; their
interests are therefore no more germane to the economic analysis of
schooling than, say, automobiles are to analyses of the auto industry.
The state, the agent for the public at large, is poorly situated to
acquire and assimilate relevant information; in fact, this is an important reason why public schools perform so badly in Bowles' and Gintis'
view. In short, the only interested party that fits the theory's needs is
the parents. Thus parents assume the role of monitors – of teachers
and other providers of educational services. Bowles' and Gintis'
approach to the school voucher question therefore disables them from
making the workers' interests their own. Their theoretical paradigm,
even as it underwrites egalitarian redistributions of ownership rights,
pushes them, at least in this instance, to side against workers' rights.
It is not surprising, then, that their plans for schooling and those of
rightwing enemies of public schools intersect.

The most immediate losers in the privatization scheme Bowles and
Gintis sketch, as in so many other privatization plans, are public
sector workers. Through them, the larger labor movement would also
lose. And if the (small-r) republicans are right, so too would everyone
who values democratic community – unless, of course, educational
providers are so heavily regulated that most of the purported efficiency
advantages of school vouchers would probably disappear. In short,
the losers are the historical agents of egalitarian change – labor and
the larger democratic movement. Therefore even if a voucher system
could be contrived that would move society in an egalitarian direction,
while making schooling work better (by producing, as it were, more
human capital), the price egalitarians would pay for this advance
could well be too great. That price is the further decapacitation of
those social groups that have provided the major impetus for egalitarian improvements in the past, and that remain the most likely agents
for further egalitarian advances.

In sum, if Bowles and Gintis are right about everything they claim
for school vouchers, their scheme would make things better in two
respects: it would advance equality and it would enhance individuals'
capacities to perform well in the emerging world economy. However,
there is nothing about vouchers that renders them especially effective
for further egalitarian aims; equality can be advanced as well by more
traditional funding mechanisms. And the more efficient production of
human capital for the world market, a dubious value for leftists to
promote, would be won at the expense of diminished ideological and

organizational resources for furthering progressive goals. Even so, if only because schooling in capitalist America today is in such dire straits, all suggestions for improvements, including proposals for school vouchers, should be seriously considered and assessed on their merits. We should be grateful to Bowles and Gintis for turning the school voucher idea on its head and making it a subject of discussion on the left. But we should also recognize that they have yet to show us why, in this case (or in any other), egalitarians should forsake deeply entrenched convictions about the beneficial roles an affirmative state can play and instead join forces with the free-marketeers of the political right in relying on private ownership and markets to solve pressing social problems.

Other Reforms

Bowles' and Gintis' plans for the privatization of public housing would have no direct effect on workers' interests or on public interests in enhancing democracy. Left capitalists can therefore be more sanguine about this proposal than about school vouchers. The idea, presumably, is that owners have more incentive than renters to maintain their quarters, and therefore that the housing stock would improve if renters became owners. This 'efficiency' has nothing to do with Pareto-optimality, strictly speaking. However, one could, again, impute a notion of 'productive efficiency' to Bowles' and Gintis' reform. If we would indeed improve public housing by privatizing it, keeping subsidy levels the same, then resources that might otherwise be 'wasted' on housing would be available for other productive uses.

I have already remarked (in note 2) that the privatization of public housing could actually have adverse effects on equality by increasing private debt. As with worker-ownership of firms, everything depends on how the plan is implemented. Let us concede, however, that public housing could be privatized in an equality-enhancing way. There are still reasons to be wary of Bowles' and Gintis' scheme.

The problem, again, is that their proposal is skewed towards matters of interest in the information-centered paradigm in which they are working. Thus Bowles and Gintis make an assumption that may not be generally applicable. They assume that the beneficial incentive effects of private ownership obtain for all individuals, regardless of their position in the actual economy. Home ownership almost certainly does have the consequences they impute for individuals who are at least fairly well-off. Thus public subsidies for private housing have worked well in the United States and throughout the developed world when the targeted constituencies have been 'middle class'. But capitalist development in recent years has marginalized ever larger sectors of the population in developed countries (not to mention the destitution it has caused elsewhere). People who would once have been integrated into the system as workers are no longer useful even as an industrial reserve army. They are not needed because the globalization of capitalist production more than suffices for depressing wage rates and removing other obstacles in the way of capitalists' profits.[17] Thus increasing numbers of people have been pushed to the margins of the economic order. Is it not fair to suppose that this phenomenon influences their dispositions to respond to ordinary economic incentives? If so, then even if political support could somehow be mobilized in favor of the subsidies required to extend home ownership to the poor, it is far from clear that poor people, especially very poor people, would respond to this asset redistribution in the way that Bowles and Gintis suppose. If they would not, institutions designed on the assumption that they would, might fail to achieve what they intend. They might even work to the detriment of more satisfactory solutions.

Bowles and Gintis appear to be oblivious to this prospect. But it is hard to imagine, say, that the majority of homeless people could be transformed into good stewards of the housing stock through a reassignment of property rights. Many of them, even if they are mentally and physically able, are too beaten down by the system. What of those who are only a rent subsidy away from homelessness? Nobody knows. It is fair to speculate, however, that the more damaging existing capitalism becomes to ever larger sectors of the population, the less susceptible it is to the kind of homeopathic remedy that Bowles' and Gintis' proposal exemplifies. This is not to say that privatization would do no good or that it has no place on a left capitalist agenda. But it is to question the merits of focusing so much attention on the allegedly beneficial incentive effects of private ownership. Solutions to the housing problems of late capitalist societies almost certainly require systematic assaults on poverty itself and on the marginalization of ever larger sectors of the (potentially) active population. For the left, including the capitalist left, the main task is to focus on this larger issue. I have suggested that doing so may be a condition for *any* 'efficiency' gain in this area; at least for people who are very impoverished and marginalized. But even if Bowles' and Gintis' plan would work as intended, there is still the worry that their reform does not address the principal cause(s) of our present predicament. This suggests yet another reason to be wary of their proposal.

Public housing in the United States and elsewhere today is in a sorry state mainly because of chronic under-funding and because the emerging world economy has left so many people poorly off; not because poor renters have fewer incentives than poor owners to take care of their dwellings. The best way to enhance 'efficiencies' in this area, therefore, is to take the economy itself in hand, in order to address poor peoples' needs. No doubt, Bowles and Gintis would agree. But their proposed reform of public housing is insensitive to this exigency. I submit that this too is an artifact of their analytical framework. For within an information-centered paradigm, there is no easy way to register the dynamic properties of the system as a whole; no way to make the economy itself, rather than particular market failures, an object of reforming zeal. Thus the politics implicit in Bowles' and Gintis' reform of public housing points away from the kind of politics the left needs to develop. If anything, it reinforces faith in the salutary consequences of private ownership and market forces, views that even left capitalists should concede partly account for our present difficulties. For anyone who would revive left-wing theory and practice at this time, institutional designs that tend in this direction are causes for concern, even if (as is far from certain in this case) they promote outcomes that the left should welcome.

This is why I am apprehensive about Bowles' and Gintis' proposals for according children property rights in their fathers' (and mothers') income streams. Whether or not their proposal is in some sense efficiency-enhancing, its impact on real world politics is a cause for concern.[18] On the face of it, however, it is hard to see what the 'efficiency' advantages of Bowles' and Gintis' proposal might be in comparison to what states already do. It is even unclear how, in practice, Bowles' and Gintis' plan would differ from current arrangements. The problem their proposal purports to address is an enforcement problem; how to get fathers (and, less often, mothers) to pay judicially mandated child-support. Why would a reassignment of property rights make this enforcement problem more tractable? I do not think that it would. In fact, I would hazard that Bowles' and Gintis' reform would make little, if any, practical difference. But it would make a political difference. For in this case too, the asset redistribution Bowles and Gintis envision reinforces an idea that the left ought to criticize: the idea that state solutions to social problems are generally self-defeating, and that markets and ancillary judicial institutions that enforce property rights somehow work better (more 'efficiently?'). This is a mark, albeit not a decisive one, against Bowles' and Gintis' plan.

I will be very brief on the last of Bowles' and Gintis' reforms – their plan for worker-ownership of firms. I have already voiced the worry that this scheme could fail to advance equality. With regard to non-equity benefits, I would venture that there are no general conclusions to be drawn. The issue, again, is the solution to principal-agent problems and the provision of appropriate incentive structures. In all likelihood, there will be cases in which the dispersion of ownership rights is beneficial and others in which it is not. When the dispersion of ownership rights is beneficial, there will doubtless be cases in which it will be useful to restrict ownership to workers in firms and others in which it is not. At the level of abstraction at which Bowles' and Gintis' reflections are pitched, there is little more to say, except to observe that, in this instance, 'efficiency' is at last used in a way that genuinely is amenable to formal economic analysis. *Productive efficiency* is evidently what Bowles and Gintis have in mind. Happily too, this is the one 'efficient asset redistribution' that Bowles and Gintis propose that is neither coincident with nor supportive of current right-wing thinking.[19]

Concluding Thoughts

When 'efficiency' is used as a place-holder term for all non-equity benefits (or at least for all non-equity benefits that have something to do with economic performance, broadly construed), then, of course, efficiency matters. Other things being equal, the more efficient institutions are, the better. But, beyond this truism, there is little to say *in general*. When there are trade-offs to be made between particular efficiencies and other values, we would need to know what is to be weighed against what. Even then, it is unlikely that anything very useful can be proposed in the way of general guidance. My worry is that, by according efficiency pride of place, the importance of other values will become obscured. I am worried especially about the values that matter most to the left; those that pertain to democratic community and the conditions for self-realization.

I have already suggested that efficiency, 'delivering the goods', can be important when there is a need to secure widespread support for egalitarian policies. However, I questioned the relevance of this consideration for the kinds of reforms that Bowles and Gintis propose. Enhancing support for the regime is, in any case, an *external* or political reason for valuing efficiency. I also observed that a condition for the *internal* or normative importance of efficiency (in virtually all of its senses) is scarcity. The more scarcity is overcome, the less urgent efficiency becomes – even if, as in Roemer's market socialism, its political importance is likely to remain strong. At the limit, abundance would render efficiency superfluous. Of course, scarcity can never be eliminated completely. But with the development of productive forces, the impact of scarcity can be substantially reduced. I suspect that scarcity is already sufficiently diminished for efficiency to matter far less than Bowles and Gintis and economists generally assume.

Whether or not this conjecture is sound, it is revealing to ponder why efficiency now seems to matter more than it did just a few years ago, despite a significant expansion of productive capacities. Over the years, few economists have addressed this question more insightfully than Bowles and Gintis. They have done much to show precisely how the answer has to do with capitalist development itself in the present conjuncture and with the diminishing capacities of states to control market forces. In these circumstances, insecurity has come to reign alongside affluence. Thus political leaders and their propagandists in the media and the universities have become able to say persuasively that what the country needs, above all, is 'global competitiveness', an idea 'efficiency' seems to capture well. But to promote this shibboleth, even if only by implication, is to participate in an assault on progressive aspirations and progressive social forces – above all, the labor movement and other victims of the new world order. The principal task today therefore is to resist the imperatives of global competitiveness. It is to seek instead to wield economic forces on behalf of all the values, not just wealth equality, that have moved the historical left. The right is mobilized against this project. In the United States, they have successfully enlisted the entire political class in their cause. This fact is reason enough to be wary of the affinities that join at least three of Bowles' and Gintis' proposed reforms to contemporary rightwing policy prescriptions. Therefore, even if Bowles' and Gintis' proposals, properly elaborated, would indeed advance equality and efficiency, the politics their reforms represent, efficiency politics, is detrimental to progressive change. How ironic that probing critics of recent capitalism, seeking to revive left politics today, should propose institutional designs that *reinforce* the very convictions that underpin capitalist development in the current period!

Notes

1. I have argued elsewhere and often for the continuing timeliness of several of the more traditional left ideas Bowles and Gintis effectively reject. See, for example, my contributions to the two preceding 'Real Utopias' conferences, 'Democratic Corporatism and/versus Socialism' in Joshua Cohen, Joel Rogers, *et al.*, *Associations and Democracy* (London: Verso, 1995) and 'Saving Socialism and/or Abandoning It' in John Roemer *et al.*, *Equal Shares: Making Market Socialism Work* (London, Verso, 1996). I treat these issues more extensively in *The End of the State* (London, Verso, 1987), *The General Will: Rousseau, Marx, Communism* (Cambridge: Cambridge University Press, 1993) and *Rethinking Liberal Equality* (Ithaca, NY: Cornell University Press, 1998).

2. For much the same reason, it is unclear whether the privatization of public housing, another of their proposals, would actually advance wealth equality.

3. At the conference at which Bowles' and Gintis' paper was discussed, the authors declared, to everyone's amazement (since there was no hint of any such plan in the paper itself), that they imagined that the proposed reassignment of property rights would be preceded by a massive, one-time redistribution of wealth. If this redistribution is sufficiently large, it would, of course, address the problem I just raised. But then other problems would arise. Everyone would realize that if wealth could be seized and redistributed *once*, it could be seized and redistributed *again*, however adamantly public officials might insist otherwise. This concern would affect economic agents' incentives, much to the detriment, presumably, of the efficiency concerns that Bowles and Gintis put forward.

4. Also upsetting to received leftwing thinking has been the uneven but undeniable economic successes registered in recent decades in parts of what used to be called the Third World. This development appears both to weaken longstanding analyses of economic imperialism and also to strengthen the case for private ownership.

5. Whoever finds certain preferences objectionable, should hesitate to regard preference satisfaction as a universal good. But even those who do find preference satisfaction (normatively) desirable for its own sake should still have difficulty endorsing Pareto-optimality, inasmuch as individuals' preferences can be in agreement for very different reasons. For example, unionized workers in a firm and the owners of the firm might both prefer that a strike take place over the continuation of protracted negotiations: the workers because they think they can win, the owners because they think they can crush the workers' union. It is hard to see how one could argue, in this case, that a strike, though unanimously preferred, would improve everyone's well-being. Similar problems for Pareto-optimality can arise in consequence of cognitive disagreements about the likely outcomes of different choices. I owe these observations to Daniel Hausman.

6. When 'efficiency' is used so loosely, the distinction between equity and non-equity concerns is itself arbitrary. Views of what is worthwhile depend on conceptions of the good society, and there is no reason in principle to exclude distributional questions from such conceptions. But this arbitrariness does not impugn Bowles' and Gintis' project *per se*: it still makes sense to investigate the consequences of more or less equality on other consequences one deems beneficial.

7. See John Roemer, *A Future for Socialism* (Cambridge, Mass.: Harvard University Press, 1994) and Roemer *et al.*, *Equal Shares*.

8. Thus Roemer would have institutions rely mainly on market incentives. The only imaginable alternative would be to rely on non-pecuniary (and non-coercive) 'moral' incentives. Some of the formerly socialist countries, those that were installed by popular revolutions, did sometimes elicit remarkable sacrifices on the part of their respective citizenries. For a time, they survived and even flourished. But nowhere was a Golden Age of revolutionary heroism and self-sacrifice indefinitely sustained. I would

venture that it is, in fact, impossible to sustain an egalitarian regime indefinitely, especially if equality is assured through extensive public interventions, if doing so requires significant voluntary sacrifices on the part of most individuals. I am sure Roemer would agree.

9. Marx, of course, believed that capitalist economies were destined to undermine the conditions for their own possibility. Because he emphasized materialist causes, he tended not to dwell on individuals' views about the legitimacy of the economic order under which they live. Nevertheless, it is plain that he expected a widespread sense of capitalism's economic shortcomings to play a role in its demise. It is ironic that, to this point, it is only socialist economies that have been undone by this kind of 'legitimation crisis'. It is ironic too that Marx's analysis of 'commodity fetishism' (in volume one of *Capital*) provides an indispensable basis for explaining this phenomenon. On legitimation crises, see, for example, Claus Offe, 'Structural Problems of the Capitalist State', in Von Beyme (ed.), *German Political Studies*, vol. 1 (Beverly Hills, Cal.: Sage, 1974) and Jürgen Habermas, *Legitimation Crisis* (Boston: Beacon Press, 1975).

10. G. A. Cohen's account of the 'distinctive contradiction of advanced capitalism' in G. A. Cohen, *Karl Marx's Theory of History: A Defence* (Oxford and Princeton: Oxford University Press and Princeton University Press, 1978) is a compelling recent example of this line of thought.

11. See Juliet B. Schor, *The Overworked American: The Unexpected Decline of Leisure* (New York: Basic Books, 1991).

12. One might also ask what it has to do with equity. Because school funding in the United States today depends heavily on local property taxes, far more money is spent to educate the children of the well-off than those of the poor. Were the state to accord each pupil a voucher of equal worth or, better yet, to provide larger vouchers to the less well-off, it would effectively redistribute public revenues in a progressive way, at the same time that it would distribute educational assets (opportunities for education) in an egalitarian direction. But we hardly need school vouchers to implement this *desideratum*. We could, for example, simply fund existing school districts on a *per capita* basis, perhaps allowing for even greater expenditures on children who suffer educational disadvantages. Bowles' and Gintis' scheme for voucher funding may or may not be preferable to this simpler alternative, but nothing that they tell us about it suggests that it would be more egalitarian.

13. In fact, *any* redesign of schooling that would make anyone worse off would be Pareto *sub-optimal*. Bowles' and Gintis' scheme, like any egalitarian program, would probably make the currently best-off worse off in the course of making the worst-off better off. Then, in comparison to the status quo, their plan would *not* be Pareto-optimal.

14. It could be argued that a school voucher system could be imagined that would enhance 'productive efficiency'; in other words, that it would give rise to outcomes less wasteful of resources than alternative schemes for financing schooling. Bowles and Gintis advance no argument to this effect. However they do suggest that better schooling, obtained through school vouchers, would enhance the productivity of students after they become workers, thereby augmenting overall productivity.

15. Thus situation A represents a *Pareto improvement* over situation B if A is *unanimously* preferred to B (or if at least one person prefers A to B and everyone else is indifferent). A situation is *Pareto-optimal* if, taking technologies, preferences, and the distribution of resources as given, it admits of no Pareto improvements.

16. It could be argued that, in general, parents are the best judges of their children's interest or, at least, that they are better judges than the state, and that institutional arrangements should reflect this fact. Bowles and Gintis do not make this argument, however; and I think they are right not to do so. Unless publicly enforced educational standards are *very* far-reaching – so far-reaching, in fact, as to weaken the argument for school vouchers that appeals to the benefits of parental choice – some children might find themselves placed by their parents in schools that indoctrinate them into religious or secular ideologies that impede the development of their critical intellectual

capacities, contrary to their interests as (future) democratic citizens. Bowles and Gintis are characteristically vague about the nature and extent of the standards public bodies would enforce.

17. For corroborating evidence, see the papers collected in Michael A. Bernstein and David E. Adler (eds.), *Understanding American Economic Decline* (Cambridge: Cambridge University Press, 1994). Bowles and Gintis have, of course, contributed importantly to current understandings of these processes. See, among many others, David M. Gordon, Thomas E. Weisskopf and Samuel Bowles, 'Right-Wing Economics in the 1980s: The Anatomy of Failure' in the Bernstein and Adler anthology *Beyond the Waste Land: A Democratic Alternative to Economic Decline* (New York: Anchor Press, 1985); S. Bowles and H. Gintis, *Democracy and Capitalism* (London: Routledge, 1986); and S. Bowles, 'Contested Exchange: Political Economy and Modern Economic Theory', *American Economic Review*, vol. 78 (1990), pp. 165–222.

18. It is far from clear, in this case too, what the impact of Bowles' and Gintis' proposal might be for equality. If what they have in mind is indeed more 'efficient' than current practices, female poverty would diminish somewhat because single mothers would be obliged to assume less of the (financial) burden of child rearing than is now the case. But fathers who resist paying child-support are usually of the same social class as the mothers they leave in the lurch. The resulting redistribution would therefore mainly be an intra-class redistribution. There may be good reasons for insisting that such transfers take place; diminishing female poverty is a worthwhile goal. But Bowles' and Gintis' plan is unlikely to do much for wealth or income equality overall.

19. It is worth noting, however that worker-ownership is not necessarily grist for right-wing enmity. Did even the *Wall Street Journal* editorial page object to the employee buy-out of United Airlines?

PART III
Specific Institutional Contexts

7

School Choice:
Theoretical Considerations

Harry Brighouse*

A natural temptation with institutional blueprints such as presented by Samuel Bowles and Herbert Gintis is to criticize them from the left, as it were, by demonstrating how far their ambition departs from the traditional socialist or left ambitions for full-blooded equality and community. However, in a period when socialist and egalitarian thinking is publicly perceived as irrelevant to contemporary politics, I think that temptation should be resisted, at least in the absence of alternative institutional proposals which explain how those values can be implemented more full-bloodedly in practice. If they are defensible, the great value of Bowles' and Gintis' proposal and others like them is not that they impugn traditional maximalist demands, but that they show that movement *in the direction of* equality is institutionally feasible at a time when even that minimalist view has very little support. Rather than engage the broader themes of their chapter, I want to focus very narrowly on one of their three innovative proposals, which involves the suggestion that equality can be promoted by appropriately designed educational voucher systems.

This chapter is structured as follows: after reviewing the state of 'choice' in the US today, I shall review and criticize Milton Friedman's case for educational vouchers. In section 3 I elaborate and partially defend two egalitarian liberal criteria which any school system should implement. In section 4 I look at Bowles' and Gintis' egalitarian voucher

*An earlier version of this chapter was presented at the 'Equality and Efficiency' conference sponsored by the Havens Center on November 3–5 1995. I am grateful for written comments from and/or discussion with Samuel Bowles, Herbert Gintis, Tim Brighouse, Lynn Glueck, Jonathan Barrett, Andrew Levine, Daniel Hausman, Francis Schrag, A.J. Julius, Erik Olin Wright, Paula England and other participants in the conference, and to John Cook for many useful discussions of these matters.

scheme and defend it against *principled* objections to vouchers. In sections 5 and 6 I further defend the egalitarian liberal criteria, and explain why it would be difficult to win majority political support for vouchers which met them. In the final section I suggest that the difficulties of winning support for egalitarian voucher schemes may arise from the fact that voucher schemes meet a transparency condition which the design of public school systems often fail; in other words that we can anticipate difficulties winning majoritarian political support for any system of schooling which transparently meets the egalitarian criteria. Ironically, it may be because vouchers are good instruments of democratic policy-making that egalitarians have difficulty with them.

First it is worth clarifying some terms. The terms 'school choice' and 'educational vouchers' are often used interchangeably in public debate. But a voucher scheme is only one mechanism for guaranteeing parents some degree of choice over what schools their children attend and, consequently, what kind of education they receive. Even programs which are usually referred to as voucher schemes rarely literally deploy vouchers: usually the government does not issue a voucher to the parents, but pays a sum directly to the school on receipt of a request from the parents.[1] In my discussion, and in Bowles' and Gintis', then, the notion of a voucher scheme is to be thought of as a perspicuous device for representing the idea of school choice and constraints upon it. Vouchers are by their nature limited – like food stamps and rationing coupons they embody the idea of what Michael Walzer calls a 'blocked exchange'.[2] When a voucher is granted it represents a sum of money which can be spent on only one thing: the schooling of a particular child. By examining the proper regulative constraints on a voucher system we can represent the proper extent of parental choice over their children's schooling. I shall usually use the terms 'voucher scheme' and 'choice scheme' interchangeably, depending on what makes the most sense in the context. I shall also use the terms 'public school' and 'private school' in the standard American usage, where 'public' means 'run by the government' and 'private' means 'run independently of the government'.

1. School Choice in the US Today

The idea that parents should choose which schools their children attend neatly appeals to both the ideological commitment to the market of the libertarian right and the 'family values' agenda of the authoritarian, or conservative, right. School choice is, for this and other reasons, a powerful idea within not only the US Republican Party but also some rightwing European political parties.[3]

As a practical policy school choice has been much less successful. While there are many instances of school districts designing their allocation formulae to give some weight to the choices of parents, only a handful of programs that give overwhelming weight to parental choice have been implemented. Those that have fall into three categories. First, trial private voucher programs run by non-profit charitable concerns (and mostly funded by large corporations) have been continuing in Milwaukee, San Antonio, Indianapolis, and New York City, since the early 1990s, and have since been established in 13 other cities. But these programs generally provide choice only among a certain range of private schools, and are directed at children of poor families. They are extremely small: in 1994/5 these programs assisted 6,572 students in 17 cities. Nor do the programs represent any kind of policy victory: they are run not by cities or school districts, but by business-people, without any kind of democratic mandate.[4]

Second, there are choice mechanisms *within* many public school districts. In part, public school choice developed in response to judicial pressure for racial integration: magnet schools in particular were often developed as responses to, or to preempt, integrationist court orders. But some public school choice schemes were devised to facilitate parental involvement in the public schools and to improve already integrated facilities. Most famously, East Harlem District No. 4 has 23 high schools organized around different themes, application to all of which is available to all parents in the district.[5] Public school choice, however, appears radical only because neighborhood schooling has become such an established part of the US public school system. Neighborhood schooling has never been elevated to the level of a guiding principle in the UK for example. The 1944 Education Act which set the framework for the contemporary state school system established that:

> The Minister and local education authorities shall have regard to the general principle that, so far as is compatible with the provision of efficient instruction and training and the avoidance of unreasonable public expenditure, pupils are to be educated in accordance with the wishes of their parents.[6]

It would be a mistake to think that public school choice, in turning away from neighborhood schooling, also turns away from the fundamental principles of public schooling.

The form of school choice most threatening to traditional understandings of public schooling is public/private school choice. Currently the US has only one public/private choice program running, in
Milwaukee: the Milwaukee Parental Choice Program.[7] In public/
private school choice parents have a choice between a range of public
schools and a specified range of private schools within the area. If a
private school is chosen then the public school district pays some
proportion of the tuition at that school. It is, in effect, a program of
public subsidy for private schools, and thus does break with the
fundamental tradition of public schooling – that the government runs
exactly those schools which it pays for through tax revenues.

The Milwaukee program is relatively modest. The total number of
students in MPCP is limited to 1.5 per cent of the children in
Milwaukee Public Schools,[8] and eligibility is limited to students from
households with incomes 1.75 per cent of the poverty line and below
who have not attended a private school (or any other school district
than Milwaukee Public Schools) in the year prior to their entry into
the program. The qualifying schools must be non-sectarian (a requirement that severely limits the attractions of the program), and are
subject to weak non-discrimination requirements in their selection
processes. The schools receive the Milwaukee Public School per-
member state aid for each eligible student enrolled.

While the MPCP is modest and the only one of its kind, there have
been attempts to establish other, more radical, schemes. California's
Proposition 174 (defeated in 1994) would have established a public/
private choice system without eligibility limits for children. Schools
would have had to meet only one requirement – non discrimination
on the basis of race – and no inspectorate would have been established
to enforce this. Religious schools would therefore have been eligible
for subsidy. It would also have established almost unattainable
supermajority requirements for future regulation of participating
schools. It would have provided a contribution toward tuition in the
form of a voucher, but the amount would have been around $1,000
less per student per year than in the Milwaukee scheme, thus ensuring
that fewer low-income parents would be able to take advantage of it.

Public/private school choice appears to threaten the principle of
public schooling as it is commonly understood because, following the
outline of a voucher scheme detailed by Milton Friedman in his classic
Capitalism and Freedom, it separates the government functions of
providing schooling and paying for schooling. Because of this, and
because it has been promoted by the political right in the US, choice
has been badly received on the left. My purpose in this paper is to

develop a left-wing – specifically an egalitarian liberal – response to school choice[9]. The left is particularly prone to criticize choice because, in subjecting public schools to competitive pressures it undermines the ideal of democratically governed public schools. I believe it is a mistake to see markets as always contrary to democracy. As Herbert Gintis says, 'The use of the market' can be 'an instrument of, rather than an alternative to democratic policymaking'.[10] As I shall argue, the serious problems with school choice lie in the difficulties of designing a school choice scheme which meets certain important egalitarian liberal constraints *and* would be persistently upheld by a majority in a democratic system. However, it is not clear that the task of designing a public school system which meets egalitarian liberal criteria is a great deal easier.

2. Friedman's Case for Vouchers

The recent interest in voucher schemes owes a great deal to the work of Milton Friedman.[11] It is not surprising, given the recent provenance of the idea, that most voucher policy proposals have emanated from the right (and the far right) of the US political spectrum, where enthusiasm for markets and pseudo-markets is great. Attention to Friedman's proposal and argument is revealing in the sense that the objectionable aspects of his proposal and arguments have shown up repeatedly in policy proposals. Considering the objectionable aspects of Friedman's view also helps us in elaborating the features that would be necessary in order for a voucher proposal to have good 'left-wing' credentials.

As I suggested earlier, Friedman's innovation is his separation of two government roles in education which are commonly assumed to be inseparable. Advocates of public schooling argue that the government has to pay for the education of minors, and also that the government should run the institutions through which they are educated. But Friedman claims that, while there is a perfectly good argument that the government should pay for (or contribute to paying for) schooling, this argument does not support the idea that it should monopolize provision of – or even play *any* direct role in the provision of – the institutions through which it occurs.[12]

The argument which Friedman thinks justifies the government paying for some schooling is that education of children has what he calls 'neighborhood effects' (what would now more usually be called 'externalities'):

A stable and democratic society is impossible without a minimum degree of literacy and knowledge on the part of most citizens and knowledge on the part of most citizens and without widespread acceptance of some common set of values. Education can contribute to both. In consequence, the gain from the education of a child accrues not only to the child or his parents but also to other members of society. It is not feasible to identify particular individuals (or families) benefited and so to charge for the services rendered. There is therefore a significant neighborhood effect.[13]

There are two important things to notice about this argument. First, as Friedman points out, it does not in itself justify what he calls 'nationalization' of schools. Some public goods may be provided efficiently only by the government but for most (including education) all that is needed is that the government play an essential coordinating role, which in this case could in principle be limited to regulation of the market and injections of financial support for the consumers. Second, Friedman believes that while maintaining social stability is properly thought of as a public good, the increased productivity of future workers through education is not, since competitive advantages to a particular worker in the labor market are overwhelmingly of benefit to that very person and of much less benefit if any to others.[14] The 'vocational' benefits of education to the individual, then, cannot be used as a justification for government funding (though he does recognize the practical difficulties in disagreggating the vocational from the civic effects of education).

Whether schooling should be run by the government depends, for Friedman, on whether nationalization will be an efficient form of delivery. He poses a voucher system as a more efficient alternative, in which the government would provide each parent with a voucher for some substantial portion of the cost of schooling and allow them to purchase schooling from private institutions. The only role of the government would be 'insuring that the schools met certain minimum standards, such as the inclusion of a minimum common content in their programs, much as it now inspects restaurants to insure that they maintain minimum sanitary standards'.[15] He elaborates a series of efficiency and equity benefits which could be expected from a voucher system.

Vouchers would, according to Friedman, widen the range of choices available to parents by permitting the establishment of a wider variety of schools and choice among them. They would also make choice effectively available to all parents, whereas under current arrangements choice is available only to those parents who can move relatively easily between and within school districts or afford the fees of private schools from their after-tax income.[16] Vouchers would also prevent the possibility of the vicious circle in school districts where parents who send their children to high-quality parochial schools apply political pressure to lower the taxes levied to fund public schools, thus worsening the quality of the public schools and giving the parochial schools even greater relative advantage. Since parents could 'express their views of schools directly by withdrawing their children from one school and sending them to another'[17] they would have more control than at present over the structure of the school and the content of the curriculum. The influence of professional educators over the structure of the profession would decline, and in particular the current uniformity of teachers' salaries would be broken up, thus enticing 'the imaginative and daring and self confident' who are currently 'repelled' from the profession.[18] The diminishing influence of teachers' unions would probably lead to lower labor costs, and at the same time the increased differentials would lead to more good teachers entering the profession.

Left-wing reformers of education will obviously react against Friedman's optimism about the effects of the market, and will be made uneasy by his anti-union bias. They will dispute the purported power of the profession over its structure, and will point out the benefits to all workers of strong teachers' unions. But these points do not bring into question his more formal claim that the argument for government funding does not in itself imply the need for government provision.

More theoretically troubling should be the very grounds on which Friedman justifies government funding of schooling. It is uncontroversial among egalitarian liberals that schooling provides a public good, and most will go beyond Friedman's framework in considering the vocational aspect of schooling as a public good. But to acknowledge that some institution produces a public good is not *sufficient* to justify having the government fund it.

It will be useful for our purposes to distinguish between two kinds of government expenditure. First is expenditure on goods which are *required by justice* – to give an uncontroversial example, spending on a court system capable of providing the right to a fair trial for all. The state bears responsibility for providing such goods in its capacity as an agent on behalf of the individual members of society: it is as moral agents that we owe one another the right to a fair trial, and the state is the mediating body through which we deliver each other that right. A second kind of expenditure is on what we might call *'mere' public goods* – goods which are indeed public in the standard senses, but which the government would not be committing an injustice in failing to provide. There is no stricture of justice which requires that the government sponsor an interstate railroad system, even though an interstate railroad system would provide a public good.

The standards of justification for expenditure on goods required by justice and mere public goods are different. As suggested, the government is required to ensure that goods required by justice are provided, and must spare no expense in making sure that they are present. But for mere public goods, not only must it be reasonable to think that the public good would not come about but for government funding, but it must also be reasonable to expect that the opportunity costs of funding the good will not exceed the benefits produced. Otherwise the expenditure is wasted.

In treating schooling as, in effect, a mere public good, Friedman fails to bring out the most important reasons for providing schooling. For egalitarian liberals the fact that schooling is a public good should be entirely irrelevant to justifying having the state pay for it. As moral agents we each have an obligation to other people's children to ensure that they get a decent education. Having the state pay for schooling through taxation is the mechanism by which we fulfill this obligation. In other words education for minors is like the right to a fair trial in that it is a good, the provision of which must be guaranteed by the state as a matter of justice: it is something which all adults are obliged to provide for each future adult. This is an *individualist* justification for state funding of education which does not appeal to the public good produced thereby. While education is a public good it is its status as a private good to which all have a right that obliges us to provide it.

3. Two Criteria

Seeing the education of minors as something which is required by justice naturally makes for suspicion of vouchers and school choice. If all adults owe education to children as a matter of justice, delivery on that obligation limits the permissible scope of parental choice. In particular, parents may not make choices which prevent children from getting the schooling owed to them by other adults. Egalitarian liberals will think, in particular, that educational institutions should be structured to insulate children's education from their parents' choices in two ways.

First, when the justification of government funding of education is seen as a matter of justice, it is easier to see how the government has an obligation to guarantee vocational education as well as 'civic' education. Vocational education affects a student's future access to resources – it is itself a resource which provides the student with competitive opportunities within the economy. If we believe in an ideal of equality of opportunity then we should be concerned that no one be unfairly advantaged in their access to resources over the course of their life. But if unequal access to resources is entirely conditioned by arbitrary factors such as the ability and willingness to pay for vocational education of one's parents, then opportunity appears to be unfairly unequal. We shall see in section 5 that it is hard to formulate a principle of equal opportunity in education which captures this moral ideal perfectly, but one criterion which an egalitarian will impose on any school system will be that it provides substantial insulation of a child's opportunities from the level of success and choices of the parents.[19]

A second way in which education should be insulated from parents' choices, for which I shall argue in detail in section 6, is that each child should be provided with realistic opportunities to become an autonomous person, regardless of the values or ways of life of their parents. The idea is that our moral commitments should not be merely impressed upon us by contingent conditioning, but should be arrived at and upheld in circumstances in which meaningful, rational reflection on them is a live possibility.[20] Autonomy with respect to our religious views or our conceptions of the good life is particularly important because they have pervasive implications for our lives, and because when we do not hold them autonomously they are not, in some important sense, truly ours. If much of our life activity is shaped by commitments which are not genuinely ours, then there is an important sense in which we are (even if we do not feel it) alienated from our lives.

Where our commitments are the result of manipulation or coercion, it is easy to see how they are not really ours. But we might be alienated even from commitments which, though not the result of coercion or manipulation, are conditioned by factors which make no reference to our conscious mental activity, especially when rational reflection would have led us to reject those commitments. Of course, if our lack of rational reflection is a matter of our own indolence we have no complaint. But rational reflection is a skill, and its absence can reasonably be attributed to indolence only when we have had a reasonable opportunity to learn it.

Schools provide a rare socially-sanctioned setting in which children can be exposed to a range of moral views and religious commitments other than those of their parents, and be equipped with the skills to reflect rationally about all of those views. Since each of us has an obligation to our fellow future citizens to ensure that they can live autonomously, we should ensure as a society that all children attend institutions in which they will receive an autonomy-facilitating education. It is not entirely obvious what demands autonomy-facilitation places on the curriculum, but presumably it would include, at the appropriate grade levels, accurate and critical teaching of history and civics; education in the history and doctrines of several religions and also of anti-religious movements; and exposure to various methods of relative evaluation of moral doctrines. For most children it will be important for their prospective autonomy to know that there are numerous 'live' moral options and that there are various ways of going about making moral choices, some of which are more rational than others.

Acknowledging that the two above-mentioned criteria are binding on a just system of education delivery explains why left-liberals are suspicious of vouchers, but does not justify principled rejection of them. Exactly *how* the state ensures that children get an education of the right kind depends on what are the most effective and self-sustaining institutions for doing so. Efficiency is also a value at least in so far as when other values can be implemented adequately by either of two schemes, the more efficient should be chosen, so that resources can be freed up for the provision of other goods. So uncovering the wrongness of Friedman's argument for government funding of schools does not serve to re-establish a strong connection between the argument for funding and widespread public provision of schooling.

The question we have to ask of any proposed system of educational delivery is how well it can be expected to meet the criteria we set. We ask this question at a time when the US education system fails quite dramatically to meet the criteria briefly mentioned above. Per-pupil spending which, other things being equal, can be taken as a very rough proxy for equality of opportunity, varies immensely among school districts.[21] Other things are not equal, of course. While *Brown versus Board of Education* requires some level of racial balance among schools within districts, it does not require the same among districts, and it does not require a balance of at-risk children or poor children except in so far as those categories coincide with racial categories. Money buys less educational opportunity in schools with a higher density of at-risk children. Not only is the US public school system radically inegalitarian, but it is possible for the wealthiest parents to opt out and purchase private education for their children in schools with very low densities of at-risk children and in which money therefore buys more educational opportunity than in the public school system.

Nor is the criterion that all children should have a realistic opportunity to become autonomous met in the current structure of US schooling. American law allows religious communities such as the Amish to withdraw their children from public schooling before they have been exposed to the kind of education which could plausibly equip them to challenge their parents' religious views in a rational manner. In the *Wisconsin versus Yoder* decision of 1972 the US Supreme Court decided that the right of Old Order Amish and Conservative Amish Mennonite parents in Wisconsin to free exercise of their religion came into conflict with the interest of the state in ensuring that all children receive education up to the age of 16.[22] Because the state did not demonstrate that its interest was compelling, it was ruled that the free exercise of the religion should take precedence. The parents 'believed that by sending their children to high school they would not only expose themselves to the danger of censure of the church community, but, as found by the county court, also endanger their own salvation and that of their children.'[23] The Yoder decision is hedged with concessions that the Amish community is successful, and that 'its members are productive and very law-abiding members of society: they reject public welfare in any of its usual modern forms'.[24] The well-being of the children is also considered, emphasis being placed on the fact that the Amish do not reject all education beyond eighth grade, only education 'of the type provided by a certified high school because it comes at the child's crucial adolescent period of religious development'.[25] The decision nevertheless conflicts with the argument presented above, which emphasizes the obligation we owe to children to equip them with the ability to choose autonomously whether to take up or reject the religious commitments prevailing in their community.[26]

Another controversial case, *Mozert versus Hawkins*, in which Christian parents objected to their children being exposed to a reading curriculum which included, among other things, reference to the objectionable Renaissance ideal of 'the dignity and worth of human beings', was found against the parents. However, those parents were able to remove their children from the public schools, and one consequence was that the publishers voluntarily excised the offending materials from the textbooks in question.[27] Another indication of the failure of American law to implement the autonomy-facilitating requirement is that in many States there are no special qualifications required for 'home schoolers', and the success of home-schooled children is tested entirely in terms of standardized tests. Finally, of course, sectarian private schools are sanctioned, and while in the US many (for example many liberal Catholic schools) probably do a better job than public schools of facilitating personal autonomy, some are quite deliberately intended by their overseers to perpetuate the sectarian faith.

4. Egalitarian Liberal Voucher Proposals

While actual voucher proposals have come mainly from the political right, and have therefore unsurprisingly failed to meet egalitarian liberal criteria, the long-term failure of the existing public institutions to meet these criteria have inclined some left-wing reformers to turn to the possibility that voucher schemes could be designed to advance egalitarian ends. I have argued in an earlier paper that there are no principled reasons for rejecting educational voucher systems. More positively, a current co-chair of the British Labour Government's educational standards commission once argued for a quasi-voucher system, moved by the consideration that in the absence of a commitment to prohibit private schooling serious educational inequalities must persist in Britain, contributing in turn to more general social injustices. Herbert Gintis and Samuel Bowles also argue for the adoption of an egalitarian voucher system, again moved largely by considerations of equality (though in their co-authored work they are also concerned with efficiency).[28]

Although Bowles' and Gintis' voucher proposal is designed with the US context in mind,[29] much of what is said is relevant also outside the US context.[30] Bowles and Gintis echo many of Friedman's themes. They point out that, since expenditure on education represents a substantial part of the economy, and education plays such a pivotal role in our lives, a failure to meet the 'needs and wants of the child' would represent, at the very least, a substantial economic shortcoming. But in the existing system of public school governance, where parents are the residual claimants of the benefit and the school leadership has control rights over provision, there is great scope for failure because there are three major barriers to enforceable agreement between the parents and the leadership. Parents will often disagree with each other about what they want and need; there is little incentive for the school leadership to enter agreement with the parents; and parents have neither reliable independent information concerning the leadership's actions nor means of enforcing whatever agreement is reached.

Because different parents (and others) make conflicting demands on the school, and because it is hard to disagreggate educational policy from other policy areas in elections, democratic voice has limited effectiveness on school policy. And because there is usually both a limited ability to leave the system (schooling is compulsory and since we have to pay for the public schools whatever we do, all alternatives are relatively expensive), and limited ability to move schools within it, it is hard for parents to make schools accountable by using an option of exit.

For Bowles and Gintis the point of a voucher scheme is to make school leaders the residual claimants on the consequences of their actions, by making school funding proportional to those enrolled, and by giving parents the realistic power to affect the number of students in the school.[31] They can achieve this consistent with egalitarian goals only if they meet four constraints: the amount of the vouchers has to be sufficient to purchase a decent education; accredited schools must be prohibited from charging anything in addition to the value of the voucher; decentralized incentives for balance of various kinds must be established; and an enhanced national certification program is required to mitigate the deleterious effects on information gathering of, for example, the grade inflation which is otherwise a likely consequence of superior mobility.[32]

The question I shall address in the next two sections is whether it is reasonable to think that an acceptable left-wing voucher proposal could be implemented and stably reproduced in a democratic capitalist state. First it is worth deflecting two *principled* objections to voucher proposals.

It is unlikely that standard principled objections to the commodification of certain kinds of goods impugn voucher schemes. Why is commodification of any good thought to be objectionable? Three reasons are very commonly offered. The first is that commodification reduces the scope for public democratic deliberation. I shall look at this objection directly in a moment. The second and third focus on the character of the good itself. A perfectionist argument is made that the good in question has a certain kind of value, and that when it is valued in the ways supported by market-exchange either a wrong is done, or the character of the good being purchased is altered resulting in a loss of an important source of value. For example, it is argued of legal prostitution that valuing sex in ways shorn of personal affective attachments is a wrong, and that having sex available on the market changes the character of sexual relations for even those people who never purchase or sell it. Similar arguments are commonly made concerning permission for commercial surrogate motherhood.

Whether such arguments work depends, of course, on the specific character of the goods in question. Sex and parenthood are two goods for which the argument does sound initially plausible, while the argument would be very strange indeed if applied to standard commodities such as television sets and cans of orange juice. What about schooling and education? Education, of course, is never bought directly. We might want to make a distinction between education and schooling parallel to the distinction between health and healthcare, and acknowledge that what is bought is schooling, while what the purchaser hopes to acquire through the purchase of schooling is education. Now, it does seem reasonable to fear that prevalence of market mechanisms might contribute to a common confusion between schooling and education on the part of consumers and proxy con-sumers. Some parents appear to believe that attendance at school should be sufficient for their children to emerge educated, whereas getting an education from schooling requires active participation which is sometimes not forthcoming.[33] But this confusion is possible under any delivery mechanism, and the way to combat it seems to be by having a clear public explanation of the character and value of education.

Like most claims concerning commodification, any claim that the value of education is distorted or destroyed by allowing significant weight to parental choice in the delivery mechanism is speculative, and so, therefore, is any denial. For that reason the question cannot be settled satisfactorily here, but I am skeptical. But at least education does not seem to be the kind of good or service which it would be *wrong* to buy or sell, in the way that recreational or reproductive sexual services might be. An extremely complex world requires that we engage in a social division of labor such that some people devote much of the working part of their lives to acquiring the skills needed to teach well. Every adult member of society is enabled to contribute to delivering justice to children by the fact that they can pay specialists to do the job. Teaching is, of course, a vocation, in the more romantic sense evoked by such cultural icons as Mr Chips and Miss Brookes. But it is *also* a job, which should be valued – and paid for – in monetary terms, as well as in other ways. If the service is not paid for, at least within a monetary economy, those who are not teachers fail thereby to value the teachers properly, as well as failing properly to value their own obligations of justice to provide education for children. It is a matter of justice to children that society designs institutions so that some people become good teachers and get paid to live their lives that way. In this sense education *must* be bought, at least, and as such differs very greatly from the kinds of services associated with prostitution and commercial surrogacy.

Finally, commodification-based arguments against markets generally presume a model on which only the market and nothing else is determining the distribution of the kind of good. But in any viable voucher scheme there are *some* other determinants: in particular, government regulation affecting both the distribution and the character of educational opportunities. Exactly how much is determined by market processes and how much by government regulation depends on the details of the scheme as well as what happens in practice when they are implemented. As we have seen in considering Friedman's argument for vouchers, choice has a role in allocation even in a system in which all schools are government schools and there is no formal role for school choice: some parents will decide among occupational and housing options on the basis of what schools those options would lead their children to be placed in. So the difference between that system and a voucher system is one of degree, not quality.

A second principled objection to vouchers is that they *replace* determination of standards through the exercise of public democratic 'voice', with the exercise of the option of private 'exit'.[34] This, too, is far from decisive against vouchers. One of the motivations of voucher proponents is that with respect to those educational goods provided by school, when the option of exit is clearly available, schools will be more responsive. Schools are relatively small institutions, and the contribution on behalf of each student is, relatively, a very substantial amount of money. As one of their several million customers spending three dollars a time, I cannot have any effect on the quality of Lipton Tea by simply refraining from buying it. Nor can I have an effect by writing and telling them that I shall refuse to buy it unless they improve its quality. But as one of only 1500 customers each contributing, say, $10,000 a year (as I would be in a voucher system) there would be a great incentive for the school to listen to me. Providing a realistic option of exit makes available better opportunities for voice in this case. The picture of parents just withdrawing their children from the school without trying to correct the features they dislike depends on an unrealistic – one might say idealistic – picture of how markets work. Although it is made possible by a voucher scheme, exit from the school is costly for the child: mid-year exit disrupts learning, as do too many moves, and children find it disruptive having to reconstruct their social life within a new school, which distracts them from work even more than their regular social life does. Concerned parents (those who are likely to *use* the option of exit) will recognize this, and will be inclined to improve conditions within the existing school if it is possible.[35] The option of exit provides the leverage which gets the voice heard. If we care about giving parents the ability to affect the behavior of the school we should not make a fetish of the means through which they are able to do that[36] – we should be concerned just that they have what is in fact the most effective means available to them.

Furthermore, there is nothing about voucher schemes which precludes considerable opportunities for governance through specifically democratic voice. We have seen that even Friedman accepts that some regulation will be necessary, and that regulation will at least be subject to democratic review. In left-wing schemes, involving more extensive regulation, the overarching regulation governing the whole school system including the curriculum will presumably be decided through standard democratic mechanisms. This fact also mitigates the possible fear that under a voucher system we shall see a general decline in lobbying on the part of parents for a general improvement in standards and conditions. There remains substantial scope for public deliberation over standards and methods. In any educational system it can be expected that parents will engage on behalf of their children at the level of the school and for general standards at higher levels of regulation. An appropriately designed voucher scheme can leave plenty of scope for both.

5. Vouchers and Educational Equality

The most powerful objection to right-wing voucher schemes which actually get proposed is that they undermine equality of educational opportunity. This is certainly true of real voucher schemes. None that have reached legislative consideration in the US has included the full cost of schooling in the voucher, and none has prohibited the use of top-up expenditure by parents. For this reason, at least, it is likely that vouchers would provide a subsidy for those who already use private schools, and would not enable most parents to get their children to private schools. Of course, a universal voucher scheme, in which vouchers were essentially the *only* means of paying for school-ing, would be different. But even in such a system, wealthy parents, being on the whole more leisured, better educated, and closer to crucial sources of information, are liable to be more effective proxy consumers of education. Their children would be more attractive to schools so there may be a tendency for different schools to stratify along class lines, with only the most promising poorer children brought into the wealthier schools. If there is an educational benefit to less able students from being educated alongside more able students, that benefit is liable to diminish.

So the mere fact of (near) universality is not enough. We would have to design the voucher scheme with built-in regulations and accreditation requirements, which are designed to prevent the tend-ency to inequality of opportunity. As Bowles and Gintis say:

> The scope for egalitarianism and pluralism is considerable, provided that the level of voucher funding be sufficient to cover the costs of quality education, and that schools accredited to receive vouchers be prohibited from charging parents additional tuition fees.

This seems right in principle; we can ensure that there is rough equality of access to schooling by equalizing the amount that people can spend on their children's education, with departures from equality sanctioned to deal with, for example, children with disabilities, and children who come from significantly disadvantaged groups. We can place require-ments for a mix of class origins, a mix of ability, and a mix of 'teachability', within each school.[37] In principle, in fact, we could make the vouchers of the children of the poor worth more than vouchers for the children of the rich, thus reaching beyond the traditional ambition that public schooling should insulate against background inequalities of wealth, and achieving some measure of redress.[38]

But it is worth noting that there are likely to be serious practical difficulties in winning public support for a voucher system so scrupu-lously designed. The central problem is that there is no public standard of opportunity by which to evaluate a claim that some institution equalizes educational opportunities.[39] Consider the following three possible accounts of equality of educational opportunity.[40]

First we might understand equality of educational opportunity in terms of equal resources being expended on each individual's school-ing. But the money value of a voucher is at best a poor proxy for the deeper notion of equality of opportunity. Consider, most tellingly, children with disabilities. Some of them have no prospect of achieving an educational output which would be equal (on any reasonable standard) to the outputs achievable by exceptionally talented students, regardless of how much money is spent on their education. It seems wrong to say of them that equal money spent on them gives them equal opportunity.

Some have tried to describe equality of educational opportunity in terms of equal outcomes. There is an obvious objection to this, which is that, in general, outcomes are a poor measure of opportunities, since individuals make different choices with respect to their opportunities, some making better and some making worse decisions, and hence equality of opportunity is liable to produce inequality of outcome. They are certainly conceptually distinct.

One response to this objection is to say that children cannot be held responsible for the quality of the choices they make with respect to their educational opportunities. They are, after all, children, and it is therefore not proper to hold them responsible for their choices in the way that we would hold adults responsible for choices.[41] But while the basis of this objection seems to be correct, it does not establish the conclusion that educational outcomes are a good measure of educational opportunities. Rather it seems to suggest that educational opportunity is at best a second-best egalitarian objective for the purposes of social policy. Furthermore, of course, the fact of disability is a problem for an equal-outcome account of equal-opportunity. Some of the disabled, who certainly should be granted more resources than the ordinarily abled (other things being equal), could never be expected to reach the level of educational attainment that some of the ordinarily abled could.

For a third account of equality of educational opportunity we might modify John Rawls' principle of fair equality of opportunity. For Rawls, fair equality of opportunity obtains when 'those who are at the same level of talent and ability, and have the same willingness to use them, should have the same prospects of success regardless of their initial place in the social system, that is, irrespective of the income class into which they are born'.[42] The parallel account of fair equality of educational opportunity might say that:

> Children with the same level of natural ability and the same level of willingness to learn should have the same prospects for educational attainment regardless of their initial place in the social system.

Notice that this interpretation of equal educational opportunity would require a considerable departure from a policy of equal educational resources: it is quite likely that more resources would have to be directed to the children of less wealthy parents than to the equally talented children of wealthier parents, and it might be difficult to win public support for a voucher system which did this.[43] But, more importantly, it seems to be too weak a principle to capture the idea of equal educational opportunity, because it fails to comment on the relationship between the prospects for attainment of children with different levels of talent. It is compatible with this interpretation of the criterion that we devote almost all our educational resources to a small elite with a very high level of talent and willingness to learn, and hardly any resources to the vast majority who range from the extremely lazy and untalented to the very (but not extremely) talented and willing. Intuitively, this violates any ideal of equality of opportunity.[44]

This shows that it is hard to elaborate a conception of equality of educational opportunity, though it certainly does not show that it is impossible. However, the task is sufficiently difficult that we can predict serious problems winning majority political support for a voucher scheme which conscientiously attempts to implement equality of properly conceived educational opportunity, and difficulty implementing the principle even if majority support can be won politically.

A full and principled account of equality of educational opportunity needs to say something about how much more must be devoted to children with disabilities than to ordinarily-abled children. Even among students without disabilities there is a range of ability levels, such that, assuming that the same level of resources is devoted to each, those in the top ability levels simply have more educational opportunities than those in the bottom ability levels. So the account must also be able to guide the distribution of resources among more and less able children within the ordinarily-abled group. If the same resources should be devoted the account needs to explain why, and why such differences do not merit the same response as the differences between the ordinarily-abled and disabled. If, as seems more likely on the face of it, differential resources should be devoted, this needs to be explained. And the parents of each group need to be persuaded of the account if their support is to be won for a voucher scheme informed by the correct conception.

It is likely to be publicly acknowledged that the disabled need to be granted more resources in order for them to have the same level of opportunity, and there is significant public support for the current policy of devoting considerably more resources to the education of students with disabilities than to those of students without disabilities. This public support is dependent on some degree of trust that experts can tell who has and who does not have disabilities.

But it is notoriously difficult to establish who are the less able and who are the more able students within the non-disabled range, and there is much less public trust in the 'experts' who claim to be able to differentiate them. Furthermore there is much less public support (and it would be much harder to generate public support) for a regime of publicly devoting differential resources to the education of the less able (but not disabled) students.

One solution might be to allow the schools to devote more resources to the less able once the students pass the school gates. But if parents have the capacity to monitor what is going on, those whose children are (quite properly from the perspective of equality of opportunity) receiving fewer resources (say in the form of less attention from teachers) within the school gates will feel that they are being cheated, because their child is receiving less in educational resources than they are contributing to the school in the form of the money value of their voucher.

A second problem is that, regardless of the conception of edu-cational opportunity we are working with, there are serious problems for parents trying to monitor how far resources are being devoted to their children within the school. Even if each student is supplied with roughly the same supplies (books, paper, desk, etc.) they are not likely to be supplied with the same amount of valuable attention. With the best will in the world the teacher cannot be sure that he is even coming close to an equal distribution of attention. Parents, who are not in the classroom, cannot know at all. Sometimes parents will know and will resent that the teacher deliberately withheld assistance from their child, and will see this as shortchanging even though in fact the decision was pedagogically well-motivated.

This is not to say that equality of opportunity is impossible to achieve through a voucher system, but just to point out potential sources of difficulty in winning majority political support for the implementation and maintenance of a system designed to achieve it.[45]

6. Vouchers and Personal Autonomy

Whatever the difficulties with meeting an equality constraint, voucher schemes are liable to have even more serious difficulties with a constraint requiring that all children receive an autonomy-facilitating education. The problem is not that parents may be incapable of or uninterested in advancing the educational success or opportunities of their children. This is a problem, but it is not the one that matters here. The objection which the liberal will raise is nicely expressed by Elizabeth Anderson: a voucher system:

> effaces the distinction between the freedom of the parents and the autonomy of the children. Many parents fear that training in argument, reasoning and imagination, in conjunction with certain kinds of knowledge . . . will enable their children to defy parental authority and challenge their parents' religious and moral ideals. A voucher system would enable parents to satisfy their ideal-based desires to indoctrinate their children rather than educate them to exercise their own judgment.[46]

Bowles and Gintis deliberately evade this question when they say, 'we shall elide the not small problem of possible differences of interest between the parents and child'. In the final section I shall look at what it would mean to give up Bowles' and Gintis' 'not small assumption'. But in this section I want to explain why we *should* give it up. One very natural response to the objection from autonomy-facilitation is to reject it: that is, to assert that the simplifying assumption is either true, or should be treated as true for the purposes of political morality. This response does not have to deny that personal autonomy is extremely valuable, but denies that providing for it is an obligation which merits denying parents the opportunity to protect their children from autonomy. This response currently has a great deal of public support, not all of it from the political right. Furthermore, it has recently become disputed ground even among liberal theorists of education, some of whom are influential on public policy in the US. For these reasons, and because it will afford an opportunity to further elaborate the case for autonomy-facilitating education, it is worth exploring the arguments advanced for it in some detail.

i) Do parents own their children?

Conservative libertarians are generally uncomfortable with the idea that the state should play any deliberate role in affecting the relationship between children and parents. The argument that parents should have the right to form their child's values is nicely put by Charles Fried.

The right to form one's child's values, one's child's life plan and the right to lavish attention on that child are extensions of the basic right not to be interfered with in doing these things for oneself.[47]

He then asks what would be implied by the suggestion that parents have no special title to determine their children's values? 'Surely such a view implies that parents' reproductive functions are only adventitiously their own: . . . they have no special relationship to the product of that reproduction.'[48] Loren Lomasky, arguing for the more moderate position that primary responsibility for the care of the child should be vested in its parents and the extended family, claims that: 'Producing children makes them one's own. That is so whether or not conception of the child was desired and intended. No other individuals stand in the same causal relation as the parents.'[49] Since 'having children is often an integral component of persons' projects' and 'regard for someone as a rights-holder is grounded in the recognition of that being as a distinct individual' and parents immediately recognize their children as distinct individuals, we are obliged to grant parents immense latitude in forming their children's conceptions of how to live.[50]

However, a 'special' title to form one's child's values can be recognized without granting *exclusive* title. That other agencies are granted *some* influence over the formation of a child's values implies neither that parents have *no* rights over their children nor that their rights are not special. So a mandatory autonomy-facilitating education does not threaten a special title, since it is quite consistent with permitting parental influence in the home. Parents may have an exclusive right to determine which church, if any, their children attend at the weekend; whether their children attend Sunday school, or Hebrew school; whether their children will be allowed to watch commercial television: none of these are threatened by a policy of autonomy facilitating education in the school curriculum.

Furthermore, even if there were a conflict, Fried is wrong to think that denying that parents have a fundamental right to the power to determine the course of their children's lives implies that they have no special relationship to their children. Parents may indeed have a special relationship to their children, which derives from their having brought the children into the world. But that specialness is probably best characterized in terms of the *obligations* they have toward the children and toward their fellow citizens who will now have to share their world with the children.[51] It is not clear why we should think that the parents have special *rights* over their children. They may indeed have the right against society that they not be prevented from fulfilling their obligations toward their children, but this does not extend to the right that the rest of society refrain from stepping in when the parents fail to fulfil their obligations. The right to be allowed to fulfil an obligation is precisely that. It does not imply the right to refrain from fulfilling that obligation, nor the right to prevent others from fulfilling their obligations to the same persons. It may well be wise to establish a presumption in favor of a rough social division of moral labor which grants parents some conditional and limited power over their children. If so, that is because this is the best available mechanism for delivering our obligations to the children, not because the parents are properly thought to have rights. But if ensuring that future citizens have the opportunity to become autonomous persons is an obligation that we all share, and that we share with parents of children, mandating autonomy-facilitating education is acceptable, even given the claim that parents have a special relationship with their children, which society is obliged to respect.

ii) Liberal neutrality

Some liberals are committed to a principle of neutrality, which says that the government should not promote policies which are deliberately designed to favor one way of life over others because the favored way of life is presumed to be intrinsically superior.[52] A principle of neutrality might seem to preclude requiring autonomy-facilitating education. When considering the next objection I shall deny that it does. But it is worth seeing how implausible the principle of neutrality is when applied to government policies concerning the upbringing of children.

With respect to adult citizens, neutrality has at least two distinct major sources of appeal. First, if the government is neutral with respect to people's conceptions of the good, it is more likely than if it does not, to be able to secure the free consent of its citizens. The free consent of the citizenry is, in turn, considered to be a condition of legitimacy. So neutrality facilitates (though it may not be a prerequisite of) legitimacy. Second is the notion that citizens should be equal in the sight of the government and that neutrality is part of what it is for them to be treated with equal respect. There is an intimate connection between people's ideas about the good and their views of themselves. This connection makes it reasonable for them to feel that when coercive force is used on them for reasons which they morally reject, the government, acting on behalf of their fellow citizens, is not only discounting their views, but, in doing so, is failing to respect them equally with others.[53]

But neither of these sources of appeal has any weight when we consider children. Children generally do not yet have conceptions of the good to which they are intimately tied, and even when they do we do not think that respecting that intimacy is either a condition of legitimacy of the state or of treating them with respect. The reason that the intimate connection between persons and their conceptions of the good impresses liberals so much is that persons are presumed properly to regard those conceptions as their own. But children should not regard their conceptions as their own – if they do have a conception of the good it is usually someone else's, since they are unequipped as yet to make it their own in the relevant sense.

It might be argued that the imposition of autonomy-facilitating education is unacceptably non-neutral with respect to the parents of the children. Again, in the next subsection I shall explain that it is not non-neutral in the *relevant* sense. But even if it were non-neutral it would be non-neutral *to the parents* only if we thought that parents had, pre-institutionally, some strong rights over their children such that whatever we do to the children has implications toward the parents. This is not the case, as we saw when dealing with the previous objection.

iii) Is the unexamined life valuable?

A third strategy for opposing mandatory autonomy-facilitating education is to argue that the case for it is simply false. In an influential recent book William Galston has argued that, while the state should promote certain civic virtues (such as toleration and 'the minimal conditions of reasonable public judgment'), through the education system, it may not mandate autonomy-facilitating education. He specifically rejects the idea that students should be taught to respect ways of life other than their own, and that they should be exposed to a wide range of ways of life and conceptions of the good, and educated as to how to evaluate them critically.

Galston's argument has two elements. First is the fact that the argument for promoting civic virtues through compulsory schools simply does not support the further measures needed for autonomy-facilitating education. Galston's argument for teaching the virtues is rooted in a requirement that the freedom-guaranteeing state has a responsibility to ensure that it remains stable, which responsibility is facilitated by teaching the virtues. However, living by those virtues is compatible, both in theory and in practice, with a quite determined and unreflective commitment to a sectarian conception of the good. As he says, 'tolerance of deep differences is perfectly compatible with unswerving belief in the correctness of one's own way of life', and civic deliberation, which only requires that 'each citizen accept the minimal civic commitments without which the liberal polity cannot long endure' is compatible with 'unshakable personal commitments'.[54] The argument for promoting civic virtues, then, does not suffice to generate permission for autonomy-facilitation.

The second element of his argument is that autonomy-facilitating education is based on the unacceptable premise that 'the unexamined life is an unworthy life'.[55] This claim is unacceptable, he thinks, because a liberal state could not build it into the system of public education without

> throwing its weight behind a conception of the human good unrelated to the functional needs of its sociopolitical institutions and at odds with the deep beliefs of many of its loyal citizens. As a political matter, liberal freedom entails the right to live unexamined as well as examined lives – a right the effective exercise of which may require parental bulwarks against the corrosive influence of modernist skepticism.[56]

Notice that for Galston the problem is not exactly that the policy is non-neutral. In his view, when a policy is required for the self-reproduction of liberal institutions (such as the promotion of the civic virtues), or for overcoming barriers to the normal development of children (such as the enforcement of laws against incestual rape), that it is non-neutral is no objection to it. But intrusions into the upbringing of children which are not required for either of these purposes are unjustifiable. And requiring autonomy-facilitation is therefore impermissible.

More recently, Galston has supplemented his argument with a direct defence of what he calls the *Diversity State*. The Diversity State acknowledges and protects the institutional preconditions of diversity, but 'beyond the unity required for and provided by shared liberal purposes, the liberal state must allow the fullest possible scope for diversity. And the promotion of personal autonomy is not among the shared liberal purposes'.[57]

However, Galston's arguments fail, for two reasons. First, there are solid justifications for requiring autonomy-facilitating education which do not rest on the premise that the unexamined life is an unworthy one, and which are therefore not non-neutral among conceptions of the good. Second, it is arguable that the liberal state has an obligation to ensure that all children have an opportunity to become the kind of person whose consent to coercive institutions matters. If it does have such an obligation (or, to put it another way, if adult citizens have this obligation toward children who will become citizens of the state those adults have maintained), then requiring autonomy-facilitation appears to be a consequence.

First, consider the alternative justifications of mandatory auton-omy-facilitating education. One weaker justification would be that it is a precondition of the worthiness of a life that it is selected in circumstances in which rational scrutiny of it and other alternatives is a meaningful possibility. Whether rational scrutiny is exercised over the life selected or the other alternatives is not important. This particular claim is, of course, as improbable as the claim that the unexamined life is unworthy. It is hard to see why, if there are worthy unexamined lives, they would be worthy only if they were selected in conditions which make rational scrutiny possible.

But there is another, more plausible, justification.

The argument starts with the premise that the basic methods of rational evaluation are significant aids to approaching the truth about the good. This is especially true in modern conditions, with, as Joseph Raz puts it,

> fast changing technologies and free movement of labour [which calls for] an ability to cope with changing technological, economic and social conditions, for an ability to adjust, to acquire new skills, to move from one subculture to another, to come to terms with new scientific and moral views.[58]

Without the capacity for autonomous rational reflection it is easy to get lost in the moral complexity of the modern world. Of course, this does not deny that some will hit upon, or at least approach, the truth, without their aid, nor does it claim that any rational deliberator is bound toward the truth. Just as with other areas of knowledge, truth may be achieved by an inspired guess, or by accepting on trust the truthful communication of another, or simply by being manipulated into believing it. And just as with other areas of knowledge, of course, rational deliberation can confront barriers. But in the absence of fortunate guesses and well-informed and truthful parents, children will be significantly more able to find worthy lives for themselves if they have the effective means to compare different ways of life rationally.[59]

The facts described in this argument suffice to support a strong presumption in favor of this form of education, and enough to make it seem that children's claims to this kind of education cannot legitimately be waived by their parents: especially when they live in a tight community which limits opportunities for other kinds of rationality-inducing exposure to a variety of ways of life, such as the Amish or Mennonite communities.[60]

Notice that this argument for autonomy-facilitating education is structured entirely differently from Galston's argument for education in the civic virtues. Unlike Galston's, this argument starts with the obligation which adults have towards prospective adults, to provide them with sufficient means to lead a good life. The state is charged not with maintaining its own stability, but with providing prospective citizens with the substantive means to select pursuit of a better rather than worse conception of the good life. The fundamental interest each individual has in living a good life yields an obligation on all to provide prospective adults with an almost essential instrument for selecting better lives: and hence to provide autonomy-facilitating education. We must attempt to meet our obligation to make available to all prospective citizens the means to live a worthy life, and we can only begin to be confident that others are living lives that are both worthy and really theirs if we make available to them the real possibility of rational scrutiny.

Nor is the argument non-neutral, at least in the relevant sense. It invokes not a controversial moral value, autonomy, but a true epistemological claim: that rational evaluation is one somewhat reliable method for approaching the truth with respect to the good. This may be a controversial claim, and the controversy concerning it will often be surrounded by other, genuinely moral controversies, but the controversy about the claim itself is not about morality but about epistemology. As I pointed out earlier, neutrality, even if it does have power as a constraint on some aspects of government policy, is not an appropriate constraint on policies concerning the development of children. My point here is that this argument would meet the constraint if it were appropriate.

Finally, it should be obvious why I have called the policy auton-omy-*facilitating* education, rather than autonomy-*promoting* edu-cation. The education is not directed at trying to ensure that students employ autonomy in their lives, any more than literary criticism classes are aimed at ensuring that students employ literary criticism in their lives. Rather it is aimed at *enabling* them to live autonomously should they wish to do so, rather as we aim to enable them to criticize poetry, do algebra, etc. without trying to ensure that they do so. Autonomy, on this account, has to be facilitated, but does not have to be promoted. (I shall note some practical problems for attempting to distinguish the policies in practice in the next section.)

Now consider the obligation that children have a real opportunity to become the kind of citizens whose consent matters for the legitimacy of liberal institutions. How does making autonomous living available to children facilitate this? By suggesting that the legitimacy of the coercive force of the liberal state depends on its acceptability to autonomous citizens I do not imply that there are no restrictions on the legitimate coercion of the non-autonomous. There are restrictions, and they are the same as those that obtain on coercion of the autonomous. However, the liberal state cannot be satisfied with the uncritical and unreasoned consent of its citizens. In judging the legitimacy of a policy being enacted by a liberal state we need to be assured that critical citizens, who have reasoned about the various options and have considered their relationship to the state, not as a given fact of nature, but as one which they endorse despite their appreciation of the fact that there are a range of feasible alternatives, even when they are on the receiving end of the coercion. There is an emptiness to the claim that a state is legitimate because its coercive actions would have been accepted by autonomous citizens unless that same state has ensured that each person has been able to become autonomous. So the state has an obligation to ensure that all future citizens have the opportunity to become such citizens, and especially has this obligation if it engages in the promotion of civic virtues designed to bring about their loyalty to it.

What, though, of Galston's Diversity State? The account I have provided shows that there *is* something special about personal auton- omy, and what is special about it justifies ensuring that all have autonomy available to them, which is not the same thing as trying to ensure that they actually live autonomously. So it is not clear that the argument I have made violates the norms of the Diversity State. But, whether it does or not, Galston is mistaken in thinking that the liberal state 'must allow the fullest possible scope for diversity'. Justice is not concerned with 'giving diversity its due', but with giving citizens and future citizens *their* due.[61] If giving them their due inhibits possibilities for diversity, that is a consequence which may or may not be regrettable (depending on the value of the set of ways of life which is disadvantaged), but which has to be accepted by someone concerned with justice.

iv) Rectifying injustice

A final, and less significant, argument against autonomy-facilitating education is worth considering. Some will argue that the survival of certain minority cultures within modern societies is threatened, and that the imposition of autonomy-facilitating education on children from those cultures would hasten their decline. We are not, now, considering cultures such as the Amish, but cultures the participants in which have suffered from longstanding and continuing injustice, such as some native American cultures, African-American cultures, etc. The argument therefore has at least more rhetorical power than those surveyed above, resting as it does on the fact of injustice toward individuals.[62]

However, it does not follow that participants in a culture who have been treated unjustly can waive, on behalf of their children, a good the provision of which is required by justice. Justice requires that we take measures to facilitate autonomy for all future citizens. If this results in the departure of children from minority cultures, that is not a cost we have any reason to take into account. Of course, the fact of injustice imposes obligations of redress on us. We should return due resources to members of unjustly-treated cultures, and should additionally compensate for oppression and discrimination. But allowing them to remove their children from autonomy-facilitating education does neither of these things – it merely allows them to perpetuate their culture among their children.

Concern about autonomy-facilitating education is often couched in terms of the tendency for autonomy-facilitation to lead to departure from sectarian ways of life. There is something self-effacing, though, about opposition to autonomy-facilitation on these grounds. The concern only arises if you think that careful rational reflection on your way of life by someone who is able also to reflect carefully on other ways of life will lead them to adopt a different one. It is not clear why it would do so, unless your way of life is not a better one than the other ones. But if the others are better, what could be objectionable about having someone adopt them rather than yours?

Furthermore, of course, since it is impossible in the modern world for sectarians to completely deprive their children of exposure to other ways of life, because as they grow children inevitably become less tied to their parents, and because most illiberal communities we are concerned with are embedded within a larger community which is tolerant of difference, they do indeed leave the ways of life that their parents prefer in significant numbers. There is no reason to suppose that autonomy-facilitating education would hasten or make these departures more numerous. What it might do, though, is alter the circumstances of and reasons for the departure. The bitter ex-Roman Catholic who is ill-equipped for the rational evaluation of the faith she abandoned is not an uncommon phenomenon. Autonomy-facilitating education might mitigate the tendency she exemplifies, with the result that when people abandon their parents' ways of life they do so not irrationally and with resentment, but with a cool appreciation of the goods and bads of both the way of life they are entering and the one that they are exiting.

7. Accommodating Autonomy

The upshot of the above discussion is that parents should not be treated as having the same interests as their children. In some crucial cases their interests diverge, and the design of the curriculum should reflect this. Every child has an interest in being able to be an autonomous person which all adults have an obligation to meet, regardless of parental preferences. How can a voucher system be constrained to ensure that autonomy-facilitating education is provided?

We saw earlier Elizabeth Anderson's claim that vouchers efface the distinction between the freedom of the parents and the autonomy of the children. This is not exactly true. Even within voucher systems it is possible, in principle, to maintain and respect that distinction by implementing regulations requiring that all accredited schools have a program of autonomy-facilitating education. But there are practical difficulties with doing this. It is important to assign responsibility for monitoring the implementation of curricular regulations. One of the advantages of a voucher scheme is that parents, those closest to the individual child, can, at least to some extent, directly monitor the education he or she receives.[63] But this advantage depends on the coincidence of interests of parents and children. Where the interests diverge parents are no longer suitable monitors. This is not to say that all, or even most, parents are interested in depriving their children of access to this form of education, just that those parents who are interested are unsuited to monitoring its implementation.

Even those parents who *are* interested in monitoring will have difficulty doing so. The methods by which we teach children how to be critically evaluative are complex, and success is hard to measure. Even suppose that the aim were to ensure that children become autonomous. Success is not measurable by standardized tests. It is not even measurable by looking at the content of the ways of life they select, since most ways of life that can be lived autonomously can also be lived heteronomously. And the process of turning a child into an autonomous person does not always seem to reflect the end of autonomy very clearly. Sometimes we present them with information about other ways of life, and expose them to other people's critical thinking about those ways of life. But sometimes we might try to get them to entertain the thoughts they would have if they were a member of a cult so as to make the contrast. And, of course, autonomy promotion would be liable to infuse the curriculum, or at least substantial parts of it.

The difficulty of monitoring is compounded by the fact that the policy we are concerned with is not one of *autonomy-promotion*, but of *autonomy-facilitation*, the problems of measuring which are even greater. Even if we knew how to measure whether or not someone had selected their way of life autonomously, finding out that they had not would not tell us whether we had failed in facilitating autonomy, since they might have learned how to live autonomously, and then rejected that option. So even parents who wanted autonomy for their children would be hard pressed to ensure that the classroom experience was doing what they want. It will also be difficult to distinguish autonomy-facilitation and autonomy-promotion in practice. It is hard to see how a teacher could impart the skills associated with autonomy without simultaneously communicating some norms concerning the virtues of autonomy. In teaching a child to play cricket one cannot teach the skills without also communicating enthusiasms and a sense that the game is worth playing, and similarly someone teaching the skills associated with autonomy is likely to communicate that autonomy is worth applying. This does not mean that all children will become autonomous, nor that there is no meaningful distinction at the level of justification between an autonomy-facilitating and autonomy-promoting policy, but it does mean that in practice the policies will be difficult to distinguish, to the detriment of attempts to monitor what is being taught.[64]

The difficulties with monitoring the implementation of autonomy-facilitating education are not exclusively a problem for advocates of vouchers, however. The natural response to these problems from the voucher proponent is to shift a burden of justification back on to the liberal opponent of vouchers. What alternative form of educational governance can do *better* at guaranteeing autonomy-facilitation? Direct democratic governance has its own problems. First of all, if autonomy-facilitating education is an obligation that we owe to our future fellow citizens, then it is not a matter over which democratic discretion can properly be exercised. That is, to use Ronald Dworkin's terminology, it is a choice-insensitive policy, in the sense that a democratic decision to withhold it would be illegitimate.[65] So the justice of mandating autonomy-facilitating education by no means automatically supports democracy as the central direct mechanism for governing schools. Second, the monitoring problems raised above appear to be as severe under direct democratic governance as under vouchers: it is no easier for concerned liberal citizens to monitor than for concerned liberal parents. This very important point is too often neglected. When raising a problem with the efficiency of a system it is not enough to point out a source of inefficiency. One has to point to alternative institutional forms which lack that source and do not introduce equivalently bad sources. But the character of the difficulty of monitoring the delivery of autonomy-facilitating education seems to make it as hard for the state as for citizens to overcome it.

Liberal opponents of vouchers may claim that democratic governance is none the less more likely to ensure autonomy-facilitating education. The idea is that democratic deliberation fosters the valuing of autonomy by enticing citizens to engage in public rational defence of their own views, and hence to rationally evaluate them. Once one engages in rational evaluation one begins to recognize its value. Furthermore, democratic governance provides assurance to those who, though they are not completely averse to having their children engage in critical reflection on their way of life, are reluctant to have that happen unless they can be somewhat confident that the children from other sectarian faiths are doing the same. Someone who might use a voucher to withdraw their children from autonomy-facilitating education might nevertheless vote for autonomy-facilitating education for all.[66]

I suspect that both these claims are true, but are also beside the point. We have seen that egalitarian liberal voucher proponents accept the need for democratic regulation, and would make autonomy-facilitating education a condition of accreditation. While democratic control is not direct, it is present, and as such it can contain the advantages referred to.

The case against vouchers will tend to be speculative, but so will the case for them. Ultimately, the most powerful case for direct democratic control against vouchers concerns the stable *reproducibility* of a system providing autonomy facilitation. It could be argued that vouchers appear to embody the idea that the parent is the presumptive arbiter of their child's interests. By contrast, a democratically accountable regulatory body which is simultaneously the provider of the service directly paid for through taxation is that it appears to embody the idea that each member of society bears a responsibility to ensure that justice is done to each child. The argument need not deny that the two ideas may be compatible, and may even both be true (which is why the autonomy objection is not, in fact, a principled objection to voucher schemes as such). It would say, though, that having the latter idea rather than the former idea embodied in our public institutions is more likely to make autonomy-facilitating education reproducible over time.

But even this argument can be met with a somewhat plausible counter-speculation. If we take the state out of direct delivery of education it is quite possible in the US context that sectarians who currently resent and fear the state might be assured in ways that relax their guard against their children's exposure to diverse moral outlooks and ways of thinking about them. The arguments I have given support that we have an obligation to ensure that each others' children get such exposure, but do not imply that we must use the state to ensure that. If we think that sectarian parents would behave better toward their children in a regime in which less pressure to behave well was applied by the state, we should have the state apply less pressure.

I think this speculation has some power. It has more when we give up the simplification I have employed throughout this paper of treating the Bowles and Gintis voucher system as a discrete proposal. In fact the proposal is part of a package of reforms which include the family-strengthening measure of assurance of some level of an absentee parent's income, housing reform, and, the centerpiece, a massive redistribution of wealth in the direction of equality. This package, especially its central egalitarian element, could be expected over time to undermine the level of insecurity, distrust, fear and ignorance within which sectarian religious views find such fertile breeding ground. The autonomy problem may wither or at least diminish of its own accord as a more just distribution takes hold. This may be a wild speculation, but if it is false, that is no succor to the liberal opponents of vouchers.

8. Concluding Comments

I have surveyed serious difficulties in designing voucher schemes which meet two egalitarian liberal criteria. In both cases there will be difficulties in winning democratic majorities for imposing the criteria, and difficulties monitoring their implementation once imposed. These difficulties may be more severe for voucher schemes than for a system of direct democratic governance, but more tellingly they raise difficulties for designing any education system which meets these criteria. If the problems *are* especially severe for vouchers, I suspect that it is partly because voucher schemes are generally more transparent than systems of direct provision. When voters regulate a voucher system they are forced to represent explicitly the criteria that they think should be met by schools. The criteria egalitarian liberals favor are hard to explain, hard to argue for, and hard to monitor, and will therefore sometimes lose in a democratic vote. Under direct provision the difficulties of scrutinizing the system and the professional discretion ceded to teachers help to ensure that even if democratic support cannot be won for liberal egalitarian criteria, it is possible to impose them partially within the system anyway. Bowles and Gintis are right to say that markets can be instruments of democratic policymaking, but in this case it is precisely because they are such clear instruments that they present problems for egalitarian liberals.

I would like to make one final observation about efficiency. Bowles' and Gintis' explicit motivation for school choice is a concern about the inefficiencies generated by the unresponsiveness of school bureaucracies to the preferences of parents. The egalitarian liberal who is impressed by the considerations I have raised does not see it as the purpose of schools to respond to the preferences of parents. Instead, the egalitarian liberal sees schools as being designed to deliver efficiently the obligations of each adult citizen to all minors, of preparing them for citizenship and moral agency, and providing them with valuable internal resources which make the opportunities they face in the world meaningful possibilities for them. Adult citizens have these obligations to all children regardless of the status or preferences of their parents, and parents are not morally entitled to refuse the resulting treatment on behalf of their children. But the egalitarian liberal cannot conclude from this that responding to the preferences of parents does not matter at all. It may well be that the efficiency gains attendant upon greater responsiveness to parents' preferences will free up resources which are then available for us to use in meeting our obligations. The more parents that act on the actual interests of their children, the more this is likely to be true.[67] And in determining public policy we should choose policies which give us the best possible chance to fulfil our obligations,[68] so that we have every reason to care about school efficiency in the sense deployed by Bowles and Gintis if we care about it in the more fundamental way suggested by egalitarian liberalism.[69] The standard hostility on the left to educational voucher schemes in general is misplaced. Vouchers are not *in principle* incompatible with basic left-wing goals for education. We should acknowledge this. But we should, at the same time, recognize the immense difficulties in designing a voucher system which can, in practice, realize those goals. Recognizing those difficulties might lead us to reject Bowles' and Gintis' proposal. On the other hand, it might lead us to recognize that it is similarly difficult to realize left-wing goals even in a public education system.

Notes

1. The Milwaukee Parental Choice Program, for example, involves direct payments from the State of Wisconsin to the schools involved. See John Witte et al., *First Year Report: Milwaukee Parental Choice Program* (Madison, Robert M. La Follette Institute of Public Affairs, University of Wisconsin, 1991).
2. Michael Walzer, *Spheres of Justice* (Oxford: Martin Robertson, 1983), see especially pp. 100–103 for elaboration of other blocked exchanges. For further discussions see Judith Andre, 'Blocked Exchanges: A Taxonomy', *Ethics*, 103, no. 1 (1992), pp. 29–47, and Jeremy Waldron, 'Money and Complex Equality' in David Miller and Michael Walzer (eds.), *Pluralism, Justice and Equality* (Oxford: Oxford University Press, 1995), pp. 144–70.
3. For the case of the British Conservative Party see Denis Lawton, *The Tory Mind in Education* (London: The Falmer Press, 1994).
4. For an account of these plans, see Terry M. Moe (ed.), *Private Vouchers* (Stanford: Hoover Institution Press, 1995). The figures are taken from his introduction to the volume (p. 14). See also Valerie Martinez, Kay Thomas, and Frank R. Kemerer, 'Who Chooses and Why: A Look at Five School Choice Plans', *Phi Delta Kappan*, (May 1994), pp. 678–88.
5. Other districts which have abolished attendance zones include Cambridge, MA and Montclair, NJ.
6. Section 76, quoted in Andy Stillman, 'Half a Century of Parental Choice in Britain?' in J. Mark Halstead (ed.), *Parental Choice and Education* (London: Kogan Page, 1994). A subsequent Ministry of Education 'Manual of Guidance' (1950) elaborated eight reasons parents could give when choosing an alternative school to that which they would otherwise be allocated by the LEA: denominational reasons; educational reasons; linguistic reasons; convenience of access; special facilities at a school such as the provision of midday meals for children whose parents both work all day; preference for single-sex or co-educational schools; family association with a school; and medical reasons. As may be apparent from the list, there is a greater variety of kinds of school within any given LEA than within most US school districts.
7. John F. Witte *et al. Fourth Year Report on Milwaukee Parental Choice Program* (Madison WI: Robert M. Lafollette Institute of Public Policy, 1995) details the plan.
8. This is the figure as of 1994/5, revised up from 1 per cent at the start of the program.
9. The designation 'egalitarian liberal' is a little artificial. The response is organized around the idea that there are two important criteria an educational system should meet: that it implement a principle of educational equality, and that it give proper due

to the idea that children have an interest in becoming autonomous adults. These correspond, respectively, to the designations 'egalitarian' and 'liberal'. They are often found together, and are most naturally connected, in my view, in the framework of contemporary liberalism. See John Rawls, *A Theory of Justice* (Cambridge: Harvard University Press, 1971); Ronald Dworkin, *A Matter of Principle* (Cambridge: Harvard University Press, 1985) and Stephen Darwall (ed.), *Equal Freedom* (Ann Arbor: University of Michigan Press, 1995).

10. Herbert Gintis, 'The Political Economy of School Choice', *Teachers College Record*, 96, no. 3 (1995), pp. 492–511.

11. Milton Friedman, 'The Role of Government in Education' in R.A. Solo (ed.), *Economics and the Public Interest* (New Brunswick: Rutgers University Press, 1955). My discussion will concentrate on the slightly more recent and updated exposition of the proposal in Milton Friedman, *Capitalism and Freedom* (Chicago: University of Chicago Press, 1962), chapter 6. Vouchers have received increased attention recently, both due to the political movements around them, and the publication of John Chubb and Terry M. Moe, *Politics, Markets, and America's Schools* (Washington DC: Brookings Institution, 1989). For a balanced discussion of the current state of the debate, and a contribution to it, see Jeffrey R. Henig, *Rethinking School Choice: Limits of the Market Metaphor* (Princeton: Princeton University Press, 1993). See also useful discussions in William H. Clune and John F. Witte (eds.), *Choice and Control in American Education: Volume 1* (London: The Falmer Press, 1990); Helen F. Ladd (ed.), *Holding Schools Accountable* (Washington DC: The Brookings Institution, 1996), chapters 5 and 6.

12. He appears to think that in some circumstances it is proper for the government to run some schools as long as these are subject to the same regulations as private schools, and as long as there are not significant barriers to entry into the market. See *Capitalism and Freedom*, p. 93. Herbert Gintis explains how the government can regulate markets in schooling to overcome the most commonly posed barriers to market-entry in 'The Political Economy of School Choice', *Teachers College Record*, 96, no. 3 (1995), pp. 492–511.

13. *Capitalism and Freedom*, p. 86.

14. Of course, there are public productivity benefits to the overall workforce being educated up to some threshold. Friedman seems to think that the requisite threshold could be achieved without government funding.

15. *Capitalism and Freedom*, p. 89.

16. *Capitalism and Freedom*, p. 91.

17. *Capitalism and Freedom*, p. 91.

18. *Capitalism and Freedom*, p. 96.

19. I argue in more detail for the idea that opportunities should be insulated from the level of success and choices of parents, and that there are mechanisms for doing so which are not in tension with the goods provided by the family, in 'Educational Equality and the Value of the Family' (unpublished manuscript).

20. For valuable discussions of autonomy and why it matters, see Gerald Dworkin, *The Theory and Practice of Autonomy* (Cambridge: Cambridge University Press, 1988); Joseph Raz, *The Morality of Freedom* (Oxford: Oxford University Press, 1986); Thomas Hill Jr., *Autonomy and Self-Respect* (Cambridge: Cambridge University Press, 1990).

21. Jonathan Kozol, *Savage Inequalities* (New York: Harper Perennial, 1992) documents and explains some of these inequalities.

22. Wisconsin versus Yoder, p. 406 U.S. 205 (1971)

23. Wisconsin versus Yoder, p. 209.

24. Wisconsin versus Yoder, p. 222.

25. Wisconsin versus Yoder, p. 223.

26. The Court evades this question in its decision, saying that there is no evidence that Amish do leave the Order, and that those who might are well enough equipped

with basic skills by their education to survive within mainstream society without becoming 'burdens on society because of educational shortcomings' (p. 224).

27. For an account of the Mozert case, see Stephen Bates, *Battleground* (New York: Simon and Schuster, 1993). For an excellent discussion of Mozert and other themes of this essay see Amy Gutmann, 'Civic Education and Social Diversity', *Ethics* 105, no.3 (1995), pp. 557–79. See also Steven Macedo, 'Liberal Civic Education and Religious Fundamentalism: The Case of God vs. John Rawls?', *Ethics*, 105, no.3 (1995), pp. 468–96 and 'Multiculturalism for the Religious Right? Defending Liberal Civic Education', *Journal of Philosophy of Education*, 29, no. 2 (1995), pp. 223–37.

28. Harry Brighouse, 'The Egalitarian Virtues of Educational Vouchers', *Journal of Philosophy of Education*, 28, no. 2 (1994), pp. 211–19; Tim Brighouse, *Private Schooling – What Is and What Might Be* (University of Keele, Dept. of Education, 1992); Herbert Gintis, 'The Political Economy of School Choice', *Teachers College Record*, 96, no. 3 (1995), pp. 492–511; Samuel Bowles and Herbert Gintis, 'Efficient Redistribution: New Rules for Markets, States, and Communities', *Politics and Society*, 24 (1996), pp. 307–342, and contribution to this volume. Sections 4–6 of this paper were stimulated by reading the papers by Bowles and Gintis, and also by some critical comments on my own previous paper kindly sent to me by Samuel Bowles.

See also an excellent non-technical discussion of the choice between public and private schooling in Francis Schrag, *Back To Basics* (San Francisco: Jossey-Bass, 1995), chapter 6. For an argument which appears to oppose school choice on principled grounds see John McMurtry, 'Education and the Market Model', *Journal of Philosophy of Education*, 25, no. 2 (1991), pp. 209–17. For an argument that markets in education are *inefficient* with respect to fundamental educational goals see Michael Strain, 'Autonomy, Schools and the Constitutive Role of Community: Toward a New Moral and Political Order for Education', *British Journal of Educational Studies*, 43, no.1 (1995), pp. 4–20.

29. See Christopher Jencks, *Education Vouchers: A Report on Financing Education by Payments to Parents* (Cambridge, MA: Center for the Study of Public Policy, 1970) for an earlier left-wing proposal. See also J. Coons and S. Sugerman, *Education By Choice: The Case For Family Choice* (Berkeley CA: University of California Press, 1978).

30. The Brighouse proposal, which is designed for the British context, would have effaced the distinction between private and state schools by 'privatizing' all schools while subjecting them all to overarching regulation, and requiring all schools to meet stringent requirements with respect to the composition of the student body. The proposal is not concerned with problems concerning autonomy. For Bowles and Gintis, as we shall see, lack of concern with autonomy reflects an important simplifying assumption, but for Brighouse it reflects an institutional context in which the idea that autonomy should be promoted by schools is almost uncontroversial among educators and politicians alike.

The Conservative government's experiments with vocational training vouchers appear to have diminished enthusiasm for vouchers both on the left and the right in Britain. For other thinking on the British left concerning school choice see David Miliband, *Markets, Politics and Education* (London: Institute for Public Policy Research, 1991).

31. In most districts school funding above a fixed level is affected by the number of students in the school, but that in turn currently depends on truancy rates, etc.

32. Bowles and Gintis appeal only to the value of improved national standards and anonymous testing for information provision. But, at least in the US context, improved national standards would have other important efficiency-enhancing effects, regardless of whether vouchers were adopted. Clear national standards and some amount of anonymous testing in accordance with them would have beneficial effects on information flows. But they would also yield significant benefits in the classroom. When the classroom teacher is entirely responsible for assigning the grade to her students, two possibilities adversely affect her relationships with parents and students: their fears (or

hopes) that her feelings about their overall behavior might affect her grading of them; and her fear that they will pressure her with respect to their grades. While classroom teacher grade-assigning sets up an incentive for parents and students to pressure directly for better grades (and thus wasting her time and energy), anonymous grading sets up an incentive for them to pressure for better and more teaching. Anonymous testing can thus be expected to improve classroom discipline, allowing more resources to be put into education and fewer into maintaining the preconditions for providing education.

33. During my first experience as a teaching assistant in a university in the US I was told by a student who had failed an exam that he should have got a passing grade because he had paid $1500 to take the course.

34. Michael Walzer makes this complaint in *Spheres of Justice*, (London: Martin Robertson, 1983), pp. 218–20.

35. I should add a qualification here – apparently some local education authorities in the UK do experience numbers of parents moving their children more than once during a year.

36. I shall express my doubts about the antecedent of this conditional later.

37. Tim Brighouse provides some detail of such requirements in the UK context, in *Private Schooling: What Is and What Might Be.*

38. There are of course many factors outside the school which affect the level of educational opportunity available to a child. Parental attention and neglect, the cultural resources within the home, how similar the interests and abilities of parents to those of their children all affect how many opportunities the child has, and none of these factors correlates perfectly with levels of income and wealth. Without removing children from the home, the schools cannot be expected to compensate for these factors, though they can provide limited insulation.

39. For an argument that the very idea of equal educational opportunity is nonsensical see John Wilson, 'Does Equality (of Opportunity) Make Sense In Education', *Journal of Philosophy of Education*, 24, no. 1 (1991), pp. 27–31. For (convincing) objections to his arguments see my 'In Defence of Educational Equality', *Journal of Philosophy of Education*, 29, no. 3 (1995), pp. 413–18.

40. It might be objected that what we should care about is a more general ideal of equality of opportunity which does not imply the specific ideal of equality of educational opportunity. I think that it is true that equality of opportunity is the more fundamental principle, and it may be correct that it does not strictly imply equality of educational opportunity. But because education is so crucial a good for the pursuit of other opportunities, I suspect that in practice at least social policies founded on a more general ideal of equality of opportunity should aim at equality of educational opportunity.

41. Kenneth R. Howe, 'In Defense of Outcome-Based Conceptions of Equal Educational Opportunity', *Educational Theory*, 39, no. 4 (1989), pp. 317–36; 'Equal Opportunity is Equal Education', *Educational Theory*, 40, no. 2 (1990), pp. 227–30; 'Equality of Educational Opportunity and the Criterion of Equal Educational Worth', *Studies in Philosophy and Education*, 11, no. 3 (1993), pp. 329–37. See also Nicholas C. Burbules, 'Equal Opportunity or Equal Education?', *Educational Theory*, 40, no. 2 (1990), pp. 221–26, and the interesting discussion in Christopher Jencks, 'Whom Must We Treat Equally for Educational Opportunity to Be Equal?', *Ethics*, 98, no. 4 (1988), pp. 518–33. On the subject of equal educational opportunity, see also Onora O'Neill, 'Opportunities, Equalities and Education', *Theory and Decision*, 7, no. 4 (1976), pp. 275–95.

42. John Rawls, *A Theory of Justice* (Cambridge: Harvard University Press 1971), p. 73.

43. It is worth noting that many teachers of young children say that they find children who are used to being given attention far more demanding of their time and energy (which are educational resources) than children who are used to being given less attention.

44. I should say that I do not think that Rawls' fair equality of opportunity proviso is vulnerable to the parallel of this objection, given the role it plays in his theory.

45. There is a separate question about the needs of children being different. Boys get far more attention in the co-educational classroom than girls do, and naughty boys get the most attention of all. Despite (or because of) the informal and formal constraints on teachers being able to discipline students informally in the classroom, discipline implementation in the form of security guards and assistant principals, exhausts enormous amounts of resources in contemporary public schools, which resources are being devoted mostly to a very few students. Is this lavishing of resources on very few students unfair? I am not sure – the point here is that it is liable to appear as an inequality of resources which will be unjustifiable to parents whose vouchers are 'worth' more than the resources being devoted to the education of their children.

46. Elizabeth Anderson, *Value in Ethics and Economics* (Cambridge: Harvard University Press, 1994), p. 163.

47. Charles Fried, *Right and Wrong* (Cambridge: Harvard University Press, 1978), p. 152. Fried was US Solicitor-General during the Reagan Presidency.

48. Fried, p. 153.

49. Loren Lomasky, *Persons, Right, and the Moral Community* (Oxford: Oxford University Press, 1987), pp. 166–7.

50 Lomasky, p. 167.

51 For an interesting discussion of obligations toward children see Onora O'Neill, *Constructions of Reason: Explorations of Kant's Practical Philosophy* (Cambridge: Cambridge University Press, 1989), chapter 10.

52. For representative formulations of this principle see Ronald Dworkin, *A Matter of Principle* (Cambridge: Harvard University Press, 1985), chapter 8, and Charles Larmore, *Patterns of Moral Complexity* (Cambridge: Cambridge University Press, 1987), chapter 3.

53. I explore the consequences of accepting a neutrality constraint on the justification of public policy in some areas of policy in 'Neutrality, Publicity, and State Funding of the Arts', *Philosophy and Public Affairs*, 24, no. 1 (1995), pp. 35–63.

54. William Galston, *Liberal Purposes* (Cambridge: Cambridge University Press 1992), p. 253.

55. Galston, *Liberal Purposes*, p. 253. Gutmann does say quite explicitly that 'a good life must be one that people live from the inside, by accepting and identifying it as their own'. 'Democracy and Democratic Education', *Studies in Philosophy and Education*, 12, no. 1 (1993), pp. 1–9. It is not clear to me that she ever goes as far as to say that the unexamined life is unworthy.

56. Galston, *Liberal Purposes*, p. 254.

57. William Galston, 'Two Concepts of Liberalism', *Ethics*, 105, no. 3 (1995), pp. 516–34.

58. Joseph Raz, *The Morality of Freedom* (Oxford: Oxford University Press, 1986), pp. 369–70.

59. See the valuable discussion in Joseph Raz, *The Morality of Freedom*, pp. 370–78.

60. Some people have *personalities* which are ill-suited to the use of rational reflection on their ways of life. Take personalities that have high levels of anxiety associated with situations of ambiguity. They might be better off living their lives in (relatively benign) traditionalist unreflective communities, and it might be that the process of learning how to be autonomous would be extremely damaging to their psyches. My surmise that such personalities would be less common in a society in which schools facilitated autonomy would be little comfort to those who remained. This is why the argument supports only strong presumption in favor of the form of education. The question is what counts as the proper bases for exemption. The important claim here is that the provision of autonomy-facilitating education should be independent of parental preference. Since there is no reason to think that such personalities naturally occur disproportionately in families with strong religious

commitments, the religious commitments of parents, and their desire to have their children exempted on those grounds, are not connected to the existence of anxious personalities. Exemptions should be sorted not by appeal to parental preference, but by the professional and trained discretion of teachers working in consultation with parents of identified children. I'm grateful to Erik Wright for raising this question.

61. Galston, 'Two Concepts of Liberalism', p. 525.

62. For discussion of the relationship between wrongs toward groups and toward individuals see Will Kymlicka, *Multicultural Citizenship* (Oxford: Oxford University Press, 1995) and *Liberalism, Community, and Culture* (Oxford: Oxford University Press, 1989) chapters 7–11.

63. This advantage plays a crucial role in Bowles' and Gintis' case for vouchers, though a less crucial role in Gintis' more extensive defense of school choice.

64. I'm grateful to Erik Wright for pointing out this difficulty.

65. See Ronald Dworkin, 'What is Equality? Part 4: Political Equality', *University of San Francisco Law Review*, 22, no. 1 (1987), pp. 1–30.

66. A standard argument for direct democratic governance of schools is the speculation that democratic participation enhances autonomy. While it doesn't seem unreasonable to think that participation enhances autonomy there are two problems with this as an argument for democratic school governance. First, democratic governance does not guarantee participation – and typically participation in school board elections, let alone lobbying and policy-formation, is very low indeed. Second, while it seems reasonable to think that participation does generally enhance the autonomy of *participants*, they are not the people whose autonomy matters with respect to determining how schools should be governed.

The autonomy-enhancement we should care about with respect to schooling is that of the students, who are not likely to be significant participants in the democratic process of governance (and in my view shouldn't be). There is no particular reason to think that democratic participation leads people to make decisions which enhance the autonomy of *others*.

67. Notice that even the religious sectarians usually care a great deal about some of their children's real interests: they often want them to read, write, be numerate, etc.

68. Subject to some unformulable constraint concerning the dynamic effects of the policy toward full justice. I discuss the relationship between medium-term reforms toward justice and the long-term goal of justice in 'Transitional and Utopian Market Socialism', *Politics and Society*, 22, no. 4 (1994), pp. 569–84.

69. It could be that this last obligation – that we should choose policies that give us the best possible chance to deliver on our obligations – suggests that progressives should be willing to compromise autonomy in the name of equality. If vouchers offer the best chance of delivering equal educational opportunity, and neither vouchers nor other forms of delivery offer much prospect of guaranteeing autonomy-facilitating education, perhaps the left should drop the autonomy demand, and make common cause with religious sectarians on the condition that the sectarians compromise on a 'no top-up' equality constraint. It will be plain from my discussion that I do not find this prospect attractive.

8

Conflict and Cooperation:
An Empirical Glimpse of
the Imperatives of Efficiency
and Redistribution
David M. Gordon

Bowles and Gintis provide an important argument for a set of redistributive policies which would both promote equality and enhance economic efficiency. I support their objectives and much of their analysis. In particular, I agree that concern for productivity deserves paramount priority – especially among egalitarians; that market-based policies pursuing both egalitarian objectives and productivity-enhancement have greater promise than public interventions 'over-riding' market outcomes; and that there exists a set of specific market-based policies which could simultaneously reduce inequality and boost economic efficiency.

In this comment I further examine the relationship between equality and efficiency by exploring concrete experiences with different kinds of labor-management systems. Bowles and Gintis provide little empirical support for their claims. As reviewed in the first section below, empirical evidence does seem to provide strong support for at least two strands of Bowles' and Gintis' argument: relatively more inegalitarian production systems indeed appear to involve heavy costs of supervision, and economies featuring such systems appear to suffer considerable economic disadvantages compared to those featuring relatively more cooperative systems.

But is *inequality* the principal disadvantage shackling these less effective production systems? And would egalitarian asset redistributions provide the principal solution to their problems? In the second section of this comment, building on the empirical evidence reviewed here, I ask whether we should focus so persistently on *equality* as an intrinsic socio-economic objective and whether other complementary and more concrete objectives – such as productivity-sharing wage bonuses, employment security, and workers' councils – do not deserve equivalent or even higher priority than the more general egalitarian objectives Bowles and Gintis explore.

The Costs of Conflictual Labor Relations

Bowles and Gintis advance a number of arguments supporting their contention that 'inequality impedes economic performance by obstructing the evolution of productivity-enhancing governance structures.'

One is that 'institutional structures supporting high levels of inequality are often costly to maintain.' In particular, private corporations face 'costs in enforcing inequality, in such forms as high levels of expenditure on work supervision and security personnel.' Even more specifically, 'the profit-maximizing labor discipline system adopted by the capitalist firm is typically inefficient in that it uses too many monitoring resources and not enough wage incentives.' A second reason is that 'more equal societies may be capable of supporting levels of cooperation and trust unavailable in more economically divided societies. Yet both cooperation and trust are essential to economic performance, particularly where information relevant to exchanges is incomplete and unequally distributed in the population.'

While many of us participating in these discussions tend to take such arguments for granted, there has been surprisingly little empirical evidence which *directly* supports these kinds of claims. For example, we repeatedly cite literature appearing to demonstrate that enterprises with relatively greater worker participation and control also feature relatively higher labor productivity.[1] However, if the additional *costs* of providing stronger wage incentives in more egalitarian settings exceed the incremental *benefits* of higher productivity, efficiency gains may not rebound. (Blinder (1990) stresses this point.) Unless, of course there were the kinds of savings from reduced monitoring costs which Bowles and Gintis anticipate.

But the available empirical literature is surprisingly mute on this question of monitoring and supervision. In my far from exhaustive search, I have found *no* systematic documentation that the intensity or costs of supervision are relatively lower in work settings featuring greater worker participation or control; given the critical importance of this dimension of the argument in favor of relatively more democratic modes of work organization, remarkably little empirical attention appears to have been paid to the impact of alternative governance structures on the scope and intensity of supervision and monitoring. Nor have I seen any kind of coherent empirical evidence supporting the proposition that 'the profit-maximizing labor discipline system adopted by the capitalist firm typically . . . uses too many monitoring resources and not enough wage incentives.' 'Too many' monitoring resources with respect to what kinds of benchmark standards? 'Not enough' wage incentives compared to what?

Bowles' and Gintis' additional claim that 'more equal societies may be capable of supporting levels of cooperation and trust unavailable in more economically divided societies', while inherently plausible, is also intrinsically difficult to test empirically. How do we properly define, much less measure 'cooperation' and 'trust'? Once again, I am not aware of compelling empirical evidence supporting this kind of claim.

Conflict and Cooperation across the Advanced Countries

Because many of the propositions in the literature on which Bowles and Gintis draw are based on microeconomic reasoning, most of the evidence exploring the productivity-effects of alternative governance structures is also based on individual case studies or micro surveys of individual enterprises. Even if such surveys paid more attention to the phenomena of monitoring and supervision than is evident, there would none the less be limits to the usefulness of that kind of evidence of variations across firms *within a single country*. As Bowles and Gintis emphasize, state policies and credit markets play a central role in shaping the alternatives facing individual enterprises. Within a single country, even within a single industry, firms with different governance structures will face essentially the same institutional environments and, therefore, the range of structural opportunities confronting them will be to some degree constrained.

I have therefore been drawn, despite the difficulties, to the possibility of adducing useful evidence on these questions from international comparisons across the advanced countries. State policies and financial structures – as well as a number of other crucial components of the institutional environment facing the firm – differ widely among the leading capitalist economies, allowing for considerable variation in the environments shaping the structure of labor-management systems. And, we think, the character of labor relations themselves differs sharply as well. Can we learn anything useful about the 'inefficiencies' of the 'labor-discipline system adopted by the capitalist firm' from cross-country comparisons? Almost all firms within the advanced economies share certain common features of capitalist organization, of course, but we may none the less find that modes of governance vary widely enough to permit generalizations about the costs and benefits of one or another approach to labor relations and the organization of production.

Pursuing such international comparisons seems to point toward four principal empirical conclusions of direct relevance for Bowles' and Gintis' claims.[2]

1 It is probably most useful to array labor-management systems among the advanced countries along a spectrum ranging from the 'conflictual' to the 'cooperative.'[3] More conflictual systems tend to feature relatively little employment security, reliance on the threat of job dismissal as a goad to workers, minimal wage incentives, and sometimes weak unions. More cooperative systems tend to feature a fair degree of employment security, positive wage incentives, often with substantial employee involvement and strong unions. As is commonly recognized, Germany, Sweden and Japan provide examples of the latter kind of approach – even though among their labor-management systems there are also important differences.[4] And, as many have pointed out in recent years, the United States tends more and more to represent the archetype of the former system, also exemplified by Canada and the United Kingdom.

A couple of formal quantitative studies provide evidence supporting the importance of this dimension of variation among labor-management systems. Using factor analysis in a study of the G–7 economies, Buchele and Christiansen (1992) derive an 'index of cooperation' from a variety of indicators of labor relations, especially including measures of workers' rights and job security. By this measure, the US, the UK, and Canada, in that order, feature the relatively least 'cooperative' systems of labor-management. Also making use of factor analysis for a broader range of countries and a wider number of variables, my own study (Gordon, 1994) derives two complementary indices of labor relations appearing to highlight two different dimensions of the conflictual-cooperative dimension. Summing the two provides a composite index of 'cooperation'. By this measure, Sweden features the most 'cooperative' labor relations while the US ranks at the opposite end of the scale.

2 There appears to be considerable variation in the intensity of supervision across the advanced countries. The difficulties of international comparison of managerial and supervisory structures are legion. Nonetheless, I believe that we can draw some reasonably robust conclusions about the rank ordering of countries along this dimension as well.

In the United States in 1993, where quite detailed occupational data are available, there were 16.6 million private non-farm employees who worked as wage-and-salary employees in various occupations labeled as either 'managers' or 'supervisors' – roughly three fifths as managers and two fifths as supervisors.[5] This comprised roughly 19 per cent of total private non-farm employment. How does this compare with other advanced countries?

Although individual countries' definitions of occupational categories vary substantially, the International Labor Organization (ILO) has devoted considerable effort to fitting the respective nations' census data into standardized occupational definitions across countries.[6] Overlaying the ILO figures with US data, we find that the category 'administrative and managerial' occupations in the ILO data corresponds precisely to the category of 'executive, administrative, and managerial' occupations in the Bureau of Labor Statistics (BLS) household surveys – or 'managers' for short.[7] The ILO data therefore allow us to compare the relative proportions of managers across countries but not the relative numbers of other employees in job slots called 'supervisors'.

Because the employment share of overhead workers is highly sensitive to the business cycle, I have chosen data for 1989, the most recent year in which most of the advanced economies were more or less at their business cycle peaks. Figure 1 compares the percentage of 'administrative and managerial' employees in total non-farm employment for nine of the leading advanced economies; data for 1989 are not available for France, Italy, and the UK.

The data in the figure suggest at least a couple of obvious conclusions:

• The bureaucratic burdens in the United States and Canada were substantially the highest among the nine countries represented here. Data available for the UK for other years suggest that it has roughly equivalent proportions of managerial employment. This provides a first strong hint that among the developed countries top-heavy corporate bureaucracies are associated with adversarial labor relations.

• Following that lead further, we can look at the managerial

Figure 1:   Comparing the Bureaucratic Burden

Managerial & administrative employees as percentage of non-farm employment, 1989

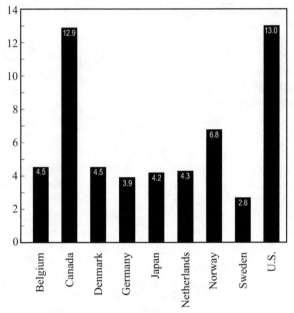

Source: ILO, *Yearbook of Labor Statistics*, 1994.

proportions for the three other economies that I have already cited as exemplifying more 'cooperative' approaches to corporate organization and labor management – Germany, Japan, and Sweden. In 1989 the relative size of the US bureaucratic burden had reached more than three times the levels in Japan and Germany and more than four times the percentage in Sweden.

Some who have seen these comparisons have wondered whether at least some of the huge gap in managerial proportions might be due to differences in the industry make-up of the various economies.

For example, if private corporations manage health insurance in the United States and the government oversees it in countries such as Sweden and the Netherlands, won't all those managers get counted in the United States but not for the others? This might be a consideration if we were looking at data just for the *private* sector. But in fact the ILO data represented in figure 1 cover the *total* non-farm economy, including the government; a separate breakdown for just the private non-farm sector is not available. So those health insurance managers are included in these figures regardless of whether they're employed by corporations or the government.

Or, if the United States and the UK have 'de-industrialized' more than other economies, shedding manufacturing jobs like flies and shifting employment into sectors such as finance where the managerial proportions may be higher, might this account for the heavier US burden? But this appears not to be a major factor affecting the comparisons either. For a few of the economies represented in the graph we can compare the percentage of managerial employees for specific industries. And the large differences reflected in the graph persist for individual sectors as well. In 1993, for example, 11.6 per cent of *manufacturing* employment worked in administrative and managerial occupations in the United States and only 4.1 per cent in Japan.[8] This almost exactly replicates the figures for the two countries for the non-farm economy as a whole.

What would these comparisons look like if we could include a broader category of employees with supervisory responsibilities who are not counted or coded as managers?

We have one important body of data that can help us examine the intensity of supervision more inclusively. Thanks to Erik Wright's pioneering efforts, we can glimpse the actual extent of supervision by employees *regardless of* their primary occupational categorization.

In order to establish benchmarks, we should look first at the US. In nationally representative surveys replicated in the United States in both 1980 and 1991, respondents were asked directly about their positions and roles in their jobs. Several different questions were aimed at highlighting occupational responsibilities from a number of different angles. Referring to their present or most recent jobs, participants were asked whether or not they were engaged in supervising others, whether or not their position was considered to be managerial or supervisory, and what kinds of authority they exercised over others. We can compare impressions from these data – afforded by what I shall be labeling for short as the Class Structure Surveys – with estimates from standard official government sources. The more recent data from the 1991 survey are the most relevant for this discussion.[9]

• In 1991, according to government establishment surveys for the US, 19.1 per cent of private non-farm employees worked in non-production or supervisory jobs. But in the 1991 Class Structure Survey, almost exactly double this proportion – fully 38.9 per cent of all private non-farm workers – reported that they 'supervise the work of other employees or tell other employees what work to do'.

● In the 1991 Current Population Survey (CPS) of households, 18.7 per cent of private non-farm workers were categorized as in either managerial or supervisory occupations. But in the 1991 Class Structure Survey, 36.3 per cent report that their position within their business or organization was 'managerial' or 'supervisory'. Of these 36 per cent, roughly half worked in 'supervisory' jobs and the other half at various levels of the 'managerial' hierarchy.

● One of the main tests of how many 'bosses' are sprinkled through the occupational category is how many employees can discipline or even fire another employee. In the 1991 Class Structure Survey, 27.7 per cent of private non-farm employees reported that they had the authority directly to 'discipline a subordinate because of poor work or misconduct'.

Why are these estimates of managerial and supervisory employment so much higher than the estimates we derive from official government sources? The Class Structure Surveys were carefully structured and weighted so that they were effectively representative of the characteristics of the population revealed in other official government surveys.[10] Consequently the differences do not appear to flow from biases in the construction of the actual surveys.

One possibility, of course, is that when asked direct questions about their role in the job, people might tend to exaggerate their importance and attribute greater authority to their own positions than they actually have. This source of bias is probably relatively minor in the Class Structure Survey, however, because estimates of managerial and supervisory responsibilities based on very different kinds of questions within the survey fall within a fairly narrow range – and are all considerably higher than the estimates from official government sources. And this problem would also presumably confound standard 'official' occupational estimates taken from the household surveys provided by the CPS.

More important as an explanation of the discrepancy between the two kinds of information, apparently, is precisely that many people besides those working in jobs officially categorized as 'managers' and 'supervisors' *also* have substantial supervisory responsibilities. Table 1 compiles the percentage of private non-farm employees in different occupational categories in the 1991 US Class Structure Survey – as those categories are conventionally defined in standard government censuses – who report that their present (or most recent) job is best described as a 'managerial or supervisory position'. As the table shows, substantial numbers of workers outside the explicit occupa-

Table 1:   Supervisory Responsibilities across the Occupations, 1991

Per cent in various private non-farm occupations with 'managerial' or 'supervisory' responsibilities

Managers	79.6%
Technicians or supervisors	59.0
Professionals	29.1
Clerical or sales workers	16.4
Skilled workers	12.0
Semiskilled workers	8.1
Unskilled workers	2.2
All employees	35.5

Sources and Notes: Author's own calculations from the Class Structure Survey for the United States, 1991. Sample is for all non-government employees not in farm occupations.

tional categories of managers and supervisors also have such responsibilities within their firms' hierarchies. Someone trained as a lawyer who is running a corporate division, for example, may get tabulated in the government surveys as a 'professional' but would be captured in the Class Structure Survey as someone who also exercises managerial responsibility.

With this benchmarking as background, we can now turn to international comparisons. For at least a few of the countries represented in figure 1, we can rely on Wright's Comparative Project on Class Structure and Class Consciousness for commensurable surveys on managerial and supervisory responsibilities. The Class Structure Survey permits a comparison of actual employee responsibilities for the US, Canada, Norway and Sweden among the nine countries included in figure 1.[11] Among these four countries, the rank order is exactly the same as with the ILO data: the United States once again features the highest percentage of employees identified as having 'managerial' or 'supervisory' responsibilities while Sweden exhibits the lowest; Canada ranks second and Norway third. In the United States, nearly 35 per cent of all employees worked in 'managerial' or 'supervisory' positions. In Sweden, according to the same definitions from the same survey instrument, only 22.5 per cent worked in such jobs.[12]

Given that these estimates are uniformly higher in the Class Structure Survey than in the ILO data – since the former encompasses everyone with managerial and supervisory responsibilities, not just those called 'managers' – the gap between the US and Sweden is roughly comparable in the two sources. In the ILO data the percentage difference of 'administrative and managerial' employees is slightly more than ten percentage points, while in the Class Structure Survey the interval between their shares of workers with 'managerial' or 'supervisory' responsibilities is roughly twelve percentage points.

3 One can apparently draw a further conclusion with a reasonable degree of confidence. As I have already suggested in my comments on the percentages of administrative and managerial employees presented in figure 1, there appears to be a fairly close association across countries between the intensity of supervision and the relatively cooperative or conflictual character of labor-relations systems.

The first indication comes from a simple bivariate comparison. I use as a measure of the intensity of supervision the percentage of administrative and managerial employment from the ILO data as presented in figure 1. I take as an Index of Cooperation, measuring the relatively conflictual or cooperative character of a country's labor relations, the sum of the factor scores on the two multivariate indices of cooperation presented in Gordon (1994). Figure 2 graphs these two measures for twelve advanced countries for which comparable data on these and several other measures used below are available. I have labeled on the graph the points for three cooperative archetypes – Germany, Japan and Sweden – and three conflictual representatives – the US, Canada, and the UK.

The bottom axis of the figure displays the Cooperation Index, ranging from -3.18 for the US to $+1.85$ for Sweden. The vertical axis measures the Bureaucratic Burden, the percentage of administrative and managerial workers in total non-farm employment, for 1980. (I use 1980 here because the data on which the Cooperation Index is based also come from around the early 1980s.) As the plots seem to indicate, the *more* cooperative the labor-management system, the *lighter* is the bureaucratic burden. The simple correlation coefficient between the two measures is -0.72, significant at 1 per cent.

Multivariate analysis appears to confirm the robustness of this association. In Gordon (1994) I examine the connection between labor-relations and the intensity of supervision across sixteen advanced countries.[13] For reasons of data availability, I study the period at the beginning of the 1980s. No matter what other factors are considered, the two composite factor indices appearing to capture the relatively cooperative character of labor relations retain a strong influence on cross-country differences in the percentage of employment in managerial and administrative employment: the more coop-

Figure 2:   More Cooperation, Fewer Bosses?

Per cent administrative-managerial employment & cooperation index

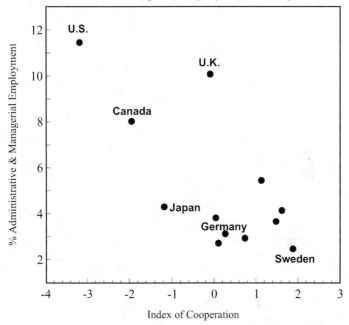

Sources: See text and notes.

erative a country's labor-management system, the fewer bosses it appears to require. In addition, the cost of job loss also has a strong positive influence on the bureaucratic burden across countries: the greater the potential costs to workers of losing their jobs, at least at the margin, the more pay-off there appears to be to a top-down supervisory approach to labor management.

Other potentially important influences do not seem to make much difference. One might have thought, for example, that another source of relatively large managerial bureaucracies in the United States would have been the vast global empires controlled by multinational corporations based in the United States – requiring huge staffing of headquarters at home. But there is no evidence that the size of a country's economy or its relative involvement in global trade have any effects on its bureaucratic burden – once the effects of labor relations have been taken into account.[14]

One final result in this more detailed study deserves mention. In terms of one's ability to explain variations across countries in at least this one measure of the intensity of supervision, two alternative explanatory models seem equally plausible – as the visual evidence in figure 2 also suggests. On the one hand, one could view the extent of cooperation in countries' labor relations as varying *continuously* along the range specified by my measures of cooperation. This approach pays attention to the simple correlation coefficient between the two indices in figure 2 and the significance of the regression coefficient on these indices of cooperation in a multivariate regression seeking to explain variations in the percentage of managerial and administrative employees. On the other hand, one could view countries as falling into either of two *categorically (and discontinuously) distinct groups* – a group with relatively more cooperative systems of labor management and another group with relatively more conflictual relations. This approach pays attention to the tight clustering in figure 1 of six of the nine countries in the lower right corner of the graph, with the distance between them and the more conflictual grouping in the upper left corner; it also suggests a multivariate model which represents labor-relations systems in the multivariate analysis by dummy variables for categorical grouping rather than by continuous scores on the cooperation indices.

In the multivariate regression analysis, the categorical approach achieves as high an explanatory power as the continuous approach, suggesting that differences between the groups of countries are at least as important as variations within the groupings, leaving us no strong empirical grounds for choosing between the two interpretive approaches. Methodologically, I tend to lean toward the categorical approach since I think that the structural influence of the logic of different approaches to labor relations is likely to push countries toward one or another kind of structure and to militate against wide variations around those basic structural options

4 One also appears to find evidence of the trade-off between supervision and wage incentives which Bowles and Gintis presuppose – in their own words, that the undemocratic firm 'uses too many monitoring resources and not enough wage incentives'.

The best comparative data on wages come from US BLS studies of wage trends across twelve of the leading advanced economies – including the G-7 powers as well as five other smaller European countries (Belgium, Denmark, Norway, the Netherlands, and Sweden). Their data provides comparable information on trends in real hourly compensation for all manufacturing employees, with

Figure 3:   Corporate Bureaucracies and Real Wage Growth

Per cent managerial & administrative employment, 1980
Per cent change, production-worker real wage, manufacturing,
1973–89

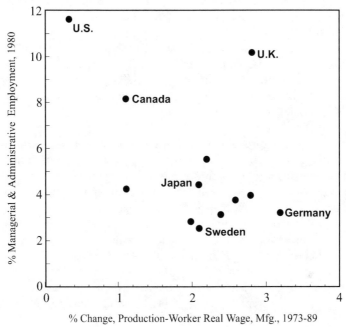

% Change, Production-Worker Real Wage, Mfg., 1973-89

Sources: See text and notes.

compensation deflated by the consumer price index for each country, which provides insight into trends directly affecting workers' living standards.[15]

For reasons I shall discuss below, I think it is more useful to look at *rates of change* of wages rather than *levels* when considering the effectiveness of wage incentives. Figure 3 arrays the rate of change of real manufacturing compensation for these twelve countries against the percentage of administrative and managerial employment.

The horizontal axis presents the average annual real wage change for workers in manufacturing between 1973 and 1989. (A more limited analysis of real wage change for the narrower interval between 1979 and 1989 yields a similar picture.) The vertical axis represents the percentage of total non-farm employment working in administrative and managerial occupations in 1980. (1980 is used here, rather than 1989 as in figure 1, in order to provide a measure for the level of managerial burden that lies *in the middle* of the time period being examined.) As in figure 2, I have labeled the six countries that many take as representatives of the conflictual and cooperative approaches respectively.

Except for the single striking case of the UK, there is a fairly strong negative association, as hypothesized, between the bureaucratic burden and real wage growth. As anticipated, the US stands out for its swollen bureaucratic burden *and* for its virtually flat real wage growth. If the UK is removed momentarily on the grounds that it seems to be such an outlier, the simple correlation coefficient between the two variables is −0.78 (statistically significant at 1 per cent). With the UK included, the simple correlation is −0.50 − still statistically significant at 1 per cent.

Again as with figure 2, however, it may make more sense to think of the countries as falling into two groupings. One group, including Germany, Japan, and Sweden and six other countries, cluster in the lower right corner of the graph. (The one country in this group with relatively slower real wage growth is Denmark; many labor economists view Denmark's system of labor management as one among several examples of a kind of hybrid case, with a relatively unsuccessful mix of cooperative and conflictual features that result in relatively higher inflation and unemployment than in most of the more cooperative countries.) The US and Canada, two of the three more adversarial economies represented here, lie in the upper left. Only the UK departs substantially from this pattern.

In short, I think that reasonable empirical support can be found for some of the conclusions which Bowles and Gintis propound. In international comparisons, relatively more conflictual systems of labor relations do appear to feature higher intensities of supervision and more moderated wage incentives.

I can offer no such direct empirical support for the second principal Bowles and Gintis claim, that 'more equal societies may be capable of supporting levels of cooperation and trust unavailable in more economically divided societies' − though I have no reason to doubt the claim either. Following fairly standard practice, I have used the term 'cooperative' to refer to the group of countries which appear to feature less conflictual labor relations. In fact, however, I am unaware of any direct evidence which in any formal or rigorous way measures the actual extent of 'cooperation' and 'trust' among workers in these different kinds of work settings. Lacking such formal quantitative evidence, we are forced to rely on qualitative assessments. And here, most experienced observers of comparative labor relations seem confident that one of the sources of the coherence of the 'cooperative' model is indeed that workers take substantial responsibility for relying on each other and effectively cooperating in their roles in production. David Soskice[16] emphasizes, for example, the mutual understanding upon which this cooperative system rests: 'The basic form of this agreement is that the unions underwrite the flexibility of the system . . . and that in return they are given a position within the system that enables them to ensure that that flexibility is not abused.' Only with and because of that understanding can the corporations' need for hierarchical authority be relaxed. In these kinds of systems, Soskice continues, unions 'act as a guarantor of work-force cooperation. . . . The national unions are able to act in this way in part because, in the last resort, they can exert sanctions on workgroups and union officials at company level. . . . [T]here is a complex balancing act which produces work-force cooperation and cooperative management worker relations.'

The Costs of Conflictual Relations

Are economies that feature relatively more conflictual labor relations also relatively less 'efficient' – whatever that might mean for cross-country comparisons? Many of us active in this literature tend to assume so, of course, but the evidence needs to be handled with care.

One problem is that international comparisons have tended to focus on a few limited measures of macro-performance such as inflation and unemployment. Another problem is that there may be a non-linear relationship between labor-relations systems and economic performance, with relatively conflictual and relatively cooperative economies both tending to outperform those with more hybrid features.[17]

My own approach to a simple assessment of comparative macro-performance has been to screen out the mixed, relatively more hybrid cases and to compare relatively more polar cases – to compare groups of countries which could with reasonable confidence be classified as featuring either 'conflictual' or 'cooperative' labor-relations systems. A number of different observers have provided us with classification or ranking schemes for dividing countries into these two categories, not all of which perfectly agree.[18] Among the twelve countries represented in figure 3, for which we otherwise have the fullest set of comparable data available, it seems reasonable, at least for the purposes of preliminary analysis, to propose Japan, Germany, the

Table 2:   Cooperative and Conflictual Economies

Average Annual Rates (by percentage), 1973–1989

	Cooperative	Conflictual
productivity growth, business sector	1.9	1.1
productivity growth, manufacturing	3.4	2.2
investment share of GDP	14.2	10.8
% change, capital-labor ratio	3.3	2.2
inflation rate, GDP deflator	5.8	8.0
unemployment rate	3.7	7.6

Note: 'Cooperative' Economies are Germany, Japan, Norway, and Sweden;
'Conflictual' Economies are US, UK, & Canada.
Group averages are unweighted arithmetic averages of country period averages.

Sources: Productivity growth for manufacturing from US Bureau of Labor Statistics, (1995),
table 1. All other indices from OECD, (1995), historical tables.

Netherlands, Norway, and Sweden as representatives of the cooperative approach and the US, the UK, and Canada for the conflictual
model. (This treats France, Italy, Belgium and Denmark as intermedi-
ate cases, economies displaying mixed features.)

Table 2 compiles a number of indicators of macro-performance for
these groups of cooperative and conflictual economies. I look at group
averages for the period covering the last two completed business
cycles, from 1973 to 1989. (I briefly consider below whether more
recent evidence would alter any of the impressions derived from this
longer period.)

The first two lines are probably the most important in assessing the
claims of relative 'efficiency'. It does indeed appear that productivity
growth has been substantially more rapid, on average, in the cooperative economies than in the conflictual economies over the medium
term, whether we look at the business sector or more narrowly at
manufacturing.

This advantage on the productivity growth front may have little to
do with the character of labor relations, of course, and may be caused
by other factors, particularly the pace of investment. There are indeed
differences in the rate of increase in capital per worker across these
countries, to which we shall return in a moment. But even after
allowing for these differences, we still find that the impact of labor
relations remains strong.

In their recent study, for example, Buchele and Christiansen study
differences in productivity growth rates among the G-7 economies
over the period from the early 1960s through to the late 1980s. They

allow for the effect of the rate of increase in the capital-labor ratio, which of course had a positive influence on productivity growth rates. Having taken capital intensity into account, they examine the effect of their own measure of the cooperative character of the countries' labor-management systems, which they derive from a factor analysis of a number of different dimensions of those systems. They find that the degree of cooperation in an economy, all things being equal, has a positive (and statistically significant) impact on productivity growth. They conclude that 'cooperation fosters productivity growth . . .'[19]

Table 2 also provides two alternative measures of comparative investment performance – the first looking at the share of gross domestic product devoted to gross fixed non-residential investment and the second at the average annual rate of change of the capital-labor ratio in the business sector. By both measures, the cooperative economies also appear to enjoy considerable advantages.

Do these differences in investment performance have anything to do with labor relations? One key to steady, stable and healthy investment performance over time, at least when viewed from a structuralist macroeconomic perspective, is that productivity growth needs to be at least as rapid as wage growth, ensuring that the profit share does not get squeezed over time. Looking at the period between 1973 and 1989 represented in table 2, we can compare the difference between the productivity growth rate and the rate of change of real wages between our groups of relatively conflictual and cooperative economies.[20] If this difference is positive, profits have been protected from excessive wage growth. If the difference is negative, wages have been squeezing into the firm's surplus that which might otherwise be available for investment. Over this period, the five cooperative economies enjoyed a decent positive productivity dividend: the rate of productivity growth was 0.4 percentage points higher than the rate of real wage growth. The three conflictual economies fares less well: over those same sixteen years, real wage growth actually exceeded productivity growth, resulting in a net deficit of −0.3 percentage points.

Traveling the 'high road', in short, the more cooperative economies are able to achieve sufficiently higher rates of productivity growth to afford and more than cover their relatively more rapid rates of real wage growth, managing the balance between productivity and wages in such a way that corporate profits are protected to help finance investment.

The final rows in table 2 provide the more familiar comparisons for inflation and unemployment. There are no surprises here. By both measures, the cooperative economies enjoyed much less stagflationary pressure in their labor markets than did the conflictual economies.

Have these advantages been sustained into the 1990s? Many have the impression that the 'social democratic' countries have more recently been paying a high price in unemployment for their relatively more rapid wage growth over the medium term and that, since the mid-1980s, unemployment rates in Europe have soared to levels dramatically higher than those in the 'jobs-miracle' United States.

These impressions are based on a casual empiricism which is misleading for our purposes here. Conflictual England is as much a part of Europe as cooperative Sweden or Germany. For our purposes of discussion, treating all European economies as if they're the same is like comparing apples and broccoli.

The concern about high unemployment in Europe therefore requires posing a much more specific question in this context: Table 2 reports that average unemployment rates over the 1973–89 period were substantially lower in the five representative cooperative economies than in the three conflictual archetypes. Does this comparison look substantially different for shorter, more recent intervals? What about the 1980s? What about the 1990s? Prevailing perceptions might lead us to expect that the cooperative economies' advantages on the unemployment front would erode or even disappear the closer we moved to the present.

This is not the case. Whatever combination of years are examined over the recent past, average unemployment rates in the five cooperative economies remain substantially lower than in their adversarial counterparts.[21] During the 1980s, unemployment rates averaged 4.7 per cent in the cooperative group and 8.8 per cent in the conflictual. During the 1990s, the gap was marginally smaller, with 5.0 per cent in the former and 8.6 per cent in the latter. Over the full period from 1980 through 1994, the cooperative economies' margin was 4.8 per cent to 8.8 per cent.[22]

What reconciles this strong unemployment performance by the cooperative economies with the alarums about massive unemployment throughout Europe? One source of the cooperative group's favorable standing, of course, is that it includes Japan – which is obviously outside Europe and has the lowest average unemployment rates among the eight countries in this continuing comparison. Even with Japan excluded, however, the average for the other four members of the cooperative group for the full 1980–94 period is 5.4 per cent, still almost 40 per cent below the conflictual average.

More important as an explanation for these apparently anomalous results is that on the unemployment front the cooperative economies clearly out-performed *other* European economies – many of them featuring more conflictual labor relations.[23] In a ranking of unemployment rates from *lowest* to *highest* across twenty OECD economies for 1991, when the European recession was hitting hard, our five cooperative representatives ranked first (best), second, fourth, fifth, and seventh among the twenty countries. Only Portugal and the United States from outside the cooperative group kept them from sweeping the top five positions. Among the larger advanced economies, two groups clustered toward the bottom of the ranking – the other conflictual economies, including Canada and the UK, and those with mixed labor-management systems, such as France, Italy, and Denmark.[24]

How Important Are Equality and Asset Redistribution?

While this fleeting review of the empirical evidence appears to provide substantial support for some of Bowles' and Gintis' specific claims, my review of that evidence has made virtually no mention of either 'equality' or the distribution of productive assets. One of Bowles' and Gintis' central conclusions is that 'a more equal distribution of assets then permits broader scope for the beneficial effects of markets and other forms of competition'. They focus consistently on the importance of increased equality as an objective and on the relatively general policy recommendation of asset redistribution. But the kind of cross-country comparisons I've just reviewed don't provide much direct support for the general importance of asset redistribution in the more cooperative economies.

In this final section I want briefly to raise some more general substantive questions about Bowles' and Gintis' emphasis on equality and asset redistribution. If alternative governance structures in production can potentially support greater efficiency than those in relatively more conflictual settings like the United States, how central is greater equality in the distribution of assets to their structure and performance?

It is certainly true that the relatively more cooperative economies featured in the preceding section also appear to display greater equality in the distribution of income and more moderated recent tendencies toward rising income inequality. The US and the UK appear to feature the greatest degree of income and wealth inequality among the advanced countries (Wolff, 1995). Perhaps more striking still is evidence on recent trends in inequality. Among the eleven countries for which Freeman and Katz (1995, table 2) present trends during the 1980s in inequality between the top and bottom of the male wage distribution, the three countries experiencing the most rapid increases are precisely those three 'conflictual' economies we have been tracking – with the US showing the greatest rise, the UK second, and Canada third. By contrast, the four of our five represent-ative 'cooperative' economies for which they present data experienced little or no increase in inequality; Germany actually displayed a *decrease* in earnings differentials. (Data were not available for Norway.) The average increase in wage inequality for the three conflictual economies from 1979 to 1990 was 0.19 index points, while the average for the four cooperative economies was less than 0.01 point. (The results for changes in the female wage distribution are comparable.)

But is this greater equality in the cooperative economies a central structural objective of their production systems or a by-product? And how much does the distribution of productive assets have to do with their comparative efficiency advantages?

It is unlikely that the operations or comparative advantages of the production systems of the cooperative economies depend fundamen-tally on an egalitarian distribution of the means of production, in the sense that Bowles and Gintis generally imply. They are all capitalist economies and the ownership of productive assets is held fairly narrowly. While the Swedish model historically featured some worker-determination of the allocation of investment funds, this feature was neither general in Sweden nor shared in the other cooperative examples.

Nor does it appear to me that an intrinsic and fundamental commitment to increased equality has been a central feature of the cooperative model. More basic and more central, in my view, have been at least four characteristics of that approach to labor-manage-ment. First, real wage growth has been steady and ample, providing direct wage incentives for production workers. Second, whether explicitly or implicitly, real wage growth has been tied in some determinate way to real productivity growth, getting as close as we come to involving production workers in the position of Bowles' and Gintis' vaunted role as 'residual claimants'. Third and critically, workers are provided with a substantial degree of employment security; indeed, various measures of employment security are cen-trally featured in the composite multivariate indices of 'cooperation' developed by Buchele-Christiansen and myself. Fourth, workers are provided direct and effective democratic channels for expressing and to some degree enacting their preferences about the organization of production through unions and works councils. Relatively high income equality appears to flow more from the commitment to steady real wage increases, including for workers at the bottom, than from an explicit much less contractual commitment to equality as an objective in and of itself.

These characteristics bear a striking resemblance to the conclusions of the recent literature evaluating the success of experiments in workplace participation in the United States. Worker involvement by itself is not enough. According to Levine and Tyson[25] and others, the success of workplace participation in promoting enhanced productivity hinges on at least four corollaries: real sharing of productivity gains with workers; significant employment security (so that workers won't worry that production innovations will result in lay-offs); substantial institutional changes to build *group* involvement, not just individual participation (since much of workers' contribution to production depends on group effort and coordination); and protection of the rights of individual employees (so that 'whistle-blowers' and 'trouble-makers' won't fear for their jobs). Neither explicit commitment to reduced inequality among wage-earners or between wage-earners and owners, nor formal conditions of employee stock ownership, seem to play an explicit role in these necessary conditions.

We get the same kind of impression if we look closely at individual cases in the United States of large firms moving toward more democratic and apparently more 'efficient' governance structures. Take the case of Magma Copper.[26]

Magma Copper, headquartered in Tucson, Arizona, is a relatively large mining corporation. In 1994 its sales totaled $890 million, its profits $87 million. It employed roughly 5,000 workers.

In the mid-1980s Magma was a wreck. The company's relations with its workers and unions teemed with conflict. It carried a huge debt resulting from its spin-off from the previous parent company. Its unit mining costs were among the highest in the industry. And, reeling from low copper prices, Magma was showing bright red on the bottom line.

Beginning in 1989 management began to explore whether the company could forge a completely different kind of relationship with its unions, one in which the workers and unions assumed a real partnership with management and effectively take joint responsibility for the success of the company. After three years of careful, sometimes halting, always delicate discussions, Magma and its unions, led by the

Steelworkers, signed in 1991 what *Fortune* called a 'revolutionary labor agreement'. The contract was to last for fifteen years, with no-strike guarantees for at least seven. It formally created joint labor-management 'work-redesign' teams to explore ways of improving productivity together with joint 'problem-solving' teams to deal with contract disputes, with the parties agreeing to submit contract disputes on economic issues to binding arbitration.

The contract, though obviously important, came more as a culmination than as an initiation of the transformational process at Magma. Workers and management had already participated in intensive efforts to change work relations, improve productivity, and transform a culture of conflict into a reality of cooperation.

In one of the major projects, a 150-member labor-management team worked for months to design new methods for mining ore from a new site, aiming to turn a questionable venture into a viable operation. The company had spent more than $150 million trying to come up with new technology to develop the new site but had abandoned the project. Within a year, by deploying new ways of organizing production and reorganizing job categories, the team had succeeded in designing an operation that then achieved productivity roughly two thirds higher than the previous best returns at the firm's principal underground mine.

By 1995, at the time of writing, Magma has become a proselyte of participatory and cooperative methods of labor management. And it has the record to justify its zeal. Over the seven years of the firm's effort to reconstruct its ways of doing business, according to company reports, productivity has increased by 86 per cent, production costs have decreased by 40 cents per pound, production has increased by 70 per cent, absenteeism and grievances have gone down dramatically, and the company's stock price has increased by over 400 per cent. In 1994, though its revenues ranked only twentieth within the top firms in the metals sector, its rate of return on revenues ranked second.

As with the more general conclusions drawn above, the carrot of cooperation could only work in the case of Magma if the workers were provided clear and manifest incentives and protections. In exchange for the union accepting limited wage increases, the company contractually agreed to grant the workers 40 per cent of all money saved as a result of productivity improvements; in 1993, the agreement earned the workers an average annual bonus of $4,700. And while there are no explicit contractual guarantees of job security, both management and labor have understood that job redesign and production reorganization must build upon the existing workforce rather than shrinking or replacing it. Without the productivity improvements, the largest mine was targeted to close within a couple of years. It now thrives.

And with the carrots in place, indeed, Magma has been able to pare its supervisory battalions. The company has reduced its organizational structure from eight levels of managerial and supervisory hierarchy to only four. 'Thanks to improved labor relations,' the *Wall Street Journal* reports, 'Magma has eliminated bosses from many shifts and crews. . . . The elimination of some supervisors [has] lowered management costs.'

Through all of this, the Magma example has featured neither an explicit commitment to increased income or wealth equality nor a formal program of employee stock-ownership or asset redistribution.

Are these distinctions without a difference? Does it matter whether increased equality is merely a by-product or a much more intentional, explicit objective of policies aimed at alternative governance structures and improved economic efficiency? Does it make any difference whether or not formal asset redistribution is part of the package? I think these distinctions probably matter for a couple of not entirely inconsequential reasons.

First, if asset redistribution as such is not even a necessary condition for enhancing workers' living and working conditions and improving economic efficiency, while other structural changes – such as real wage incentives, greater employment security, and explicit instrumental channels for workers expressing their 'voice' – are necessary conditions for achieving such objectives, then we should pay more attention to the latter and less to the former.

Second, from a more opportunistic political perspective, it may be that increased equality and asset redistribution are not even objectives which the vast majority of workers and citizens intrinsically value. Survey evidence is notoriously contingent, but studies such as Kahneman (1994) lead me to suspect that people are more concerned about *changes* in their own working and living conditions than they are in the *levels* of those conditions either absolutely or in relationship to others. If so, then those of us who would hope to promote progressive or even radical political change in countries such as the United States may be headed down the wrong alley if we focus primarily or excessively on equality of condition as an intrinsic objective and might consider placing a higher priority on *improvement* in working and living conditions for the vast majority – independent of their effects on the level of equality – instead.

What then of the value which many of us would place on increased equality and asset redistribution as part of a longer-term, perhaps explicitly socialist agenda? I consider myself an egalitarian and a socialist, but I'm tempted at least in the spirit of devil's advocacy to suggest that neither increased equality nor asset redistribution as such need parade at the top of our agenda, at least in the medium-term and even the shorter long-run. If they are not keys to a program which would both improve people's lives and livelihoods and enhance economic efficiency, they may not be essential ingredients of a progressive or even radical strategy. And if they are not high on the majority's intrinsic list of objectives, why should they be high on ours?

I can imagine that Bowles and Gintis might answer that asset redistribution might not appear to be a necessary condition for the kinds of advantages which relatively more cooperative economies and workplaces have enjoyed but that it could conceivably offer a sufficient condition at the site of production. (They of course propose crucial redistributions in other domains as well.) If there were effective, egalitarian redistribution of productive assets, they might argue, then workers would find it necessary to institute real wage-growth incentives tied to productivity change, employment security, and effective democratic instruments for expressing their 'voice' in order to maximize the value of their owned assets. I'm not persuaded this is the case, but it might be. But if it's easier politically to push for these more concrete objectives directly than to hope to achieve them indirectly through pushing for asset redistribution, we might want to consider pursuing the more direct route.

I pose these concerns not as hostile criticisms of Bowles' and Gintis' argument but as friendly and mostly speculative questions. Bowles and Gintis do not offer much evidence to support many of their claims for the benefits of their asset redistribution strategy. When we look for such evidence, in my experience, we find those benefits redounding to a 'cooperative' structure of labor relations. Neither increased equality nor asset redistribution appear to play a central role in the structure and performance of those relatively more 'cooperative' systems. Perhaps we ought to concentrate on achieving what seems to work according to the available evidence. I do not view this as an anti-utopian position so much as one which values the lessons of experience.

Notes

1. A common citation, as in Bowles and Gintis, is the useful survey provided by Levine and Tyson (1990).

2. Unless otherwise noted, all of the evidence and characterizations presented here draw upon the detailed discussion in Gordon (1996), especially chapters 3 and 6.

3. The literature supporting this kind of generalization is fairly broad. For a useful recent review of the issues and the relevant literature, see Adams (1995).

4. For a compact discussion of some of the principal differences among these three countries in their systems of labor management, see Appelbaum and Batt (1994), chapter 3.

5. These data for the household surveys are based on the author's own tabulations from the Current Population Surveys microdata samples for March 1993, including only private non-farm wage-and-salary employees. For this tabulation I include all those from the general category of 'executive, administrative, and managerial' and all those in specific categories, scattered throughout the census occupational codes, designated as one kind of 'supervisor' or another.

6. International Labor Organization, *Yearbook of Labor Statistics, 1994* (Geneva: ILO, 1994), table 3.

7. In 1989, there were 14.8 million 'administrative and managerial' employees tallied for the US in the ILO compilation. This exactly equaled the total number of 'executive, administrative, and managerial' employees identified in the BLS tabulations from the 1989 household surveys. (*Employment and Earnings*, January 1990.)

8. ILO, *Yearbook of Labor Statistics, 1994*, table 2C.

9. All the following data are based on the author's own tabulations from the 1991 US survey organized under the auspices of Erik Olin Wright's Comparative Project on Class Structure and Class Consciousness. The survey was conducted by the Survey Research Center of the University of California–Berkeley under the direction of Michael Hout, Erik Olin Wright and Martin Sanchez-Jankowski. For an introductory background to the data and their methodological purposes, see Wright (1985). For a more recent discussion, including both a discussion of the survey methodology and an overview of the results from the 1991 survey, see Wright (1996), especially chapter 2.

10. See the detailed discussion of the representative character of the surveys in Wright (1997), chapter 2.

11. There is also a survey for Japan, but it covers only Tokyo and its environs, which leads Wright to worry about its comparability with the other surveys. See Wright (1997), chapter 2 and appendix II.

12. For some brief but useful speculation about precisely these dimensions of difference between the US and Sweden, see Esping-Anderson (1990), pp. 202–3.

13. A more detailed unpublished version of the paper, including a full data appendix, is available under the same title as Working Paper No. 46 (Department of Economics, New School for Research, February 1994).

14. See the longer working-paper version of Gordon, (1994), for a report of these tests. Data are not available to test directly the effect of the percentage of a country's corporations that are multinational, so the indirect country-size and trade-involvement measures must serve as proxies.

15. US Bureau of Labor Statistics (1995), table 13.

16. David Soskice (1990), pp. 190–91.

17. See, for example, Calmfors and Drifill (1988).

18. See, for example, Adams (1995), chapter 6; Dell'Aringa and Lodovici (1992); and my own classification in Gordon (1994).

19. Buchele and Christiansen (1992), p. 95.

20. Based on author's calculations from OECD data. The productivity measure is for real business sector per employee, while the wage rate is annual business-sector compensation per employee. Group figures are unweighted averages of individual country average annual arithmetic growth rates for the years 1974–89.

21. As is standard in these kinds of cross-country comparisons, the unemployment rates for Germany are those for the former West Germany only, in order to avoid distortions from the integration of the former East Germany. For our purposes here, this practice is especially important, since analysts would refer only to labor relations in West Germany as reflecting historically cooperative structures.

22. Based on standardized unemployment rates, OECD (1995), annex table 22.

23. The underlying framework generating the expectations of a trade-off between unemployment on the one hand and wage and productivity growth on the other may also be inadequate, since it largely builds on assumptions of perfectly competitive labor markets. For a careful analysis which, in spite of its predictions, fails to find evidence of the expected trade-off between unemployment growth and productivity growth among the G–7 economies, see R. J. Gordon (1996).

24. OECD (1994), vol. I, chart 1.14.

25. Levine and Tyson (1990), pp. 144ff.

26. This vignette about Magma Copper is based on a range of journalistic and company sources; see Gordon (1996), chapter 3, for further detail and documentation.

References

Adams, Roy J., *Industrial Relations Under Liberal Democracy: North America in Comparative Perspective* (Columbia, SC: University of South Carolina Press, 1995).

Appelbaum, Eileen and Rosemary Batt, *The New American Workplace: Transforming Work Systems in the United States* (Ithaca, NY: Cornell University ILR Press, 1994).

Blinder, Alan S., 'Introduction', in Alan S. Blinder (ed.), *Paying for Productivity: A Look at the Evidence* (Washington, D.C.: Brookings Institution, 1990), pp. 1–13.

Buchele, Robert and Jens Christiansen, 'Industrial Relations and Productivity Growth: A Comparative Perspective', *International Contributions to Labor Studies*, 2 (1992), pp. 77–97.

Calmfors, Lars and John Driffill, 'Bargaining Structure, Corporatism and Macroeconomic Performance', *Economic Policy: A European Forum*, no. 6 (April 1988), pp. 13–61.

Dell'Aringa, Carlo and Manuela Samek Lodovici, 'Industrial Relations and Economic Performance', in Tiziano Treu (ed.), *Participation in Public Policy-Making: The Role of Trade Unions and Employers' Associations* (Berlin: Walter deGruyter, 1992), pp. 26–58.

Esping-Andersen, Gösta, *The Three Worlds of Welfare Capitalism* (Princeton: Princeton University Press, 1990).

Freeman, Richard B. and Lawrence F. Katz, 'Introduction and Summary', in Freeman and Katz (eds.), *Differences and Changes in Wage Structures* (Chicago: University of Chicago Press, 1995).

Gordon, David M., 'Bosses of Different Stripes: Monitoring and Supervision across the Advanced Economies', *American Economic Review*, 84, 2 (May 1994), pp. 375–9.

——, *Fat and Mean: The Corporate Squeeze of Working Americans and the Myth of Managerial 'Downsizing'* (New York: Martin Kessler Books/The Free Press, 1996).

Gordon, Robert J., 'Is There a Tradeoff between Unemployment and Productivity Growth?' in Dennis J. Snower and Guillermo de la Dehesa (eds.), *Unemployment Policy* (1996).

Kahneman, Daniel, 'New Challenges to the Rationality Assumption', *Journal of Institutional and Theoretical Economics*, 150, 1, (March 1994), pp. 18–36.

Levine, David I. and Laura D'Andrea Tyson, 'Participation, Productivity and the Firm's Environment', in Alan S. Blinder (ed.), *Paying for Productivity: A Look at the Evidence* (Washington, D.C.: Brookings Institution, 1990), pp. 183–237.

Organization for Economic Cooperation and Development, *The OECD Jobs Study* (Paris: OECD, June 1994).

——, *Economic Outlook* (June 1995), country historical tables.

Soskice, David, 'Reinterpreting Corporatism and Explaining Unemployment: Co-ordinated and Non-co-ordinated Market Economies', in R. Brunetta and C. Dell'Aringa (eds.), *Labor Relations and Economic Performance* (New York: New York University Press, 1990).

US Bureau of Labor Statistics, Office of Productivity and Technology, 'Output per Hour, Hourly Compensation, and Unit Labor Costs in Manufacturing, Twelve Economies, 1950–1993', unpublished tables (February 1995).

Wolff, Edward N., *Top Heavy: A Study of the Rising Inequality of Wealth in America* (New York: The Twentieth Century Fund Press, 1995).

Wright, Erik Olin, *Classes* (London: Verso Books, 1985).

——, *Class Counts: Comparative Studies in Class Analysis* (New York: Cambridge University Press, 1997).

9

How Do We Support Children?
Paula England

Children suffer higher rates of poverty in the United States than in most industrialized nations, and these rates have been increasing for about two decades. A major explanation for the increase is that, because of increases in divorce and non-marital births, more children are supported by their mothers with little or no help from their fathers. In 1960 about 8 per cent of children lived with a single parent; by 1991 the figure was 25 per cent overall and over 50 per cent for black children.[1] Given that one parent usually earns less than two, and given women's relatively low earnings, the result is often poverty. Indeed, about half of children in households without adult men are in poverty.[2] All this would be very different if child support were always awarded and paid, but more than half of all children potentially eligible for child support receive nothing from their fathers.[3] It would also be different if the US had a system of public provision of health care, child care, or family allowances as many industrialized nations do.

Bowles' and Gintis' paper, while emphasizing the redistribution of firm ownership, also contains a proposal regarding the support of children. In my reaction to this proposal, I make four related points: 1.) What is most productivity-enhancing about getting more financial support to children is the increase in their human capital, very broadly construed. 2.) What they propose is not very different from what is now on the books but not well enforced. 3.) The fact that enforcement of child support is productivity-enhancing will probably not make it more politically feasible. 4.) I will argue in favor of a more universal and redistributive but still targeted approach to public provision for the support of children.

1. What is Productivity-enhancing about the Reform?

Bowles and Gintis favor redistributions of property that are 'efficient' or 'productivity' enhancing. Put simply, they want to redivide the pie in a way that also makes it grow. The reasons for this preference are that growth is an effective way to help those at the bottom (a goal of redistribution), and that productivity-enhancing reforms will be more politically acceptable.

The reform their paper discusses at greatest length is that of the state providing loans or grants to workers that seek to buy their companies and run them as democratic, worker-owned firms. Such firms, they argue, would be more productive because workers can monitor each other with less cost than owners can monitor workers. The reform would solve a problem of information (the fact that owners can't costlessly see if workers are being conscientious) by putting ownership (and hence motivation to increase profits) in the hands of those who most efficiently observe and control the exertion of effort.

Regarding children, they propose that the state give children property rights in the income streams of their parents. Thus, in cases where one parent lives with the child and provides care, and the other parent is not a member of this household, some fixed amount per child plus a fraction of the parent's income would be owed by the non-custodial parent to the parent living with the child. The state would enforce this transfer.

Hereafter I will shift to gender-specific language for ease, and assume the mother has custody and the father is failing to pay child support, since this is a typical case, and to remind us of the gendered consequences of doing or failing to do the redistribution. However, their proposal, while not gender-neutral in its effects, is gender-neutral in its treatment of cases. That is, it would also redistribute to the child via a check to the father in a case where he had custody.

What are the commonalities between proposals for 'money to the workers to buy the firms' and 'money to the mothers' that makes them productivity-enhancing? And what, in their view, led to the inefficiency to be corrected by the policy in each case?[4] The inefficiency in the current system of child-support, they argue, is that the person who has the *de facto* responsibility to enforce men's support obligations is the mother, but mothers are not the ones with a comparative advantage in enforcing rules. The state is.

What sorts of enforcement costs, now faced by mothers, are they talking about? There are costs of a lawyer to obtain the support award to begin with. There may be costs of finding the father. Even if found, he may refuse to pay, whether or not she has a child-support award. Her state may or may not automatically deduct awards from wages (this was rare until recently). If his income and/or the cost of living goes up dramatically, there is no automatic increase in the award without hiring a lawyer and going to court again to get one. Many women just give up. Note that the problem they are talking about could not be solved by prior contracts. That is, even if women never had sex with men without a written contract that the men would contribute to the support of any resulting children, women would still have a hard time enforcing the contract.

Bowles and Gintis think the state could enforce this more efficiently. (Whether it would be the federal or state governments is beside the theoretical point.) Since revenue departments already exist with payroll deductions for taxes, the principle of economies of scale suggests that collecting awards is more efficiently done by the state than individual mothers. The state also holds the exclusive right to seize assets or imprison.

They are *not* advocating state enforcement because women don't have the money to incur the costs of getting fathers to pay up and the state does; that may be a reason to support it, but it is not the one that flows from their theoretical logic. They are saying that the state can do it more efficiently (i.e. get more results per dollar spent) than mothers can (this is what it means to say the state has a comparative advantage at enforcement of rules). I have no quarrel with this claim.

However, I think there is also another way in which any reform that diverts more money from other kinds of consumption to support-ing children is productivity-enhancing, and that the magnitude of the gains from this are probably much larger. If more money goes into the rearing of children, one consequence will be greater human capital development, *very* broadly construed. This will increase the produc-tivity and welfare of the children in their adulthood. I do not only refer to human capital in a narrow sense of skills that help one earn more because they increase productivity, although that is certainly included. I intend human capital to include physical and psychological health, intellectual skills for citizenship and work (paid and unpaid, including parenting), and habits of civil rather than anti-social behav-ior (the latter create costs for society in the form of crime). Money isn't everything, but with more of it mothers could do more for all these aspects of children's development. Adequate child-care could be paid for where now it is inadequate, health insurance could be purchased, housing in better school districts could be afforded, housing in a neighborhood less likely to induce youth into crime would be more possible, mothers could afford to be choosier about whether to marry or cohabit with prospective mates based on how well they treat the children, and so forth. Not all mothers will use the money for the children, but many will. Indeed, there is evidence that children who live with two parents are more successful as adults, and that some of the difference is due to differences in income (McLanahan and Sandefur 1994).

2. How Does Their Proposal Differ from Current Law?

Unlike their proposal to encourage worker-ownership of firms, Bowles' and Gintis' proposal for child support differs little from current law. The main difference is semantic. They make a point of the distinction between redistributing property and redistributing income, and it is clear that their proposal regarding firm ownership is very different from, say, a guaranteed minimum income. But when it comes to the proposal for supporting children, the difference between property rights to some specified amount of the income-stream of one's parents (their terms) and the right to some specified amount of child-support seems only semantic to me. And it is precisely what we have on the books in every state in the United States and have had since about the turn of the century (Friedman 1995). The difference between their proposal and current *law* is little; there is considerable difference between how they envision their proposal working and how current *practice* works. That is, laws requiring that non-resident fathers support their children are not well enforced, while they envision that the state would really enforce the law, bearing whatever costs of enforcement are necessary. In the case where the state could not collect from the absent parent, they envision the state paying the amount. This would create a guarantee to child-support.

I agree with them that the state has a greater 'comparative advantage' in enforcing universal rules than do individual mothers. However, that is not to deny that the state faces huge costs of enforcement. I presume that Bowles and Gintis would agree, since their argument is very much in the spirit of the new information economics, with its emphasis on such transactions costs.

Given that the state faces problems of information and enforcement, we can't assume that creating a legal right necessarily means that the state will enforce it no matter what the costs are. Some degree of non-enforcement, as well as procedures that push some of the transaction costs onto those whose rights the state purports to uphold, are the rule rather than the exception in most areas of law. For example, we have anti-discrimination laws, but if the Equal Employment Opportunity Commission (EEOC) doesn't choose to take a plaintiff's case, s/he can only find redress by paying a lawyer to take the case. In many areas of the law, there is no analog of the EEOC. If someone fails to repay a loan, the creditor must hire a lawyer to get relief, and even then a court decision ordering someone to pay doesn't guarantee that the state will seize assets for the creditor if the debtor doesn't pay (it will under some circumstances). The general point is that most laws that create a right to income or property end up requiring individuals to bear some of the transaction costs of enforcement, and sometimes remain unenforced because of the transaction costs. Child-support is no exception.

For Bowles' and Gintis' proposal to constitute any significant departure from the status quo would mean that the state would have to bear more enforcement costs in the area of child-support than at present. For example, automatic assignment of payments and wage garnishment starting at the point of divorce (or birth in the case of a non-marital birth with a non-resident father) with either a federal system or cooperation between states would increase payments dramatically – but at a substantial cost. But even this wouldn't always get the payment to the child. Thus, to really provide a guarantee, the state would also need to provide some minimum income to families with children where a parent was absent and the state could not get him to pay.

The last twenty years have seen successive steps by the federal government in the direction of tightening up enforcement of child-support by the states. A succession of federal laws from the 1970s to the late 1980s gave money to states that were willing to take certain steps, and mandated other steps. The Family Support Act of 1988 (PL 100–485) went even further, requiring all states to withhold payments from paychecks from the outset by 1994. It also authorized federal payment for 90 per cent of the costs of blood tests used to establish paternity. Yet few states have implemented universal withholding and all states are a long way from universal establishment of paternity. Crossing state lines remains an effective way to avoid a child-support obligation. There is no state or federal assurance of benefits in the case where collection from the non-custodial parent fails. (Garfinkel et al. (1994) provide an assessment of the effects of these changes so far, mainly by comparing across time and across states that have instituted various parts of the reforms unevenly and at different times.)[5]

Bowles' and Gintis' proposal is very much in the spirit of these recent initiatives by the federal government, but is not significantly different from the status quo, with more devoted by the state to enforcement, and the state providing a guarantee of the award if the parent can't be made to pay.

3. Are Redistributive Reforms that Make the Pie Bigger More Politically Popular?

One reason Bowles and Gintis give for preferring redistributive reforms that increase productivity, as compared with redistributive reforms that do not, is that the former will be more popular and thus politically feasible. In the absence of growth, redistribution is zero-sum, and, if we assume self-interest, the losers can be expected to resist. If a reform simultaneously makes the pie larger while redistributing it, the losers could possibly be compensated for their loss by their share in the growth. At the least, even if they aren't fully compensated, they will lose less (by whatever amount is their share of the gains from growth) than with a redistribution of similar size that creates no growth.

If the gains from state enforcement and guarantee of child-support are simply that the state does it more cheaply than mothers, it is hard for me to imagine that non-custodial fathers' gain from their diffused share of this would be greater than what they would lose in payments extracted from them. Thus, non-custodial fathers, an increasingly politically organized group, might be expected to oppose the reform. Even if you grant that the growth-enhancing effects are larger than just those from comparative advantage in enforcement, because they will affect children's human capital (as I have argued), it still isn't clear that the father's share in this will offset his losses. The children, who would gain, can't yet vote.

Also, while the income streams themselves would usually come from the fathers, the enforcement costs and costs of payments where the fathers couldn't be made to pay would be covered by the state to a degree that they aren't now, or the reform would not change anything. Thus the state would need to raise more tax or shift monies from present programs to these reforms. Thus, those whose creed is 'no new taxes' would resist. (They don't say 'no new non-productivity-enhancing taxes'!) If one agrees with the argument that most proposals that shift money to supporting children are productivity-enhancing via effects on human capital, then given that more children live with mothers than fathers, it follows that any reform that shifts money to women is productivity-enhancing. But that hasn't made affirmative action for women more popular. Nor has it led to shifting Medicare money, now used to prolong the last weeks of elders' lives, to education or children's allowances of some kind.

Even more important is how muddled citizens' perceptions of such matters are. Bowles and Gintis are working with theoretical logic that emphasizes the effects of imperfect and asymmetric information. But if one fully appreciates this, then it is clear how hard it is for citizens to see what the costs and benefits of a particular policy change are for various groups.

In sum, I agree that, *ceteris paribus*, if citizens believe that something is 'good for growth' it is more politically popular. But I doubt that subtle points, like the efficiencies of having the state do what is its comparative advantage or of investments in children, do much for the political feasibility of a proposal. (Such arguments may be much more effective among economists, given their training in converting issues into optimization calculations.)

4. A More Universal Approach to Supporting Children

Bowles' and Gintis' proposed reform, like current policy, aims to shield children from the consequences of whether their parents live together. Since children in mother-only families are disproportionately poor, the policies are to a greater extent redistributive the more enforcement is accomplished. However, there is another type of redistribution attempted by neither their proposal nor current policy. (Recall that I have argued that their proposal and current policy are the same in principle.) Both keep the linkage of children's economic fates to those of their parents fully in force.

I advocate a system that is redistributive along this dimension as well as between those children living in mother-only and two-parent families. A much more redistributive reform would be analogous to the Social Security and Medicare system. We would decide that children in our society have property rights in a proportion of the earning stream of the adult generation. Put another way, we would decide to provide for the support of children collectively. Each adult's earnings are taxed through payroll deductions or, preferably, progressive income taxes. (I would include all adults with income, including non-parents and parents who are supporting their own children.) However, I would decouple child's benefits entirely from the amount contributed by his or her parents. This decoupling is done partially but not completely with Social Security; those who pay in more get more, but less so than they would if benefits were proportional to contributions. All children would have access to medical care, regardless of economic need (whether adults would be included could be debated separately). Cash benefits from this fund would be transferred to the custodial parent or parents in the event that the income in the children's household fell below a specified level, with a sliding scale type arrangement for when payments are discontinued that makes it like a negative income tax. This payment would be available whether one or two parents were present. Child-support awards providing some award above and beyond this could continue as usual. Note that whatever the state's efficiency in enforcement that is the merit of Bowles' and Gintis' proposal is present in this proposal as well.

What I propose is really just a more generous safety net (at least for households with children) combined with universal medical care (at least for children). A much more elaborately worked out proposal more specifically geared to child-support in one-parent families has been offered by Garfinkel.[6] His proposal would make payroll deductions from all parents not living with a child (the tax would fall primarily upon non-custodial fathers), and use it to provide a minimum in cases where it was not being provided by the child-support system. Both what I have proposed and Garfinkel's proposal (but not Bowles' and Gintis') have the equity problem that an adult who is supporting his or her child through child-support is taxed the same as one who is managing to avoid such payments. My proposal makes this true for a parent in residence supporting a child as well. But, while regrettable in one sense, this is analogous to the fact that adults who currently contribute to the support of their elderly parents are also required to pay into the fund that, in a pay-as-you-go manner, is supporting current retirees. The place where the analogy breaks down is that Social Security is not means tested, so if I give my elderly parent some amount of money per month, they do not thereby lose part of their Social Security check. As I put in my proposal above, the income of the household in which a child lived might become too high to be eligible for as much of a state-provided benefit if a father who hadn't been paying child-support started doing so. However, if done with a negative-income-tax (sliding scale) sort of arrangement, the households with children would never lose a dollar for every dollar gained in earnings or child-support.

To my mind, the important political choice is between something as universal as what I am proposing and something more universal in the sense of non-means tested. The more universal option is child-allowances for all families with children regardless of need. While I favor universal health care, collectively financed (if for no other reason than to get the 'notch effect' out of the current welfare system),[7] I favor a more targeted approach to cash-support of children. This is because I fear that any truly universal child-allowances would end up being set at significantly less than today's welfare levels, much less welfare plus Medicaid. Even to set them at the current welfare level would multiply the costs of the current welfare program many dozens of times, while doing little or nothing that isn't already being done to reduce poverty or redistribute assets.

The argument for an even more universal strategy is that it is the only way such payments will have political support in the way that Social Security has compared to 'welfare' – because the average middle-American sees the program as something for 'people like me' that 'I have paid into', rather than a dole for 'those people'. The risk of a more targeted strategy is that it will not have this political support. In effect, Garfinkel's proposal would target the benefits to those with high need, but also target the tax on non-custodial parents. This has different kinds of political risks – it would certainly mobilize the already organized Fathers' Rights groups against it, but might get more support from other middle-class people. Who would prevail is unclear. The hope of any of these schemes is that they would be accepted as a kind of risk-sharing against adversities that don't allow children to be well supported. This would be aided by an understanding that society has even more reason to insure children than adults against adversity since they are never to blame for their own poverty, and, where children are being supported, consumption is also investment to a greater extent than is true for adults.

Perhaps any scheme that redistributes to children will be opposed for reasons of self-interest on the part of those who would pay, or because of moral disapproval of the adults subsidized by such arrangements, heightened in some cases by racism since single mothers are disproportionately (though not in the majority) black. In this, my proposal, or Garfinkel's, would face obstacles similar to the obstacles that are now faced in raising welfare benefits to even the poverty line. But I have argued that Bowles' and Gintis' proposal is not immune to problems of political unpopularity, because abstractions about 'productivity-enhancement' are unlikely to move many people. Any effort to use the state to divert more to children requires persuading people to care about investing in the welfare and productivity of children other than their own. Perhaps the political hurdles are no greater for a more universal scheme that would reduce poverty and inequality more. I prefer to aim in this direction.

Notes

1. Garfinkel *et al.* (1994), chapter 1.
2. US Bureau of the Census 1993.
3. Garfinkel *et al.* (1994), chapter 1.
4. One commonality that immediately struck me is that both reforms get money into the hands of the people actually doing the work – the workers in one case, or the mothers who care for the kids in the other. But, that is really not the theoretically salient commonality, because, while they argue that worker-ownership makes workers more productive (because they have both the incentive and ability to monitor each other), they don't argue that getting the money to mothers improves their mothering. They don't identify as a problem that the absent father can't monitor the mother, and nothing about their proposal would increase his ability to do so. So, whereas with the firm, they look for a reform that will increase workers' motivation to put forth effort, they do not take that approach with parenting. They tacitly assume that some amount of altruism is forthcoming from mothers. The problem they identify is that children get less adequate financial support than they would if men's incentives were more aligned with the residual claimancy situation. In plainer language, men have little incentive to bear the costs of their role in procreation.
5. Despite these efforts, child-support collections were lower in 1989 than in 1978. A smaller percentage of children living apart from one parent had awards, and the average amount awarded and received was smaller. Hanson *et al.* (1995) show that one reason for the lower proportion of awards was the increase in the proportion of births that were non-marital. Awards have always been less likely in these cases than in divorces. They also show that one reason for the decline in awards was fathers' declining incomes. Thus, they conclude that the legislative changes probably did help, but it was upstream swimming against other trends.
6. 1992; Garfinkel *et al.* (1994).
7. The 'notch effect' refers to the fact that access to medical benefits are present or absent, and thus cannot be easily incrementally decreased, like cash payments can, as other income goes up. Thus, there is always a point at which when one earns one more dollar, all medical benefits are lost, and one is worse-off working unless one gains employer-paid health insurance at that point.

References

Friedman, Debra, *Towards a Structure of Indifference: The Social Origins of Maternal Custody* (New York: Aldine de Gruyter, 1995).

Garfinkel, Irwin, Sara McLanahan and Philip Robins (eds.), *Child Support and Child Well-Being* (Washington, DC: The Urban Institute Press, 1994).

Hanson, Thomas, Irwin Garfinkel, Sara S. McLanahan and Cynthia Miller, 'Trends in Child Support Outcomes', Working Paper Series, paper 95–8 (Princeton University, Office of Population Research, 1995).

McLanahan, Sara and Gary Sandefur, *Growing Up with a Single Parent* (Cambridge, Mass.: Harvard University Press, 1994).

US Bureau of Census, *Poverty in the United States: 1992*, Current Population reports, Series P-60, no. 185 (Washington, DC: US Government Printing Office, 1993).

PART IV

Criticisms of the
Economic Model

10

The Limits of
Private-property-based Egalitarianism
John E. Roemer

There is much that I find admirable in the proposals of Samuel Bowles and Herbert Gintis for efficient redistribution. I believe the tripartite division of responsibility for 'governance' among the state, the market, and the community is well motivated; it sounds like the right solution to the generalized monitoring problem. But, in the spirit of constructive criticism, I wish to sound a note of caution with respect to the proposal.

I believe that Bowles and Gintis are unduly optimistic with respect to the degree of egalitarianism that can be achieved under an exclusively private-property regime. The so-called Second Theorem of Welfare Economics states that, under specified conditions on preferences and technologies, any Pareto-efficient allocation can be achieved with an appropriate redistribution of private property rights. This theorem is usually interpreted as saying that the issues of equity and efficiency can be entirely separated. The Bowles–Gintis paper is part of a growing literature arguing that efficiency and equity cannot be so neatly separated: indeed, efficiency may not be achievable unless the distribution of private property rights is in a certain degree egalitarian.[1] But I would go further and claim that neither efficiency nor equality (in a certain degree) can be attained as long as the ubiquitous form of property is private.

Of course, this may sound like the classical Marxian call to abolish private ownership in the means of production. But it is not. We all recognize that the Bowles–Gintis proposal is the intellectual product of an historical experience that tried to implement that call, a product which comes at the end of a series of steps in an argument that began with *Das Kapital*. I do not mean that achieving egalitarianism requires nationalizing the means of production, but rather that forms of property other than private and state will be needed to achieve what we aim for.

The modern view of property was first enunciated, perhaps, by Wesley Hohfeld (1919), was developed significantly by the legal realists, among whom Robert Hale (1937) was a prominent figure, and is further elaborated today by the critical legal theorists, including Thomas Grey (1980), Duncan Kennedy and Frank Michelman (1980), and Joseph Singer (1988). I shall not attempt here to summarize the views of these writers, but shall simply concentrate on one aspect, which is that property consists in the sets of rights that persons have with regard to things, the delineation of torts against persons involving things, and the delineation of types of contract that persons can write with regard to those things. It is frequently thought, by social scientists, that private property consists in having unlimited rights with respect to the use of a thing, but this is clearly false: a private owner of a thing is not allowed to use it in ways that infringe on certain rights of other persons. (My right to wave my fist in the air stops somewhere short of your nose.)

The Bowles–Gintis argument for efficient redistributions has, at its core, the view that efficiency requires bundling together the rights to the residual income flowing from, and to control of, the use of the thing in question in one person or sets of persons. Thus, for example, workers in a firm with physical assets, who, by their location control the use of those assets, should be assigned the rights to residual claimancy in the firm's income. Tenant farmers, who control the use of the land, should be the residual claimants in the income stream produced by the farm. (The verb 'should' in these two sentences is implicitly modified by the phrase 'in order to achieve efficiency'.)

There is another right of private property which I believe must be significantly attenuated to achieve efficiency and equality, and that is the right to transfer the rights one has in a thing to another person: we frequently refer to this right using the reified language, that an owner has a right to 'sell the thing' to another. (This is reified language, because what one is selling is a certain bundle of rights with respect to the use of the thing.) Bowles and Gintis do not discuss the need to attenuate this right. Indeed, it might be fair to say that their argument suggests this right should *not* be attenuated, for one of the reasons owners of houses or of firms have the incentive to 'maintain their property' (again, a reified usage) is to maintain its resale value. In a word, since the right to 'sell a thing' is viewed as one of the defining rights of 'private' property in the thing, I am claiming that efficiency and equality require the attenuation of private property.

In addition to attenuating the unlimited right to 'sell property', there are certain obligations with respect to who uses the thing, which do not exist with private property, that it may perhaps be necessary to require in order to achieve efficiency and equality: I refer to an obligation that the owner himself be the one who uses the thing. Thus, for example, a person may not own a share in a worker-owned firm unless she works in the firm; under the Homestead Act of 1867 in the US, a person could not 'own' a piece of land unless he worked it himself.

William Simon has named the property form in which rights to sell are attenuated and obligations to use are required, social-republican. He argues that social-republican property engenders the production of local public goods which may not be produced under the private property form. Owners of apartments who must live in them may have a greater interest in improving the neighborhood than either an absentee landlord or a tenant. One who owns a share in a firm, and is obliged to live in the town where the firm operates (another possible social-republican obligation), may have more incentive than an absentee owner to instal pollution-control devices – or, somewhat more realistically, if all the owners of a firm live in the town, then social, as well as legal and financial, pressure may be brought to bear against them to keep the firm green.

Although attenuating the right to sell a thing may, *ceteris paribus*, reduce the incentive to maintain it, there are often counteracting incentive effects. The easier it is for me to sell my property, the more I may use 'exit' rather than 'voice' in reacting to a local public bad in my environment. (If I can easily sell my house and move to a town with better schools, I may be disinclined to organize for better schools in my own town.) In recent writing, I have suggested that this argument may apply to a nation's firms,[2] to wit, that all citizens should be obliged to hold a roughly equal share of ownership (in the sense of rights to residual income and control) in the nation's firms. The argument rests on the claim that there are a variety of 'public bads' whose levels are postively correlated with aggregate profits of firms, including fast assembly-line speeds (i.e., poor or unsafe working conditions), environmental degradation, dishonest or manipulative advertising, and imperialist wars. If a small class of wealthy individuals receive the lion's share of profits in the nation's firms, I argue that this class will have an incentive to fight, through the legislative process, for lax restrictions on the levels of these public bads: the disutility they would suffer from these bads would be more than compensated for by the profits they thereby accrue. If, in contrast, profits are equally distributed among the citizenry, then, although some citizens would desire higher levels of public bads than they would were they to receive no share of profits, there would be no powerful political force, as in the first scenario, calling for permission to produce very high levels of these bads. Equality of share ownership would, I argue, tend to align the level of public bads desired by politically powerful interests more closely with the level of public bads desired by the majority of citizens. (Non-economists should remember that the goal is not to eliminate public bads, but rather to bring their level to that which most citizens optimally want. We do not, for example, wish to eliminate pollution, but to produce a socially optimal amount of it.) Another public bad whose level may be reduced by maintaining roughly equal citizen shares in the nation's profits is the social disruption caused by runaway shops. Citizens who receive roughly 20 per cent of their income from profits (assuming that profits constitute roughly 20 per cent of national income) may be more prone to support legislation restricting the rights of firms to move to other countries than are politically influential capitalists, who have vastly more to lose by such restrictions.

Suppose shares in profits of the nation's firms were equally distributed to all citizens, and were held as traditional private property, including, in particular, the right to sell. It is likely that a quite high degree of concentration of such shares, in the hands of the wealthy, would quite rapidly ensue, for three reasons: (1) many citizens would, myopically, underestimate the long-run income stream that would return to these shares, and would prefer to sell them; (2) the poor, who 'should' be more risk-averse than the rich, may wish to hold assets, like government bonds, that are less risky than corporate stock, and hence would sell their shares to the rich; and (3) many low-income citizens, who might overestimate the probability of succeeding in small business, would sell their shares in order to finance a small business. But if many low- and middle-income citizens sell their shares to the rich, a small class of wealthy individuals who would own the lion's share of the nation's profit stream would thereby be created, with the consequent deleterious effect on the level of public bads, as outlined above. In a word, the unrestricted right to sell shares of firms creates a free-rider problem: it is (perceived to be) individually optimal by most citizens to sell their shares, but in the aggregate, the consequence is a level of public bads which makes the vast majority of citizens worse off than they would have been had they not been able to sell their shares to the rich.

Bowles and Gintis, in their discussion of efficiency, are concerned with the micro-management of physical assets: maintaining houses, keeping effort levels high on the shop floor. In the last several paragraphs, I have been concerned with efficiency of a different kind, that which comes from having socially optimal levels of public goods and bads; I have argued that private property redistributions, of the kind Bowles and Gintis have recommended, will not suffice to bring about this second kind of efficiency. Somewhat loosely, there is a 'quality of life' associated with having high levels of public goods (and low levels of bads) that I think is unattainable if all property in productive assets is held privately. I also believe that that life-quality is unattainable if all assets are held by a state controlled by a party which is not politically accountable to the citizenry. What I am arguing for is the necessity of developing property forms which are neither private nor state.

With respect to the ownership of a nation's firms, a number of such property forms, besides worker ownership, have been recently proposed. Leland Stauber (1987) proposes that there be created hundreds, or thousands, of investment funds owned by local government organs, which become the corporate owners of the nation's firms. Corporate stock would be traded on a market in which only these investment funds participate. The income from stock would finance local government activities, and/or could be rebated directly to citizens. Pranab Bardhan (1993) has proposed a system of firm-ownership modelled after the Japanese *keiretsu*, in which firms would be owned by other firms in a corporate group, and by other institutions, such as pension funds, and would be monitored by main banks that would be state owned. I (1994a, 1994b) have proposed a system in which adult citizens would receive coupons with which they could purchase corporate stock. Citizens could trade stock on a market in which only coupons were an allowable currency, and they could not liquidate stock for money: this institution, while not locking individuals in to the ownership of the shares of any particular firm, would prevent citizens from divesting themselves of an interest in the nation's aggregate corporate profits, thus perhaps solving the free-rider problem discussed above. This is not the place to evaluate these proposals: the salient point is that a variety of property relations have been suggested which partition the rights associated with firm owner-ship in ways differently from how those rights are partitioned in the private, public, and labor-owned property forms. Some of these proposals may well be superior to private ownership in the levels of public goods and bads that they engender, through the political economy.

Finally, I take issue with the view, suggested by Bowles and Gintis, that worker-ownership can, or should, be the ubiquitous property form for large firms. (Almost all egalitarian proposals these days include a stipulation that private ownership is acceptable or desirable for small firms.) Bowles and Gintis have raised the important point that worker-owned firms may be too risk-averse; I have another point in mind. The average amount of capital per worker in the US today is approximately $100,000. If the corporate sector were ubiquitously worker-owned, then, on average, each worker would have to own $100,000 of physical equipment and property. This would mean, in the event, that the average worker would hold a mortgage in her capital equipment considerably larger than the average house mortgage. Aside from the difficulty of financing such mortgages through the banking sector, it would be decidedly irrational for the average worker to hold such a large position in one risky asset. Jacques Drèze (1993) gives the example of an oil tanker, typically worth tens of millions of dollars, which requires a labor force of only a dozen. It would be extremely unwise for these workers to mortgage themselves to the required extent, given the riskiness of the business. (There might be periods of months with no revenue, during a Gulf War, for instance.) What this means is that, in practice, workers in firms with high capital-labor ratios will rationally not want to entirely own the capital equipment they use: they will want others to own (at least a large share of) it, and to be *residual* claimants in the firm's income stream. (The problem with simply financing the firm's equipment and property with bonds or loans is that bond-holders and creditors are legally entitled to a steady stream of income from the firm; in other words, they can require that the assets of the firm be sold in the event that the income stream cannot finance the required payments.) Thus, rational workers will want to issue equity in such firms. But equity holders (at least in the US and the UK) require (some substantial degree of) control of the firm: the *quid pro quo* for being only the *residual* claimants is to give substantial rights of control of the use of the physical assets to those claimants. Thus, we are back to the publicly held, privately owned corporation.

I have just argued that worker-ownership, in the sense of giving both residual claimancy and rights of control to the workers in a firm, is not a workable option, on average, in economies with high capital-labor ratios (i.e., all advanced economies). Perhaps one could suggest a kind of public, or non-private, ownership of the equity in firms that would permit workers to be residual claimants, and would therefore allow the alignment of residual claimancy and control that Bowles and Gintis argue is important for micro-efficiency in the firm. I am skeptical, but I do not wish prematurely to foreclose the discussion of such a possibility. It is arguably the case that, in Japan, many providers of equity have no say in the operation of the firm: I refer to the fact that banks, rather than common stockholders through the board of directors, typically control firm management. This is not an example of worker-control in the presence of publicly held corporate stock, but one, more weakly, of non-stockholder control of a joint-stock company. In any case, my conclusion is that some form of corporate property other than worker-ownership will be required in the 'new society'.

Let me conclude with a simple observation. Both the Marxists and the Hayekians have had, I believe, a simplistic notion of property; that it consists in assigning all of the rights with respect to the use of a productive asset to a particular (corporate) person. (By this I mean that it is not the case that some rights be given to one [corporate] person and other rights to another.) I believe that property entails no such restriction, and furthermore, that unbundling property rights, as I have discussed, may well be necessary for further progress along both the equality and efficiency dimensions. Such unbundling has, in some degree, been the result of class and democratic struggles in capitalist countries during this century. 'Regulation', the bane of conservative policy makers, is nothing but a transfer of certain property rights from firm owners to other citizens. Minimum wage laws are, likewise, a property relation: they restrict the kinds of contract that a firm may write with a worker. The taxation of firm profits, and the allowable use by government of tax incentives to induce firms to invest in certain ways are, as well, unbundlings of rights in the income streams of firms. Laws that require firms to notify workers several months in advance of a plant closure implement a change in property relations, as do laws that require firms to pay substantial amounts to displaced workers. Perhaps Marxism's simplistic view of property lies at the source of its adherents' traditional underassessment of the achievements of Nordic social democracy, which inaugurated many of these changes in property relations in regard to productive assets.

While I believe that some progress can be made by reallocations of private property, as Bowles and Gintis advocate, I think that we must experiment with a variety of 'new' (i.e., unbundled) property relations with regard to both productive assets and housing.[3] Indeed, the voucher proposal for education that Bowles and Gintis describe is an unbundling of the traditional state ownership, in which not only schools are controlled by the state, but the assignment of pupils to schools is, as well. There is not just a 'third way' towards progress, but a continuum of possible ways that we must experiment with and study.

Notes

1. A recent, elaborate statement of the view that distribution affects efficiency is found in Stiglitz (1994).
2. Roemer (1994a).
3. For a thoughtful proposal for unbundling property relations with respect to housing, which the authors call 'limited equity housing cooperatives', see Kennedy (1994) and Kennedy and Specht (1994).

References

Bardhan, P. K., 'On tackling the soft budget constraint in market socialism', in P. K. Bardhan and J. E. Roemer (eds.), Market Socialism: The Current Debate (Oxford: Oxford University Press, 1993).

Drèze, J., 'Self-management and economic theory: Efficiency, funding, and employment', in P. K. Bardhan and J. E. Roemer (eds.), Market Socialism: The Current Debate (Oxford: Oxford University Press, 1993).

Grey, T., 'The disintegration of property', in Roland Pennock (ed.), NOMOS, 22 (New York University Press, 1980), pp. 69–85.

Hale, R., Freedom through Law: Public Control of Private Governing Power (New York: Columbia University Press, 1952).

Hohfeld, W., Fundamental Legal Conceptions (New Haven: Yale University Press, 1919).

Kennedy, D. 'Neither the market nor the state: Housing privatization issues', in G. S. Alexander and G. Skapska (eds.), A Fourth Way? (Routledge: New York and London, 1994).

——and F. Michelman, 'Are property and contract efficient?' Hofstra Law Review, 8 (1980), pp. 711–70.

——and L. Specht, 'Limited equity housing cooperatives as a mode of privatization', in G. S. Alexander and G. Skapska (eds.), A Fourth Way? (Routledge: New York and London, 1994).

Roemer, J. E., A Future for Socialism (Cambridge, MA: Harvard University Press, 1994a).

——,'A future for socialism', Politics and Society, 22 (1994b), pp. 451–78.

Simon, W., 'Social-republican property', UCLA Law Review, 38 (1991), pp. 1335–1413.

Singer, J., 'The reliance interest in property', Stanford Law Review, 40 (1988), pp. 611–751.

Stauber, L., A New Program for Democratic Socialism (Carbondale, IL: Four Willows Press, 1987).

Stiglitz, J., Whither Socialism? (Cambridge MA: MIT Press, 1994).

Redistribution of Assets Versus Redistribution of Income

Karl Ove Moene and Michael Wallerstein *

1. Introduction

Samuel Bowles and Herbert Gintis advance two core propositions in making the case for asset-based redistributive strategies. The first is the claim that redistributive programs that enhance efficiency stand a better chance of being adopted than redistributive programs that reduce efficiency. The second proposition is that the redistribution of assets can be 'productivity-enhancing' while the redistribution of income is 'productivity-dampening'. Together, the two propositions constitute an argument for an egalitarian strategy that focuses on attacking inequality in the ownership of assets instead of the traditional remedy of taxing income and using the proceeds to provide transfer payments or welfare services.

In this comment, we accept the first proposition and question the second. We compare the asset-based approach of Bowles and Gintis with the alternative approach associated most closely with social democracy but followed in all advanced industrial societies to some extent. The social-democratic approach is based primarily on the redistribution of income, leaving the distribution of assets largely untouched.[1] The asset-based approach is to redistribute assets, letting the distribution of income be whatever results.

It is misleading to think of social democracy and the asset-based approach proposed by Bowles and Gintis as alternative blueprints, however. Social democracy, as we know it today, was not the result

* This is a revised version of a paper that was presented at the Real Utopias Project on Efficiency and Equality Conference, University of Wisconsin, Madison, 3–5 November, 1995.

of implementing a carefully constructed plan but a process of piece-meal reforms with continual adjustments and modifications that were politically expedient. One can learn a lot – both on the positive and on the negative side – from the long string of trials and errors in Northern Europe as social-democratic governments struggled to find ways to reduce poverty and increase workers' security while maintaining economic prosperity and political support. Social democrats displaced their rivals on the left because their program was superior in terms of political feasibility, not necessarily because it was more efficient.

Consider, for example, the choice between worker-owned firms and unions. Workers' cooperatives competed with unions as the organizational form for enhancing workers' position in the labor market throughout Europe in the nineteenth century. Robert Owen in Britain, Pierre-Joseph Proudhon in France, and Ferdinand Lassalle in Germany all shared the view that workers' cooperatives were the most effective solution to workers' exploitation–deprivation. The German Social Democratic Party's program called for government aid for the establishment of worker-owned firms until the adoption of the Erfurt Program in 1891 (Lindemann 1983). Establishing cooperatives required capital, however, while organizing unions mostly required activists. Since the labor movement had little capital but was richly endowed with talented organizers, the choice to concentrate on organizing unions rather than producer cooperatives is understandable for reasons that have little to do with economic efficiency.

Nevertheless, we agree with Bowles and Gintis (and Gary Becker) that efficiency-promoting redistributive policies are more likely to succeed politically than efficiency-retarding policies, other things being equal. Indeed, much of the success of social democracy is due to the ability of social democrats to find ways of pursuing efficiency and equality at the same time. Where we disagree is with the claim of Bowles and Gintis that efficiency considerations, and therefore political considerations, clearly favor the redistribution of assets over the redistribution of income. In our opinion, both economic and political considerations favor a mixture of the two, with a greater weight on the redistribution of income than Bowles and Gintis acknowledge.

The paper by Bowles and Gintis is unbalanced in that they emphasize the benefits of asset-redistribution and the costs of income-redistribution. Our comment is equally unbalanced in the opposite direction. We emphasize the efficiency gains from policies of income redistribution and the economic and political costs of policies to redistribute assets. What counts in nutrition is the overall balance of a diet as a whole, not the nutritional balance of any individual meal. We trust the same is true in this volume. In section 2, we begin our discussion with the efficiency gains associated with social democratic policies that redistributed income rather than assets. In section 3, we discuss some of the economic and political costs of asset-based redistributive policies, as revealed by the social democratic experience. In section 4, we explore the tension between equality among insiders and the opportunities of outsiders that appears in both income and asset-based redistribution schemes. We compare asset-based and income-based redistributive policies in terms of the political support for redistribution in section 5. Section 6 concludes.

2. The Benefits of Redistribution

The asset-based approach of Bowles and Gintis emphasizes the problems posed by the separation of use from ownership. In situations where the user of an asset is not the owner, where the owner's wealth can be increased by actions which are costly to the user, and where the user's actions are difficult or costly to monitor, the transfer of ownership to the user can increase aggregate efficiency. If the user is made the residual claimant, the user internalizes the full costs and benefits of his or her actions. The efficiency of use rises and monitoring costs disappear. The two examples of efficiency-promoting asset transfers that Bowles and Gintis discuss are the transfer of home ownership from the landlord to the tenants and the transfer of firm ownership from outside investors to the workers.[2] The social-democratic approach emphasizes, instead, the provision of social insurance and, in Scandinavia, the reduction of wage inequalities through collective bargaining. Both the social-democratic welfare and wage policies can be advocated on efficiency grounds, albeit in response to different market failures than the agency costs emphasized by Bowles and Gintis.

The efficiency argument for the compression of inter-plant and inter-industry wage differentials is based on the potential inefficiency of wage differentials. In the 1950s, two Swedish trade union economists, Gösta Rehn and Rudolf Meidner, argued that decentralized wage-setting resulted in wage differentials that reflected different levels of productivity between and within industries (Rehn 1952). If wages are higher in more productive firms and lower in less productive firms, the wage structure serves to tax the most efficient and subsidize the least efficient employers. Since employers understand that new investment raises their workers' bargaining power as it enhances productivity, the profit-maximizing level of investment is inefficiently low with decentralized bargaining. A uniform wage imposed by centralized wage bargaining that ties wages to average productivity, but not to the productivity of plant in particular, can increase both equality and investment simultaneously, provided the uniform wage is low enough to maintain full employment (Agell and Lommerud 1993; Moene and Wallerstein 1995a, 1995b).

That some degree of wage compression increases efficiency and profits finds empirical support in studies of the Swedish post-war experience. The goal of 'leveling the playing field' by reducing inter-industry and inter-plant wage differentials was shared by both employers and unions in Sweden in the 1950s and 1960s (Swenson 1989). Recent statistical work by Douglas Hibbs and Håkan Locking (1995) on wage differentials and productivity in Sweden concludes that wage compression between plants is associated with above average growth in productivity while wage compression within plants is associated with below average productivity growth. From 1960, the earliest year in which data on wage differentials in Sweden are available, until the early 1970s, Hibbs and Locking find that the benefits of wage compression between plants outweighed the cost of wage compression within plants. In contrast, Hibbs and Locking find that productivity growth suffered as the negative effect of within-plant wage compression overwhelmed the positive effect of between-plant wage compression after the early 1970s. Thus, the empirical evidence suggests that wage compression in Sweden was carried beyond the level that maximized productivity growth in the 1970s. Rising opposition from both employers and skilled workers forced an end to the policy in Sweden in the 1980s.

The efficiency argument for the welfare policies associated with social democracy is that private markets for insurance often fail to be efficient. Insurance against many potential calamities, such as lack of adequate retirement income, job loss, work-related accidents or ill health, are generally not provided at efficient levels with private insurance markets because of adverse selection and moral hazard (Barr 1992).

Adverse selection refers to the problem that can occur when consumers of insurance have private information about their risk. Consider the case of health insurance. The need for expensive medical care differs greatly among individuals. A voluntary insurance plan that provides full insurance for all at the same rate is unstable. Any competitor could profit by writing a policy with less insurance and lower premiums that is attractive only to the relatively healthy. The plan that provides full insurance would then be left with those who anticipate large medical expenses, which raises costs and forces the premium up. The only stable equilibrium with private insurance entails less insurance than consumers would like.

Moral hazard refers to the problem that exists when insurance reduces efforts to avoid the state for which insurance is sought. Private unemployment insurance, for example, faces problems of both adverse selection (those who expect to be laid off will be the most eager to purchase insurance) and moral hazard (the presence of insurance reduces the effort taken to find new employment or to reveal to the insurance company that new employment has been found). It is difficult enough for the government to know whether those receiving unemployment benefits are really unemployed and looking for work. Monitoring the job-search efforts of the unemployed would be impossible for a private insurance company. In the case of unemployment insurance, the private market fails to exist entirely.

It is, perhaps, less clear that private markets fail in the provision of pensions. All who save for retirement, however, are subject to the risk that the value of their savings will be reduced by unanticipated inflation (in the case of defined benefit plans) or unexpected investment losses (in the case of defined contribution plans). The government, which can use current tax revenues to fund current pensions, is better able to offer insurance against monetary and financial risk than any private company.

Bowles and Gintis are well aware of the efficiency arguments for the public provision of insurance through welfare programs, as their discussion of health and unemployment insurance indicates. Indeed, Bowles and Gintis acknowledge that the need for insurance may increase with the redistribution of assets. Workers whose non-human capital is tied up in the same firm as their human capital are less able to insure themselves through diversification of their holding than workers in a traditional capitalist firm. In addition, Bowles and Gintis accept the criticism that less diversified owners may be less innovative because of their reluctance to take risks. What Bowles and Gintis do not recognize is how much of current welfare spending is dedicated to the funding of social insurance programs. It is wrong to identify current welfare spending as tax and transfer policies designed to mitigate the consequences of concentrated ownership. Social-democratic welfare policies are better understood as policies designed to provide social insurance in contexts where private insurance is inefficient.

3. The Costs of Redistribution

Both the asset-based approach (assuming the policy instrument is the provision of subsidized credit) and the provision of social insurance must be financed by taxation. It is important, in both cases, to consider the costs as well as the potential benefits. As an example, consider the proposal of Bowles and Gintis to encourage owner-occupied housing. It so happens that the housing policy adopted by the Norwegian social democrats in the post-war period accomplished exactly what Bowles and Gintis advocate. In 1990 as much as 78 per cent of all dwellings in Norway were owner-occupied, largely a consequence of the government's housing policy. This is the second highest fraction in Europe (after Ireland with 81 per cent) and should be compared to 52 per cent in Denmark, 40 per cent in Sweden, 38 per cent in (the western part of) Germany, 54 per cent in France and 67 per cent in Italy (Statistics EU 1993, Statistics Norway 1990). Some 19 per cent of the dwellings in Norway, included in the 78 per cent owner-occupied, are owned by housing cooperatives (most common in the larger cities).

Norwegian housing policy worked through the provision of cheap credit for the construction of private homes and to housing cooperatives associated with the social democratic party. Credit from the governmental bank for housing *(Husbanken)* implied a substantial subsidy. The subsidy for a private home owner in 1987 who obtained credit in *Husbanken* that year was calculated to be around $30,000. Since 1987, interest rates in *Husbanken* and commercial banks have converged.

Subsidized credit for the construction of private homes was not means tested. Instead, credit was rationed on the basis of the kind of house being built. Houses above a specified size and cost were ineligible for the subsidy. In addition, the interest rate charged by *Husbanken* had an increasing profile over time. This made the subsidy particularly attractive to less wealthy, credit-rationed households and less attractive to the rich who could easily borrow elsewhere.[3]

Subsidized houses could be sold freely on the market. Since most houses of a similar type were either subsidized or not, the policy did not allow the beneficiaries to capitalize the subsidy by selling the house *ex post*. Access to new units in the housing cooperatives, mostly apartments in the cities, went to members of the cooperative (who paid a small membership fee) according to their place in line. Units in the housing cooperatives could be sold, but at a price determined by the cooperative. Rental units, whether built with the subsidy or not, were subject to rent control.

Was the Norwegian policy a success? Yes, in the sense that the government accomplished the twin goals of increasing the supply of modest housing and making private or cooperative ownership of dwellings almost universal. But the policy does raise questions concerning both the criteria used to allocate the subsidy and the cost of the program.

First, it proved difficult to design rationing schemes which did not imply unjust allocations. Means-testing of the builder would not have worked as well to increase the supply of modest housing, since it might be most profitable for entrepreneurs of modest means to use the subsidized credit to build luxury houses for immediate sale. Means-testing with restrictions on subsequent transfers of ownership would also have efficiency costs in terms of restricting mobility and reducing the incentive of owners to maintain the quality of their property and their community. To allocate credit on the basis of cost favored those with access to cheap land. Policies of asset-based redistribution as well as policies of income-based redistribution pose difficult questions of rationing if they cannot be offered to all.

Secondly, and more importantly, the allocation of credit for housing meant that less credit was available for other purposes. The housing policy was part of the general controls over credit used by the Norwegian government to steer investment. Because the government did not use the rate of return as the sole criterion for allocating capital, the average rate of return on investment in Norway suffered. This does not necessarily indicate a policy failure. Why have controls except to impose an allocation that differs from what the market would generate? Yet, the cost may have been large. Norway ranked nineteenth out of nineteen OECD countries in terms of the rate of growth of productivity of capital between 1960 and 1990 (OECD 1991). While Norway grew rapidly in per capita terms, in part by investing an extraordinarily high share of national income, the rate of growth could have increased or the same rate of growth could have been achieved with less sacrifice of current consumption if capital had been invested more efficiently.

The social-democratic experience has less to say about the other policy of asset redistribution advocated by Bowles and Gintis: the promotion of worker-owned firms. Unlike the US or the UK, social-democratic governments have not encouraged the growth of worker-owned firms through tax subsidies. It is obvious, however, that the same question of the opportunity cost of government funds applies here as well. Policies that are potentially self-financing, like the provision of government-supplied credit to worker-owned firms at cost, do not solve the underlying problem. If the government simply provided credit for worker-owned firms, for example, the government would face the same moral hazard problems as private banks. Worker-owners with none of their own money invested in the company, have an incentive to engage in overly risky ventures (since they capture all of the gains if the venture succeeds and can simply default on their loan if the venture fails) whether their financing comes from private banks or the government. The debacle in the US with the savings and loan industry illustrates how serious the moral hazard problem can be.

It should be noted that, in the 1970s, the Swedish unions did propose a major redistribution of corporate ownership. The Meidner plan called for a fraction of profits in large firms to be converted to shares of stock and placed in union-controlled funds. As the plan was originally proposed, it was estimated that the wage-earner funds would own a majority of Swedish industry within twenty-five to fifty years (Meidner 1978). The wage-earner fund proposal was adopted after the social democrats came to power in 1982, but in a diluted form that precluded majority ownership (Esping-Anderson 1985). In the debate over the funds, the social democrats discovered that the threat of workers' ownership mobilized the bourgeois opposition, and failed to generate much enthusiasm among workers. Indeed, the bitterness of the conflict over the funds undermined the cooperative relationship between the unions and the employers' associations and contributed to what became, in the 1980s, a general political offensive by employers against the entire corporatist framework of Swedish collective bargaining.

Since the Meidner plan envisioned workers' ownership through centralized funds rather than ownership of the particular firm in which they worked, it was very different from the type of policy advocated by Bowles and Gintis. Nevertheless, the political history of attempts to redistribute assets through the forced sale of stock, even a limited amount of stock at the prevailing market price, is not encouraging. Both managers and owners fought hard to maintain the dominance of outside stockholders in firms' governance structure. In Sweden, the social democrats were able to obtain widespread support for the expansion of welfare programs, but when they proposed establishing workers' ownership on a large scale through the conversion of wage increases into shares of stock, they suffered a smashing defeat. One of the political lessons of social democracy is that policies designed to redistribute wealth generate much greater political resistance than policies to redistribute income.

4. Insiders Versus Outsiders

One of the criticisms of union-imposed wage compression is that employers who must pay the same wage to all will try to avoid hiring less productive workers. Less productive workers benefit from a compressed wage schedule if they obtain employment, but the compressed wage schedule makes finding employment more difficult for such workers. At a more aggregate level, some have noted that the high degree of equality within the Scandinavian countries achieved through both wage and welfare policies was accompanied by strict controls on immigration.

Similar conflict between equality among insiders and the opportunities of outsiders may arise with worker-owned firms. For a variety of reasons, worker-owned firms are likely to adopt more egalitarian distributions of income within the firm than is typical when wages are set unilaterally by management hired by outside owners. First, fairness is likely to play a more significant role in pay determination when the pay scale is decided collectively through some democratic procedure. To persuade others, one must present arguments in terms of either common interests or commonly held principles. Conceptions of fair or equal distributions of pay are likely to serve as focal points in a situation where no equilibrium based upon purely self-interested voting exists. Second, democratic enterprises foster feelings of community and equality which make it difficult to allocate revenues too unevenly among the members.

Internal equity, however, may have an adverse impact on how outsiders are treated. If all cooperative members receive equal pay, cooperatives will try to avoid admitting members with lower-than-average productivity. The smaller the internal wage differentials, the greater the pressure to avoid giving membership to less productive workers. Thus, highly productive workers would cluster in enterprises with other highly productive co-workers while cooperatives with less productive workers are only able to recruit other less productive workers. There may be important complementarities involved in the sense that the marginal contribution of a highly productive worker is higher the higher the average productivity of the cooperative members. In addition, enterprises with highly productive workers may be better able to improve their technology or overall efficiency than other firms. Thus, initial differences in workers' quality may magnify income inequalities over time. Greater equality of pay within the enterprise may lead to greater inequality of pay between enterprises.

Internal pay equality can affect the quantity as well as the quality of desired cooperative members. If cooperatives adjust the number of members in the long run to maximize income per member, the optimal number of members is determined by the condition that the marginal contribution of the last member equals the average income per member. If the marginal contribution is more than the average, insiders would benefit as a group by recruiting more members. If the marginal contribution is below average, insiders would let the membership decline, perhaps through attrition. If the cooperative is established by purchasing capitalist firms at their market price without subsidies from the government, the cooperative would start with fixed costs that can only be recouped by maintaining the same number of workers as a profit-maximizing firm would choose. If the cooperative is established from scratch or is bought up with the help of subsidies, however, there may be pure rents to be shared among members. The existence of such rents reduces the optimal size of membership since more members means dividing the rents among more individuals.

Two negative consequences follow. The first is that workers are not allocated efficiently across enterprises, since the marginal product of labor in highly productive firms will exceed the marginal product of labor in less productive firms. This is a loss of efficiency, since if workers were reallocated from less productive to more productive firms, total production would increase. The second negative consequence is a reduction in the demand for labor in the cooperative sector. This means either lower wages or more unemployment among workers who are not cooperative members. Again, these consequences are the result of an internally egalitarian pay policy. If cooperatives discriminated against new members, cooperatives would maximize the income of existing members by mimicking the employment practices of profit-maximizing firms and admit new members at the market-clearing wage.

5. The Politics of Redistribution

There are, at least, two important political issues that need to be considered in evaluating redistributive policies. The first is the impact of redistribution on other aspects of government policy. The second is the impact of redistributive policies on the extent to which redistributive policies can sustain political support.

The redistribution of assets will not eliminate the need for political interventions. No matter how the ownership of assets is distributed, the state will still be called on to provide public goods, like education, and prevent public bads, like environmental degradation. One of the standard arguments for a more egalitarian distribution of wealth is that concentrated wealth makes democratic political control more difficult.[4] It is possible, however, that the reverse is true. Less concentrated ownership may make the political regulation of asset holders more difficult in a democracy.

Let us illustrate the point with a simple example. Oslo is surrounded by low-lying mountains that have been protected and preserved for the enjoyment of hikers, mountain bikers and cross-country skiers. The strict controls on development were facilitated by the fact that almost all of the land was owned by a single landlord, whose interests were easily overridden for the sake of preserving the natural environment. If the land had, instead, been owned in small pieces by thousands of families, policies that prevented landowners from realizing the full potential commercial value of the property would have faced much stiffer resistance.

In general, social-democratic governments have preferred to deal with concentrated asset-holders than with many small asset-holders. As health-care reformers discovered during the battle over health care in the US, it is easier to work with large corporations than with small businesses. In part, large corporations are more willing to live with mandated benefits. In part, large corporations are less fearsome political opponents. In a democracy, it is an advantage when your opposition represents a constituency that is a small share of the electorate. Of course, the disadvantage of being small in numbers may be offset for concentrated asset-holders by the influence they exert through financial contributions to political parties or candidates. The dependence of parties and politicians on private financing, however, is not universal among democracies and can be eliminated with reform of the electoral system. The power of numbers is inherent in majority rule.

The second political consideration concerns the political sustainability of redistributive policies. Two aspects of social-democratic
policies of income redistribution have important consequences for the
level of political support. The first is the universalistic design of major
welfare programs, particularly pensions, health care and child-
support. Benefits are provided to everyone, not just to the poor. The
second is the continuity of policies to redistribute income as opposed
to the one-shot character of asset-redistributions.

The universalistic feature of social-democratic welfare policy is a
good example of the fortuitous way in which the social-democratic
model evolved. Although the social democrats reaped the political
advantages of universalism in welfare policy, social democrats were
often not the primary advocates of universalism. For example, the
Swedish pension reform of 1946 instituted a uniform pension to be
paid to all elderly people regardless of wealth or income. The social-
democratic government was strongly committed to the establishment
of a national pension system, but not necessarily to a universalistic
pension with uniform benefits. It was Swedish employers who lobbied
for a pension that would be provided on a universalistic basis
(Swenson 1995). Employers' support for universalism stemmed from
their desire to avoid any reduction in the supply of labor. Employers
opposed pension plans that would encourage older workers to retire
by making pension benefits contingent on lack of income. Swedish
employers lobbied for the uniform payment to minimize administrative costs.

From the point of view of economic efficiency, universalistic
programs have well-known advantages and disadvantages over
means-testing. Universalistic programs avoid the disincentive effects
of high implicit marginal tax rates that occur when benefits are
reduced as income rises. In addition, universalistic programs have
much lower administrative costs than means-tested programs, since
there is no need to verify recipients' eligibility. The disadvantage of
universalistic programs is that the absence of means-testing greatly
increases the cost of providing a given level of benefits in terms of
government revenues. From the point of view of political sustainability, universalistic programs have the great advantage of not dividing
the population into two disjointed categories of welfare recipients and
tax payers. The more welfare policy works as a redistributive policy,
where some groups benefit and others pay the cost, and the less that
welfare policy works as an insurance policy where most benefit *ex
ante* (even if only a minority benefits *ex post*), the lower the political
support.

The political difference between an ongoing policy of income redistribution versus a single-shot policy of asset redistribution is best explained by analogy with the choice between bridges and ferries to connect people living on islands (or, in Norway, separated by fjords).[5] Ferries require an annual subsidy. A bridge, in contrast, requires a much larger initial subsidy, but minimal maintenance costs once built. With ferries, the islanders are continually mobilized in support of subsidies sufficient to maintain reliable service. Once the inhabitants of an island have a bridge, however, they have no reason, apart from altruism, to support further government spending on either ferries or bridges for others. While the islanders might prefer a bridge (since a ferry service can be discontinued while a bridge will not be torn down), broad political support for a policy to subsidize transportation among islands is easier to sustain with ferries.

Suppose that the government was able to encourage a significant growth of worker-owned firms by providing subsidized credit for the establishment of cooperatives. Some of the newly created worker-owned firms would thrive and their owners would become rich. Others would go bankrupt and their owners would be left without assets once again. Would those who succeeded in building successful firms continue to support a policy that favored the establishment of new cooperatives? Or would those who succeeded attribute their success to their own superior skills and hard work and fight against continual hand-outs to those unable to survive the rigors of market competition?

A social insurance system suffers from the same difficulty, but to a lesser degree. Once people become sufficiently successful that they are almost certain never to collect from the social insurance system, they would like to cancel their policy. But the ongoing need for insurance and the difficulty of self-insuring for most provides some basis for long-term support for policies that redistribute income. In contrast, current asset-holders receive nothing from a policy that encourages the spread of asset-holding to those without assets.

6. Conclusion

The objections that we have raised to the proposals of Bowles and Gintis should not obscure our support for their project of designing policies that reduce inequality and enhance efficiency at the same time. Altruism is not absent from political choice, but redistributive policies whose support depends exclusively on the altruism of the majority are fragile. Developing politically-robust redistributive programs requires finding ways to extend the benefits to the majority of voters.

Although we have concentrated on where we disagree with Bowles and Gintis, emphasizing costs of asset redistribution and benefits of income redistribution that they neglect, it is unlikely that the optimal redistributive policy would rely exclusively on one or the other. The reforms advocated by Bowles and Gintis increase the need for social insurance, in which case we need to think of asset-based redistribution as an addition to current welfare policies, not as a replacement for the welfare state. Moreover, the efficiency case for workers' ownership varies with the characteristics of the industry such as entry barriers, capital requirements and the difficulty of monitoring performance. Asset-based redistribution may have an important role to play in particular policy areas, such as housing, without being the single solution to all distributional problems.

Notes

1. Social-democratic governments, at times, have implemented policies for altering the distribution of assets, particularly housing as we discuss below.
2. Bowles and Gintis suggest four examples of asset-based redistribution: worker-owned firms, ownership of housing, property rights for children in parents income and school vouchers. Property rights for children and school vouchers are not really examples of asset-based redistribution, in our opinion. The school voucher proposal may or may not be a good idea, but that is an issue of introducing competition in the supply of public services rather than the redistribution of assets. Property rights for children is also an issue that doesn't fit. Current practice in the US and elsewhere does, more or less, give children a property right in their parent's income. The problem is that the property right is not enforced, but enforcement is not addressed in the Bowles and Gintis proposal.
3. The credit subsidy can be understood as a scheme to implement an efficient redistribution through distorting taxation as suggested by Hoff and Lyon (1995).
4. This argument has been formalized by Roemer (1993).
5. In Norway, this is an important choice decided by parliament.

References

Agell, Jonas and Kjell Erik Lommerud, 'Egalitarianism and Growth', *Scandinavian Journal of Economics* 95 (1993), pp. 559–79.

Barr, Nicholas, 'Economic Theory and the Welfare State: A Survey and Interpretation', *Journal of Economic Literature* 30 (1992), pp. 741–803.

Becker, Gary, 'A Theory of Competition Among Pressure Groups for Political Influence', *Quarterly Journal of Economics*, 98 (1983), pp. 371–400.

Bowles, Samuel and Herbert Gintis, 'Efficient Redistribution: New Rules for

Markets, States and Communities', unpublished paper (Amherst MA: Department of Economics, University of Massachusetts, 1994).

Esping-Andersen, Gøsta, *Politics Against Markets: The Social Democratic Road to Power* (Princeton: Princeton University Press, 1985).

Hibbs, Douglas A. Jr. and Håkan Locking, 'Solidarity Wage Policies and Industrial Productivity in Sweden', *Nordic Journal of Political Economy* 22 (1995), pp. 95–108.

Hoff, Karla and Andrew B. Lyon, 'Non-Leaky Buckets: Optimal Redistributive Taxation and Agency Costs', *Journal of Public Economies* (1995), forthcoming.

Lindemann, Albert S., *A History of European Socialism* (New Haven: Yale University Press, 1983).

Meidner, Rudolf, *Employee Investment Funds* (London: Allen and Unwin, 1978).

Moene, Karl Ove and Michael Wallerstein, 'Collective Bargaining versus Workers' Ownership', *Journal of Comparative Economics*, 17 (1993), pp. 628–45.

——, 'How Social Democracy Worked: Labor Markets Institutions', *Politics and Society*, 23 (1995a), pp. 185–211.

——'Solidaristic Wage Bargaining', *Nordic Journal of Political Economy*, 22 (1995b), pp. 79–94.

Organization for Economic Cooperation and Development, *OECD Economic Outlook*, no. 49 (Paris: OECD, 1991).

Rehn, Gösta, 'The Problem of Stability: An Analysis of Some Policy Proposals', in Ralph Turvey (ed.), *Wages Policy under Full Employment* (London: W. Hodge, 1952).

Roemer, John E. 'Would Economic Democracy Increase the Amounts of Public Bads', *Scandinavian Journal of Economics*, 95 (1993), pp. 227–38.

Swenson, Peter, *Fair Shares: Unions, Pay and Politics in Sweden and West Germany* (Ithaca: Cornell University Press, 1989).

——, 'Swedish Employers Supported the Universalistic Social Democratic Welfare State', unpublished manuscript (Evanston IL: Department of Political Science, Northwestern University, 1995).

The Crisis of Egalitarian Policy and the Promises of Asset-based Redistribution

Peter Skott *

Economic inequality has been increasing in many parts of the world since the late 1970s, and there is a widespread perception that existing egalitarian models impose unacceptable costs in the form of high taxation, low productivity and reduced growth rates. The failures and recent collapse of central planning in the Soviet Union and Eastern Europe have undoubtedly contributed to a general shift of opinion against western social democracy. However, the policy reversals and attacks on the welfare state predate the Soviet collapse and must be explained primarily by developments within the capitalist countries.

In an important and thought-provoking essay Bowles and Gintis build on and extend their earlier work.[1] Applying an agency-theoretic approach to egalitarian policy issues, they suggest that there are good reasons why social democracy (and traditional egalitarian models in general) lack credibility. These traditional strategies have, they argue, focused on the redistribution of income, a strategy which ultimately must impair economic performance. Asset-based redistribution is offered as an alternative strategy. Unlike income redistribution, an egalitarian strategy based on asset redistribution can, they argue, be productivity-enhancing. Hence, it may become possible to gain broad political support for this kind of egalitarian redistribution.

As pointed out by Bowles and Gintis, ' "equality pessimism" finds little support in the empirical record of macroeconomic performance'. The data are often shaky and the methodology questionable,[2] but existing studies typically suggest that, if anything, equality and

*This version of the paper has benefited from the comments of participants in the conference on Efficiency and Equality, University of Wisconsin, November 1995.

economic performance are positively correlated. Thus, the roots of the crisis of egalitarian policy are not immediately obvious in the data, and to explain the crisis Bowles and Gintis focus on two sets of issues. They suggest that: (1) egalitarian policies during the 'golden age' were linked to closed-economy, left-Keynesian beliefs in the expansionary effects of egalitarian redistribution; (2) these beliefs have been gradually undermined by the increasing integration of national economies in the world market. As a result, attention has shifted to the supply side: productivity and wage costs are now regarded as the key determinants of international competitiveness, and anti-egalitarian, low-wage policies appear attractive.

A correct diagnosis is important for an evaluation of possible solutions, and in some respects the account by Bowles and Gintis seems incomplete or even misleading. In this paper I consider, in section 1, the links between Keynesian employment policy and inequality, while section 2 takes up the effects of international integration. The analysis of the background to the changes is followed in section 3 by a brief discussion of the proposals for worker-owned firms. Worker-ownership may indeed overcome some of the constraints on traditional egalitarian policy. But one should not exaggerate the differences between the Bowles and Gintis approach and social-democratic policy. Schemes of industrial democracy and increased worker-ownership were developed in a number of countries, and the fate of these proposals testify to the opposition and transitional difficulties that would meet any scheme of this nature. A final section summarizes the conclusions.

1 Egalitarian Policy and Left Keynesianism

During the golden age, Keynesian policies were seen as important in smoothing out the trade cycle and preventing deep depressions, and the promise of full employment through Keynesian policy also gave credibility to a reformist and pragmatist approach, thereby strengthening social democrats against attacks from both radical socialists and the right.[3] In this sense the Keynesian promise may well have been essential for egalitarian policy. Moreover, good economic performance in the form of both high employment and high rates of productivity growth made the implementation of egalitarian policies easier during the golden age. But, at least in Europe, Keynesian demand arguments played a very limited role in the direct justification of welfare-state programs. This is not surprising. The links between distribution and growth in some Kaleckian and left-Keynesian models have never been widely accepted,[4] and in any case the links would be largely irrelevant if other policies could (and did) ensure full employment. Furthermore, the models did not apply (without significant modification) to small open economies, and social democrats and mainstream Keynesians in the small west European countries have always been keenly aware of the openness of their economies.[5]

Growth considerations did play a role in the policy discussions but not in the form of left-Keynesian demand-driven growth models. When egalitarian policies were linked to productivity and growth, the arguments usually focused on the supply side. Wage increases, it was argued, would put pressure on employers to innovate and ensure high-quality jobs and technological progressiveness; shorter hours would be compensated by an increase in the quality and intensity of work; educational programs would raise productivity, labor-market policies increase flexibility, and social programs bring women into the work force and reduce workers' opposition to productivity increases and structural change.

The demise of the golden age was followed by a breakdown of the consensus behind both Keynesian demand policy and egalitarian redistribution. Macroeconomic problems made their appearance in the late 1960s with a pronounced increase in strike activity and general social unrest in most OECD countries. These developments were accompanied by rising inflation, reduced productivity growth and low profitability, problems which were later exacerbated by the oil shock.

Broadly speaking, the initial policy response aimed at maintaining full employment and at dealing with inflation and balance of payments problems through some combination of incomes and exchange-rate policies. In the late 1970s, however, priorities started to change, inflation was given top priority and unemployment was allowed to rise. Monetarist and new classical theories were used to justify the change. Market mechanisms, it was argued, automatically and quickly bring the economy back to full employment following a shock, and Keynesian policy, consequently, becomes unnecessary or even harmful: attempts to push income beyond the full employment level merely lead to rising inflation, and informational problems and policy lags defeat all possibilities of fine-tuning, making attempts in this direction destabilizing.

Having denied the need for aggregate demand policy, the rise in unemployment was followed by supply-side criticisms of trade unions and of the disincentive effects of high taxes, generous unemployment benefits, high minimum wages and a low dispersion of wages. Although 'all too often based on a superficial analysis of economic behavior and unsupported by rigorous empirical evidence' (Atkinson, 1993) these criticisms have been influential, and the 1980s and 1990s have been characterized in many countries by labor-market reforms, attacks on unionized labor, tax reforms and the restructuring or curtailment of welfare programs.[6]

Although Kaleckian and left-Keynesian ideas played, at best, a limited role as motivation for egalitarian policies, other aspects of Kalecki's work may help explain both the decline of the golden age and the policy reversals: the broad pattern of the post-war period can be seen as part of a Kaleckian long wave. As long ago as 1943 Kalecki predicted that 'the *maintenance* of full employment would cause social and political changes' as '"the sack" would cease to play its role as a disciplinary measure' and that, as a result, 'a powerful block is likely to be formed between big business and the rentier interests, and they would probably find more than one economist to declare that the situation was manifestly unsound'.[7]

From this Kaleckian perspective, egalitarian policies in the post-war period were not the means to ensure high aggregate demand and full employment. The main direction of causation went the other way: full employment generated ever-increasing egalitarian demands for reform during the golden age while high unemployment after the golden age paved the way for increasing inequality. The breakdown of the golden age is itself explained endogenously. High employment not only compressed the distribution of income, it also caused, more generally, a deterioration of the business climate, and this deterioration gradually undermined the full-employment policy.

The Kaleckian long-wave argument can be represented mathematically in the form of a two-dimensional system of differential equations (Skott, 1993). This system implies that fluctuations in 'business climate' lead fluctuations in employment by about a quarter of a cycle.[8] Using profitability and strike activity as indicators of business climate, the post-war evidence for the OECD countries is consistent with this prediction. The late 1950s and early 1960s were characterized by high-profit rates, low strike activity and falling unemployment. In the late 1960s and early 1970s unemployment was low but profit rates were falling and strike activity increasing. This period was followed in the mid 1970s to early 1980s by low profitability, high strike activity and rising unemployment. Finally, from the mid 1980s to the early 1990s profit rates have been rising and strike activity falling while unemployment (especially in Europe) has fluctuated around a high level.

Kalecki's argument is essentially that any economic system which relies on markets and private accumulation must maintain a satisfactory business climate, and that if full employment causes a deterioration of this climate then traditional social democratic attempts at taming the capitalist beast are bound to falter. From a long-term perspective, however, institutions cannot be taken as given, and institutional reform may affect the compatibility of full employment and an egalitarian income distribution with successful, market-based accumulation. This kind of institutional transformation can be seen precisely as 'social democracy's historic challenge',[9] while events over the last twenty years indicate the failure so far to meet the challenge and achieve this kind of transformation.

In the present context the interesting question is whether or to what extent the breakdown of the golden age and the increase in inequality could have been averted through a strategy of asset-based redistribution. Or looking ahead, whether asset-based redistribution can be a key element of an institutional transformation to overcome the accumulation constraint on egalitarian policy. I shall return to this question in section 3.

2 International Integration

Many of the developments of the post-war period have been common to all OECD countries, and this (imperfect) synchronization may have been reinforced by increasing international integration. In Europe, for instance, the policy reversals after the golden age came early in the UK, and the UK changes contributed to the pressure for change elsewhere.

Bowles and Gintis emphasize the limitations that international demand leakages and capital mobility impose on traditional domestic demand policy. I think this emphasis may be misplaced. Trade and capital mobility have profound effects on the conduct of Keynesian demand policy, and the policy game between different countries will typically lead to suboptimal outcomes. It is not clear to me, however, why the demand-side complications should give a strong inegalitarian bias. 'Social democracy in one country' may come up against international constraints, but the main constraints are not the conditions for aggregate demand policy.

Open economies may try to solve their demand problems through beggar-thy-neighbour policies, and at the world level these policies may lead to aggregate demand problems which could have been solved by coordinated expansion (problems of this kind may well play a role in the European experience). But international competitiveness does not in itself dictate an uneven distribution of income. The domestic-income distribution will influence the sectoral trade pattern, but arguably there can be dynamic advantages to an egalitarian strategy involving the specialization in skill and knowledge-intensive products as opposed to inegalitarian strategies of price competition in low-skill products.

Certain forms of increased competition can, of course, have inegalitarian effects. This is the case, for instance, in high-income countries when low-skill products meet intensified competition from new producers in low-income countries. Structural changes of this kind, which figure prominently in current debates (e.g. Wood, 1995), will clearly put a strain on egalitarian policies. But internationalization has had additional, direct effects on the domestic 'bargaining game': changes in reference groups and in international mobility have affected both the attitudes and bargaining position of the rich. The logic of this argument can be presented in terms of a simple, stylized example.

Consider first a closed economy and assume that

i. random shocks cause the incomes of individual agents to deviate from the average income.
ii. redistribution is possible using proportional taxes to finance lump-sum transfers.
iii. redistribution may be costly in the sense that the average level of income may depend inversely on the rate of redistributive taxation.
iv. agents are risk-averse; they are prepared to buy insurance (in the form of a lower expected value of income) in order to reduce the variability of income.

In the special case with costless redistribution, the optimal outcome is complete redistribution: the tax rate is set equal to one and all agents receive the same post-redistribution income. With costly redistribution the optimal tax rate will typically lie between zero and one, the exact solution depending on the degree of risk-aversion, the distribution of the random shocks and the costs of redistribution.

Now introduce a second country and assume that initially the two countries are identical and that a country may restrict immigration but cannot prevent emigration. Each country sets its own redistribution scheme, but now agents in each country may escape the implications of the scheme by emigrating to the other country *after* learning the value of their individual income. Emigration involves private costs, and agents weigh these costs against the possible gains in income (after redistribution).

In the extreme case without migration and redistribution costs, the implications for egalitarian policy are devastating. If country 1 has chosen a tax rate $t_1 > 0$, country 2 may raise the income of *all* its citizens by reducing its tax rate marginally below t_1. High-income agents in country 1 will then wish to emigrate, and the inflow of high-income agents increases the average income and enables the country to raise its lump-sum transfers. Incomes in the high-tax country, on the other hand, drop as a result of the emigration. Thus, on plausible assumptions the game between the policy makers in the two countries produces an outcome with $t_1 = t_2 = 0$, that is, without any redistribution.

With positive migration costs each country retains some leeway for redistribution, and in general one would expect the degree of redistribution to vary directly with the level of migration costs and inversely with the level of redistribution costs. Internationalization may have affected the potential for egalitarian redistribution through both of these channels. The reduction in the costs of migration (both tangible and mental) is straightforward. Increasing similarities of education, improved language skills, cultural homogenization and legal changes combine to increase the job opportunities abroad, and improved transportation and communication make it possible to retain close links with family and friends in the home country.

The costs of redistribution have also been affected by the process of internationalization. Internationalization has altered the composition of the reference groups of, in particular, high-income groups: the weight of domestic low-income groups has declined and the weight of foreign high-income groups increased. As a result the general consensus behind egalitarian policies has been eroded. Comparing their own net income with those of foreign managers, lawyers or professors, high-income agents no longer show the same willingness to accept domestic redistribution. Changes of this kind in general attitudes almost inevitably lead to increased tax evasion and intensified attempts to exploit loopholes of the system. The result is a rise in the costs of redistribution.

In addition to these changes in the costs of migration and redistribution, the argument also implies the existence of international policy spillovers. The migration condition sets an upper limit to the difference in taxation. Hence, a domestic shift in priorities leading to lower taxes in any single country can make it impossible for other countries to pursue their previous policies. In this way the consequences of Mrs Thatcher can spread internationally.

In Europe, these effects of increased internationalization have, I think, been much more important for distributional policy than the external leakages of traditional Keynesian demand policy. The US, where changes in international mobility have been less pronounced, might seem to require a different explanation. In fact, however, the basic reasoning behind the example may be particularly relevant for the US. High domestic mobility is combined in the US with the financing of many programs at the state or local level. This combination severely circumscribes the possibilities of redistribution using traditional European-style policies. Thus, although other factors have undoubtedly been important, this institutional element alone may help explain the relatively low level of redistribution in the US throughout the post-war period. In the US, redistributional programs that would have been viable in the absence of mobility, instead cause a fiscal crisis for the local authority that tries to implement them. High mobility makes it essential that redistributive programs are financed centrally and that they are structured in a reasonably uniform manner. From this perspective the current US trend towards increasing decentralization of welfare programs threatens to produce a further weakening of egalitarian policy.

3 Asset-based Redistribution

The analysis in section 1 raises a number of questions with respect to the asset-based strategy advocated by Bowles and Gintis. From a Kaleckian perspective, the main question is whether asset-based redistribution presents a hitherto neglected way of achieving egalitarian objectives without violating the accumulation constraint. There are at least three ways in which this might happen.

Productivity increases, first, may relax the accumulation constraint if they take the right form. If capital goods come to be used more efficiently (if the output–capital ratio increases) then less investment is required to generate any given rate of growth of output and employment. But an increase in the rate of growth of labor productivity, on the other hand, raises the investment requirements for full employment growth.[10]

With asset-based redistribution, second, the conflict over the functional distribution of income would presumably be greatly attenuated. If workers are the sole residual claimants (and all economic activity were to be organized in worker-owned firms) a distinction between profits and wages would be irrelevant. In itself this does not necessarily remove all conflict: the distinction between wages and profits might not matter under these circumstances, but the distinction between saving/accumulation and consumption remains. More fundamentally, asset-based redistribution will affect both the identity and characteristics of the decision-makers. Thus, the relevant definition of 'business climate' cannot be assumed unchanged, and depending on the detailed institutional set-up of worker-owned firms the investment criteria will change too.[11]

The net effect of these changes is uncertain, and the precise institutional implementation of the reforms could be critical for the outcome. More importantly, even if on balance an egalitarian wealth distribution with widespread worker-ownership could overcome the accumulation constraint, a comparative analysis of this kind is insufficient. Distributional conflict may be attenuated once the redistribution of assets has been accomplished, but the transitional process of asset redistribution will be characterized by intense conflict. In this connection it is interesting to note that proposals for increased industrial democracy and worker-ownership were developed by social democrats in a number of countries in the 1970s.

In Denmark the debate started after proposals from the trade unions in the early 1970s, and in 1977 an official commission was formed under the Ministry of Labor to examine the various possibilities for extending worker-ownership. The commission's report acknowledges that industrial democracy may be desirable for a variety of reasons but focuses on economic aspects, touching on some of the same issues that come up in relation to the Bowles and Gintis proposals. Thus, it is argued that increased worker-ownership may reduce distributional conflict, increase worker motivation and productivity, and increase the saving rate and the supply of finance for industry.[12]

Unlike in Sweden, none of the Danish proposals were carried out. They never gained widespread popular support, and by the early 1980s the debate had faded completely in the face of high unemployment, inflation and balance of payments problems. The lack of public support may be attributed partly to the collective funds which were prominent in the trade-union proposals. These collective funds were easy targets for attacks from employers and rightwing parties as well as from the new left. Bowles and Gintis reject central funds (I expect), but while central funds may have clear political drawbacks, involve real dangers of bureaucratization and nullify some of the incentive benefits of worker-ownership, one should not overlook the fact that there are also strong arguments in their favor. Risk considerations and the desirability of raising additional finance provide part of the motivation for this feature of the plans, and a concern for the unity and internal solidarity of the workers' movement also played a role: the introduction of central funds would make it possible to ensure that all members of the labor force, private and public employees as well as the unemployed, could receive shares in the funds while the control rights associated with the gradual build-up of worker-owned capital in private companies could be vested locally with the workers of the companies.

If nothing else, the fate of these plans for industrial democracy and extended worker-ownership illustrate the political obstacles to drastic changes in property rights. The proposals appeared in response to escalating worker militancy and declining profitability and business confidence. In the Scandinavian case the proposals were backed by powerful unions and strong social democratic parties, yet they failed. The proposals were seen as a massive threat to the existing order, and the radical political nature of the plans may have contributed to subsequent attacks on the traditional welfare state.[13] The general lesson is that social democrats – like other would-be reformers – face a dilemma. Fundamental institutional reform may be required to achieve egalitarian objectives and maintain full employment without violating the accumulation constraint, but the very attempt to bring about any such fundamental reforms easily provokes a political backlash.

Turning briefly to the problems associated with international integration, Bowles and Gintis claim that asset-based redistribution will reduce the international mobility of capital. Again the transitional process would seem to raise problems, but leaving aside the transitional issues the argument seems plausible. If redistribution consisted of a once and for all reallocation of existing assets without any subsequent intervention, the result might even be a removal of the migration constraint altogether. In practice, however, asset-based redistribution will not have this character. Although Bowles and Gintis give few details of what they have in mind, they do accept the need for 'continuing redistribution of property rights to overcome the disequalizing consequences of luck, increasing returns to scale, differences in individual abilities, and other forces contributing to uneven development'.[14] In practice, therefore, the policy may not be dramatically different from traditional social democracy in this respect.

Social-democratic policies have clearly involved income redistribution, but asset redistribution seems at least as important: education and health are obvious examples, but social expenditures like unemployment insurance or universal, state-backed pension rights would also seem to fit the asset category. In fact, the distinction between income and asset-based redistribution is somewhat blurred. Policies which from the point of view of an individual involve asset redistribution (e.g. the right to a minimum old-age pension, the right to unemployment benefits, or the right to a 'home ownership grant at the age of twenty') show up at the national level as a stream of 'contractual income transfers'. If by asset redistribution one meant a one-off redistribution of existing physical assets the distinction would be clear, but on a broader interpretation of asset redistribution it seems wrong to identify social democracy with income redistribution.

4 Concluding Remarks

An agency-theoretic perspective does not provide final answers and complete blueprints. It highlights questions that should be asked of any organizational structure. It is perhaps indicative of the 'openness' of the underlying framework that the most important example in the paper – worker-owned firms – remains somewhat sketchy and underspecified. Asset-based redistribution may have important advantages but the information and incentive problems are complex and, as pointed out by Bowles and Gintis, the interaction of effort, financing and risk issues complicates the design of worker-owned firms.

The Bowles and Gintis proposals concerning housing, education and children are more concrete, but complications also arise in these areas. Owner-occupation, for instance, carries many benefits (at least for stable households), and housing projects often have social problems, high crime rates, poor physical environment etc. But the incentive structure in renting may be only a minor part of the problem. To a large extent the high concentration of poverty in public housing in the US is a result of changes in eligibility and rent structures during the post-war period, and the physical deterioration of many housing projects has been exacerbated by the underfunding of housing authorities in the wake of falling rental incomes.[15] Post-war policies in favor of owner-occupation may also have contributed to the 'ghettoization' and concentration of social problems in public housing. They facilitated a process in which traditional working/middle class tenants started to leave for the suburbs. Once this process began, the resulting deterioration of the stability and general environment of the projects increased the incentives for anybody else to get out. Quite apart from these policy effects and vicious circles, owner occupation suffers from its own incentive problems and market failures: the level of property maintenance and neighborhood activities of any single owner affects the property values of all neighbours. Some of the coordination problems that these externalities give rise to are more easily solved by a housing authority. A housing cooperative may be an even better solution but the individual ownership incentives stressed by Bowles and Gintis get weaker the larger the cooperative.[16]

The big question, however, concerns the implementation of asset redistributions. Bowles and Gintis do not discuss implementation in any detail, but there appears to be a certain tension in their treatment of transitional issues. Thus, the expansion of worker-ownership will not, they argue, take place unless 'supported by government policy' and the redistribution of assets must make use of the 'ability of the state to define and assign property rights'. But the state does not operate in a vacuum, and as pointed out by Bowles and Gintis in a number of places, the potential productivity-enhancing effects of asset redistribution may not overcome the resistance to these changes from powerful groups.[17]

The relative neglect by Bowles and Gintis of transitional questions is reflected also in some of their general arguments for the productivity-enhancing nature of asset redistribution. Trust and cooperation, for instance, may improve economic performance, and the existence of high levels of trust and cooperation may be correlated with low levels of inequality. But the causation is unclear. An 'equal distribution of property holdings may foster the social solidarity necessary to support cooperation and trust' but could it not be argued, conversely, that trust and cooperation are indispensable for the feasibility of egalitarian policies and outcomes? The existence of a positive correlation between trust and equality does not necessarily imply that attempts at radical redistribution will raise the level of trust.

In order to address the transitional questions one needs to analyze the reasons for the observed crisis in egalitarian policy, and in these comments I have focused on two sets of influences: a Kaleckian long wave of endogenously changing worker militancy and business confidence, and the effects of international integration and increasing mobility. Both of these sets of influences are, I believe, important at a general level, but internationally the empirical picture is quite diverse.

The policy reversals and the tendency to increasing inequality are by no means uniform, and traditional welfare policies retain strong popular support in many countries.[18] This international diversity of institutions and political conditions is important. It is difficult to transplant successful schemes from one part of the world to another, and policy proposals need to be given concrete shapes that take into account the local conditions. Proposals that fit the current US situation may be unsuitable for a North European reality, and vice versa. One general conclusion, however, seems safe: radical changes in property rights will provoke immense opposition and any scheme of asset-based redistribution needs to address this political reality.

In conclusion, the concept of asset-based redistribution encapsulates some important implications of post-Walrasian, agency theory for egalitarian policy, and I have found Bowles' and Gintis's analysis and proposals immensely stimulating. Perhaps they try to differentiate their product a bit more strongly than is really warranted from traditional social-democratic policy but that is a minor point. Overall, if I have doubts about the paper, they concern not the central message but the neglect of some complications and problems. Transitional issues, in particular, would seem to require much more attention.

Notes

1. For example, Gintis (1976), Bowles (1985), Bowles and Gintis (1993).

2. Different studies have produced strikingly different results. ILO (1984), for instance, includes only eight developed countries but the most equal country (Japan) in the Bowles and Gintis data has a higher Gini coefficient in the ILO data than the US, the most unequal country according to Bowles and Gintis, and the rankings of the other countries also differ greatly. And both the Bowles and Gintis and the ILO figures differ from the Luxembourg Income Study which was designed specifically to overcome the comparability problems involved in international studies (Atkinson et al., 1995).

3. See Scharpf (1991) and Glyn (1995).

4. In fact, neither theoretical nor empirical arguments have convinced me of the relevance of wage-led growth, even in closed economies. See Auerbach and Skott (1988) and Skott (1989).

5. The question of international competitiveness has probably been the most dominant theme in political-economic debates in Denmark in the post-war period.

6. The careful studies in Atkinson and Mogensen (1993) of the disincentive effects of the welfare state in Sweden, Germany, Denmark and Britain lead to the conclusion that 'a number of the effects which have been identified are relatively small in size. Perhaps more importantly, there are relatively few situations in which a disincentive effect has been clearly established: there are many areas where we have a great deal still to learn. To dismantle the welfare state on the grounds that it causes disincentives would risk losing its very definite distributive advantages for the sake of an uncertain pay-off in terms of improved economic performance' (Atkinson (1993), p. 297).

7. See Kalecki (1971 [1943]), pp. 141–4.

8. Incidentally, the cyclical implications of the Kaleckian argument suggest that the

current phase of high unemployment and increasing inequality will give way to phases with increasing employment and then, with a lag, to decreasing inequality. So perhaps some of the current pessimism on the left is unfounded or at least exaggerated.

9. See Glyn (1995), p. 5.

10. This adverse effect may be offset by an aspiration effect: a higher growth rate of income may lower workers' demand with respect to the wage share if there is inertia in the formation of real wage aspirations. See Skott (1991).

11. As discussed, for example, in several contributions to Bardhan and Roemer (1993).

12. See Udvalget Om Lønmodtagernes Ejendomsret (1978), pp. 14–15.

13. Discussing the Swedish case, Glyn (1995, p. 20) notes that the proposed policies 'impinged on the authority and freedom of action of business which was supposed to be guaranteed in return for full employment and the welfare state. This seems to be at the root of the employers' repudiation of the Swedish model'. Thus, full employment 'generated demands which violated the prerogatives of capital. This provoked a backlash which forced social democracy to abandon not only its radical, and system-reforming proposals but also full employment itself'. A similar argument is made by Lundberg (1985).

14. Le Grand (1989), who addresses some of the same issues raised by Bowles and Gintis, offers a couple of interesting suggestions, e.g. a universal 'poll grant' financed by wealth taxation and paid to everyone at the age of majority.

15. The average annual income for public housing residents in Chicago has dropped from 33 per cent (in 1980) to less than 10 per cent of the median income in the city in 1994. This concentration of low-income households in public housing has 'isolated public housing politically as well as spatially' (Kamin, 1995).

16. Similar problems arise with respect to work place organization; see Aage (1995).

17. Solow (1987, pp. 181–2), hardly a radical socialist, goes as far as to claim that 'the Reagan and Thatcher people do not really care about macroeconomic performance' but about 'the redistribution of wealth in favor of the wealthy and of power in favor of the powerful'.

18. A Danish survey from 1994 showed little change compared with earlier studies. Only 28 per cent of the population thought the welfare system had gone too far while 63 per cent disagreed with this view; faced with a choice between tax reductions or further increases in public sector services, only 44 per cent opted for tax reductions (Goul Andersen, 1995).

References

Aage, H., 'The optimum size of brigades', *Advances in the Economic Analysis of Participatory and Labor-Managed Firms*, 5 (1995), pp. 139–57.

Atkinson, A.B. and G.V. Mogensen, *Welfare and Work Incentives* (Oxford: Clarendon Press, 1993).

——T.M. Smeeding and L. Rainwater, *Income Distribution in the OECD Countries: the Evidence from the Luxembourg Income Study*, *Social Policy Studies*, vol. 18 (Paris: OECD, 1995)

Auerbach, P. and P. Skott, 'Concentration, Competition and Distribution', *International Review of Applied Economics*, 2 (1988), pp. 42–61.

Bardhan, P.K. and J.E. Roemer, *Market Socialism: the Current Debate* (Oxford: Oxford University Press, 1993).

Bowles, S. 'The Production Process in a Competitive Economy', *American Economic Review*, 75 (1985), pp. 16–36.

—— and H. Gintis 'The Revenge of Homo Economicus', *Journal of Economic Perspectives*, 7 (1993), pp. 83–102.

——'Efficient Redistribution: New Rules for Markets, States, and Communities' (University of Massachusetts, 1994).

Gintis, H., 'The Nature of the Labor Exchange and the Theory of Capitalist Production', *Review of Radical Political Economics*, 8 (1976), pp. 36–54.

Glyn, A. 'Social Democracy and Full Employment', WZB Disc. Paper FS I (1995), pp. 95–302.

Goodwin, R.M., 'A Growth Cycle', in C.H. Feinstein (ed.), *Socialism, Capitalism and Growth* (Cambridge University Press, 1967).

Goul Andersen, J., 'Velfærdsstatens folkelige opbakning', *Socialforskning* (August, 1995), pp. 34–45.

ILO *Income Distribution and Economic Development*, (Geneva 1984).

Kalecki, M., 'Political Aspects of Full Employment', in M. Kalecki, *Selected Essays on the Dynamics of the Capitalist Economy* (Cambridge University Press, 1973 [1943]).

Kamin, B., 'Concentrations of Poverty Result from US Laws on Eligibility', *Chicago Tribune* (20 June, 1995), p. 8.

Le Grand, J., 'Markets, Welfare, and Equality', in J. Le Grand and S. Estrin (eds.), *Market Socialism* (Clarendon Press, 1989).

Lundberg, E., 'The Rise and Fall of the Swedish Model', *Journal of Economic Literature*, XXIII (March 1985), pp. 1–36.

Scharpf, F.W., *Crisis and Choice in European Social Democracy* (Cornell University Press, 1991).

Skott, P., *Conflict and Effective Demand in Economic Growth* (Cambridge University Press, 1989).

——'Efficiency Wages, Mark-up Pricing and Effective Demand', in J. Michie (ed.), *The Economics of Restructuring and Intervention* (Edward Elgar Publishing, 1991).

——'Class Conflict and Accumulation', in G. Mongiovi and C. Ruhl (eds.), *Macroeconomic Theory: Diversity and Convergence* (Edward Elgar Publishing, 1993).

Solow, R., 'The Conservative Revolution: A Roundtable Discussion', *Economic Policy* (October 1987), pp. 181–5.

Udvalget Om Lønmodtagernes Ejendomsret, *Lønmodtagernes Ejendomsret* (Copenhagen, 1978).

Wood, A., 'How Trade Hurt Unskilled Workers', *Journal of Economic Perspectives*, 9 (Summer 1995), pp. 57–80.

PART V

Extensions of the Economic Model

Associational Redistribution:
A Defense

*Steven N. Durlauf**

I

One of the most important conclusions of recent theoretical work on the economics of inequality is the recognition that equity and efficiency represent complementary policy goals in many contexts. Samuel Bowles and Herbert Gintis have, in 'Efficient Redistribution: New Rules for Markets, States, and Communities' (1996), written a masterful survey of the possibility that egalitarian redistribution policies will improve aggregate productivity.[1] The underlying theme of their analysis, as well as in other work – Bowles and Gintis (1994) for example – is that highly unequal distributions of assets or income can create incentive problems which militate against the efficient employment of available resources. Intuitively, a wide range of economic activity, ranging from workplace effort to contract fulfillment, contains the potential for principal/agent conflicts as the goals of economic actors diverge. Such divergence may be lessened by egalitarian redistribution, due to the confluence of interests between economic actors which are thereby induced.

In this essay, I examine possible complementarities between equality and efficiency from the perspective of the redistribution of memberships in various socioeconomic associations. Associations refer to

* This paper was prepared for the Real Utopias Project Conference on Equality and Efficiency held at the University of Wisconsin, November 1995. I thank Ann Bell, Samuel Bowles, William Brock, Kim-Sau Chung, Glenn Loury, Alexandra Minicozzi, Susan Nelson, Paula Voos, Michael Wiseman, Erik Wright and especially Donald Hester for comments on earlier drafts and the National Science Foundation for financial support. Some of this work was completed while I was visiting the Santa Fe Institute, whose hospitality I gratefully acknowledge. All errors and opinions are mine.

those units into which agents organize themselves. Examples of such associations include firms, neighborhoods and schools. From the perspective of inequality, the critical feature of associations is that they define (at least partially) isolated socioeconomic environments for their members. Differences across socioeconomic environments in turn produce differences in socioeconomic outcomes for individuals across groups. This link suggests that policies which alter the private market determination of associations can ameliorate inequality. Examples of policies which directly alter the formation of associations include affirmative action admissions and hiring policies, school busing to achieve racial integration, and location decisions for public housing.

The role of associational interactions in creating and perpetuating inequality has been the focus of a number of recent theoretical papers in the economics literature. Bénabou (1993, 1994, 1995) and Durlauf (1996a, b, c) have shown how neighborhood interactions can lead to persistent inequality across generations; Kremer and Maskin (1994) have shown how worker interactions within firms can explain growing wage inequality; Lundberg and Startz (1993) have shown how neighborhood and employment interactions can interact to explain racial income differences.

What distinguishes this new research from much previous work on inequality is its emphasis on the role of interaction environments in determining inequality. In particular, rather than focusing on individual characteristics in isolation, this body of theory focuses on the ways in which the endogenous organization of individuals determines how these individual attributes translate into economic achievement. Hence, the role of an individual's education in determining his labor-market prospects cannot be known without understanding who his co-workers are and the sort of firm in which he is employed.

This emphasis on group-level determinants of inequality in turn leads to a different perspective on redistribution policies. While conventional redistribution schemes such as progressive taxation (and even the more exotic policies advocated by Bowles and Gintis) focus on the transfer of income or wealth across individuals, the sorts of redistribution suggested by this new literature lead to a consideration of interventions in the market determination of socioeconomic interaction environments for individuals. I therefore refer to such policies as attempting to achieve *associational redistribution*, to distinguish them from other types of equality-enhancing policies.

I will argue that associational redistribution can lead to substantial increases in the average productivity of the economy. Building on previous work by Bénabou (1993, 1994, 1995) and Durlauf (1996a, b, c), which has described the role of local interactions on inequality and efficiency, powerful channels are identified through which policy interventions can promote equality and efficiency as complementary goals. Complementarity occurs because market forces produce assignments of individuals to associations which are stratified beyond the level dictated by economic efficiency. Intuitively, the presence of interaction effects within an association creates incentives for more able or more affluent or more educated individuals (depending on the association in question) to isolate themselves from others. One obvious case of such stratification occurs in neighborhood formation. In this case, since the distribution of incomes across families in a neighborhood helps determine school quality, neighborhoods become economically stratified as affluent families seek out affluent neighbors. The interaction structure underlying various associations, however, means that when individuals sort themselves without considering the consequences of their actions on others, the isolation of agents with high levels of these attributes can have adverse aggregate consequences.

While capable of producing substantial efficiency and equity gains, associational redistribution policies are much less likely to be politically appealing than the class of redistribution schemes envisioned by Bowles and Gintis. As a result, while efficiency considerations may be useful, a politically efficacious defense of associational redistribution will need to rely largely on ethical considerations. I therefore consider the ethical justification for associational redistribution as well.

II

Much of the justification for considering associational redistribution policies stems from the growing recognition in economics that socio-economic interaction environments produce powerful effects on the economic prospects of individuals. A distinguishing feature of the new economics of interactions is the emphasis on those interactions which occur directly between individuals rather than through the mediation of markets.

An important class of association-level influences is often referred to as social capital, a term introduced in Loury (1977). Social capital has been characterized by Coleman (1990) as 'the set of resources that inhere in family relations and in community social organizations and that are useful for the cognitive or social development of a child or young person' (p. 300). Since social capital is intangible and exists only in the context of relationships between one individual and others, the level and allocation of social capital are directly determined through association formation. Components of social capital can range from labor-market connections to role models. Notice that while the emphasis in the economics and sociology literatures has usually been on intergenerational issues, social capital effects can also be contemporaneous. For example, when one considers the interactions of workers within a firm or students within a school, the social norms within either group can determine the way in which actions are coordinated. In other words, distinct configurations of otherwise identical workers across firms will induce different productivity effects through social capital-type mechanisms. Within a firm, workplace attitudes are interdependent, both with each other and with each worker's social capital; within a neighborhood, group behavioral characteristics such as out-of-wedlock birth rates will be influenced by social capital as well.

Interaction effects are important for reasons beyond the influence of social capital *per se*. In many socioeconomic contexts, an individual's pay-off from a particular behavioral choice depends directly on the actions of members of one's reference group. For example, dropping out of school may be more desirable when one's classmates do the same. In this case, social capital, if constituted as a social norm favoring education, can militate against this effect. Other examples of direct interdependence of pay-offs include team production, where each member of a team of workers receives an equal share of a common effort.

Finally, association composition matters for the distribution of the stocks of physical and human capital. One obvious case is the assignment of workers to firms, which implicitly allocates the stock of human capital across production functions. The link between the allocation of capital stocks and group formation provides an additional reason to focus on the role of associational redistribution in overcoming inequality. For example, within a firm each individual's productivity is affected by the educational level of co-workers. In this case, individual-level interactions are at least partially mediated through labor markets as the wage mechanism determines worker assignments. Nevertheless, the process of worker allocation across firms has critical implications for the distribution of wages.

This perspective on income determination thus embodies several potential links between group membership and inequality. Appendix 1 outlines a formal model of interactions and inequality. The intuition

behind the model is straightforward when one considers the different
interaction structures in the economy. Association-based interactions
help determine inequality at two levels.

An initial level of interactions occurs at the level of a neighborhood.
Neighborhood composition matters for inequality in two contemporaneous respects. First, the level of educational expenditures is determined by the preferences and incomes of neighborhood members, as
aggregated through the political process. Further, social capital represents a collective neighborhood-level resource whose nature is
determined by the characteristics of the neighborhood's population.
Components of social capital that are relevant at the neighborhood
level include role models and attitudes towards work, each of which
will influence individual choices on school and job-market effort.
Each of these neighborhood influences partly determines the skill and
productivity levels of neighborhood offspring, when they become
adults.

A second level of interactions occurs at the level of the firm. The
assignment of a particular worker to a particular firm is based upon
productivity-related characteristics, which were determined by the
human and social capital obtained while young. In particular, an
individual's social capital embodies characteristics such as social
norms and information which help determine both productivity and
access to job opportunities; neighborhood-level influences during
youth determine firm-level interactions as an adult. There is thus an
intertemporal link between neighborhood and firm associations. In
turn, the allocation of workers across firms determines incomes, and
by implication neighborhood memberships of families. Once families
are located across neighborhoods, those group-level forces come into
play which help determine the distribution of human capital and
income for the next generation of adults.

In response to the presence of interactions, economic actors in
many contexts attempt to organize themselves in order to produce
environments with favorable social capital allocations. A standard
example of this is the pursuit of 'good' neighborhoods by parents. As
shown by Bénabou (1993, 1994) and Durlauf (1996a, b), the presence
of associational spillover effects creates incentives for families to
stratify themselves by income.

Stratification and interactions combine to produce persistent inequality. This is most clear in the case of neighborhoods, where the
differences in the social capital and per capita educational expenditures between rich and poor communities transmit inequality across
generations: children in poor neighborhoods grow up to be poor due

to educational and labor-market handicaps. In Durlauf (1996b) an example is given in which the equilibrium configuration of families across neighborhoods is that which maximizes (in a well-defined sense) intergenerational inequality between the richest and poorest families in the economy.

Many empirical studies have produced evidence consistent with the claim that interaction effects are significant determinants of economic success. Most of these studies have focused on neighborhood interactions. In one study, Crane (1991) shows that the percentage of managerial and professional workers among adults in a community correlates negatively with both the high school dropout and teenage pregnancy rates. Corcoran et al. (1989) find that the percentage of families on public assistance in a neighborhood lowers the expected adult wage of children in the neighborhood. Datcher (1982) finds that black economic status is sensitive to the degree of segregation experienced in youth. Additional evidence may be found in the context of so-called natural experiments, which examine the consequences of exogenous changes in neighborhood sorting rules. Studies of the Gautreaux program (Rosenbaum and Popkin, 1991), in which a number of inner-city families from Chicago were provided with public housing in adjacent suburbs, indicate that a number of socioeconomic outcomes of the transplanted families were greatly improved.

It is important to recognize that this empirical work is far from decisive. The empirical literature on interaction effects has been subjected to powerful criticisms concerning the way in which the studies have dealt with identification issues (Manski, 1993a, b). In addition, there appears to be a lack of robustness of the findings of neighborhood feedbacks (Jencks and Mayer, 1990). A fair reading of the empirical literature seems to be the following: while the evidence is very suggestive of substantial interaction effects, it is sufficiently plagued by statistical problems that one's prior beliefs ought strongly to be affected by the body of existing empirical work. However, because the interaction effects are consistent with the formal evidence, and are furthermore very plausible, their implications for redistribution are worth examining.

The basic interaction structure described above illustrates how the sorting of individuals has important implications for the study of productivity-enhancing redistributions. In particular, different levels of interaction – neighborhood, school and firm – suggest the importance of focusing on redistribution policies that attempt to alter associational structures, rather than attempt to alter the contemporaneous distribution of wealth through direct monetary transfers. One obvious case is educational opportunity. An interactions-based perspective alters the redistributive focus away from policies designed to equalize per student expenditure to those that attempt to equalize the total school environment. Even if expenditure equalization is important in producing equality of opportunity, the efficacy of such policies may depend on the available social capital in a school, again suggesting the need for associational redistribution.[2]

III

The relationship between persistent inequality and stratification does not address the implications of stratification for the productive efficiency of the associated allocation of economic actors. In fact, one might even expect that there exist broad conditions under which stratification is required for productive efficiency. In particular, a link between stratification and efficiency might be expected when complementarities exist between agents, that is, when the marginal product of a group's production function with respect to one person's ability is an increase in the ability levels of others. In this general case, it is possible that maximum productivity requires placing high-ability agents together in order to take advantage of spillovers among them. These intuitions are formalized in analyses of particular economic environments by Becker (1973) and Kremer (1993), each of which finds that the presence of complementarities is a sufficient condition for the efficiency of stratification.

However, Durlauf (1996c) shows that stratification may be inefficient even in the presence of complementarities across all agents, when one considers a broader range of economic environments than those studied by Becker and Kremer. In particular, it is demonstrated that the link between complementarities and the efficiency of stratification depends on the additional assumptions that, first, all groupings are constrained to be of equal size, and, second, that the productive input supplied by each individual to a group is independent of the composition of that group.

Neither of these assumptions holds when one considers neighborhoods or firms. Such groups obviously can vary in size. Feedbacks from the allocation of agents across groups to the level of productive inputs will occur whenever the composition of groups affects individual effort. Such feedbacks occur when school effort is affected by the presence of neighborhood role models or worker effort is affected by the skill level of co-workers. The important implication is that even in the presence of positive interaction effects, stratified configurations can fail to be output-maximizing, relative to some integrated alternative.[3]

To be sure, under some configurations of technologies and ability distributions, stratification will be efficient. The point is that the connection between stratification and efficiency is not a necessary consequence of some qualitative set of features of the economy such as the presence of a particular type of interaction structure – i.e. complementarities – among all agents. On the other hand, for a much wider range of economic environments than those in which stratification is efficient, the equilibrium allocation of agents will nevertheless be stratified. Thus, there exist cases where the gains from productivity-enhancing associative redistribution may be considerable.

The adverse productivity consequences of stratification may be associated with analogous welfare effects. The model of binary choices with spillovers studied in Brock and Durlauf (1995), which applies directly to phenomena such as out-of-wedlock births, dropping out of high school, and entry into crime, exhibits precisely this feature. In that model, individuals choose between a pair of possible actions in order to maximize a utility function which includes both a private component, corresponding to individual economic pay-offs from a course of action, and a social component, corresponding to the desire to conform to the behavior of one's community or reference group. When the private utility difference between the two choices is below some threshold, the social utility component allows the existence of multiple equilibria in community choice levels. However, if the private utility differences are large enough, these conformity effects cannot induce multiplicity. From the perspective of that model, social capital within a community may coordinate individual choices in a way that leads to a socially efficient equilibrium. The model implies that, by rearranging individuals across communities in order to reduce the number of communities which exhibit multiple equilibria, it is possible to improve average utility in the economy. The model also shows that poor economic fundamentals and a culture of poverty constitute complementary rather than alternative explanations of underclass behavior.

It is possible for a reorganization of an initially stratified configuration of communities to induce increases in utility for all members of the society. Bénabou (1995) describes conditions under which the economic integration of neighborhoods makes all families better off because of dynamic improvements in the quality of the labor force. The possibility of uniform utility improvements relies on strong intergenerational utility ties, as occurs when descendants find themselves members of a better-trained workforce.

In general, associational redistribution can enhance aggregate productivity either by facilitating the solution of coordination problems resolving other market imperfections, or by obviating the necessity to solve such problems. Some simple algebraic examples of these possibilities are given in Appendix 2, where the characteristic that differentiates economic agents is ability. When these examples are studied from the perspective of a market equilibrium, it is easy to verify that an allocation of agents which integrates high- and low-ability agents across coalitions will never occur. The reason is straightforward: high-ability agents always have an incentive to match themselves with other high-ability agents. This phenomenon is in fact quite general. Intuitively, stratification emerges as an equilibrium phenomenon in contexts ranging from neighborhoods to firms, despite adverse output or welfare consequences, because individual agents seek association configurations that maximize their own pay-offs, without regard for the effects of such isolation on the total productivity of the society. However, the efficient allocation of individuals across coalitions requires that the net effect on the welfare of all agents from moving any set of agents across groups be zero or negative, which is clearly a very different condition.[4] In this respect, interaction effects operate in ways either analogous or equivalent to externalities.[5]

A concrete example of the general claim that associational effects create a tendency towards stratification is the allocation of families across neighborhoods. While affluent families have an incentive to isolate themselves from the poor in order to maximize school quality, the desirable consequences for poor families who were placed in such a community may nevertheless outweigh any deleterious effects on the affluent (in the sense that the affluent can be compensated in such a way that everybody is made better off). This inefficiency is attributable to the presence of externalities and attendant coordination problems which impede educational effort among the poor, rather than through any of the principal-agent issues emphasized by Bowles and Gintis (1995).

The allocation of individuals across associations so as to maximize aggregate output provides a productivity-based justification for a number of public policies that have fallen into disfavor in the last two decades. From the interaction effects at a neighborhood or school district-based level, integration of communities through redistricting, busing or explicit public housing strategies[6] can have potentially powerful static or dynamic efficiency effects, depending on the time horizon under consideration. Affirmative action policies may have similar consequences.[7] If role-model or labor-market connection effects are important determinants of economic success, then affirmative action can, by altering the way in which workers are sorted across occupations and firms, be productivity-enhancing.

Whether they are intended to ameliorate inequality or to increase per capita output, it is a clear implication of the new literature on neighborhood effects and inequality that redistribution schemes must deal with the questions of sorting and group formation. While equilibrium stratification by income or skill will, in the presence of positive interaction effects, typically generate substantial contemporaneous and persistent inequality, such stratification is justified by considerations of economic efficiency only in a relatively narrow range of cases.

IV

In a recent piece of research, Glenn Loury has argued that associational redistribution programs such as affirmative action may have adverse productivity consequences. His analysis is conducted in an economic environment in which the various interaction effects I have discussed are absent, so that there is no clash *per se* in the arguments each of us makes. At the risk of doing an injustice to the depth of his work, I briefly comment on and attempt to answer the main thrust of Loury's arguments on his own terms.

In suggesting that affirmative action may have adverse productivity considerations, Coate and Loury (1993) and Loury (1995) focus on potential adverse incentives for investment in education. Specifically, these papers argue that the presence of race-based quotas can lead minority workers to reduce investment in education due to the possibility of obtaining high-paying jobs through quotas rather than through education-based qualifications.

My own view is that this problem is unlikely to have great empirical salience. First, this argument requires that individuals are willing to take jobs for which they know they are unqualified. This seems improbable, particularly if the commonplace argument that these policies stigmatize successful minorities is correct. After all, successful on-the-job performance is the one certain way to show that any stigma is unjustified. In the context of the Coate–Loury model, high educational investment to avoid stigma can completely eliminate any disincentive effects, because education investment is a fixed cost; when the investment costs are an increasing function of the level of education, these investments designed to avoid stigma limit the extent of the disincentives without necessarily eliminating all education investment effects. Additionally, the Loury argument supposes that affirmative-action policies will not positively influence education investment by creating the perception of a fairer workplace environment. Descriptions of African American attitudes such as Cose (1993) suggest that affirmative-action policies are perceived by African Americans as partially ameliorating unjust hiring practices, and that the beneficiaries do not perceive themselves as suddenly possessing a chance to succeed regardless of merit. Such perceptions imply that education investment among African Americans ought to increase in response to some forms of associational redistribution.

Second, the economic environments which Coate and Loury study presuppose that once an individual is employed, his position and compensation within the firm are independent of his performance. Clearly, firms are able to structure internal promotions incentives in such a way as to encourage high productivity. The question raised by Coate and Loury is not whether affirmative action creates adverse education incentives, but rather how affirmative-action policies ought to be structured. I read their arguments as suggesting that affirmative-action policies should be primarily directed at entry-level positions; Loury (1995) in fact develops related arguments in respect of the timing of affirmative-action policies.

Third, the efficiency argument in Loury's work presupposes that sorting mechanisms in the economy are efficient before affirmative action. To the extent that the ability to succeed through family connections is diminished through affirmative action, then the current beneficiaries to non-meritocratic sorting should increase their efforts to obtain education. Put simply, if affirmative-action policies reduce the incentives for minorities to work to gain admission to Ivy League schools, they should similarly increase the incentives for the offspring of alumni, whose places are in jeopardy. There is no theoretical calculation for predicting whether this net effect on incentives will enhance or reduce average education investment across the labor force, when considered as a whole.

V

The potential for associational redistribution policies to secure general public support is questionable, however, given the widespread unpopularity of mechanisms such as affirmative action. Productivity-enhancing redistributions are claimed by Bowles and Gintis to be relatively politically efficacious on the grounds that such redistributions can make the entire population better off. However, the indivisible nature of the burden created by associational redistribution makes it especially unlikely to produce such uniform welfare improvements, at least without a set of (implausible and unwieldy) compensatory arrangements for those advantaged-group members who lose out.[8] Further, because the retention of any meritocratic aspects to the allocation of societal positions is likely to protect those in the upper tail of either the skill or ability distributions, associational redistribution is likely to hurt some members of the advantaged group, in particular those who are relatively less advantaged.

Further, it is probable that associational redistribution policies will remain unpopular regardless of their productivity consequences, unless they can be shown to be just. It seems clear that much of the opposition to affirmative action is predicated on the belief that it is unfair. The standard formulation of this claim is that those affected by affirmative-action policies are neither responsible for nor the victims of the discrimination which is being addressed. The assumptions of this argument are obviously correct. Certainly, the evidence in Verba et al. (1987) on American attitudes towards egalitarian policies suggests that the level of support for associational redistribution as defined by affirmative action is weaker than that for other forms of income redistribution. Associational redistribution policies thus face a much higher hurdle to public acceptance than the policies studied by Bowles and Gintis.

My own view is that the most likely prospect for a politically successful defense of associational redistribution lies in the development of an ethically based defense on equality-of-opportunity grounds. From an ethical perspective, one appropriate goal of redistributive policy is the reduction of the dependence of forecasts of adult socioeconomic outcomes, when defined over all factors, on those variables over which the adult has no control. Obvious candidates for such variables include race or neighborhood of residence in youth. This idea is a variant of the notion of equality of opportunity defended by John Roemer because it emphasizes that equality of opportunity is properly defined relative to the salience of particular causal explanations of inequality. This formulation also has the benefit of forcing explicit consideration of the way in which different variables affect outcomes, which is likely to be as politically contentious as the determination of which variables should be considered to be under an individual's control. In addition, the conditional probability structure forces explicit consideration of how to handle unobservable variables such as effort. Of course, appropriate notions of equality become difficult to define in the presence of nontransferable attributes such as genetically determined ability.

The concept of equality of opportunity resonates strongly across political boundaries in American society, especially when applied to the prospects of children. Given this resonance, associational redistribution policies may be required to achieve accepted notions of justice and fairness and may therefore be defended as necessary actions despite the ethical concerns raised above. Such policies will be defensible even when associational redistribution increases some contemporaneous inequality among adults.

A formulation of equality of opportunity which provides a specific defense of associational redistribution has been developed in an important series of papers by Roemer (1993, 1995a, b). In this work, Roemer argues that equality of opportunity requires equalization of the performance of different societal groups when compared percentile by percentile, when these groups are defined by characteristics which are beyond individual control. An obvious case is that of opportunities such as school admission or employment when affected by circumstance of birth. Notice that one need not take a stand on the propriety of rewarding differences in genetic endowment to argue that neighborhood-based or ethnic-group-based effects should have no independent role in determining the allocation of opportunities in a society. One important contribution of Roemer's analysis is the demonstration of how performance-based notions of equality of opportunity may be reconciled with requirements of personal responsibility.

An ethical defense of associational redistribution must rest to a large extent on a particular view of the mechanisms that explain the cross-section and intertemporal income distribution. In particular, following Roemer's reasoning, associational redistribution is defensible when it acts to reverse the influence of factors which are beyond an individual's control in producing unequal outcomes. Such reasoning immediately applies to affirmative-action policies that are implemented to counter discriminatory behavior, because any redistribution is merit-rewarding and equality-enhancing.[9] Similarly, to the extent that neighborhood-level differences create substantial persistence in economic status, the equalization of neighborhood influences by interventions in the private market allocation is again defensible because neighborhood membership is imposed upon a child.

This argument does not require that past discriminatory behavior is responsible for consigning a subset of the population to environments with low social capital. For example, if an ethnic group is admitted as refugees, do the current members and future offspring of that group have a lesser claim on society's resources because our society bears no past responsibility for their parents' condition? Clearly not, because the act of admission to our society presumes admission as a fully equal member.

The argument also does not require that effects of low social capital be permanent. Even if market forces are certain eventually to eliminate the effects of contemporaneous social capital imbalances on inequality, interventions to equalize social capital across groups may still be justified because of the potential harm to the current young. In this respect, I disagree with Loury (1987), who argues that irreversibility of the effects of past discrimination is important in justifying government remedies to group inequality. The degree of persistence of cross-group inequality is germane only when one is accounting for competing dimensions of equity and efficiency which are adversely affected by associational redistribution. As a practical matter, irreversibility is virtually impossible to verify through formal statistical procedures; some of the reasons for this are described in Bernard and Durlauf (1996). So it seems that Loury's condition is very unlikely ever to be met empirically, ethical issues notwithstanding.

The strength of ethical objections to associational redistribution must be sensitive to the relative importance of different determinants of inequality. First, if one accepts the argument made by Rawls (1971) and others that differences in talent or productivity have no implications for the justice of compensation differences *per se*, inequality due to differences in ability versus inequality due to differences in tastes need to be distinguished. Second, even if one accepts that some differential rewards due to differential ability are ethically defensible, the question of the fairness of the reward scheme currently observed in society remains. If the financial rewards to high education are due to monopoly rents, then the income distribution induced by meritocratic admissions criteria cannot be said to be just.[10] To the extent that associational redistribution ameliorates an unjust income distribution induced by the compensation rules of society, the argument that the reward of merit is a competing claim on the design of institutions is, of course, weakened. Certainly, the recent work of Frank and Cook (1995) on the rise of winner-take-all compensation schemes is suggestive that this is more than a theoretical possibility.

VI

An ethically based equality-of-opportunity argument for associational redistribution differs from a number of previous defenses. For example, it does not rely on any notion that associational redistribution represents just compensation for previous discrimination. As a number of authors, including Amdur (1979), Loury (1987) and Roemer (1995a, b), have emphasized, such a defense fails for several reasons, including the absence of identity between victim and recipient. These arguments appear to be persuasive, although it should be noted that current members of disadvantaged groups are suffering the consequences of previous discrimination. Second, it does not rely on, but of course would be strengthened by, the claim that overt contemporaneous discrimination is influencing the sorting mechanisms of the private economy.

A criticism of the equality-of-opportunity argument could be made, however, on the grounds that associational redistribution itself violates a prior right of individuals to pursue private lives; an extreme version of this argument underlies Nozick (1974). Ethical limits on the right of government to interfere with private interactions must imply bounds on the degree to which associational redistribution may be implemented. An obvious example (due to Glenn Loury) is marriage, where no one would seriously propose that the observed patterns of segregation should be explicitly interfered with by the government.

For two reasons, neither work nor education represents a case where the right to private association may be deemed to be absolute.[11] First, the social interactions embedded in such institutions are in large measure auxiliary to their goals, as opposed to something such as private social clubs or marriage. The primary goal of a firm is the generation of profit, not the creation of a workplace in which individuals can socialize; similarly, the primary goal of schools is the education of students, not the creation of a social environment *per se*. From this perspective, the inviolability of private associations such as friendships and families is irrelevant to the question of government interventions in the workplace or education environment. Little qualitative difference exists between the regulation of an industry with pollution that creates production externalities and the regulation of an industry with employees who provide role models to the young. Second, the fundamental relationship between education, economic success, and one's perceived value as a member of society (Shklar,

1991) provides a compelling reason to interfere with private social interactions in these cases. As argued in Nagel (1979b), while a persuasive defense of egalitarianism would seem to require a concession that equality is only one of many desiderata for a society, equality of opportunity is not necessarily subordinate to other values, such as those embedded in a natural right to all private associations.

The case of neighborhood formation is somewhat more problematic, because a neighborhood's interaction environment is an objective of community formation. However, any right of adults to private neighborhood formation will conflict, due to spillover effects, with the right of all offspring to equal opportunities, as manifested in equality in neighborhood influences. Unless the parents of all offspring have equal initial opportunities, justice would seem to require that the latter rights take precedence.

Further, if individual neighborhood choice is made on the basis of the desire for a particular school composition, then it is unclear what weight should be assigned to adult associational preferences, because it is the offspring whose social interaction environments are being defined. In forming neighborhoods for schools, parents are acting (at least partially) as agents for their offspring. Preferences of the parents for certain types of neighborhood composition which do not promote their children's interests create a tension between the parents' right to private association and the interests of their offspring which needs to be adjudicated. Therefore the right to private neighborhood associations is not absolute in this case. Can a parent's pursuit of a racially homogeneous neighborhood ever coincide with a child's interests? If this pursuit is based on prejudice, then the answer is presumably no, since minors cannot be said to possess full powers of moral reasoning. On the other hand, if racial homogeneity avoids racial conflict, then the answer is not so clear.

A possible ethical limitation on arguments for associational redistribution does arise in the broader context of the question of the justice of rewards to individuals (in this case memberships in schools, neighborhoods, etc.) for characteristics which are not choice variables. The difficulty arises from the need to define what is an 'essential' person (to use a word employed by John Roemer in this regard) whose attributes are those which may be justly rewarded. An overwhelming ethical consensus exists that one should not be penalized on the basis of race or gender, given ability, in labor-market outcomes. In this context, race or gender is inessential. Conversely, a relationship between an individual's effort and compensation is, by consensus, justified because effort reflects individual preferences, which are clearly essential. On the other hand, one's genetic ability endowment is difficult to disassociate from the 'essential' person in any meaningful context, which is one reason why arguments in favor of eliminating this factor as a source of inequality differences through associational redistribution are often rejected, even in the writings of liberals such as Walzer (1983).[12] Associational redistribution alters the rewards to a number of individual characteristics, ranging from family and group background to genetic endowment, not all of which are necessarily on a comparable ethical footing. In this respect, associational redistribution is typically a second-best policy.

VII

In summary, it is important to recognize the extent to which associational redistribution may be necessary to achieve a substantially more egalitarian income distribution. Equalization of school expenditures may be unlikely to produce much equalization of human capital without attendant changes in the unequal distribution of social capital. The development of an ethically based defense of social capital redistribution is, in my view, an essential corollary to achieving the politically efficacious defense of the redistributive policies suggested by Bowles and Gintis.

At the same time, one must acknowledge that the importance of associational redistribution policies says nothing about how such policies ought to be designed. Any interference in the private market sorting process may create behavioral responses in associational choice that will undermine the original policy. Such responses are potentially serious in two respects. First, the policies themselves may be rendered ineffective. The white flight out of school districts which implemented racial-integration plans is a prominent example of this possibility. Similarly, even if school populations are integrated, within-school segregation can emerge in response to interschool integration. Second, associational redistribution policies, by providing insurance against adverse background, might undermine mechanisms by which family-level and neighborhood-level investment in offspring occur. The challenge to economists (at least in terms of comparative advantage) is to identify specific associational redistribution mechanisms with equilibrium consequences that will contribute to the joint goals of equality and efficiency.

Appendix 1: Formalization of Dynamic Inequality Model

To see how associational interactions collectively influence inequality, I briefly outline a model based upon ideas in Bénabou (1993, 1994, 1995), Durlauf (1996a, b, c), and Kremer and Maskin (1994). The model characterizes the joint determination of human capital and income. The interested reader is advised to consult these papers to see how the various behavioral equations can be justified.

In this model, the evolution of a stable population of individuals is studied. The population consists of I family dynasties. Individual i, $t - 1$ denotes the member of dynasty i born in period $t - 1$. Each individual is assumed to live two periods, corresponding to youth and adulthood. Individual i, $t - 1$ possesses adult human capital $H_{i, t}$, which is determined by four components: the human capital of his parent, $H_{i, t - 1}$, the educational investment level of the neighborhood in which he grows up, $ED_{n, t - 1}$, sociological spillovers such as role model effects, with consequences measurable by the income distribution among adults in the individual's neighborhood during youth, $F_{Y, n, t - 1}$, and random individual-specific effects such as genetic endowment, $\xi_{i,t - 1}$. These arguments interact to produce a human capital equation

$$H_{i,t} = \phi(H_{i,t - 1}, ED_{n,t - 1}, F_{Y,n,t - 1}, \xi_{i,t - 1}). \tag{1}$$

The direct contribution of $F_{Y, n, t - 1}$ to $H_{i, t}$ proxies for such social capital effects as role models. In this context, social capital interacts with educational expenditure, parental background and individual ability to determine an individual's human capital.

An adult individual's income is determined by the particular firm in which he works. An individual's productivity and compensation are determined by the number of and skill levels of co-workers as well as through his own human capital. If individual i, t is employed by firm f, then his income may be modelled as

$$Y_{i,t} = \xi(H_{i,t}, H_{j,t}, \text{A } j \neq i \text{ employed by firm } f \text{ at } t). \tag{2}$$

In order to close the model, it is necessary to specify the mechanisms by which families are sorted into neighborhoods and individuals are sorted into firms. Denoting $n(i, t)$ as the equilibrium neighborhood assignment of the family containing the adult i, $t - 1$ and child i, t, then

$$n(i, t) = \gamma\, (Y_{i,\,t},\, Y_{j,\,t},\, A\, j \neq i). \tag{3}$$

This equation captures the idea that neighborhoods are determined by the entire cross-section distribution of family incomes. This occurs because family-level preferences over neighborhood configurations are converted into actual neighborhoods through the interactions of families in housing markets. Embedded in this equation is the determination of the number of distinct neighborhoods. Typically, the dynamics implied by this equation lead to substantial stratification of neighborhoods by income, as wealthier families attempt to isolate themselves from poorer ones due to associational spillovers and local public finance effects.

To complete the model, it is necessary to specify the assignment of workers across firms. Individual i, t's firm assignment, $f(i,t)$, as a function of the hiring decisions of all firms in the economy, which will in turn depend on the human capital distribution for workers across the economy.

$$f(i, t) = \zeta\, (H_{i,\,t},\, H_{j,\,t},\, A\, j \neq i). \tag{4}$$

This holds because the value of a particular worker to a firm depends on the co-workers at the firm, which in turn depends on the supply of workers of different human capital levels. This equation will determine the degree to which individuals possessing high and low human capital levels are isolated from each other. It implicitly contains incentives for the formation of large firms due to increasing returns from specialization, as well as incentives for the formation of small firms if the productivity of high human capital adults is reduced through interactions with low human capital co-workers. For a wide range of technologies and compensation rules, this equation will produce stratification of firms by human capital.

This framework thus unifies the allocation of families across neighborhoods and workers across firms in a way which can produce complex income-distribution dynamics. Observe that in this framework relating intergenerational inequality and associational spillovers, no explicit account has been taken of race or gender. These factors can be added to the rules for firm and neighborhood formation to generalize the stratification induced by income and human capital which the model already embeds. Notice that if a self-reproducing demographic group is the victim of past discrimination, the associational effects in this model mean that the consequences of this discrimination will persist.

Appendix 2: Inefficiency of Stratification by Ability

The possibility that stratification can be inefficient (where efficiency is defined as maximizing per capita pay-offs) is illustrated in the following example, taken from Durlauf (1996c). Suppose that a group of individuals must be assigned to coalitions of size two. Each coalition has a set of rules which determine the compensation for each coalition member which exhaust the coalition's output. Hence average compensation is $\frac{1}{2}$ of the total output of each coalition, so that aggregate output can be studied by looking at average compensation across individuals. Each individual has an ability level $a_i \, E \, \{1, 6\}$ and makes an unobservable effort choice $e_i \, E \, \{1, 2\}$. Suppose that the compensation rule within a coalition comprised of agents i and j is

$$\Phi(a_i, a_j, e_i, e_j) = 10 + a_i \cdot a_j \cdot e_i \cdot e_j - 5e_i + 1000(e_i - 1)(e_j - 1) \quad (5)$$

It is straightforward to verify that any agent matched with a high-ability agent will choose $e_i = 2$; similarly a high-ability agent will always choose $e_i = 2$ even if matched with a low-ability agent. On the other hand, when two low-ability agents are matched together, the joint effort levels $e_i = e_j = 1$ and $e_i = e_j = 2$ both constitute noncooperative equilibria. Therefore, the average pay-off when the agents are stratified by ability is 1074 if the less able agents coordinate on $e_i = e_j = 2$, or 575 if the less able agents coordinate on $e_i = e_j = 1$. On the other hand, integrated coalitions which match high- and low-ability agents will produce an equal pay-off of 1024 for each agent.

Two features of this example are worth noting. First, the success with which a pair of agents is able to coordinate on the high pay-off equilibrium can be influenced by the presence of social capital related to work norms. Second, integrating high- and low-ability agents can maximize average per capita pay-offs, if the probability of a coordination failure among low-ability agents is high enough. Thus, if a deficit of social capital leads to coordination failure, in the sense that low-ability workers are matched and choose $e_i = e_j = 1$, integration can eradicate this effect by eliminating the potential for a coordination problem.

Observe that if the less able agents were able to coordinate on $e_i = e_j = 2$, then stratification would again maximize per capita pay-offs. For this example, associational redistribution, in the form of requiring integration of ability levels, is therefore a second-best policy from the perspective of maximizing per capita output. However, it is straight-forward to construct examples where integration maximizes per capita pay-offs. For example, if the individual pay-offs are altered so that

$$\Phi(a_i, a_j, e_i, e_j) = 10 + a_i \cdot a_j \cdot e_i \cdot e_j - 5e_i + 1000(e_j - 1)^2, \qquad (6)$$

then $e_i = e_j = 2$ is ruled out as an equilibrium when two low-ability agents are matched. In this case, integration will be the unique (average) pay-off maximizing allocation of agents. Notice that, in this second case, multiple equilibria in individual behavior no longer exist because the effort levels when low-ability agents are uniquely deter-mined. This indicates how associational redistribution can lead to productivity increases due to other market frictions beyond those which prevent economic agents from coordinating actions. In the present example, the friction consists of the fixed compensation rules.

Notes

1. Other arguments supporting a positive relationship between inequality and productivity have been made by Murphy, Shleifer, and Vishny (1989), who argue that high degrees of inequality can lead to a demand structure inconsistent with high production.

2. A great deal of empirical controversy exists over the effects of increased per capita spending on educational and economic outcomes. Without assessing the contro-versy, it seems fair to say that a possible explanation of the lack of strong empirical evidence for these links is the failure of the relevant empirical work to adequately control for social capital effects. At a minimum, it is simple to choose parameterizations of equations (1) to (4) in Appendix 1 such that educational expenditures have significant human capital effects which become unobservable due to their interaction with social capital levels.

3. See Lundberg and Startz (1983) for an alternative perspective on the efficiency gains from affirmative-action policies that alter equilibrium labor-market allocation based on the effects of imperfect information on hiring decisions.

4. Again, it is important to emphasize that efficiency is being equated with maximization of per capita pay-offs, which is different from the usual procedure in economics of equating efficiency with Pareto Optimality. The integrated allocation does not Pareto-dominate the stratified allocation for either of the pay-off functions I consider, because the high-ability agents are made worse off in both cases by integration.

5. For example, no market exists to compensate good role models and thereby induce their efficient allocation across neighborhoods.

6. Massey and Kanaiaupuni (1993) show how the location strategy for public housing projects in Chicago since 1950 has been a contributing factor to the concentration of poverty within the inner city. The contribution of government policies in explaining the current level of residential racial segregation in the United States is explored in Massey and Denton (1993).

7. This possibility is explicitly recognized in Loury (1987, 1992) in his analyses of

the ethical bases for affirmative action. Unlike the present discussion, though, Loury focuses on the role of social capital in perpetuating inequality, rather than on productivity issues. One aspect of these spillovers, role model effects, figured in the defense of affirmative action argued on behalf of UC Davis in the Bakke case, which led to the Supreme Court rejecting numerical quotas as unconstitutional (as discussed in Dworkin, (1985).

8. Erik Wright (private communication) has suggested that the creation of additional slots in organizations such as schools can overcome the indivisibility aspect of associational redistribution.

9. The failure to consider the specific mechanism by which ability differences are translated into income differences indicates the vacuousness of the Herrnstein–Murray (1994) view that a society which rewards the more able over the less able is somehow self-evidently just. If the entire GNP in the US were annually rewarded to the citizen with the highest recorded IQ, the resulting distribution would be putatively merito-cratic, though obviously indefensible.

10. This argument is inspired by Nagel (1979a).

11. The line of reasoning followed here and below is supported by the brilliant critique of Nozick developed in Cohen (1995). In particular, Cohen gives a broad defense of government interventions to alter private market-determined income distri-butions based on the argument that a set of individual economic transactions, each voluntary and putatively just, can lead to an unjust outcome due to interaction effects. The interaction effects discussed in the present paper are a clear example of this phenomenon.

12. Walzer specifically argues that self-realization is too closely connected to the objects of associational redistribution to justify these policies; but such an argument is powerful only to the extent it is the 'essential' person who is under discussion. I believe John Roemer would disagree with my assessment of the role of genetic endowment in what constitutes an essential person, from the perspective of labor-market outcomes.

References

Amdur, R., 'Compensatory Justice: The Question of Costs', *Political Theory*, 7 (1979), pp. 229–44.

Becker, G., 'A Theory of Marriage: Part I', *Journal of Political Economy*, 81 (1973), pp. 813–46.

Bénabou, R., 'Workings of a City: Location, Education, and Production', *Quarterly Journal of Economics*, CVIII (1993), pp. 619–52.

——'Education, Income Distribution and Growth: The Local Connection', *National Bureau of Economic Research*, working paper no. 4798 and forthcoming, *Review of Economic Studies* (1994).

——'Heterogeneity, Stratification, and Growth', mimeo (New York University and forthcoming American Economic Review, 1995).

Bernard, A. and S. Durlauf, 'Interpreting Tests of the Convergence Hypothesis', *Journal of Econometrics*, 71 (1996), pp. 161–74.

Bowles, S. and H. Gintis, 'Escaping the Efficiency-Equity Tradeoff: Productivity Enhancing Asset Redistributions', mimeo (Department of Economics, University of Massachusetts at Amherst, 1994).

——, 'Efficient Redistribution: New Rules for Markets, States, and Communities', *Politics and Society* (1995) and this volume.

Brock, W. and S. Durlauf, 'Discrete Choice with Social Interactions I: Theory', mimeo (Department of Economics, University of Wisconsin, 1995).

Coate, S. and G. Loury, 'Will Affirmative Action Policies Eliminate Negative Stereotypes?', *American Economic Review*, 83 (1993), pp. 1220–40.

Cohen, G. A., *Self-Ownership, Freedom, and Inequality* (Princeton: Princeton University Press, 1995).

Coleman, J., *Foundations of Social Theory* (Cambridge: Harvard University Press, 1990).

Corcoran, M., R. Gordon, D. Laren and G. Solon, 'Effects of Family and Community Background on Men's Economic Status', NBER working paper no. 2896 (1989).

Cose, E., *The Rage of a Privileged Class* (New York: Harper Collins, 1993).

Crane, J., 'The Epidemic theory of Ghettos and Neighborhood Effects on Dropping Out and Teenage Childbearing', *American Journal of Sociology*, 96 (1991), pp. 1226–59.

Datcher, L., 'Effects of Community and Family Background on Achievement', *Review of Economics and Statistics*, 64 (1982), pp. 32–41.

Durlauf, S., 'A Theory of Persistent Income Inequality', *Journal of Economic Growth*, 1 (1996a), pp. 75–93.

——'Neighborhood Feedbacks, Endogenous Stratification, and Income Inequality', in Dynamic Disequilibrium Modelling, W. Barnett, G. Gandolfo, and C. Hillinger, (eds.), (Cambridge University Press, 1996b).

——'Stratification and Efficiency', in W. B. Arthur, S. N. Durlauf and D. Lane (eds.), *The Economy as a Complex Evolving System II* (Redwood City: Addison-Wesley, 1996c).

Dworkin, R., *A Matter of Principle* (Cambridge: Harvard University Press, 1985).

Frank, R. and P. Cook, *The Winner-Take-All Society* (New York: Free Press, 1995).

Herrnstein, R. and C. Murray, *The Bell Curve* (New York: The Free Press, 1994).

Jencks, C. and S. Mayer, 'The Social Consequences of Growing Up in a Poor Neighborhood', in L. Lynn and M. McGreary (eds.), *Inner-City Poverty in the United States* (Washington DC: National Academy Press, 1990).

Kremer, M., 'The O-Ring Theory of Economic Development', *Quarterly Journal of Economics*, CVIII (1993), pp. 551–75.

——and E. Maskin, 'Segregation by Skill and the Rise in Inequality', mimeo (Massachusetts Institute of Technology, 1994).

Loury, G., 'A Dynamic Theory of Racial Income Differences', in P. Wallace and A. LaMond (eds.), *Women, Minorities, and Employment Discrimination* (Lexington: Lexington Books, 1977).

——'Why Should We Care About Group Inequality?', *Social Philosophy and Policy*, 5 (1987), pp. 249–71.

——'The Economics of Discrimination: Getting to the Core of the Problem', *Harvard Journal of African American Public Policy*, 1 (1992), pp. 91–110.

——'Conceptual Problems in the Enforcement of Antidiscrimination Laws', mimeo (Department of Economics, Boston University, 1995).

Lundberg, S. and R. Startz, 'Private Discrimination and Social Intervention in Competitive Labor Markets', *American Economic Review*, 73 (1983), pp. 340–7.

——'On the Persistence of Racial Inequality', mimeo (University of Washington, Seattle, 1993).

Manski, C., 'Identification Problems in the Social Sciences', in P. Marsden (ed.), *Sociological Methodology*, vol. 23 (Cambridge: Basil Blackwell, 1993a).

——'Identification of Endogenous Social Effects: The Reflection Problem', *Review of Economic Studies*, 60 (1993b), pp. 531–42.

Massey, D., and N. Denton, *American Apartheid* (Cambridge: Harvard University Press, 1993).

Massey, D., and S. Kanaiaupuni, 'Public Housing and the Concentration of Poverty', *Social Science Quarterly*, 74 (1993), pp. 109–22.

Nagel, T., 'Rawls on Justice', *Philosophical Review*, 82 (1973), pp. 220–34.

——'The Policy of Preference', in *Mortal Questions* (Cambridge: Cambridge University Press, 1979a).

—— 'Equality', in *Mortal Questions*, (Cambridge: Cambridge University Press, 1979b).

Nozick, R., *Anarchy, State, and Utopia* (New York: Basic Books, 1974).

Rawls, J., *A Theory of Justice* (Cambridge: Harvard University Press, 1971).

Roemer, J., 'Equality of Talent', *Economics and Philosophy*, 1 (1985) pp. 151–87.

—— 'A Pragmatic Theory of Responsibility for the Egalitarian Planner', *Philosophy and Public Affairs*, 22 (1993), pp. 146–66.

—— 'Equality of Opportunity: Theory and Examples', mimeo (Department of Economics, University of California at Davis, 1995a).

—— 'Equality of Opportunity and Affirmative Action', mimeo (Department of Economics, University of California at Davis, 1995b).

Rosenbaum, J., and S. Popkin, 'Employment and Earnings of Low-Income Blacks Who Move to Middle Class Suburbs', in C. Jencks and P. Peterson (eds.), *The Urban Underclass* (Washington DC: Brookings Institution Press, 1991).

Sen, A., 'Equality of What?', reprinted in S. Darwell (ed.), *Equal Freedom: Selected Tanner Lectures on Human Values* (Ann Arbor: University of Michigan Press, 1995).

Scanlon, T., 'The Significance of Choice', reprinted in S. Darwell, (ed.), *Equal Freedom: Selected Tanner Lectures on Human Values* (Ann Arbor: University of Michigan Press, 1995).

Verba, S., S. Kelman, G. Orren, I. Miyake, J. Watanuki, I. Kabashima and G. Ferree, *Elites and the Idea of Inequality* (Cambridge: Harvard University Press, 1987).

Walzer, M., *Spheres of Justice* (New York: Basic Books, 1983).

14

Redistributions of Assets and Distributions of Asymmetric Information

Ugo Pagano*

Introduction

'What new configuration of state, communities, and markets would be permitted by a more egalitarian distribution of residual claimancy and control rights? Among these would any be productivity-enhancing?' (Bowles and Gintis, 1994, p. 21)

Bowles and Gintis observe that the answer to these questions depends on two factors: *factor (1)* 'on the types of information available to some people and not to others, the way in which the information can be acquired, hidden and shared'; *factor (2)* 'the way in which governance institutions and property-rights distributions alter the information structures of social interactions'. (Bowles and Gintis, 1994, p. 22.)

Bowles and Gintis offer two compelling reasons for which the differential access to information should be central to any attempt to answer their question. The first is that much information is 'naturally' asymmetric: individuals know their own preferences,[1] needs, personal skills and productive capacities better than other people and, sometimes, it is impossible or, at least, very costly to transfer this private information. The second is that, in a world where everyone knows

* University of Siena. This paper was written for the Conference on 'Equality and Efficiency' held in Madison Wisconsin that was based on the issues raised in Bowles and Gintis (1994). I thank the participants to the workshop for their stimulating comments, and Massimo D'Antoni, Maurizio Franzini, Luigi Luini and Antonio Nicita for useful suggestions. I am grateful to C.N.R. for funding part of the costs. The usual 'caveats' apply.

the same things, such different governance structures as markets and central planning (as well as firms based on different distribution of assets) turn out to be equivalent.

Bowles and Gintis argue that, under some conditions, in spite of any 'risk-aversion' argument, egalitarian redistributions of assets may be productivity-enhancing because they abate the agency costs that are associated to asymmetric information. Or, in other words, given a certain information structure *factor (1)*, egalitarian redistributions can improve efficiency. This argument seems to be based on an exogenously given information structure. There are some good reasons for which this may be a good assumption: much information is 'naturally' asymmetric independently of the ownership of assets and of their governance. Thus, one may argue that egalitarian redistributions may decrease the agency costs due to exogenous asymmetric information.

Still, *factor (2)* is also very important: asymmetric information is also endogenous in the sense that it is partially determined by a given distribution of assets and governance system. When this type of asymmetric information exists, we cannot judge the efficiency of the present distribution of assets on the basis of the existing distribution of information. A distribution of assets may be efficient when a distribution of information is taken as given (and, vice versa, a distribution of information may be efficient when a distribution of assets is assumed to exist). However, changing both the distribution of information and that of physical assets may improve efficiency. In this case, obtaining an efficient redistribution is difficult for two related reasons: on the one hand one needs to identify and change together the 'complementary' distribution of assets and of asymmetric information; on the other hand a change that fails to deal with these 'complementarities' may produce inferior 'hybrids' where the distribution of assets does not match the distribution of information.

Economic literature has concentrated its attention on the source of incentives (including the distribution of assets) that allows us to deal better with a given structure of asymmetric information. In the first section of this paper we will show that, unlike the theory of economic agency, the 'scientific management' literature and, perhaps, a relevant part of actual management practice, has focused on the opposite problem: how to achieve the distribution of information that fits a given distribution of assets.

In the second section, we will consider a typical example of the economic approach due to Alchian and Demsetz. In their approach the 'optimal' distribution of assets is determined on the basis of a given distribution of asymmetric information. On this basis Demsetz argues that inequality, favouring an 'optimal' concentration of assets, promotes efficiency.

In the third section, Bowles' and Gintis' egalitarian claims are contrasted with the conclusions of Alchian and Demsetz. They are defended on the basis of arguments relying on the endogenous nature of much asymmetric information. We will argue that Alchian and Demsetz may deduce the efficiency of inequality from technological conditions that presuppose its existence.

In the fourth section the argument is developed within the framework of 'organizational equilibria'. We argue that competition may inhibit the 'speciation' of more egalitarian 'organizational equilibria' even when these equilibria are more efficient.

In the concluding section we argue that, while the hypothesis of endogenous asymmetric information may reinforce the argument for an egalitarian distribution of assets, its complementarity with the distribution of information poses serious problems for redistribution policies. In order for dangerous situations of 'organizational disequilibrium' to be avoided, these policies should as much as possible incentivate technological conditions complementary to more egalitarian allocations of economic resources. Finally, we argue that, in some cases, 'unbundling' ownership rights may be preferable to the redistribution of *given bundles* of ownership rights considered by Bowles and Gintis.

1 Braverman's Analysis of Taylorism: An Example of an Endogenous Re-distribution of Asymmetric Information

According to Braverman, the approach of 'scientific management', that was started by Taylor at the beginning of this century, has had a lasting impact on the development of the organization of work under capitalism. Taylor realized that the traditional system of management was badly suited to increasing workers' effort. Traditional management relied on the knowledge of the workers in the sense that the managers believed that the workers knew better than they did how to perform their jobs. Under traditional management, the workers could work less than 'fairly' by maintaining that a certain time was required to perform a certain job. The situation of 'asymmetric information', existing under traditional management, implied that the managers had no means to challenge this sort of statement. Taylor's solution to this problem was straightforward: the managers (and not the workers) should know how the jobs could be best performed, plan how they should be executed and give the workers detailed instructions about their execution. Only by gaining the control of the labor process could the managers invert this situation of asymmetric information and control workers' effort.

Braverman summarises the content of Taylorism in three different principles:

1. *dissociation of the labour process from the skills of the workers.* This is implicit in the following quotation from Taylor: 'The managers assume . . . the burden of gathering together all the traditional knowledge which in the past has been possessed by the workmen and then classifying, tabulating, and reducing this knowledge to rules, laws, and formulae . . . .'[2]

2. *separation of conception from execution.* This can be found in the following statement: 'All possible brain work should be removed from the shop and centred in the planning or laying-out department . . .'[3]

3. *use of this monopoly over knowledge to control each step of the labor process and its mode of execution.* This is clearly pointed out by Taylor when he states that, under scientific management the managers should give the workers detailed instructions about each task to be performed.

'The most prominent single element in modern scientific management – ' Taylor writes – 'is the task idea. The work of every workman is fully planned in advance, and each man receives in most cases complete written instructions, describing in detail which is to accomplish, as well as the means to be used in doing the work . . . This task specifies not only what is to be done, but how it is to be done and the exact time allowed for doing it . . . Scientific management consists very largely in preparing and carrying out these tasks'.[4]

According to Braverman, the analysis of Taylorism is essential to the understanding of the real-life capitalist economy because in Taylor's work 'lies a theory which is nothing else than an explicit verbalization of the capitalist mode of production'.[5]

The prominent role that Braverman gives to Taylorism has been the object of numerous criticisms.[6] However, what is relevant for our argument is simply that Taylor's scientific management provides an example of a possible way of changing the distribution of information; under the new distribution of information a capitalist system can increase its efficiency. The capitalist system inherits from systems characterized by a different distribution of assets[7] a distribution of information that is poorly attuned to capitalism. That part of the information that is unequally distributed (i.e. that information that is asymmetric) is to an 'intolerable' degree 'privately' held by the workers. Because of the distribution of assets, the workers have little incentive to use their private information in the interest of the organization. The 'Taylorist' solution is to 'expropriate' the workers of their private information and change the distribution of information in favor of the owners and management. Under the new distribution of information, the capitalist system can efficiently operate or, in other words, under the new situation of asymmetric information the capitalist distribution of assets is now efficient: the holders of private information are now the owners of the physical assets of the firm or few managers that it is relatively easier to motivate.

In spite of some considerable limitations in his analysis, Braverman has the merit of providing an example of causation opposite to traditional agency theory. In traditional agency theory the distribution of information is exogenously given. The problem is to determine endogenously the incentive structure or the distribution of assets that can best solve the agency problem. In Braverman the distribution of assets is exogenously given and the problem of Taylorism is to determine endogenously the best distribution of information given that distribution of assets. When, under a certain ownership system, because of asymmetric information, the use of a technology is particularly costly, there will be attempts to devise technologies that imply a distribution of information that better fits that system.

In Braverman's analysis, under capitalist-ownership relations, there is a tendency to devise technologies that, inverting preexisting information asymmetries, make labor an easy-to-monitor factor. A similar process occurs for the specificity of assets. The three principles of Taylorism also imply that much of the specific knowledge, used by the workers, is made redundant by introducing a technology under which the workers are ordered to perform homogeneous tasks requiring only generic skills.

Observe that both the difficult-to-monitor character of resources and their specificity attributes define high-agency-cost resources in the sense that they involve high agency costs when other individuals employ them in situations of goal incongruence. In general, any property-right system tends to use technologies that minimize on high-agency-cost resources owned by individuals that have goals different from (or even conflicting with) those of the owners of the firm. Thus, under 'classical capitalism' workers tend to become low-agency-cost resources.

By contrast, under 'classical capitalism', similar inhibitions do not hold for the owners of resources who have rights on the organization or can be, somehow, motivated to share its goals. Thus, under 'classical capitalism' employers and managers have a tendency to become high-agency-cost resources.

A similar process occurs for physical capital.

The owners of physical capital control the production process. Thus, incentive problems do not prevent them from using capital that is difficult to monitor in the sense that its user-induced depreciation could not be easily estimated by observing the state of machinery before and after use. The choice of a technology so that work is easy to monitor cheapens the use of difficult-to-monitor capital: the user-induced depreciation of machines can be easily checked by observing the actions of the workers. At the same time, employers and capitalists can well trust the fact that they will organize the production process in such a way to take into account the user-induced depreciation of their own difficult-to-monitor machinery.

A similar argument holds for the specificity of the non-human assets: the owners of machinery, controlling the organization, can be sure that the specific nature of their machinery will be taken into account in the future decisions of the firm and that they will be safeguarded against the possible opportunism of the other agents.

The joint implication of the monitoring and of the specificity arguments is that, unlike the workers, machines and employers tend to become high-agency-cost factors. According to Taylorism, any technology that increases the private information held by the workers, is very costly. By contrast, the increase of private information that is necessary to manage the workers and the machinery is not considered to be as costly because it is held by individuals that identify their goals with those of the organization.

2 Exogenous Asymmetric Information and the Optimality of Capitalist Inequality

Typically, economic theory has followed a route opposite to that which we have just considered.[8] It has taken as given a technology characterized by a certain distribution of information and specificity attributes and it has analyzed the rights, the incentives and the safeguards that can best suit this technology. A famous example of this approach can be found in Alchian's and Demsetz's famous explanation of the nature of the firm. We will reconsider their theory for two reasons. Firstly it offers a causation mechanism opposite to that which we have just considered.[9] Secondly, following this direction of inquiry, Demsetz reaches a conclusion contrary to that advanced by Bowles and Gintis: according to Demsetz, only inegalitarian distribution of assets can ease agency problems and can allow high productivity and accumulation of wealth.

Alchian and Demsetz begin their famous article by concentrating their attention on a simple agency problem concerning the loading of weights. Because of the existence of teamwork, the marginal products of team members cannot be directly measured and remunerated. In this situation individual contributions can only be estimated by observing the behavior of the individuals working in the team.[10] However, obtaining this information is costly and it may not pay each member of the team to monitor the activities performed by the other team members.

Under these conditions, each member of the team has an incentive to shirk because some of the costs of her increased leisure will be borne by other team members who cannot, individually, detect shirking at costs lower than the benefits of detection. The result is that each team member will end up shirking. This happens in spite of the fact that each of them would prefer a situation where nobody shirks and where she would realize the trade-off between income and leisure which maximizes her utility.

How can team members overcome this problem?

Alchian's and Demsetz's answer is that they can agree to have some individual specializing in the monitoring of their activities.

'But who will monitor the monitor?'[11] This potentially infinite regression is cut by assuming that the monitor has an incentive to behave efficiently or, in other words, that she would monitor herself. According to Alchian and Demsetz this assumption can hold true if the team members agree that the monitor should have the right to the residual earnings of the team. This agreement, coupled with competition among monitors, constrains the monitors' incentive to shirk. Thus, the foundations for the rationale of the classic capitalist firm are similar to those used by Hobbes to justify the existence of the state:[12] the workers accept capitalist ownership and control because they want to exit from a situation of unfettered freedom where each worker damages the other workers.

In Alchian's and Demsetz's view, the entrepreneur-monitor must not only be given the right to the net earnings of the team but also the right to hire and fire each individual team member. For this reason the residual claimant will also have the right to terminate and start contracts defining the terms of team membership. An asymmetry does therefore characterize the position of the monitor and that of the other team members.[13] Each team member can only terminate his own contract and leave the team. By contrast, only the monitor can terminate the employment of any team member, can employ new members and sell his right to be the residual claimant of the team. These rights of the monitor define the 'ownership (or the employer) of the classical (capitalist, free enterprise) firm'.[14]

Alchian's and Demsetz's analysis of the classical capitalist firm is completed by explaining the efficiency reasons for which the owner-monitor does also usually own some of or even all the physical capital employed by the organization. They offer two arguments.

The first argument is based on the idea that the employer-owner must be able to demonstrate his ability to pay to the owners of the inputs employed in the firm. This can be better done by investing in physical capital instead of human capital because property rights in other people cannot be easily enforced. For this reason, they argue, they will invest in the capital equipment of the firm. There is something unconvincing about this argument. For, as Alchian himself has subsequently admitted, this 'appears to be incorrect since the owner could supply credibility by using some of his assets completely unrelated to the production process, such as treasury bonds, for collateral'.[15]

The second argument is more interesting. It is also more consistent with the analysis outlined above because it hinges again on monitoring costs. Alchian and Demsetz observe that the employment of a durable resource involves a user-induced depreciation. In some cases, this user-induced depreciation is difficult to detect by observing the resource before and after its use. In order for this user-induced depreciation to be detected it is necessary to observe the resource during its use, for instance by watching the care with which the resource is utilized. In this case, if the resource is rented, its depreciation will be charged according to some expected depreciation. But, under these conditions, careless use is more likely because the person renting the resource does not pay for careless use, inducing greater depreciation. By contrast, if the user owns the resource she will take into account the cost of any misuse. Renting the resource will therefore be more costly than owning it.

A possible objection to this argument is that, instead of renting machines, the workers may borrow money, buy the machines and use them as collateral. Still, this objection can be answered by observing that difficult-to-monitor machines are less valuable as collateral than easy-to-monitor machines. The agency costs are simply shifted. The lender will now have to sustain the high costs of monitoring the user-induced depreciation of difficult-to-monitor capital.[16]

In general, when net-input performance is difficult to detect without monitoring the use of the input in the production process, owner use will replace contractual arrangements where the input is rented (or other contractual arrangements limiting the ownership rights of the user and involving the use of the input as collateral). For, the owners of a resource, having an incentive to use it efficiently can save on these monitoring costs. This proposition does not only complete the explanation of the rationale for the classical capitalist firm. It also throws light upon Alchian's and Demsetz's explanation for the existence of profit-sharing firms where the residual-claimant is not the owner of physical capital. This occurs when the situation, examined above, is inverted and labor is the input that is relatively more difficult to monitor. In this case monitoring costs can be decreased by giving the workers some form of joint ownership of the firm and by making them the residual claimants.

> In 'artistic' or 'professional' work watching a man's activities is not a good clue to what he is actually thinking or doing with his mind. While it is relatively easy to manage or direct the loading of trucks by a team of dock workers where input activity is so highly related in an obvious way to output, it is more difficult to manage and direct a lawyer in the preparation and presentation of a case. Dock workers can be directed in detail without the monitor himself loading the truck, and assembly-line workers can be monitored by varying the speed of the assembly line, but detailed direction in the preparation of a law case would require in much greater degree that the monitor prepare the case himself.[17]

Thus, unlike dock workers, 'difficult-to-monitor lawyers' will form partnerships and, possibly, hire the relatively more easy-to-monitor capital equipment. According to Alchian and Demsetz, in these cases, if the size of the team is not large and the incentive of profit-sharing is not too diluted, instead of classical capitalist firms, profit-sharing firms will provide an appropriate organizational solution.

Developing the arguments expressed above, Demsetz has expressed the view that wealth inequality can be beneficial for efficiency. If many firms are characterized by the existence of difficult-to-monitor capital and easy-to-monitor labor (and especially when large size is advantageous), the capitalist firm can offer the most appropriate monitoring system.

However, only individuals, who own a considerable percentage of the shares of a firm, will be willing to exercise this monitoring function.

By contrast, 'a diffuse ownership structure discourages this undertaking because of the well-known free-rider problem.'[18] Even in societies as rich as the US, an egalitarian distribution of wealth would not allow investors to own a sufficiently large share of the capital of the big firms to induce them to monitor the firm. 'If wealth were distributed equally, we would need to either forsake effective control of efficient sized firms or forsake large-scale production where size is important to efficiency. The lower is the per-capita wealth relative to the financial size of efficient productive units, the greater is the degree of inequality in its distribution that is required to maintain effective control.'[19]

Alchian (1987) and Williamson (1985) construct a similar argument that explains the nature of rights and safeguards by referring to the specificity attributes of the resources. The owners of the more specific resources tend to acquire the ownership and control of the organization. Thus, in 'New Institutional' economic theory, Braverman's argument (and, in general, the 'radical Argument')[20] is completely inverted. In Braverman, owning factors tend to become high-agency-cost resources. By contrast, in the New Institutional approach, high-agency-cost resources get the rights on the organizations for efficiency reasons. In particular, the distribution of asymmetric information is not influenced by ownership relations but it is the factor that explains their existence and their relative efficiency. In the case of Demsetz's argument, this efficiency-explanation of ownership-relations includes the necessity of an unequal distribution of assets.

3 Endogenous Asymmetric Information and Bowles' and Gintis' Claims

Alchian's and Demsetz's approach relies on exogenous asymmetric information or, in other words, on the characteristics of the distribution of information that are independent of the effects of a given ownership system. According to them, the capitalist firm is so widespread because it is the best answer to the large majority of the situations of exogenous asymmetric information.

Exogenous asymmetric information can explain why large capitalist firms are more successful in some sectors than in other sectors.[21] For instance, the nature of the distribution of asymmetric information in agriculture makes it very difficult to have specialized and centralized monitoring for the simple fact that it is not possible to concentrate the agriculture workers in the same location. In industry, the workers are relatively easier to monitor because the concentration of many workers in the same location does not, in general, decrease efficiency. Finally, the service sector does often share many monitoring attributes with agriculture: in many cases, the absence of a physical product that can be moved from the production to the consumption location implies that the worker must be where the service is consumed; again, specialized and centralized monitoring becomes more difficult and large-scale capitalist enterprises may become less viable.

Thus, an approach based on exogenous asymmetric information can be very valuable to understand the relative efficiency of different ownership relations in different sectors of the economy; moreover we have seen that an interesting prediction of this approach is that the more intensive the use of difficult-to-monitor skilled labor the less appropriate the traditional capitalist firms.

According to Alchian and Demsetz, the conditions under which capitalist firms would be the best organizational solution, are the most common ones. One can argue that sectors different from industry (as well as some industrial sectors) do not seem to meet such conditions.

However, in order for Bowles' and Gintis' claims to be sustained, one should also challenge the double claim that, under some conditions, capitalism is the most efficient organization and that an unequal distribution of assets is a necessary condition for the minimization of agency costs.

Observe that the agency-cost argument, outlined above, defends the efficiency of capitalism in a way different from that considered by Bowles and Gintis. According to them, whereas the risk-aversion argument may favor the capitalist enterprise, the agency-cost arguments favors the democratic firm. By contrast, Alchian and Demsetz believe that, under some conditions, the capitalist firm is superior from an agency-cost point of view: their argument is that, when physical capital is difficult-to-monitor and workers are easy-to-monitor, then giving the status of residual claimant to a centralized monitor (who also owns the difficult-to-monitor capital) minimizes agency costs.

Bowles and Gintis offer two general arguments that are intended to show the superiority of the democratic firm and that can be used against the claims of Alchian and Demsetz.

The first argument can, indeed, be viewed as a direct criticism of the view advanced by Alchian and Demsetz. Bowles and Gintis argue that the workers can be more effective than a centralized monitor in controlling their own activities. They justify this claim by observing that 'workers have access at low cost to information concerning the work activities of their fellow workers'. However, if workers are easy-to-monitor, these advantages may be less important than the disadvantages that are due to the fact that each individual worker may have very little incentive to monitor the other workers. In this situation a centralized capitalist monitor, having a stronger monitoring incentive, may overcome this free-rider problem. The capitalist monitor may also exploit the fact that easy-to-monitor workers cannot hide much private information or actions. Moreover he may also easily take advantage of the economies to scale that are likely to characterize the monitoring activities. The situation is different when the distribution of asymmetric information involves that the workers are difficult to monitor; here Bowles' and Gintis' claim becomes convincing but it does not contradict the argument advanced by Alchian and Demsetz.

The second argument, developed by Bowles and Gintis, relies on the idea that the capitalist firm is typically inefficient in that it uses too many monitoring resources and not enough wage incentives. The worker-owners would not replicate this inefficient choice of the capitalist firm for the obvious reason that they will regard paying themselves to be more convenient than hiring monitors. However, the amount of extra monitoring employed by the capitalist firm is unlikely to be very relevant when work is an easy-to-monitor factor. Moreover the advantages of highly specialized and large-scale monitoring, performed by strongly motivated agents, may again imply that the capitalist firm enjoys lower agency costs.

The advantages of having a centralized capitalist monitor do not only depend on the easy-to-monitor characteristics of work but also on the difficult-to-monitor nature of managers, capitalists and physical capital. We have seen that the distribution of specificity attributes can have effects similar to those due to the distribution of asymmetric information and that the distribution of both attributes determines the low- or high-agency cost nature of the resources. Thus, the objections to the Bowles and Gintis argument can be summarized by saying that, when labor is a relatively low-agency-cost factor, traditional forms of capitalist organization may be superior and inegalitarian distribution of assets, allowing the concentration of ownership, may increase efficiency.

The Bowles and Gintis paper contains some more suggestions that could be used to answer the objections considered above. However, I would like to develop a particular point advanced in their paper. This point is related to the idea that the distribution of information is endogenous and it cannot be taken for granted as it is implicitly by Alchian and Demsetz.

Bowles and Gintis (1994) summarize the implications of their papers in three major claims:

Claim 1: *Inequality impedes economic performance by obstructing the evolution of productivity-enhancing governance structures.*

Claim 2: *Where hard work, innovation, maintenance of an asset and other behaviors essential to high levels of economic performance cannot be specified in costlessly enforceable contracts, the assignment of control rights and residual claimancy status influences the kinds of exchanges that are possible and costs of carrying out these exchanges.*

Claim 3: *Some distributions of property rights are more efficient than others; in particular there exists an implementable class of distributions that are both more egalitarian and more efficient than the concentrations of asset holding observed in most capitalist economies.*

Bowles and Gintis observe that the three claims are strictly interdependent and they form a logical chain where each ring supports the subsequent rings. Claim 2 is the essential one. It can be made stronger by pointing out that the efficiency of the present assignment of control rights and residual claimancy status should not be judged taking as given the present nature of the assets and the present distribution of information. By contrast, it should be compared to that which would be possible to develop under the governance system that one could set up in a more egalitarian society. In this way, we can challenge the anti-egalitarian argument developed by Alchian and Demsetz.

In order to develop this analysis, we need to reconsider the rationale of Braverman's analysis of Taylorism. If one considers a system that has undergone the redistribution of knowledge skills and other information suggested by Taylor, one could easily buy Alchian's and Demsetz's argument: in a 'Tayloristic' organization an inegalitarian distribution of resources would need to minimize agency costs. One could visualize their argument as follows:

> Tayloristic information and agency attributes
> $\rightarrow$
> Need for concentrated capitalist ownership   (F1)
> $\rightarrow$
> Efficiency of an unequal distribution of assets.

However, according to Braverman, the 'Tayloristic' distribution of information and the other agency attributes are not natural characteristics of technology. They are themselves the result of the unequal distribution of assets that characterizes the capitalist system. Indeed, Braverman's argument can be visualized by a causal chain that runs in a direction opposite to that of Alchian and Demsetz:

> Unequal distribution of assets
> $\rightarrow$
> Concentrated capitalist ownership   (F2)
> $\rightarrow$
> Efficiency of the Tayloristic information and agency
>   attributes.

If we join together (F1) and (F2) we obtain:

> Unequal distribution of assets
> $\rightarrow$
> Concentrated capitalist ownership   (F3)
> $\rightarrow$
> Efficiency of the Tayloristic information and agency
>   attributes.
>
> Tayloristic information and agency attributes
> $\rightarrow$
> Need for concentrated capitalist ownership
> $\rightarrow$
> Efficiency of an unequal distribution of assets.

Thus, Alchian and Demsetz may just be claiming that the efficiency of inequality is justified by its own existence in the sense that it induces a distribution of information and other resource attributes under which inequality is efficient.

In spite of the fact that the distribution of information and the other agency attributes seem to justify their argument in favor of inequality, the claims advanced by Bowles and Gintis may be right: it is possible to improve welfare by changing both the distribution of assets and that of asymmetric information.

In the Tayloristic firm, inequality does not seem to impede efficiency. It seems to favor governance structures associated to distribution of assets such that high-agency-cost resources get the appropriate incentives. Under the Tayloristic technology, observing and sanctioning workers is cheap and standard labor-market contracts can work very well; it may seem that the incentives of residual claimancy can be left to the owners of the other resources. But this may be mere appearance. One should take into account the efficiency-loss that is due to the choice of a technology where workers can be employed by using standard market contracts. The 'complete' market contracts, existing for labor, may hide the choice of an inefficient technology.

For instance, the employment of the Tayloristic techniques may sacrifice the advantages of teamwork: unlike the case considered by Alchian and Demsetz, genuine teamwork does often imply that it may become very difficult for an external observer to understand the values of individual contributions. Moreover, in the case of 'non-primitive teams', each individual becomes specific to the skills of the other members of the team. If genuine teamwork is necessary to increase productivity, then the cost of the Tayloristic organization can only be evaluated by comparing its net benefits with those of alternative systems.

For example, when one compares Taylorism or Fordism with Toyotism where teamwork is highly developed, one may observe that under the latter system standard employment contracts cannot be easily used. A different system of rights is a necessary condition for operating this system. The fact that a traditional system of capitalist ownership impedes this type of technology is a relevant opportunity cost of these rights. Even if 'classical' capitalist rights are the best rights under the existing technology, this is no proof of their overall efficiency.

4 Organizational Equilibria and the Distribution of Assets

(F3) describes an organizational equilibrium[22] where technology, distribution of assets and distribution of information reinforce each other. In this section we will consider the nature of organizational equilibria and we will try to clarify the role of the distribution of assets on the selection of a particular organizational equilibrium.

We have already observed that, according to Braverman (and,

indeed, according to almost all the Radical literature), owning factors have a greater tendency to become high-agency-cost factors. This is due to the fact that an owning factor has no 'inhibitions' to become firm-specific nor to develop situations of asymmetric information under which it becomes a difficult-to-monitor factor. The incentives due to ownership allow a saving of the agency costs that would otherwise arise in these situations.

In some ways, changes in property rights have an effect similar to changes in relative prices. They increase the agency costs of using the non-owning factors relative to those of the owning factors. Thus, similarly to changes in relative prices, changes in property rights have a substitution effect: the high-agency-cost resources of the non-owning factors tend to be substituted away; for this reason non-owning factors tend to become low-agency-cost factors. Or, in other words, they tend to become less firm-specific and more difficult to monitor than owning factors.

Thus the redistribution of asymmetric information and of the specificity attributes (that, according to Braverman, occurs as a consequence of the process of capitalist concentration) can be explained by a familiar mechanism of standard economy theory. A change in the distribution of wealth induces a form of concentrated capitalist ownership under which it is a convenient process of technological substitution that tends to make labor a low-agency-cost resource. Denoting property rights by P and technology by T the radical assumption can be summarized by saying that property rights (P) determine the characteristics of the technology (T), or:

$$P \rightarrow T \qquad\qquad\qquad (F4)$$

In particular, in Braverman's analysis, capitalist property rights (P^c) bring about a technology (T^c) characterized by a distribution of asymmetric information and specificity characteristics such that capital and management tend to become a high-agency-cost-factor and labor tends to become a low-agency-cost factor; or:

$$P^c \rightarrow T^c \qquad\qquad\qquad (F5)$$

In the Radical approach it is also assumed that, in the long run, under a property-right system P^L, where the workers have some rights in the organization, there would be a tendency to develop an alternative technology T^L, under which labor, instead of capital and management, tends to become a relatively high-agency-cost factor:

$$P^L \rightarrow T^L \qquad\qquad\qquad (F6)$$

Also the New Institutional Assumption can be explained by a familiar mechanism of economic theory: for any given technological combination of factors it will be convenient for the high-agency-cost

factors to buy out the low-agency-cost factors. For a given technological combination the high-agency-cost factors can save more on
agency costs when they own the organization and can therefore offer
the highest price for the control of the organization. Or, in other
words, according to the New Institutional assumption:

$$T \rightarrow P \qquad \qquad (F4')$$

that is, technology explains property rights.

In particular, a technology T^c characterized by the employment of
much high-agency-cost capital and little high-agency-cost labor will
favor capitalist rights P^c because, under those property rights this
technology involves lower agency costs; that is:

$$T^c \rightarrow P^c \qquad \qquad (F5')$$

Likewise, according to the New Institutional approach, technologies characterized by a high intensity of high-agency-cost labor explain
the existence of firms where the workers have property rights on the
organization:

$$T^L \rightarrow P^L \qquad \qquad (F6')$$

We assume that both the Radical Assumption and the New
Institutional Assumption are simultaneously true. Following David
(1975), we assume that, in the short run, the agents know only the
combinations of factors that they are actually using and that exploring
new technologies may require time and effort. Thus, the existing
property rights shape technology; knowing and applying the technological combination associated to alternative property rights takes
time: the substitution effect of new property rights can only work in
the long run. At the same time, the existing technology can be
operated with minimum agency costs; when, for some combinations
of factors, agency costs can be saved by shifting control from some
agents to the other, the agents will find that it is their mutual interest
to do so.

We say that we are in an *organizational equilibrium* when both the
Radical and New Institutionalist assumptions are simultaneously
satisfied: in an organizational equilibrium the behavior of the firm
under particular ownership conditions must bring about technologies
characterized by factor intensities that do not upset the initial
ownership conditions. We can therefore give the following definition
of an organizational equilibrium.

Definition of Organizational Equilibrium

An institution of production is an *organizational equilibrium* when it
is defined by a system of property rights P and a technology T such

that T is the technology that maximizes rent under the property rights system P, and P is the property-rights system that maximizes ownership rent with the factor intensities associated with T.

In other words, in an organizational equilibrium (F4) and (F4') are simultaneously satisfied. Therefore, the existing property rights and the technology will be mutually consistent or:

$$\rightarrow P \rightarrow T \rightarrow P \rightarrow \qquad (F4'')$$

In particular we will be in a capitalist organizational equilibrium when (F5) and (F5') are both satisfied and capitalist rights P^c and capitalist technology T^c imply each other (F5''):

$$\rightarrow P^c \rightarrow T^c \rightarrow P^c \rightarrow \qquad (F5'')$$

and we will be in a labor organizational equilibrium when (F6) and (F6') the labor rights P^L and the labor technologyh T^L are such that (F6''):

$$\rightarrow P^L \rightarrow T^L \rightarrow P^L \rightarrow \qquad (F6'')$$

In a 'capitalist' organizational equilibrium capitalist property rights P^c maximize ownership rent given the 'capitalist' technology T^c and vice versa the capitalist technology T^c maximize profits given the capitalist property rights P^c. Likewise, labor property rights P^L are the best given the 'labor' technology T^L and vice versa the labor technology T^L maximizes profits given the labor property rights P^L. It follows that the situations of organizational equilibrium are always superior to the situations of organizational disequilibrium. In other words, the organizational equilibria defined by capitalist rights and technology ($P^c\ T^c$) and by labor rights and technology (P^LT^L) yield higher rent than the organizations characterized by the hybrids ($P^L\ T^c$) and (P^cT^L).

Organizations share some 'formal' characteristics with natural species: in the same way in which in each organizational equilibrium technology and property rights tend to fit optimally with each other, in each natural species each gene tends to be optimally adjusted to the other genes.

The analogy between the emergence of new organizational equilibria and speciation – that is the formation of a new species – can be fruitful because the emergence of new organizational equilibria satisfies one of the typical aspects of speciation: the inferiority, or even the impossibility, of the 'hybrids' between the two groups that is a necessary condition for differentiating them into different species.[23] For instance, in our simple model any combination of capitalist rights and labor technology 'genotypes' produces an organizational 'phenotype' that is inferior to both capitalist and labor organizational equilibria.

The analogy between organizational equilibria and natural species turns out to be useful to answer the following fundamental question: *does competition select the most efficient organizational equilibrium?*

Indeed, the analogy with natural species may even help to clarify the meaning of the question above. In natural selection the pressure of competition helps to select the best members of a given species; however, the effects of competition on speciation are much more controversial. Our question is related to the case of speciation: we are not asking whether competition can select the best member of a given species of organization but whether it can help the formation of a new more efficient species of organization characterized by a different technology and property rights 'genotypes'.

Each species is characterized by important 'development constraints': the fitness of each mutation is constrained by the other characteristics of the species. This implies that many evolutionary paths may be blocked. Unfortunately, in the case of organizational equilibria these obstacles may work exactly against those changes that may otherwise lead to the formation of a superior species of organization. Suppose that there are some efficient alternative potential owners that could get a higher ownership rent than the present owners. These alternative owners are efficient because their employment by the present owners involves very high agency costs that could be saved if they own the organization. For this reason, the factors of the potential alternative owners are promptly replaced by factors that are cheaper for the present owners. In other words, an 'anti-speciation' mechanism is embodied in each 'species' of organizational equilibrium and it has the unfortunate characteristic that its strength is related to the efficiency of the alternative potential species.[24]

However, suppose that this 'anti-speciation' factor is overcome and one of the characteristics of the old species mutates into one characterizing also a potentially more efficient new species of organization. For instance, some organizations are characterized by new property rights that (coupled with the associated optimal new technology) could form a new more efficient organizational equilibrium. Until this new technological combination is developed and employed, we will have a situation of organizational disequilibrium or, in other words, an inferior hybrid between the new property rights and the old technology. If the pressure of competition by the members of the old species is strong, the hybrid is likely to be wiped out before it has any chance of turning into the new superior species.

However, even if specification is successful, the survival of the new species can be endangered by a strong competition by many members of the old species.

In the first place, if there are few members of the new species, 'interbreeding' with the many members of the old species will be very frequent and will produce numerous inferior hybrids. In these conditions interbreeding may lead to the extinction of both mutations. When the new technology is imitated and run under the old property-rights system it turns out to be inferior and, vice versa, when the new rights are influenced by the old technology they also turn out to be inferior.

Secondly, in nature, the efficiency of each species depends on its frequency. Also organizations share the same characteristic. For instance, network externalities in property rights and in technologies may imply that few firms characterized by different organizational equilibria are not viable: they would be outcompeted by firms that, even if inferior when they exist with the same frequency, can better benefit of network externalities because of their present large number.

Summing up, the same competitive pressure, that favors the 'micro-mutations' improving the fitness of a given species, may inhibit the 'macromutations' that are necessary for the beginning of a new species.

Speciation theory offers a useful framework for understanding the dynamics of organizational equilibria and the effects of competition. Organizational equilibria cannot gradually evolve into superior organizational arrangements. Because of the 'institutional stability' of these equilibria we should expect that long periods of 'stasis' characterize these equilibria that may be 'punctuated' by periods of sudden changes to new 'species' of organizations.[25] Thus, the analysis of the emergence of different organizational equilibria seems to be closer to that of the 'punctuated equilibria' discussed by Eldredge and Gould (1972) with reference to the evolution of new species than to any 'gradualist' approach.[26]

In natural species as well as in organizational equilibria, after a period of one-by-one changes, because of the selection mechanism, each part of the whole may well become optimal given the nature of the other parts: for this reason, after this point, a better arrangement cannot be approached by a gradual change of each one of the parts but it requires simultaneous complementary changes. In this context no gradual tendency to move away from inefficient equilibria can arise. Because of the 'complementarities' that are necessary for successful macromutations, these macromutations may never occur; if they do, they will be characterized by abrupt changes leading to the formation of other species that have a substantial number of different features. Like the evolution of natural species, the history of organizations is likely to be 'punctuated' by long periods of stasis and by sudden changes. In both cases, their 'efficiency' will be limited by the sequence of the mutations that were actually made or, in other words, by their own history.

Since competition can inhibit the formation of new species, speciation is likely to be characterized by 'allopatric' conditions; or, in other words, it occurs when for an initial period a physical barrier protects the mutants from the competition of the members of the original species. Competition may be very important to select the one-by-one changes that improve the fitness of a given species of organization but a temporary protection from competition may well be necessary for the speciation of 'new organizational equilibria' requiring the complementary change of property rights and technology.

The analogy with natural selection, considered above, has some implications that support the claims put forward by Bowles and Gintis. Because of the endogenous nature of asymmetric information and of the other characteristics of the technology we cannot expect from competition an efficient reallocation of assets that decreases agency costs. Although competition can be very useful in selecting the micromutations that improve the efficiency of a given species of organizations, it can inhibit those redistributions of assets that are the necessary ingredients of successful macromutations. We cannot rely on *laissez-faire*. An active policy of asset redistribution may well be justified.

Conclusion

The argument that we have developed supports policies of redistribution of assets also in cases where the existing technological and information conditions may seem to imply the contrary. However, the same rationale implies that a policy that focuses only on the redistribution of assets is likely to fail.

Even if the present system of asset distribution is efficient only relative to its own endogenous information and technological features, it is still true that these characteristics will be inherited by the new system. Indeed a redistribution of assets is likely to generate the formation of inferior hybrids. Or, in other words, after the redistribution of the assets, there could be a situation of 'organizational disequilibrium' that referring to (F3) can be characterized as follows:

Egalitarian distribution of assets

→

Concentrated or dispersed workers' ownership

→

Efficiency of the Tayloristic information and agency attri-
butes.   (F7)

Tayloristic information and agency attributes

→

Need for concentrated capitalist ownership

→

Efficiency of an unequal distribution of assets.

According to the characteristics of each sector the more equal
distribution of assets would, perhaps, create forms of concentrated or
dispersed workers' ownership.[27] This would *not* imply any more the
efficiency of 'Tayloristic' information and agency attributes. In this
sense we would have a situation of 'organizational disequilibrium': an
inferior hybrid between the new rights and the old technology would
now exist. In these conditions the existing Tayloristic information and
agency attributes would still require a concentrated capitalist ownership that would imply the efficiency of an unequal distribution of
assets.

Thus, under the conditions that we have considered, a policy of
egalitarian distribution of assets produces a situation of organizational
disequilibrium. This situation of organizational disequilibrium may
be very undesirable from the point of view of economic policy for
two reasons.

In the first place, the situation of organizational disequilibrium is
likely to be a hybrid inferior to the initial organizational equilibrium.
Thus disequilibrium is costly in terms of economic resources. Moreover a long duration of disequilibrium will give the impression that
the policy of asset redistribution is not going to work.

In the second place, the situation of organizational disequilibrium
does neither imply that the 'speciation' of a new organizational
equilibrium is necessarily guaranteed nor that there is some 'natural'
tendency to move towards the new equilibrium. By contrast, it is
possible to go back to the old organizational equilibrium. While the
new rights are 'pushing' for a new technology, the old technology is
'pushing' for the old rights and, in principle, it is not clear in which
way the disequilibrium is going to be eliminated. A failure to complete
the transition to the new equilibrium would have dramatic consequences for egalitarian policies. The poor results, due to the inferior

hybrid, could be attributed to the final outcome of the redistribution policy.

Thus, a policy of egalitarian asset redistribution must try to avoid as much as possible situations of organizational disequilibrium. This may only be achieved by taking into account the complementarities between the assets and the distribution of information and specificity characteristics.

Together with asset redistribution it is necessary to improve the quality of education and the skills necessary for alternative management and production systems. Moreover, a policy of asset redistribution must go together with the development of new technologies that do not refrain from relying on skilled labor and teamwork even when they involve the intensive use of high-agency-cost labor.[28] Finally, these policies must provide incentives for the new technologies even when the property-rights structure is not yet best attuned for their employment.

In other words, it is necessary to act simultaneously on rights and technology. We should stick to the elementary principles of economic policy according to which the number of policy instruments should not be inferior to the number of objectives.

The successful speciation of new organizational equilibria does not only require that each firm deals successfully with the complementarities between its own rights and technology. Because of network externalities there are also important complementarities among the organizational models adopted by different firms.

The existence of network externalities can cause a homogenization of technology.[29] A single technological standard may be the only possible equilibrium outcome when common inputs produced under a regime of economies to scale are used by all the firms.

Although the case of property rights has not received the same attention, network externalities can also cause the homogenization of ownership systems. For all the firms using the same system of property rights, some pieces of legislation, and the skills that are necessary to its application and enforcement, are common inputs produced and used under a system of pronounced economies to scale. A piece of legislation can be used an infinite number of times without being destroyed.

For instance, the legislation on limited liability has been very important for the development of all joint-stock companies and for the quality of collective governance by shareholders. By contrast, the legal instruments by which workers could exercise their governance are relatively underdeveloped. As Bowles and Gintis claim, redistributing assets to the workers should not imply going back to small-scale production. However, the institutions by which the workers should exercise their control in large firms are still unclear at theoretical and practical level. For instance, these institutions should face the fact that the interests of the workers are much less homogeneous than those of shareholders. For this reason, the means by which collective decisions should be taken are necessarily more complex.[30]

The complementarity between technology and property rights that is encompassed by the concept of organizational equilibria implies that network externalities can act indirectly on property rights via technology and also indirectly on technology via property rights. Network externalities among firms' technologies may also imply the homogenization of property rights. Vice versa, networks externalities among the ownership system may also imply the standardization of technologies. When these complementarities between technological and property-rights standards exist, the speciation of few alternative organizational models may become very difficult. Redistribution policies become fairly complex because they should deal with both inter-firm and intra-firm complementarities between rights and technologies.[31]

Finally, a policy of asset redistribution must be better specified. It can involve the redistribution of given bundles of rights (on which Bowles and Gintis focus their contribution) and/or the 'unbundling of rights' and their attribution to different agents. Even if this form of asset redistribution has not yet received the attention that it deserves,[32] it has had great practical relevance and it has often had the effect of increasing both equality and efficiency.

In real-life capitalist economies the workers have often acquired two types of rights with respect to the work that they perform. In some cases (that are very frequent in the 'company workers' type of capitalism' characterizing the Japanese economy) they have the right on some unspecified job in a particular organization for a long time and, in some cases, until retirement. In some other cases (that are typical of 'the unionized type of capitalism' that has been developed in the German economy) a union of workers can have the exclusive right to perform some well-specified jobs in all organizations but the single worker does not have the right to a job in a particular organization; the specification of the contents of these jobs and the relative training is to be agreed by the unions and employers' associations.

The cases, considered above, correspond to different types of 'unbundling' and redistributions of the rights on physical assets existing under 'classical Tayloristic capitalism'.[33]

Consider first the case of 'company workers' capitalism'. If a worker has some job security, the owners of the physical assets do not have the right to employ the assets of the firm without that worker. Thus, employers do not have a right on physical assets that they have under 'classical capitalism'. In other words, 'company workers' capitalism' involves the 'unbundling' and the redistribution of a right on physical assets that belongs to the employers under 'classical capitalism'.

Likewise, in the case of 'unionized capitalism', if only the workers having certain qualifications and belonging to a certain union can work in a certain trade, the owners of assets do not have the right to employ the asset with other workers. Moreover, if the employers' associations and the unions have the right to specify and standardize the nature of the jobs across the firms, then the ownership of physical assets does not entail the right to employ the assets with any organization of production; also under 'unionized capitalism', some rights that are held under 'classical capitalism' by the owners of the assets, are 'unbundled' and redistributed from the single asset-owner to the workers' union and to the employers' association.

The unbundling and redistribution of rights, considered above, is likely to dilute the incentives of owners of the employers to invest in the high-agency-cost physical assets.

However, the same unbundling and redistribution of rights is likely to have positive incentive effects on the high-agency-cost human capital. In the case of 'company workers' capitalism' job security can favor investments in firm-specific human capital that is safeguarded against the threat of 'unfair' termination. And, in the case of 'unionized capitalism' the standardization of jobs across firms, safeguarding the generality of learning acquired by doing, favors investments in human capital that can be utilized in other firms in case of job termination (or, in other words, this system of rights creates a market for skilled workers).[34] In both cases, the sense of belonging to a firm or to a craft-union and the satisfaction of learning by doing should make 'difficult-to-monitor' jobs less costly.

Observe that, in both cases, the 'unbundling' and redistribution of rights is likely to shape the nature of resources in a self-sustaining manner.

In both systems the truncation of the rights of the asset-owners may cause the underemployment of high-agency-cost physical capital. In turn, this underemployment may have the consequence that the asset-holders value less the rights on the physical assets that have been redistributed to the workers. If the new rights are allowed to survive for a sufficiently long period then, after some time, we would have a lower intensity of high-agency-cost capital or, in other words, a technology that is consistent with the new rights.

A similar self-reinforcing process holds for human capital. In the case of 'company workers' capitalism' the increased employment of firm-specific human capital will, in turn, increase the value of the firm-specific job rights for the workers. Under 'unionized capitalism', the increased employment of general-purpose (but trade-specific) human capital will, in turn, induce the workers to give greater value to the rights that their union has in that particular trade.

Under both systems the workers will have a greater incentive to acquire the knowledge that can be useful to perform their jobs; by contrast, the incentives of managers and asset-holders to acquire the knowledge to direct the labor process will become weaker. In other words, in both cases, the unbundling and the redistribution of rights on the physical assets will also have a tendency to induce a redistribution of asymmetric information.

Thus, the definition and the distributions of physical assets, defining 'classical Tayloristic capitalism', 'company workers' capitalism' and 'unionized capitalism' characterize alternative 'organizational equilibria' that involve very different degrees of (in)equality and welfare. In principle, the unbundling and redistribution of rights that occurs in the transition from 'classical capitalism' to either 'company workers' capitalism' or 'unionized capitalism', can increase equality and enhance efficiency. It is an open question as to which unbundling of rights is more likely to achieve these objectives. It is also an open question whether redistributions based on the unbundling of rights are more likely to achieve these goals than the redistributions of given unbundled rights on physical assets.

Thus, the choice among alternative redistribution policies is very complex. It must take into account the institutional characteristics of the country where it is supposed to take place and, in particular, whether some unbundling of rights on physical assets has already occurred in that country. In other words, the complementarities that we have seen to characterize the distribution of assets and the distribution of asymmetric information must be studied in the contexts of different economies. Different redistribution policies may well turn out to be appropriate for different countries.

In spite of these difficulties, an egalitarian redistribution of physical assets and asymmetric information that improves efficiency belongs to the world of real utopias. It is certainly reasonable to believe that there are not only trade-offs but also complementarities between efficiency, equality and democracy: a more egalitarian distribution of assets and a more egalitarian distribution of information and decision-making are very likely to support each other. In some cases, they are also likely to improve productivity.

Appendix

We assume the existence of a standard production function Q $(k,$ K, $l,$ L) such that the output Q can be produced with different combinations of low-agency-cost capital and labor $(k,$ $l)$ and high-agency-cost capital and labor (K, L). Q (.) can be interpreted as a 'long-run' production function. Thus, the substitution effects induced by property rights are not immediate and it is possible to have short-run mismatches between property rights and the associated technology.

We assume that when workers own the organization they pay an additional agency cost Z in order to employ a unit of difficult-to-monitor or specific capital K – a cost that is saved when K is employed under capitalist ownership. By contrast, when the capitalists own the organization, they pay an additional agency cost H when they employ a unit of difficult-to-monitor or specific labor L – a cost that is saved when L is employed under labor-ownership. No such additional costs are paid for easy-to-monitor and general-purpose labor and capital k and l when they are employed by either capitalists or workers.

We denote by r and w the prices of respectively easy-to-monitor and/or general capital and labor and by R and L the prices (net of agency costs) of respectively difficult-to-monitor and/or specific capital and labor. We also set the price of output equal to 1. Thus, we can formulate our 'Radical' assumption as follows:

Radical Assumption:

Under capitalist ownership, firms maximize profits equal to:

$$R^c = Q (k, K, l, L) - [rk + RK + wl + (H+W)L] \quad (1).$$

Under labor ownership, firms maximize profits equal to

$$R^L = Q (K, K, l, L) - [rk + (Z + R)K + wl + WL] \quad (2).$$

This way of formulizing the 'radical assumption' makes it very clear why property rights influence technology in a way similar to changes in relative prices: for instance, the relative prices of the high-agency-cost factors are (H+W)/R under capitalist-ownership and W/

(Z+R) under workers' ownership. Thus, under standard assumptions, the intensity of high-agency-cost capital relative to the intensity of high-agency-cost labor is higher under capitalist-ownership than under labor-ownership. Observe that in this framework, the value of the elasticity of substitution among factors becomes a measure of the 'strength' of the effects of changes of property rights on the nature of the technology.

We have seen that the 'New Institutionalist Assumption' runs in a direction opposite to that of the 'Radical Assumption'; taking as given a certain technology the firm is supposed to be owned by that factor which can earn the highest ownership-rent. This rent is equal to the difference between the cost of employing the factor in a firm that is property of the owners of the factor and the cost of employing it in a firm that is property of other owners.

New Institutional Assumption:

For any given combination of factors employed in the firm, ownership of the firm will be acquired by the factor which can get the highest ownership-rent. Therefore: capitalist property rights can prevail if, given the factors currently employed, $R^c \geqslant R^L$ or, alternatively,
$$ZK - HL \geqslant O, \tag{3}$$
workers' property rights can prevail if, given the factors currently employed, $R^L \geqslant R^c$, or alternatively,
$$HL - ZK \geqslant O \tag{4}.$$

Conditions defining organizational equilibria

There will be a capitalist organizational equilibrium (COE) if there is a technology that maximizes (1) and satisfies (3) and there will be a labor-organizational equilibrium (LOE) if there is a technology that maximizes (2) and satisfies (4).
Let:
$$(k^c, K^c, l^c, L^c) = \text{argmax } R^c (k, K, l, L) \tag{5},$$
$$(k^L, K^L, l^L, L^L) = \text{argmax } R^L(k, K, l, L) \tag{6},$$
Then a firm will be in *a capitalist organizational equilibrium* (COE) if:
$$ZK^c - HL^c \geqslant O \tag{7},$$
and in *a labor organizational equilibrium* (LOE) if:
$$HL^L - ZK^L \geqslant O \tag{8}.$$
Condition (7) has an immediate intuitive meaning. Suppose that a firm is under capitalist ownership and the technique of production is

such as to maximize profits. Condition (7) implies that, *with this technique*, the ownership-rent occurring to capitalists is at least as great as the rent which workers could obtain if they owned the firm. Hence, *with this technique of production*, the workers would have no incentive to buy out the capitalists. This is what is meant by a capitalist organizational equilibrium. Condition (8) has an analogous intuitive meaning.

The conditions for COE and LOE can also be written in the following equivalent ways:

$$K^c/L^c \geqslant H/Z \qquad\qquad (7'),$$
$$K^l/L^l \leqslant H/Z \qquad\qquad (8'),$$

Conditions (7') and (8') have also an intuitive meaning. Observe that K/L is the ratio of high-agency-cost (H–A–C) capital to H–A–C labor or *the H–A–C capital intensity*; observe also that H/Z is the *agency-cost ratio* between the capitalist's extra-cost in employing H–A–C labor and labor's extra-cost in employing H–A–C capital. Thus (7') means that a COE is feasible when the intensity of H–A–C capital is greater than the agency-cost ratio and (8') means that a LOE is feasible when the intensity of H–A–C capital is lower than the agency-cost ratio. For instance, high-agency costs per unit of labor could be compensated by the employment of a great amount of H–A–C capital and make it a feasible COE.

Under standard assumptions, the high-agency-cost capital intensity will be higher under capitalist ownership or:

$$K^c/L^c \geqslant K^l/L^l \qquad\qquad (9).$$

The value of the agency-cost ratio H/Z either falls in the interval defined by these two values or outside it.

Let us first consider the case in which it falls in this interval. In this case H/Z is such that:

$$K^c/L^c \geqslant H/Z \geqslant K^l/L^l \qquad\qquad (10).$$

Then both (7') and (8') are satisfied and we have multiple (capitalist and labor) organizational equilibria.

Consider now the cases in which H/Z does not fall in this interval. H/Z may be smaller than the high-agency-cost capital intensities. Or:

$$K^c/L^c \geqslant K^l/L^l > H/Z \qquad\qquad (11).$$

Then (7') is satisfied but (8') is not satisfied. In this case only a COE exists.

By contrast, if H/Z is such that:

$$H/Z > K^c/L^c \geqslant K^l/L^l \qquad\qquad (15)$$

(8') is satisfied but (7') is not satisfied. In this case only a LOE exists.

Observe that since the ratio H/Z must necessarily fall in one of the three intervals considered above, for any H/Z ratio at least one organizational equilibrium must always exist.

We can visualize the three possibilities considered above in the following figure 8. For H/Z that goes from zero to infinity we first have unique COE equilibria, then multiple equilibria and, finally, LOE unique equilibria.

$$O\_\_(COE)\_\_K^L/L^L\_\_((LOE+COE)\_\_K^c/L^c\_\_(LOE)\rightarrow\infty \quad (F8)$$

(F8) 'assumes' a certain value of the elasticity of substitution and it can give us some intuition of the effects of its change. An increase in the elasticity of substitution widens the values of the agency-cost ratio for which multiple equilibria exist. It moves K^L/L^L leftwards and K^c/L^c towards the right, widening the interval of multiple equilibria defined by them. Within this interval any initial set of property rights will induce technologies such that their interaction will define organizational equilibria. Thus, an increase of the elasticity of substitution widens the interval where property rights can shape technologies in a self-sustaining manner. Because of the 'Radical Assumption', the higher the elasticity of substitution the more powerful the effects of ownership on technology.

Notes

1. One should not only consider preferences for consumption of goods but also the preferences for alternative ways of carrying production activities. In this respect, traditional neoclassical theory can be very misleading because it includes leisure and not directly working activities among the arguments of the utility function. The asymmetric nature of the information on preferences for working activities can be a powerful argument for the redistributions of assets that is not considered by Bowles and Gintis. Observe that the asymmetric nature of this information underlies a fundamental asymmetry between (physical) capital and labor. Capitals (or their owners) do not get any *direct* utility from its allocation in production. By contrast, the workers get an *indirect* utility (via the utility of the product of labor) and also a *direct* utility from the fact that different allocations of labor involve different working activities to which they are unlikely to be indifferent. On this point see Pagano (1985).

2. F. Taylor, quoted in Braverman (1974), p. 112

3. F. Taylor, quoted in Braverman (1974), p. 113

4. F. Taylor, quoted in Braverman (1974), p. 118

5. Braverman (1974), p. 86

6. In the first place, Braverman has been criticized for seeing Taylorism as the only typical form of organization under capitalism. Other authors have limited the field of application of Taylorism either to an historical phase or capitalism (Edwards, 1979 and Gordon, Edwards and Reich, 1982) and/or to a certain countries (Elbaum and Wilkinson, 1979 and Littler, 1982) or to certain sections of the working class (for a survey see Sawyer 1989, part 2). This point is strictly related to the second criticism: Braverman has ignored successful workers' resistance to Taylorism and the fact that, because or even independently of this resistance, the capitalists themselves have found ways of controlling the workers which are more efficient than Taylorism (Edwards,

1979 and Friedman, 1977). Finally, Braverman has been criticised for his thesis that de-skilling has in fact occurred in reality. It has been pointed out that, if some skills have disappeared, new skills have been created in the course of the development of capitalism. The sheer extension of formal training for the majority of the workers seems to prove that re-skilling has occurred (Wood, 1982).

7. Following Marx, Braverman (1974) observed how the organization of work had been substantially inherited from preceding modes of productions characterized by a more dispersed concentration of ownership; the distribution of information corresponded to technologies that were suited to these types of organization were the asymmetric distribution considered by Taylor was not damaging. The new system of concentrated ownership favours technologies characterized by a different distribution of information.

8. A related point is considered by Basile and Casavola (1994).

9. The Marxian theory contains both causation mechanisms. Their integration is one of the most stimulating problems of this theory. Some Marxists have emphasized the 'primacy' of the productive forces whereas others have given more importance to the influence of property rights on technology. For instance Cohen (1978) defends this 'primacy' whereas Brenner (1986) criticizes it. Roemer (1988) offers a useful survey of both.

10. 'When lifting cargo into the truck, how rapidly does a man move to the next piece to be loaded, how many cigarette breaks does he take, does the item being lifted tilt downward his side?' (Alchian and Demsetz, 1972 p. 121)

11. Alchian and Demsetz (1972), p. 125.

12. As Bowles (1985, footnote n.3) has observed, it constitutes 'an economic analogue to the Hobbesian position which asserts that uncoerced citizens in state of nature would in their own interest commit themselves to obey the dictates of the state'.

13. The asymmetry between the contractual position of team members and the owner of the classical capitalist seems to give little support to the claim that no form of authority characterizes this organization – a claim which is made by observing that 'the employee can terminate the contracts as readily as the employer . . .' (Alchian and Demsetz, p. 125). In fact, this is the only element of symmetry of the relation because, as they well underline, many more contractual options are open to the owner of the firm. He can terminate the relationship with each individual member without terminating the relations with other team members. By contrast, the option of terminating the relation with the owner but continuing the relationship with the other team members is not open to any other individual than the owner-monitor. Or in other words the owner can 'fire' each team member, but no one of them can 'fire' the owner. Alchian and Demsetz maintain that no difference exists between the relationships between employers and employees and between us and our grocers. According to them, firing employees is not different from the fact that 'I can fire my grocer by stopping purchases from them . . .' (Alchian and Demsetz, p. 119). But this is playing with words. I cannot stop one particular grocer from cooperating with other grocers whereas the employer can obtain this result when he terminates his contract with one particular team member. The ownership of an organization and the possession of hiring and firing rights implies a form of asymmetric power which differentiates it from the ordinary grocer-consumer relationship.

14. Alchian and Demsetz (1972), p. 125.

15. Alchian (1984), p. 247.

16. A similar argument holds for the case of specific capital. The workers could borrow money, buy the firm-specific machines and use them as collateral. However, specific machines are less valuable as collateral than general purpose capital because the value of specific capital will therefore be also cheaper than arrangements where the lenders of monetary capital have some rights in the case of bankruptcy. In general, the agency costs of using positive-agency-cost capital can only be eliminated by giving the full ownership rights to its users.

17. Alchian and Demsetz (1972), p. 129.

18. Demsetz (1988), p. 231.

19. Demsetz (1988), p. 232.

20. Besides Braverman and the literature streaming from his book, a similar direction of causation is considered by Marglin (1974), Rowthorn (1974), Pagano (1985) and Bowles (1985 and 1989).

21. In Marxian words, in some cases, the 'primacy' of productive forces may be a good working assumption.

22. For a more detailed analysis of the properties of 'Organisational Equilibria', see Pagano (1991, 1992 and 1993) and Pagano and Rowthorn (1994). Bowles and Gintis (1994), p. 39.

23. If the hybrids between two species were at disadvantage, 'selection would act to increase the reproductive isolation because each form would do better not to mate with the other and produce disadvantageous hybrids: speciation would be speeded up by selection in sympathy. The process is called *secondary reinforcement*. It is secondary if the reproductive isolation has partly evolved allopatrically, and is then reinforced on secondary contact. The process by which selection increases reproductive isolation independently of the history of the populations is simply called *reinforcement*' (Ridley, 1993, p. 412). Reinforcement is a necessary condition for the new species not to merge if they happen to share the same territory but it is not a sufficient condition for speciation. By contrast 'the theoretical conditions for speciation to take place by reinforcement are difficult' (Ridleyk, 1993, p. 414).

24. The strength of this mechanism depends on the elasticity of substitution that also determines the multiplicity and the efficiency of organizational equilibria. For a formal intuitive argument see the appendix to this paper. For a more complete analysis see Pagano and Rowthorn (1994).

25. For a complete analysis of the analogies between economics and evolutionary biology see Hodgson (1993).

26. However, as Mayr (1991) points out, even the 'speciational evolution', considered by Elredge and Gould, is in some sense gradual. 'Such speciational evolution, because it occurs in populations, is gradual in spite of its rapid rate and therefore is in no conflict whatsoever with the Darwinian paradigm.' (Mayr 1991 p. 154). However, it is in sharp contrast with the view of some geneticists who see evolution as a gradual change of gene frequencies in populations and do not see the abrupt nature of speciation and the long periods of stasis that characterize the evolution of species (Mayr 1991, p. 137).

27. Bowles and Gintis leave this point open. In some cases, a redistribution to the workers may make it more efficient to break the capitalist firms; in other cases, unified governance is still convenient after changing property rights.

28. These technologies and rights based on teamwork may help the development of a sense of community that is also highly complementary to the new organizational equilibrium. Other policies, favorihg this sense of belonging to communities, may, in turn, help the new right and technologies. The concept of organizational equilibrium should be somehow extended to take into account these factors. An attempt to move in this direction is made in Pagano (1995).

29. See Agliardi (1991) and Arthur (1989).

30. For this reason, the 'influence costs' considered by Milgrom and Roberts (1990) could be relatively high in the 'democratic firm'.

31. The existence of these complex complementarities characterize also the privatization policies in the former socialist economies that, because of their different socialist experiences, inherit different distributions of asymmetric information. On this point see J. Earle, R. Frydman, A. Rapaczynski (1993). On the notion of complementarities see Milgrom and Roberts (1992).

32. An exception is Roemer (1995). I have also benefited from his comments during the conference.

33. For a more precise definition of 'classical capitalism', 'company workers' capitalism' and 'unionized capitalism' see Pagano (1991). For a (very short) explanation

of the reasons why the three major western economies have developed alternative 'organizational equilibria' see the concluding section of Pagano (1993).

34. Thus, the unions and the employers' associations that are usually seen as impediments to the unfettered working of efficient markets can, at the same time, be institutional preconditions for a system of property rights that allows the existence of markets for skilled labor. On this point see section 4 of Pagano (1991).

References

Agliardi, E., *Essays on the Dynamics of Allocation under Increasing Returns to Adoption and Path Dependency* (Ph.d. Thesis, University of Cambridge, 1991).

Alchian, A., 'Specificity, Specialization and Coalitions', *Journal of Institutional and Theoretical Economics* (1984), pp. 34–9.

——'Property Rights' in J. Eatwell, M. Millgate and P. Millgate (eds.), *The New Palgrave* London: (Macmillan, 1987), pp. 1031–34.

——and H. Demsetz, 'Production, Information Costs and Economic Organisation', *American Economic Review*, 62 (1972), reprinted in Demsetz, H., *Ownership, Control and the Firm. The Organisation of Economic Activity*, vol. I (Oxford: Blackwell, 1988), pp. 777–95.

Arthur, B., 'Competing Technologies, Increasing Returns, and Lock-in by Historical Events', *Economic Journal*, 99 (1989) pp. 116–31.

Basile, L. and P. Casavola, 'The Firm as an Institution: Recent Evolution in the Contractual Perspective', *Recherches Economiques de Louvain*, no. 2 (1994), pp. 249–70.

Bowles, S., 'The Production Process in a Competitive Economy: Walrasian, Neo-Œobbesian, and Marxian Models', *The American Economic Review*, 75 (1985), pp. 16–36.

——'Social Institutions and Technical Change', in M. Di Matteo , R. M. Goodwin and A. Vercelli (eds.), *Technological and Social Factors in Long Term Fluctuations* (New York: Springer-Verlag, 1989).

——and H. Gintis, 'Efficient Redistribution: New Rules for Markets, States and Communities', mimeo, Amherst; paper submitted for the Conference on 'Equality and Efficiency', Havens Centre, Madison (1994).

Braverman, H., *'Labor and Monopoly Capital'*, *Monthly review Press* (New York, 1974).

Brenner, R., 'The Social Basis of Economic Development', in Roemer, *Analytical Marxism* (Cambridge: Cambridge University Press, 1986).

Cohen, G.A., *Karl Marx's Theory of History: A Defence* (Oxford: Oxford University Press, 1978).

Darwin, C., *The Origin of Species* (Harmondsworth: Penguin Books, 1968).

David, P.A., *Technical Choice, Innovation and Economic Growth* Cambridge: (Cambridge University Press, 1975).

——'Why are Institutions the "Carriers of History"? Path Dependence and the Evolution of Conventions, Organisations and Institutions', *Structural Change and Economic Dynamics*, vol. 5, no. 2 (1994), pp. 205–21.

Demsetz, H., 'Towards a Theory of Property Rights', *American Economic Review. Papers and Proceedings*, no. 2 (1966), pp. 347–59.

'The Control Function of Private Wealth', in H. Demsetz (ed.), *Ownership, Control and the Firm, The Organisation of Economic Activity*, vol. I (Oxford: Blackwell, 1988).

Dosi, G., 'Sources, Procedures and Microeconomic Effects of Innovation', *Journal of Economic Literature*, vol xxvi (September 1988), pp. 1120–71.

Edwards, R., *Contested Terrain* (New York: Basic Books, 1979).

Earle, J., R. Frydman and A. Rapaczynski, *Privatisation in the Transition to a*

Market Economy. Studies of Preconditions and Policies in Eastern Europe (London, Pinter Publishers: 1993).

Elbaum, B., and F. Wilkinson, 'Industrial Relations and Uneven Development: a Comparative Study of the American and the British Steel Industries', *Cambridge Journal of Economics*, vol. 3, No 3 (1979), pp. 275–303.

Eldredge N., and S.J. Gould, 'Punctuated Equilibria: an Alternative to Phyletic Gradualism', in T.J.M. Schopf, (ed.), *Models in Paleobiology* San Francisco: Freeman Cooper & Co, 1972), pp. 82–115.

Friedman, A.L., *Industry and Labor* (London: Macmillan, 1977).

Gordon, D.M., R. Edwards and M. Reich, *Segmented Work, Divided Workers* Cambridge: Cambridge University Press, 1982).

Hodgson, G.M., *Economics and Evolution. Bringing Life Back into Economics.* (Oxford: Polity Press, 1993).

Inkster, I., *Science and Technology in History* (London: Macmillan, 1991).

Little, C.R., *The Development of the Labor Process in Capitalist Societies* (London: Heinemann, 1982.

Marglin, S., 'What Do Bosses Do?', *Review of Radical Political Economy*, vol. 6 (1974), pp. 60–112.

Mayr, E., *One Long Argument. Charles Darwin and the Genesis of Modern Evolutionary Thought* (Cambridge Mass.: Harvard University Press, 1991).

Milgron, P., and J. Roberts, 'Bargaining Costs, Influence Costs and the Organization of Economic Activity', in J.E. Alt and K.J. Shepsle (eds.), *Perspectives on Positive Political Economy* (Cambridge: Cambridge University Press, 1990).

——*Economics, Organisation and Management* (New Jersey: Prentice Hall, 1992).

Nelson, R. and S.G. Winter, *An Evolutionary Theory of Economic Change* (Cambridge Mass.: Harvard University Press, 1982).

Pagano, U., *Work and Welfare in Economic Theory* (Oxford: Basil Blackwell, 1985).

——'Property Rights, Asset Specificity, and the Division of Labor under Alternative Capitalist Relations', *Cambridge Journal of Economics*, vol. 15, no. 3 (1991), pp. 315–42, reprinted in G.M. Hodgson, *The Economics of Institutions* (Cheltenham: Edward Elgar, 1993).

——'Organisational Equilibria and Production Efficiency', *Metroeconomica*, vol. 43, no. 1–2, (1992), pp. 227–46.

——'Organisational Equilibria and Institutional Stability', in S. Bowles, H. Gintis and B. Gustafson (eds.), *Markets and Democracy* (Cambridge: Cambridge University Press, 1993).

——'Can Economics Explain Nationalism?' in A. Breton *et al.*, *Nationalism and Rationality* (Cambridge: Cambridge University Press, 1995), pp. 173–204.

——and R. Rowthorn, 'Ownership, Technology and Institutional Stability', *Structural Change and Economic Dynamics*, vol. 5, no. 2 (1994), pp. 221–43.

Ridley, M., *Evolution* (Oxford: Blackwell Scientific Publications, 1993).

Roemer, J.E., *Analytical Marxism* (Cambridge: Cambridge University Press, 1986).

——*Free to Lose. An Introduction to Marxist Economic Philosophy* (London: Radius, 1988).

——'Unbundling The Private Property Relation: A Comment on "Efficient Redistribution" by S. Bowles and H. Gintis', paper submitted for the conference on 'Equality and Efficiency', Havens Centre, Madison (1995).

Rowthorn, R., 'Neo-classicism, Neo-Ricardianism and Marxism', *New Left Review*, vol. 86 (1974), pp. 63–82.

Sawyer, M.C., *The Challenge of Radical Political Economy* (London: Harvester Wheatsheaf, 1989).

Williamson, O.E., *The Economic Institutions of Capitalism* (New York: The Free Press, 1985).

Wood, S., *The Degradation of Work?* (London: Hutchinson, 1982).

15

On the Economics of Realizing and Sustaining the *Efficient Redistribution* of Productive Assets

Michael R. Carter

In 'Efficient Redistribution', Samuel Bowles and Herbert Gintis characterize the contemporary age as one in which an equality pessimism – which doubts the efficacy of traditional, demand-oriented income transfer and redistribution policies – has reduced economic policy in countries rich and poor to a least common denominator of *laissez-faire*. Arguing that this new world of economic quietism will simply reproduce and deepen inequalities and class cleavages, Bowles and Gintis argue for a suite of asset redistributions, including a redistribution of productive assets. Such redistributions, they argue, will not only redress problems of poverty and inequality, but will also offer efficiency gains to the economy – a property which Bowles and Gintis argue will enhance the political feasibility of what might otherwise seem like a hopelessly utopian project.

This paper examines more closely the role of asset markets in aiding or impeding the realization and sustainability of efficient redistribution of productive assets. The role of asset markets in the perpetuation of inequality, and whether they can be 'reformed' and used to realize and sustain asset redistribution, is at the center of contemporary debates concerning decidely nonutopian proposals to redistribute land assets in low-income agrarian economies. Drawing on insights from this debate, this paper offers a series of considerations about the scope and form of any sustainable asset redistribution.

As a starting point, it is useful to note that Bowles' and Gintis' call for an active redistribution of productive assets to those employed to use those assets rests on two propositions:

1. *Sensitivity of Economic Productivity to the Distribution of*

Assets: Because effective or efficiency labor cannot in general be costlessly extracted from a given amount of purchased labor-time, non-labor assets are utilized more productively when combined with the labor-effort of individuals who are self-monitoring (self-extracting) because they own the residual-claim rights to the specific asset with which they are working.

2. *Inadequacy of Market-Mediated Asset Redistribution:* Second, despite this productivity differential which would seem to motivate market-mediated transfer of assets to lower wealth agents (workers), countervailing failures in capital and insurance markets (which result from asymmetric and costly information) tend to block the realization of those transfers.

In this 'multiple market failure environment',[1] asset redistribution will tend to enhance both efficiency and equality, as Bowles and Gintis explain. While in 'Efficient Redistribution' (and their other related work) Bowles and Gintis have explored point (1) extensively, their treatment of point (2) is more cursory. The goal of this paper is to complement their analysis with an exploration of the role of asset markets in affecting the realization and sustainability of asset redistribution.

Policies to foment efficient asset redistribution through land reform have of course been long debated in low-income agrarian economies. Interestingly, although land reform disappeared for some time from official policy debate as the world went *laissez-faire*, the World Bank has of late emerged as a proponent of 'market-assisted' land reform in Southern Africa and Latin America (see Binswanger et al. 1994). Motivated by the proposition that efficiency-labor considerations of the sort discussed above create the basis for a strong competitive advantage for low-wealth producers in asset markets, policies for market-driven land reform try to relax the financial or other constraints which are hypothesized to suppress the underlying pressure for market-mediated efficient redistribution. A series of questions confront market-driven efficient redistribution policies, but in simplest terms most of these questions ask whether the policies are sufficient to achieve the desired redistribution and whether any redistribution achieved will persist over time if assets are freely marketable by their new owners.

The remainder of this paper is organized as follows. First, core concepts and ideas about the economics of asset-market competitiveness will be developed in the context of a single-period endowment-continuum model, analogous to that put forward by Bowles and Gintis. Second, the functioning of the asset market will be reconsidered on the basis of insights which follow the generalization of the theoretical framework to a multi-period, dynamic general-equilibrium model. Finally, the paper will conclude by summarizing implications of the analysis for the scope and design of efficient asset redistribution.

Class Competitiveness in 'Romerian' Endowment-continuum Models

The work of John Roemer (1982a, 1982b) spawned a series of what might be termed 'endowment-continuum' models – that is, models which analyze the interacting economic choices of heterogeneously endowed agents who are distributed along a wealth or endowment continuum, as opposed to models cast in terms of representative households and firms. True to their roots in neoclassical economics, these models portray individual behavior as determined by the outcome of individually rational choice. Among other things, Roemer shows that under rational choice, a class correspondence emerges in which specific locations along the endowment-continuum map into class positions which can be defined in terms of relations of exploitation. Class structure thus depends on the distribution of agents along the endowment continuum. Moreover, when endowment-continuum models are extended to include intrinsically imperfect markets of the sorts suggested by the economics of information and contested exchange, the distribution of agents along the endowment continuum affects the level of aggregate economic productivity, and efficient – or at least productivity-enhancing – redistribution would appear possible (see for example Eswaran and Kotwal 1986 and Dasgupta and Ray 1986). After reviewing the microeconomic basis for efficient redistribution in single-period endowment-continuum models, this section queries one such model for insights about how markets in productive assets might work, and about whether or not initial levels of asset-equality or inequality tend to be self-perpetuating.

The microeconomic core of efficient-redistribution models is the proposition that for a given set of prices and market access rules,[2] the privately rational economic behavior of the agents located at different points along the continuum is systematically different in economically relevant ways – e.g., less wealthy agents may utilize productive assets differently (with different rates of return) than wealthier agents. *Given* those prices and access rules, the aggregate performance of the economy would depend on the number of agents located within each class or strategy regime.

Bowles' and Gintis' analysis in 'Efficient Redistribution' of risk-taking, project quality and labor incentives is a good example of the core microeconomics of efficient redistribution. Labor-extraction costs discourage high-wealth agents from hiring all the labor needed to fully utilize their productive assets. Imperfect capital and insurance leave low-wealth agents to self-insurance strategies which lead them to forgo socially desirable, but risky investment projects. Interestingly, given this differentiated behavior of low versus high-wealth agents, Bowles and Gintis identify the socially optimal wealth distribution as one that is neither perfectly egalitarian, nor perfectly inegalitarian. Instead, they argue that there is a degree of (not too severe) inequality which optimally mediates the trade-off between labor incentives and risk-taking. But would a market in productive assets tend to autonomously realize that optimal distribution over time? Ultimately an answer to this question requires an understanding of the differential asset-market competitiveness of different classes or agents, or of what this section will simply label as the 'class-competitiveness regime'.

The notion of class competitiveness can be developed through numerical simulation of an endowment-continuum model which brings into play the core labor and financial market imperfections which underlie the Bowles and Gintis analysis. In this model, which is developed more thoroughly in Carter and Mesbah (1993) and Carter and Zimmerman (1998), agents are distributed across a two-dimensional asset space based on their initial endowments of liquid wealth and a productive asset (land). Each agent has a fixed amount of labor time which they can either sell on the labor market and/or utilize to bring their land into production using a constant returns-to-scale technology which requires the productive asset plus inputs of labor and raw materials. Production is roundabout in the sense that the financial costs of labor and raw material inputs must be financed from either own savings, loans, or by contemporaneous labor-market earnings. Labor and loan markets are inhibited by the sorts of transactions costs and asymmetric information described by Bowles and Gintis. That is, hired labor is less productive per-unit time than is self-supervising own labor, and fixed transactions costs make small loans more expensive then large loans.[3] In addition, agents who desire to sell a large portion of their labor time on the market are presumed to face lower marginal employment probabilities. In short, low-wealth agents who have sufficient labor to run their own production processes have an efficiency labor advantage over high-wealth agents, while the latter have a financial market advantage.

Figure 1 portrays what can be called the 'class map' for this model.

Figure 1: Class Map

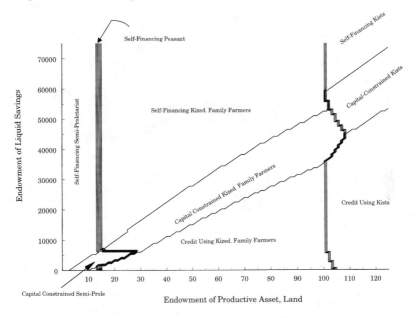

Drawn for a given set of market prices and access rules, the class map displays the optimal strategy which would be adopted by an individual located at any point within the space of initial endowments. Agents located within common sub-regions of the endowment space share the same endowment necessitated behavior, or class position in the sense of Elster (1985). As can be seen, agents located near the origin of the endowment space, tend to adopt proletarian or semi-proletarian strategies, and those without large private stores of liquid savings tend also to be capital-constrained in their own production process. (Capital-constrained here means that financial constraints prevent these agents from allocating the levels of variable inputs to their production processes which they would like to.) Moving away from the origin, higher-wealth agents begin to hire in labor, although labor-extraction costs bind the productivity of their land assets.[4]

The behavioral heterogeneity reflected in the class map – which creates the possibility for an economy in which efficient redistribution is possible – could be further explored by looking at indicators of resource-use and productivity. For example, for given prices, each position in the endowment space could be shown to map up into a third dimension measuring, say, the level of output achieved per unit

Figure 2:   Class Competitiveness in the Asset Market

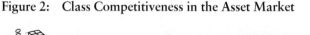

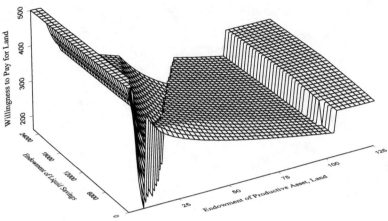

of the productive asset. For purposes here, it is useful to examine indicators not just of resource use, but also of how agents located across the endowment space would value – how much they would be willing to pay for – an additional unit of the productive asset. This mapping from endowment positions to willingness to pay for a unit of the productive asset can be called the 'class-competitiveness regime' inasmuch as it indicates the relative economic ability of different classes to compete in an asset market.

Figure 2 illustrates a class-competitiveness regime for this model. The vertical distance above the plane of initial endowments shows willingness to pay for an extra unit of the productive asset under a fairly simple present-value valuation. Specifically, the asset prices shown on the vertical axis are the discounted present value of the stream of additional income which could be earned at each endowment position with an additional unit of the productive asset.

Not surprisingly, the topography of this class-competitiveness regime reflects the underlying multiple-market imperfections. The extremely high values close to the origin and running parallel to the liquid savings axis reflects agents' relatively high willingness to pay for land when they have access to (their own) cheap labor. Further out in wealth space, willingness to pay flattens out as high-wealth agents face the same supervisory problem and can either self-finance or borrow to finance the production process. In between these two lies a trench of relatively low willingness to pay for additional units of land.[5] Indeed, as can be seen, except for those agents with relatively large savings of liquid wealth, the drop-off in willingness to pay occurs quite quickly. In short, this trench cutting across the endowment space *appears* to be a barrier to asset-accumulation by low-wealth agents – and to efficient market-mediated redistribution – of the sort described by Bowles and Gintis. While the next section of this paper will deepen the analysis of accumulation incentives and class competitiveness, the trench in figure 2 is a useful heuristic for emphasizing the point that an efficiency-labor advantage alone does not necessarily create asset-market competitiveness for low-wealth classes.

Before turning to that fuller consideration of accumulation incentives and barriers, one final point can be made using the single-period endowment-continuum model discussed in this section. The discussion so far has implicitly treated the set of prices in the economy as exogenous, or at least independent of the initial distribution of endowments.[6] Yet since initial asset distribution influences production and resource use in this model economy, it will also influence prices for inputs and outputs. With different prices, both the class map and the class-competitiveness regime change. For example, a relatively higher price for the output of the production process would encourage agents to begin borrowing at lower land-endowment levels. Correspondingly, the accumulation barrier or trench shown in figure 2 would begin to diminish in size with some numbers of lower-wealth agents becoming competitive in the asset market.

This potential relationship between initial endowment distribution and class competitiveness thus suggests an intriguing question about whether, say, initially inegalitarian distributions endogenously generate equilibrium prices which tend to render low-wealth agents non-competitive in asset markets. Conversely, are the prices generated by an initially more egalitarian economy such that lower-wealth agents are more competitive in asset markets. If such is the case, initial levels of inequality create economic forces which tend to perpetuate and ratify themselves.

While this linkage between initial endowment distribution and class competitiveness may seem a bit obtuse, the contrasting experience of Latin American versus East Asian agriculture at least appears to be consistent with it. Latin American agrarian history is replete with examples in which low-wealth agrarian households have been squeezed out through patterns of what is sometimes called 'exclusionary' growth. Microeconometric analysis of several recent Latin American agrarian growth booms indeed suggests that the lower-wealth agents have been unable to compete given the set of prices and market-access rules (Carter and Zegarra 1995, Carter *et al.* 1996). By contrast, small, often tiny farms in East Asia formed the stable core of agrarian growth and transformation. While government policies may have had a lot to do with the differential competitiveness of small-scale farming, the notion of a class-competitiveness regime which is sensitive to the initial endowment distribution is intriguing. More pointedly for the general issue of efficient redistributions, consideration of economically self-reproducing asset distributions is significant for thinking about the longevity and minimum-scale requirements for a sustainable asset redistribution.[7]

Dynamic Endowment-Continuum Models: Market-mediated Efficient Redistribution or Class Polarization?

The prior discussion introduced ideas concerning the sorts of forces which tend to perpetuate or undercut a particular endowment distribution over time. Note that these same forces could limit the economic sustainability of even a state-mandated redistribution if assets were allocated to an uncompetitive class position. However, the prior section relied upon insights squeezed from single-period endowment-continuum models. A deeper look at the perpetuation of inequality (and, relatedly of a class structure) requires more explicit attention to intertemporal or dynamic decision-making by heterogeneously endowed agents.

In simplest terms, adding dynamics to an endowment-continuum model gives more choice, or degree of freedom, to agents by permitting them to trade-off current consumption for future levels of asset holdings. The work to be briefly reviewed here suggests that the addition of dynamic choice to an endowment-continuum model creates two opposing forces: one (the strategic value of accumulation as a way to circumvent market failures) favors accumulation by low-wealth agents; the other (risk) may cut the other way.

First, in the context of the countervailing market-failure analysis of Bowles and Gintis, lower-wealth agents may have a greater incentive to suppress current consumption and accumulate assets because additional assets carry what might be termed a strategic value beyond the increased future income they directly permit. This strategic value emanates from the fact that additional accumulation may permit agents to circumvent the market failure (e.g., credit rationing) which otherwise constrains their income. Streufert and Ray's (1994) dynamic nutritional wage-theory model is a good example of this phenomenon.

In their model, a subset of low-wealth agents (whose asset, income and nutrition levels are so low that they cannot qualify for wage-labor employment) will actually suppress their consumption and nutrition yet further in order to slowly accumulate the assets which will eventually permit them to get around the market failure which keeps them from earning a return on their labor power.[8]

Carter and Zimmerman (1998) show a similar result for their dynamic version of the endowment-continuum model discussed in the prior section. In the dynamic version of the model, agents allocate their income earned in each production period between consumption and accumulation of the stocks of the two assets (liquid savings and land).[9] Over time, agents thus choose their trajectory around the endowment space illustrated in figures 1 and 2. One obvious accumulation strategy suggested by the topography of the static class-competitiveness regime in figure 2 is for low-wealth agents to suppress current consumption, accumulate liquid savings (in order to better capitalize their production process) and work their way around the trench. Numerical simulation of the model for an initial asset distribution which is highly unequal shows that there is indeed a tendency for this to occur. Over a hundred-year simulation, there is a clear tendency of the asset market to autonomously move the economy toward a more egalitarian (and more productive) distribution. However, the process is clearly slow and inhibited by the set of prices which position the trench in front of low-wealth agents. As suggested earlier, an interesting and important question concerns whether or not the price sequence generated by an initially more egalitarian distribution would tend to place fewer barriers in the accumulation path of low wealth producers. More generally, however, from the perspective of efficient redistributions, these first dynamic considerations suggest that there may be other constraints which may inhibit asset-market led efficient redistribution.

Risk is of course one of those additional considerations. When future income is uncertain, holdings of even unproductive assets[10] (e.g., cash or grain stores) can become desirable (Besley 1995 gives a nice introduction). In multiple-asset models (such as that just described), risk can differentially affect ('distort') portfolio choice depending on an agent's initial wealth level. Low-wealth agents may allocate a disproportionately large share of their wealth to grain stores, while wealthier agents acquire more entrepreneurial portfolios (see Rosenzweig and Binswanger 1993, Carter and Boucher 1995 and Murdoch 1995). Zimmerman and Carter (1997) presents accumulation trajectories which result from the simulation of a dynamic stochastic general-equilibrium model which is similar in structure (but simpler) than the non-stochastic model described in the previous paragraphs. Each individual in this economy receives a common, or covariate, shock each period (e.g., weather) as well as an individual specific or idiosyncratic shock.[11] Following the realization of income each period, individuals make a similar wealth-allocation decision between consumption, asset and savings. Savings are assumed to be in kind (a grain store). The productive asset will generate an expected positive, but risky rate of return. The asset price is endogenous to supply and demand each period. Again individuals maximize an infinite stream of (expected) utility with rational expectations on price distributions.

As opposed to the slowly equalizing trajectories generated by the non-stochastic model, the economy bifurcates toward two stable asset positions. Central to the operation of this model is the covariance between the asset price and the shared or covariate shock. That is, low-wealth individuals are driven toward safe but low-yielding port-folios not just because of production risk *per se*, but also because endogenous asset-price movements make it hard to use the productive asset to smooth consumption (i.e., when the weather is bad, asset prices are low; when the weather is good, asset prices are high). The net result is that low-wealth agents retreat to a low-yielding but defensible asset position, while higher-wealth agents head in the opposite direction. Market-based asset-redistributions in this model actually lead the economy to a position of lower aggregate productivity. However, perhaps the important point of this analysis is the attention it calls to risk and asset-price issues. Both are affected by the severity of covariate risk and the breadth of the market in which productive assets can be sold.

Scope and Design-efficient Redistribution

Where then do asset markets fit into the call for efficient redistribution of productive assets? Contemporary 'market-assisted' land reform proposals are predicated on the notion that asset markets can serve as the vehicle of efficient redistribution, at least in low-income agrarian economies. At the heart of such proposals are policies designed to (1) facilitate the operation of the land market by reducing transactions-costs barriers, especially those which inhibit transactions between high- and low-wealth agents; and (2) improve the access of low-wealth agents to long-term (mortgage) finance so that they are able to purchase land assets. For such proposals to work, and actually realize an efficient redistribution of assets, it must be the case that low-wealth agents are not fundamentally uncompetitive in the asset market. In terms of the topography of the class-competitiveness regime illustrated in figure 2, these proposals depend upon a regime which is downward sloping as one moves from lower to higher wealth classes.

Consistent with suggestions of Bowles and Gintis in 'Efficient Redistribution', the analysis here indicates that there may be significant asset-accumulation barriers to low-wealth agents, even when the labor supervisory advantages of the latter would seem to make market-mediated asset redistribution possible and desirable from the perspective of aggregate economic productivity. Moreover, while low-wealth agents may in theory be willing over time to work their way around accumulation barriers, their economic willingness to pay for risky productive assets is called into further question if missing or imperfect financial and insurance markets require that individuals use their productive assets in part to smooth out their consumption over time in the face of income shocks. Note further that these same class-competitiveness considerations confront the economic sustainability of an asset-redistribution initially carried out through administrative fiat.[12] Together, these considerations suggest that the class-competitiveness regime needs to be carefully tended, and itself perhaps reshaped with a judicious mix of ancillary capital and insurance market policies if efficient redistribution is to be either realized or sustained.

The analysis here additionally suggests, though quite tentatively, that the scope or extent of asset redistribution may matter via its impact on the equilibrium prices which shape the relative asset-market competitiveness of different wealth agents. An incremental redistribution may work differently (economically) to a large-scale redistribution.

Finally, note that the analysis summarized here has been cast in terms of constant returns-to-scale production technology so that any agent can run a small-scale production process without technical disadvantage. While perhaps adequate as a description of agricultural technologies, constant returns to scale seems inappropriate as a description of industrial processes. In this case, the potential efficiency gains to the redistribution of industrial assets will accrue only when there is a large and simultaneous transfer of firm-specific assets to the specific individuals who work with those assets in production. Realizing and sustaining efficient redistribution thus faces an additional problem of collective action among the workers within a firm.

Notes

1. Both these areas of work explicitly dispute the assumptions which underlie the standard welfare theorems of neoclassical economics, they might be grouped together as the economic analysis of actually existing capitalism. The term *multiple* market failures is used to emphasize that when there is only one problematic market (e.g., the labor market), the equilibrium-resource allocation and productivity will not be perturbed by the initial endowment distribution since market transactions can transfer the assets to where the labor is, even if sales of labor to asset-owners is inhibited by labor-extraction problems. Feder (1985) draws this point out nicely in constant returns-to-scale technology model.

2. Reference is made here to 'market access rules' to account for the possibility that some agents may be quantity-rationed in some markets, implying that the set of market prices is a not a complete representation of their economic opportunities.

3. The model works the same way under the assumption that low-wealth agents are simply rationed out of the loan market, perhaps for the sorts of reasons discussed in Carter (1988).

4. The model permits agents to choose between two labor-monitoring technologies. The capitalist producers are those who monitor workers with a hierarchical system which has fixed and variable costs. Capitalist family farm producers informally monitor workers while working next to them in the actual production process. While cheap, this monitoring mode ceases to be effective if the scale of operation grows too large.

5. Basically the trench is there because under the equilibrium prices in the economy, smallholders are unable to borrow given the structure of transactions costs in financial markets. Low-wealth agents are hence unable to productively employ more than small amounts of the productive asset. The value of additional units of that asset to such agents is correspondingly low.

6. In fact the prices used to generate figures 1 and 2 emerged from a general equilibrium simulation of the model under the assumption of an inegalitarian initial asset distribution.

7. That is, if post-redistribution prices fail to ratify the asset-market competitiveness of the new asset holders, they may find it difficult to defend their asset holdings. The Central Valley of Chile is a good example of 'indefensible redistribution' as some three-quarters of those households who received individual assignment of property rights to land eventually sold off their assets (see Carter et al. 1996). Note also that a modest redistribution which leaves relative prices untouched, and lower-wealth agents disadvantaged, may work differently to a large-scale redistribution in which prices change.

8. Obviously for this accumulation strategy to be physiologically feasible (much less individually desirable), the damage done by severe undernutrition must be reversible.

9. Asset prices are also endogenous in the model, and agents are endowed with a type of rational expectation about how prices will evolve over time in their economy.

10. 'Unproductive' means the rate of return is less then the discount rate.

11. The results discussed presume the existence of a subsistence minimum. Consumption below that minimum is presumed to irrevocably damage future utility possibilities.

12. For this reason, land-reform programs sometimes impose alienability restrictions on redistributed assets – e.g., reform beneficiaries are permitted only to sell reform assets to eligible low-wealth agents. However, to the extent that such restrictions make the asset market thinner, the problems of asset price covariance discussed above could become worse, and the willingness of low wealth agents to pay for the restricted asset would diminish.

References

Besley, Timothy, 'Savings, Credit and Insurance', in J. Behrman and T.N. Srinivasan (eds.), *Handbook of Development Economics*, vol. 3 (North Holland, 1995), pp. 2123–207.

Binswanger, Hans P. and Klaus Deninger, 'South African Land Policy: The Legacy of History and Current Options', *World Development*, 21, 9, pp. 1451–75.

Bowles, Samuel and Herbert Gintis, 'Efficient Redistribution', *Politics and Society*, (1995) and this volume.

Carter, Michael, Bradford Barham and Dina Mesbah, 'Agro-Export Booms and the Rural Poor in Chile, Guatemala and Paraguay', *Latin American Research Review*, (1996).

Carter, Michael R. and Steve Boucher, 'Consumption Smoothing at What Cost? A Household Portfolio Model of the Financial Efficiency Gap and the Economic Space for Financial Market Innovation', (1995), 35 pgs.

Carter, Michael R. and Eduardo Zegarra, 'Reshaping Class Competitiveness and the Structure of Agrarian Growth with Well-Sequenced Policy Reform', U.W. *Agricultural Economics Staff Paper 379* (revised 1995).

Carter, Michael R. and Fredric Zimmerman, 'The Dynamic Costs and Persistence of Asset Inequality in An Agrarian Economy', University of Wisconsin Agricultural and Applied Economics Staff Paper no. 416, 39pp., (1998).

Dasgupta, P. and Debraj Ray, 'Inequality as a Determinant of Malnutrition and Unemployment: Theory', *Economic Journal*, 96, (1996), pp. 1011–34.

Elster, Jon, *Understanding Marx* (Cambridge University Press, 1985).

Eswaran, Mukesh, and Ashok Kotwal, 'Access to Capital and Agrarian Production Organization', *Economic Journal* 96, (1984), pp. 482–98.

Feder, Gershon, 'The Relation between Farm Size and Farm Productivity: The Role of Family Labor, Supervision and Credit Constraints', *Journal of Development Economics*, 18, (1985), pp. 297–313.

Murdoch, Jonathan, 'Income Smoothing and Consumption Smoothing', *Journal of Economic Perspectives*, 9, 5, (Summer 1995), pp. 103–14.

Roemer, John, 'Origins of Exploitation and Class', *Econometrica*, 50 (January 1982b), pp. 163–92.

Roemer, John, *A General Theory of Exploitation and Class*, (Harvard University Press 1982a).

Rosenzweig, Mark and Hans Binswanger, 'Wealth, Weather, Risk and the Composition of Agricultural Investment', *Economic Journal* (January 1993).

Streufert, Peter and Debraj Ray, 'On the Perpetuation of Unemployment, Undernourishment and Inequitable Land Ownership in Dynamic General Equilibrium', *Economic Theory*, (1993).

Zimmerman, Fredric and Michael Carter, 'Dynamic Portfolio Management under Risk and Subsistence Constraints in Developing Countries', University of Wisconsin Agricultural and Applied Economics Staff Paper no. 402 (revised), 45pp., (1997).

16

Market Failures and the
Distribution of Wealth:
A Perspective from the
Economics of Information
*Karla Hoff**

All societies have unequal wealth and income dispersion, and there is no positive basis for criticizing any degree of market determined inequality.

US Congress, Joint Economic Committee[1]

[We seek] to identify the aspects of concentrated ownership of assets that give rise to perverse incentives and costly enforcement strategies.

Samuel Bowles and Herbert Gintis[2]

Incentive problems arise in credit and labor markets whenever individuals have private information or their actions are difficult to monitor. Incentive problems entail economic costs. This essay addresses the question: How, taking account only of such incentive problems, does the distribution of wealth affect efficiency of resource use, and by how much?

One reason this question appears so interesting is that a growing body of recent work shows that in situations where lenders have imperfect information about borrowers, or employers or landowners have imperfect information about workers, *low-wealth individuals*

*I am indebted to Sam Bowles for comments on an earlier draft and Abhijit Banerjee, Dilip Mookherjee, Joe Stiglitz, and participants at conferences at the University of Wisconsin and the University of Massachusetts for helpful discussions. Financial support is gratefully acknowledged from the MacArthur Foundation.

may be entirely shut out of capital markets or out of labor contracts and land rental contracts that elicit high effort.[3] The breakdown of exchange in turn causes a loss of national income. In this way, high inequality of wealth can lead to low long-run growth.[4]

Thus, whereas in the standard neoclassical paradigm of a market economy with perfect information the allocation of resources is efficient for *any* initial distribution of wealth,[5] and whereas a tradition associated with Nicholas Kaldor emphasizes the positive effect that inequality has on long-run growth if it raises savings rates,[6] recent work in the *economics of information* suggests an entirely different view, as Samuel Bowles and Herbert Gintis emphasize. Recent work in the economics of information shows that a highly concentrated wealth distribution may restrict individuals' opportunities to be productive. The economics of information, sometimes called the *information-theoretic approach to economics* or the *information paradigm*, relaxes the assumption of perfect information made in the standard neoclassical paradigm, and thereby overturns its central results that market equilibria are always efficient and that distribution and efficiency considerations are separable.[7]

The purpose of this essay is to identify some of the major channels through which the distribution of wealth affects efficiency in situations of imperfect information, as well as some empirical evidence of the magnitude of these effects. I can summarize the ideas in this essay by describing the following thought experiment. Among a set of individuals with identical aspirations and indistinguishable abilities to be productive, let there be a lottery awarding high wealth to some and little or no wealth to others. How will the losers in the lottery fare? They may be unable to invest in human capital or to become self-employed (results 1 and 5 below) and unable to participate in contractual arrangements that elicit high effort (results 4 and 5). The most effective corrective policy may be neither taxes nor subsidies (the standard approach to correcting a market failure) but policies that redistribute income so as to overcome the obstacles to mutually beneficial exchange (result 2).

I also argue that wealth in the form of collateral plays a kind of *catalytic* role rather than a role as *input* that gets used up in the process of producing output. In a setting of imperfect information, a tax-transfer policy that provides a riskless and therefore easily collateral-izable form of wealth can improve the efficiency of the allocation of capital resources and sometimes yield Pareto improvements (result 3).

Every field has its central analytical tools. In the economics of information, the central tool is the theory of principal and agent.[8] The canonical agency relationship is as follows. A principal puts a resource into an agent's hands. The agent can make good use of it, or not. His characteristics and/or his actions are not fully observable by the principal. That is, information between principal and agent is *asymmetric*. The problem is to devise a contract that structures incentives so that the agent can cooperate to produce something valuable. This specification captures the essence of information problems that often arise between a lender and borrower, an employer and employee, a landowner and tenant farmer, a franchisor and franchisee, or among partners in a firm. What is emphasized in this essay are the following implications of principal-agent theory:

1. Transactors' wealth affects contract form because, for example, it affects the ability to post collateral.
2. Contract form affects the profitability of exchange by providing incentives to exert effort and to reveal private information.
3. Therefore the distribution of wealth affects productivity and the feasible set of exchanges.

The remainder of this essay is divided into four sections. Section 1 analyzes an incentive problem in capital markets and shows that an individual with low net worth may have no effective access to credit.

Section 2 analyzes an incentive problem in transactions involving labor. It presents a model in which an individual's *labor* productivity depends on his initial *financial* wealth and reviews two studies of tenant farmers in low-income countries that suggest that these effects are large.

Section 3 brings incentive problems in both credit and labor into a single model based on Patrick Legros and Andrew Newman.[9] Within the model, the initial distribution of wealth determines the organization of work and the technical efficiency of resource allocation. This model illustrates one possible way in which 'a more equal distribution of assets [may permit] broader scope for the beneficial effects of markets and other forms of competition,' in the language of Samuel Bowles and Herbert Gintis. Section 4 points to future directions of research.

1 Wealth Effects in a Credit Market

Collateral increases a borrower's stake in the success of his project. In so doing, it conveys information about the quality of his project. The following example shows how for lack of collateral, an individual may lose effective access to the credit market altogether.[10]

Example. Suppose that individuals are each able to undertake a risky project. To undertake a project requires that they expend effort in what may be called the *preparation stage*: one can think of it as a stage in which an individual draws up a business plan. Without preparing, an individual will never succeed in his project. A by-product of preparing is that an individual learns his probability of success and therefore can make a more informed decision about whether the project is worth undertaking.

An individual makes two choices: first, whether or not to prepare a project and second, having learned the project's success probability, whether or not to invest capital in it. A project has a fixed capital requirement, so that low-wealth individuals must obtain outside finance to undertake a project. There is a perfectly competitive financial market.

For simplicity, suppose that every project has the same pay-off R if it succeeds and a pay-off of zero if it fails, but projects differ in their probability of success, p. If i and j are two individuals and if $p_i > p_j$, then individual i is said to have a better project than j. If a project fails, the borrower has no income and so defaults. Suppose that individuals care only about the expected value of gains; that is, they are risk-neutral.

The central information problem in this model is that borrowers know the success probabilities of their projects, but lenders do not. In a competitive market, the interest rate charged to borrowers who post a given collateral will reflect the *average* probability of default of those borrowers. The best projects therefore cross-subsidize the worst, which induces entry by individuals with negative-value projects. Some individuals with negative expected value projects will undertake them because it is the lender that suffers the downside risk. But since the lender must break even on average, the expected default rate is reflected in the interest rate he charges. Through this 'default premium', the bad risks raise the interest rate and lower the expected return to *all* borrowers with whom they are classed (that is, all borrowers who offer the same collateral).

If each individual's project is an independent draw from a density function denoted by *h* in figure 1, then the expected return from preparing a project can be depicted as the area S-L in the figure. The social return to a project whose success probability is p and whose fixed capital requirement has an opportunity cost of one is pR − 1. Thus, a project with p > 1/R yields a positive social return. In the

Figure 1:   The Dependence of Investment Returns on Entrepreneurs' Wealth

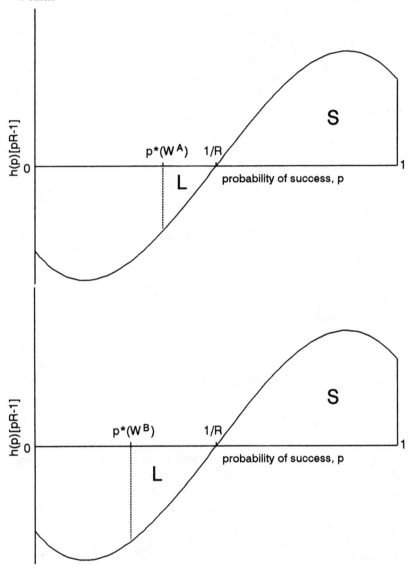

For a given cut-off success probability, denoted by p*, the expected gain from a risky project is the area S less the area L. If Astor has greater wealth than Bart (that is, W^A > W^B), then a lender will correctly infer that Astor is more selective in accepting a project: p*(W^A) in the top panel is greater than p*(W^B) in the bottom panel. As a result, the lender will charge a lower default premium to Astor than to Bart.

Figure 2:   The Minimum Wealth Level Required for
Entrepreneurship

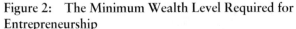
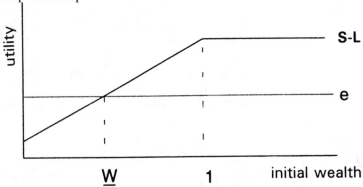

In choosing whether or not to prepare a project, an individual compares his expected
gain, S-L, with the fixed cost e. Knowing the high default premium he would be
charged if he borrowed, it does not pay an individual for whom W < $\underline{W}$ to prepare a
project.

figure, p*(W) denotes the *reservation success* probability of a borrower, that is, the lowest probability of success at which he would
find it worthwhile to undertake a project. Recalling that borrowers
are willing to undertake projects with negative social return, we have
p*R − 1 < 0, as depicted in each panel of the figure.
    The lower a borrower's wealth, the lower his losses if the project
fails, and hence the lower the success probability p* at which a project
will be, for him, just worth undertaking. Consider two prospective
borrowers, Astor and Bart, where Astor's initial wealth exceeds Bart's:
W^A > W^B. *By observing the stake that each has in his project (his
wealth, W), a lender can infer his reservation success probability, p*.*
Conditional on the information available to a lender, Astor has a
higher probability of repaying his loan than Bart does and, accordingly, Astor will be charged a lower interest rate. The lower interest
rate raises Astor's surplus from preparing a project relative to Bart's
surplus.
    Now consider the effect of a reduction in Bart's wealth. As it falls,
so too does p*, the probability of success at which he finds it just
worthwhile to undertake a project. As in the comparison provided by
the two panels of figure 1, the area L becomes larger. *The expected
gain, S-L, from preparing a project is thus a decreasing function of an
individual's initial wealth.*[11, 12] There may exist a level of initial
wealth, denoted by $\underline{W}$ in figure 2, for which p* is so low and, hence,

the interest rate is so high that the expected surplus S-L falls below the cost of effort e to draw up a business plan. $\underline{W}$ is in effect the minimum wealth level needed to participate in the credit market, since for $W < \underline{W}$, agency costs dissipate the full expected surplus from a project. This result is summarized below:

Result 1: When an individual who undertakes a project knows more about his success probability than lenders do, there may exist a critical wealth level such that individuals whose wealth is below the critical level do not borrow and do not invest in projects.[13]

It would seem natural for government to respond to the problem of under-investment by credit subsidies or loan guarantees. But loans taken out in response to such policies will tend to be of low quality (as discussed further below). And a tax on credit will increase the minimum wealth level $(\underline{W})$ below which no investment in projects occurs at all. The next result is the statement that any resources available to government to subsidize credit or to provide loan guarantees for low-wealth individuals would be better spent in the form of grants that can be pledged as collateral.

Result 2: In a setting of adverse selection where the marginal borrower has the lowest quality project, a transfer to low-wealth individuals strictly dominates a credit subsidy or loan guarantee. A transfer can increase both overall efficiency and the welfare of the low-wealth individuals, but a credit subsidy or loan guarantee cannot.[14]

In this model, wealth in the form of collateral plays a kind of *catalytic* role rather than a role as *input* that gets used up in the process of producing output. This helps to explain the result that a tax on risky incomes that finances grants, which individuals can then pledge as collateral, can increase the welfare of all affected individuals.

Result 3: In the setting described in result 2, there exist simple redistributive policies that are Pareto-improving.[15]

This result assumes that there are instruments available to government that are not available to individual transactors in the credit market: the government can impose universal taxes and make transfer payments; private lenders cannot make exclusive agreements with individuals that impose taxes and provide a one-time transfer. If government finances the transfers with labor taxes, the taxes will create a distortion in the labor market. But the grants, by providing a riskless and therefore easily collateralized form of wealth, will improve the efficiency of the allocation of capital. As a result, each individual, assessing his lifetime possibilities at the beginning of his life, becomes strictly better off.

Empirical results: The central implication of the model is that net worth affects access to credit and that for sufficiently low net worth, access to credit is lost. This implication has been derived from a variety of models of asymmetric information and is consistent with much empirical evidence, particularly for start-up firms and for small firms.[16]

For example, one implication of asymmetric information models is that wealth affects an individual's decision to become an entrepreneur. David Blanchflower and Andrew Oswald find that an inheritance of £5000 ($10,000) doubles a typical British young person's likelihood of setting up in business.[17] Jane Black et al. find that a 10 per cent rise in the value of collateralizable housing assets in the United Kingdom increases the number of new start-up businesses by 5 per cent. These authors conclude, based on a variety of different data sets, that 'there appears to be a large pool of untapped entrepreneurial talent' that cannot start a business for lack of collateral.[18]

Yet loan guarantees to start-up firms do not seem to be the answer. In a recent loan guarantee program in the United Kingdom, for example, the default rate for borrowers who had not invested personal assets in their business was much higher than for those who had (the respective proportions being 40 and 14 per cent).[19]

Lawrence Summers, a leading macroeconomist, has argued that historical experience suggests that recessions, and certainly depressions, involve breakdowns in exchange.[20] Bruce Greenwald and Joseph Stiglitz have shown that such breakdowns may occur when relative price changes or other shocks cause many firms to have low net worth, and that this can explain the observed properties of US business cycles.[21] A direct test of that theory is Glenn Hubbard and Anil Kashyap's analysis of investment behavior by US farmers in the past century.[22] They find that changes in net worth have had a large effect on aggregate farm investment spending, but *only* in periods when farmers' net worth was low. They conclude that 'standard symmetric-information models should work well [as predictors of aggregate investment behavior] in 'good times' and poorly in 'bad times' [when net worth is low]'.

For individuals whose net worth is low, all times may be 'bad times'; their actual market opportunities may be much more limited than standard symmetric information models would suggest.

2 Wealth Effects in Agency Relationships with Moral Hazard

The preceding section illustrated wealth effects on agency costs when individuals have private information, giving rise to a problem of *adverse selection*. This section illustrates wealth effects on agency costs when individuals' actions are difficult to monitor, giving rise to a problem of *moral hazard*.

Example: Suppose that an individual (the 'agent') who has been engaged as an employee or tenant farmer has discretion over some set of actions that are not observable by his employer or landlord (the 'principal'). For simplicity, suppose that what is unobservable is only the agent's level of effort, denoted by e, and that there are only two possible consequences of the agent's effort: a good outcome y^g or a bad outcome y^b. A higher level of effort by the agent increases the probability π of the good outcome: that is, $\pi = \pi(e)$, with the derivative $\pi' > 0$.

The agent dislikes effort. Associated with any level of effort, he experiences a disutility $D(e)$. The joint gains (or *surplus S*) from the principal-agent relationship are then

$$S(e) = \pi(e)y^g + [1 - \pi(e)]y^b - D(e).$$

The socially efficient level of effort is that which maximizes the surplus. Assume that the agency relationship is potentially profitable to both parties, in the sense that if the agent chooses the efficient level of effort, then the relationship can make both parties better off. The efficient level of effort, e_o in figure 3, corresponds to the effort level at which the marginal gain from higher effort, $\pi'[y^g - y^b]$, is just equal to the marginal disutility of higher effort, D'.

If there were perfect information, the principal would make a contract providing the agent a wage in exchange for effort e_o. But under our assumption that some dimension of effort is unobservable, an agent who is paid a fixed wage has no incentive to supply such effort. The principal must offer the agent a contract so that it is in the employee's self-interest to work hard. Such contracts are called *incentive contracts*, and they take a wide variety of forms in actual markets. They include:

Figure 3:   The Dependence of Labor Effort on Labor's Share

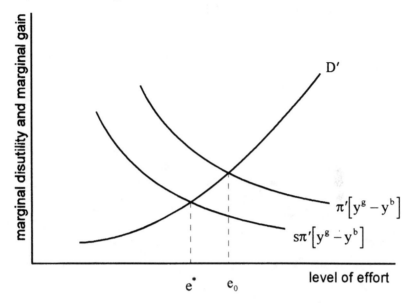

The efficient level of effort is at e_0, where the marginal disutility of effort to the agent, D', equals the expected marginal social gain, $\pi'[y^g-y^h]$. If an agent bears the full marginal cost of effort but receives less than the marginal gain, his effort will fall below e_0. The figure depicts the case of a sharecropper receiving a share $s < 1$ of output, and therefore exerting effort $e^* < e_0$.

1. Profit-sharing, commission payments based on sales, or share contracts in agriculture.
2. An incentive bond paid in the form of a contribution by the agent to the capital costs of production or in the form of a payment for the right to join a firm. The bond is foregone by the agent if output is low, but is returned to him if output is high.
3. A transfer of partial ownership to employees in order to give them the incentives that owners have to care about the value of the firm as a whole.

The contract discussed in the remainder of this section can be interpreted as an example of 1 or 2. The contracts discussed in the next section are examples of 2 and 3.

In the simple setting considered here, a contract is completely described by a pair of values (w^g, w^b), where the agent earns w^g if the good outcome occurs and w^b if the bad outcome occurs. y^b and w^b

may be negative, but I make the natural assumption that the agent's consumption must be non-negative. This limits his ability to absorb losses in the event that the bad outcome occurs: $w^b \geq -W$, irrespective of the magnitude of any losses. The principal chooses the contract (that is, the values of w^g and w^b) that provides the principal the greatest profit subject to the agent's wealth constraint and the constraint that the agent is willing to be hired. The agent then chooses a level of effort.[23]

This model conveys a simple insight: *the principal's ability to provide incentives that do not come out of the principal's own profits depends on the agent's wealth.* When the agent's initial wealth is low, so is his ability to absorb losses. If the agent's limited ability to absorb losses is a binding constraint on the contract that the principal offers, then it is in the principal's interest to deliberately forego the opportunity to induce the surplus-maximizing level of effort.[24]

This model has been used to explain the persistence of sharecropping contracts among the poor in developing countries. Under a contract in which the farmer receives a share s of output and pays a fixed amount F, the farmer earns $w^g = sy^g - F$ if the harvest is good, and $w^b = sy^b - F$ if the harvest is bad. Any incentive contract (that is, any pair w^g, w^b) is equivalent to a share contract with

$$s = \frac{w^g - w^b}{y^g - y^b}.$$

Under a pure rental contract, $s = 1$, the farmer receives the full marginal product of effort, and therefore he chooses the efficient level of effort. Under a wage contract, $s = 0$, $-F$ is the wage, and the farmer has no incentive to exert effort that is not observable. With a share contract, $0 < s < 1$, the farmer receives less than the full marginal product of effort and chooses $0 < e^* < e_o$ – see figure 3.

Will a landlord then offer a fixed rental contract to a low-wealth tenant? If the landlord requires payment of the rent in advance, a tenant with low wealth would not be able to pay. If the landlord agrees to payment after the harvest and the harvest turns out to be bad, the contract would be unenforceable.[25] In this case, it can be shown that a pure rental contract with the rent set so low that the tenant could always pay it will be *less* profitable to the landlord than a contract in which the tenant makes a higher payment to the landlord when the harvest is good than when it is bad. Compared to a pure rent contract, a share contract attenuates the farmer's incentives (though obviously it provides much better incentives than a fixed-wage payment). An implication is the following:

Result 4: When effort is not fully observable, individuals with greater initial wealth (a) enter into contracts that provide greater incentives for effort, and therefore (b) produce greater output conditional on the level of observed inputs.

Empirical results: A direct test of Result 4 was undertaken in a rural area of Tunisia by Jean-Jacques Laffont and Mohamed Matoussi (1995).[26] In this area, the main economic activity is farming, and landlords contract with tenants to cultivate the land. Tenant farmers have incentive contracts in the form of the share of output that they retain (the remaining share being paid to the landlord). The tenant's output share was observed to take one of four values: a half, two thirds, three quarters, or one. Laffont and Matoussi establish two results. First, the higher the tenant's wealth at the beginning of the period, the closer to a rent contract he had. Thus, a pure rental contract was observed as long as the tenant was sufficiently wealthy. Second, holding all observed inputs constant, a non-share contract relative to the average share contract was associated with an increase in output of 50 per cent. It might be argued that this difference reflects ability differences because more able tenants have earned more in the past, have greater wealth, and so were more likely to obtain rental contracts. But when the analysis was restricted to young tenants for whom wealth holdings reflected primarily inherited wealth, similar results were obtained. While there may still be unobserved differences between sharecroppers and renters, the results are highly suggestive: farmers with low wealth seem to produce less output than farmers with greater wealth because their limited wealth, working through the resulting contractual structure and pattern of incentives, means that they have limited incentives to work hard. This idea is not novel.[27] What is novel are rigorous attempts to determine the magnitude of wealth effects on output.

The estimates of Laffont and Matoussi would appear to promise huge gains from policies that shift the division of agricultural output in the tenants' favor. An empirical test of precisely that idea was afforded by the agricultural tenancy reform implemented by the Indian state of West Bengal after 1977. Before 1977, sharecropping contracts in West Bengal generally involved 50 per cent output shares to the tenant for the approximately 2 million sharecroppers in the state. In 1977, a new administration was elected to power:

What the new administration did as soon as it came to power [was] to give highest priority to the enforcement of a tenancy law which stipulated that: (a) The tenant would be given the choice of registering with the government. (b) Those tenants who have registered themselves cannot be evicted from the land as long as they pay the landlord a minimum legally stipulated share-rent (namely, 25 per cent of output). ... [There] was a massive drive by the administration to go village by village offering tenants the choice of registering themselves.[28]

The result of the reform was to increase many tenants' output share from 50 per cent to 75 per cent.[29]

In the decade following this reform, West Bengal achieved a breakthrough in agricultural growth.[30] The fact that the effective availability of registration of tenancies proceeded slowly across villages and across districts is the key to identifying the effect of the change in tenants' share on agricultural production. Abhijit Banerjee and Maitreesh Ghatak estimate that 36 per cent of the total growth in agricultural production in West Bengal in the period 1968–81 was due to the tenancy reform.[31]

3 Wealth Effects on the Organization of Work

Many economists, particularly the celebrated economists associated with the University of Chicago – including Gary Becker, Milton Friedman, and Ronald Coase – have viewed private actions as ones that in the long run lead to socially efficient outcomes. The most famous expression of that view is the Coase theorem, which holds that regardless of the initial allocation of property rights and initial set of markets, individuals will make agreements that lead to efficient outcomes. But the Coase theorem abstracts (fatally) from information problems. The preceding two sections suggested that in the presence of information problems, even a *marginal* change in an agent's wealth can relax the constraints on an individual's ability to obtain high returns from his capital and to enter into contracts that elicit high effort.[32]

This section presents a less intuitive result. It shows that when inequality of wealth is sufficiently high, firms may form that are technically inefficient. By a reorganization, they could produce the same output with fewer inputs, but no forces in competitive equilibrium will induce such a reorganization. This section illustrates Bowles' and Gintis' argument that 'inequality impedes economic performance by obstructing the evolution of productivity-enhancing governance structures.'[33] Pressures of competition, contrary to the view of the Chicago school, need not ensure technically efficient firms.

This result is demonstrated in the following model due to Patrick Legros and Andrew Newman.[34] The model makes three principal assumptions, which are labelled A-1, A-2, and so forth, below. First:

(A-1) *Production technology.* To work means to work on a risky project, which entails a fixed capital cost. If n individuals work together on a project, its probability of success is π_n. π_n initially has increasing returns with respect to n, and then decreasing returns.

(A-1) is a way of formalizing a firm. The assumed properties of π_n mean that individuals are more productive working with other people than working alone, and that the returns to increasing firm size diminish as firms become large.

Individuals within a firm choose whether to work or shirk, and the disutility of work is normalized at one.[35] The next assumption is that there exists a technology for monitoring the performance of individuals in the firm:

(A-2) *Monitoring technology.* There is a monitoring technology that, for a fixed capital cost to the firm, makes the effort of each individual in the firm observable. Without the monitoring technology, an individual's effort is not observable to others.

It follows that there exist potentially two types of firms. One type of firm elicits effort through incentive contracts, exactly as work was elicited in the example of section 2. Call these firms *partnerships*. A second type uses the monitoring technology that makes individuals' actions observable; call these firms *hierarchies*.

A key property of this model is that the incentive payment needed to elicit effort in a partnership exceeds, in expected value, the disutility of effort (see Appendix A). That is, every partner must be paid a pure economic rent (or must post a bond) if he is to have an incentive to work. *Whether it is feasible to do so depends, in general, on the endowment wealth of the partners.* Appendix B derives the minimum level of wealth that a set of individuals must have in order to form a partnership.

If there were no information problems in the capital market, then any group of poor individuals, though they might not have sufficient wealth to form a partnership, would yet be able to form a hierarchy. But it is more realistic to make the alternative assumption, which can be derived from a wide variety of models of credit markets with imperfect information, such as the model of Section 1:

Figure 4: The Dependence of Organization of Work on Wealth Distribution

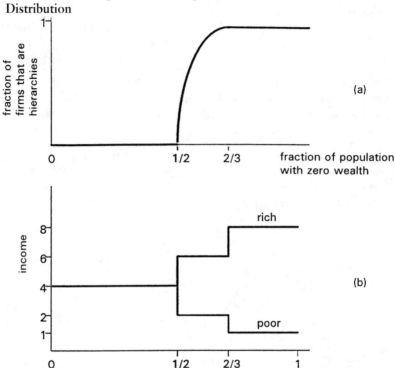

The figure shows the relationship between the fraction of the population with zero wealth and two other variables: in panel (a), the fraction of firms that are hierarchies as opposed to partnerships; and in panel (b), the expected incomes provided by a firm to an individual with high wealth ('rich') and to one with zero wealth ('poor').

(A-3) *Imperfect information in the credit market.* There is an information asymmetry between firms and outside lenders that makes the cost of borrowing a decreasing function of the net wealth of firm members.

Given (A-3), the initial wealth of firm members is used to solve two distinct incentive problems. It provides *collateral to lenders*, which reduces the informational risk that they face (as in the example of section 1), and it makes possible the *incentive payments* that elicit effort from partners in a setting where effort is not observable (as in the example of section 2).

Individuals match with others through voluntary association to create firms. Figure 4 illustrates the properties of the equilibrium for a specific technology[36] in an economy where individuals start out either poor (with zero wealth) or rich (with sufficient wealth to create a firm). The poor are unable to match together to form a partnership or hierarchy. Lacking initial wealth, they cannot make the incentive payments needed to run a partnership, and they do not have the collateral needed to borrow in the capital market at an interest rate at which a hierarchy would be profitable. Thus, the poor have to match with the rich in order to work at all.

Consider the thought experiment where aggregate wealth of the economy is held constant, but the fraction of the population that is initially poor is varied. If the fraction is below a half, the demand by the rich for partners in two-person partnerships exceeds the number of poor individuals, and all firms are partnerships – see figure 4(a). Competition for partners ensures that every individual in the zero-wealth class obtains the same expected income from a firm as a rich person does – see figure 4(b).[37]

As the fraction of the poor increases above a half, the demand by the rich for partners falls short of the number of poor. The rich no longer need to share profits equally in order to attract partners. In equilibrium, the income received by the poor will fall to the minimum incentive payment needed to elicit effort – see panel (b) of figure 4. A fraction of firms will be two-person partnerships, and the remaining firms will be three-person hierarchies that pay wages equal to the expected value of incentive payments made in partnerships. The fraction of firms that are hierarchies is determined by the requirement that the demand for labor equal the supply.

As the fraction of the poor increases beyond two thirds, then even after all the rich match with the poor in hierarchies, there are still unmatched poor in equilibrium. *Unemployment now exists among the poor.*[38]

But this is not the end of the story, nor the most interesting part. Unemployment depresses the competitive wage of the poor to the disutility of work (= 1). As it does so, the gap widens between the wage needed to hire labor in a hierarchy and the incentive payment that a partnership must pay. *This, in turn, makes the hierarchy form of organization more profitable to firm owners, even where the partnership form is technically more efficient.* When the fraction of the poor exceeds two thirds, all firms will be three-person hierarchies, and the rich will receive much greater expected incomes from the firm than the poor; see figures 4(a) and (b), respectively. In this economy, it would be feasible for all three-person hierarchies to reorganize as three-person partnerships and produce the same output with the same labor and less capital. But the hierarchy form of organization lowers the wage bill. It may do so by enough that even after allowing for the extra capital expenditures of the hierarchy, it leaves a larger residual in profits. As illustrated in the figure, only hierarchies exist in equilibrium when wealth is concentrated in the hands of one third or less of the population.

The example on which figure 4 is based is intended to highlight the kinds of forces that it seems important not to ignore in economies where monitoring technology can substitute for incentive payments and where low-wealth individuals lack the collateral to obtain a large enough loan to be productive in self-employment. I summarize below the results that follow from the assumptions A-1, A-2 and A-3 above:

Result 5: (a) *Breakdown of the marginal productivity theory of income.* Differences among individuals in labor earnings need not reflect differences in their marginal products. They may instead arise from differences in initial wealth, since initial wealth affects an individual's access to capital and also the contract form through which an individual is employed.

(b) *Formation of technically inefficient firms.* An increase in the concentration of wealth tends to lower the competitive wage and thereby to lower the wage bill of the hierarchy relative to the labor costs of the partnership. A fall in the wage rate may in turn induce the formation in equilibrium of hierarchies that are technically inefficient, in the sense that they could reorganize as partnerships to produce the same outputs at lower resource cost. But competitive forces will not induce such a reorganization.

The model of Legros and Newman offers one way to resolve what has been called the 'Chicago question', after the Chicago school of economists: *If a worker-owned firm is more productive, why don't the capitalists sell the firm to the employees?* Similarly, *if owner-cultivated farms are more productive than tenant-cultivated farms, why don't the landlords sell their land to the tenants?* In the absence of moral hazard, adverse selection, or enforcement problems, that is precisely what would happen. But in the presence of these problems, the incentive issues associated with relationships within the firm, or within the agricultural tenancy relationship, would simply be displaced by incentive issues associated with debt repayment to persons outside it, and the transfers of ownership are blocked.[39]

The Legros-Newman results are related to a long line of work[40] that emphasizes that imperfections (information asymmetries) in *capital* markets depress the *labor* opportunities of low-wealth individuals; an individual's labor opportunities are tied to his endowment of wealth. This is consistent with a frequently made observation of the contrasting experiences of Latin American countries. For instance, Enrique Iglesias observes that:

> countries such as Colombia and Costa Rica have a large agricultural sector and a relatively equitable distribution of land. Not coincidentally, they also have an equitable distribution of income. [Noting that the wage at the floor of the income pyramid is determined by the wage for day labor in agriculture,] if most farm workers are farm owners, the wage will have to be equal to what the worker could have earned farming his own land . . . In the opposite case, where many farm workers have no land, the minimum wage tends towards the subsistence level and land owners reap high profits.[41]

4 Conclusion

In the standard neoclassical model, there are no problems of information that impede exchange: no problems of commitment, of hidden characteristics relevant to a market exchange, or of incentives. In that model, the market system leads individuals as if by an 'invisible hand' to allocate resources efficiently, regardless of the initial distribution of wealth.

There is an alternative paradigm of the market, the *economics of information*, that relaxes the assumption of perfect information in the standard neoclassical paradigm and that *derives* the scope of feasible exchanges from more basic assumptions about information and technology. In this paradigm, low wealth endowment may imply constraints on an individual's ability to make productive investments and to enter into contractual arrangements that elicit high effort. A person's wealth takes on new roles – providing incentives for the intended exchange – that can mitigate problems of information.

The models of imperfect information presented in this essay are highly stylized, and some of the most dramatic empirical results reported here are from developing countries. There is obviously a considerable distance to go before it will be possible to assess the general importance of the links between distribution and efficiency that the models capture, and to design desirable and politically feasible policy. A particularly strong assumption is the existence of increasing returns in the production opportunities open to the individual or firm.[42] While the value of collateral in expanding individuals' access to credit is uncontroversial, more research is needed to see how important increasing returns are in practice.

Two further, key assumptions were made in order to keep the analysis simple. First, individuals were treated as risk-neutral. In situations where individuals are risk-averse, their willingness to bear risk is an important additional channel through which the distribution of wealth determines contract form and efficiency; this is outside the scope of this essay. One reason that the empirical results presented in section 2 are so interesting is that they show that in at least some contexts, the implications of simple agency models that ignore risk-aversion are borne out by the evidence.

A second key, simplifying assumption of the models presented here is that they implicitly restrict attention to one-period settings. The scope for providing appropriate incentives is larger in multiperiod relationships and when reputation mechanisms exist. But under most reputation mechanisms, there is a tension between the strength of reputation effects and the competitiveness of the market. Markets in which reputation effects are strong are not likely to be characterized by large numbers of actors and easy entry, so that the postulate of perfect competition is inapplicable. In markets sufficiently thick to be competitive, reputation effects are likely to be weak, an idea that I have explored elsewhere.[43]

A promising area for policy research, highlighted by Samuel Bowles and Herbert Gintis, is the design of redistributional policies that mitigate the inefficiencies created by private information. The theory presented here, in which individuals with low wealth face restricted opportunities to fully engage in productive activities, suggests that it may be possible to design policies that are both *efficiency-enhancing* and *self-targeting*. A self-targeting program would provide a set of benefits and costs to participants that dominate the market opportunities available to low-wealth individuals but that do not dominate those available to higher-wealth individuals. As a consequence, only the truly low-wealth groups would choose to participate, so that government would not need to have information on individuals' wealth to implement the policy. I intend to address this issue in future work.

In conclusion, the work reviewed here represents an early step toward understanding how the distribution of wealth affects the efficiency with which a competitive market system allocates resources. The central argument is that wealth in the form of collateral or incentive bonds can make up for failures of the price system that arise when parties to an exchange have asymmetric information. For lack of wealth, individuals may lose access to the markets and to the contracts that would permit them to fully use whatever endowments of resources, talent, and industry they may have to achieve their own ends.

Joseph Stiglitz has argued that 'assuming away information costs in an analysis of economic behavior and organization is like leaving Hamlet out of the play.'[44] What the information paradigm does is to make the scope of markets a subject of inquiry, with implications for empirical research, policy, and the ethical evaluation of a market system in which wealth is highly concentrated.

Appendix

Part A proves that the expected value of the incentive payment needed to elicit effort in a partnership exceeds the disutility of effort. Part B establishes the level of initial wealth that individuals must have in order to form a partnership.[45]

A. Incentive payment
Recall that each partner's effort contributes to the probability that the project jointly undertaken by the partners is a success. The greatest scope for incentives is obtained where, in the event that the project fails, each partner is held liable to the full extent of his wealth and receives no income from the partnership. Let y denote the income he enjoys in the event that the project succeeds. The problem is to find the minimum value of y that will induce a partner to expend effort.

Incentive contracts for n partners induce a game in effort levels in which it is an equilibrium for every partner to work if, for each partner, the expected pay-off from working exceeds that from shirking, that is, if

$$\pi_n y - 1 \geq \pi_{n-1} y$$

or, equivalently, if

$$[\pi_n - \pi_{n-1}]y \geq 1.$$

This inequality says that the difference that any one partner's effort makes to the overall success of the project on which his partners are working (= $\pi_n - \pi_{n-1}$) must increase the expected value of his own gain by enough to offset the disutility of effort (= 1). This inequality implicitly defines a minimum value of the incentive payment, denoted $\underline{y}$, that will induce effort. Thus, the expected value of the payment to each partner required to elicit his effort, $\pi_n \underline{y}$, is

$$\pi_n \underline{y} = \frac{\pi_n}{\pi_n - \pi_{n-1}} \tag{1}$$

By inspection, $\pi_n \underline{y}$ exceeds one, the disutility of effort, as was to be shown.

B. Minimum wealth to form a partnership

A partnership is feasible if its revenues less its debts cover the required incentive payments that are made in the event that the project succeeds. For simplicity, suppose that the partnership's project either succeeds, earning revenues R, or fails, earning zero revenues. Then incentive payments to the n partners are feasible if

$$R - [1 + i]\left[K - \sum W_i\right] \geq n\underline{y} \tag{2}$$

$\sum W_i$ denotes the aggregate initial wealth of the partners. If $K > \sum W_i$, then the left-hand side of (2) is interpreted as firm revenues less principal and interest due on the smallest possible loan that the partnership could take out and still cover its initial capital costs, K. If $K < \sum W_i$, then the left-hand side of (2) is interpreted as the combined revenue of the partners both within the firm and from lending outside the firm.

Denote by r the riskless rate of return paid to savers, and by i the interest rate charged a borrower. Competition in the lending market means that lenders just break even on average, so that i and r are related as follows:

$$\pi_n[1 + i] = 1 + r,$$

or, equivalently,

$$1 + i = \frac{1 + r}{\pi_n} \tag{3}$$

I have abstracted from all problems of asymmetric information between firms and lenders. Thus, the minimum wealth level derived here reflects *only* incentive problems among the partners, not those that may exist between the partnership and outside lenders.

Substituting (1) and (3) into (2), and rearranging, yields

$$\sum W_i \geq \frac{1}{1+r}\left[\frac{\pi_n n}{\pi_n - \pi_{n-1}} - [\pi_n R - (1+r)K]\right] = \underline{W}_n \tag{4}$$

Equation (4) says that the minimum, initial wealth that any group of n individuals must have to create a partnership is equal to the excess, if any, of the expected value of incentive payments (n times $\pi_n y$ derived in (1)) over the expected revenues ($\pi_n R$) less capital costs $[(1+r)K]$. The factor $1/[1+r]$ enters in order to discount dollars at the end of the period (revenues and incentive payments) relative to dollars at the beginning of the period (initial wealth $\sum W_i$ and fixed capital costs K).

Notes

1. US Congress, Joint Economic Committee, 'The Mirage of Economic Equality' (May 1995).
2. Samuel Bowles and Herbert Gintis, 'Efficient Redistribution: New Rules for Markets, States, and Communities', this volume.
3. I discuss theoretical and empirical work below. Theoretical work includes Ben Bernanke and Mark Gertler, 'Financial Fragility and Economic Performance', *Quarterly Journal of Economics*, 105 (1990), pp. 87–115; Karla Hoff and Andrew Lyon, 'Non-Leaky Buckets: Optimal Redistributive Taxation and Agency Costs', *Journal of Public Economics*, 58 (1995), pp. 365–90; Patrick Legros and Andrew Newman, 'Wealth Effects, Distribution, and the Theory of Organization', *Journal of Economic Theory*, 70 (1996), pp. 312–41; and Philippe Aghion and Patrick Bolton, 'A Theory of Trickle-Down Growth and Development', *Review of Economic Studies* (forthcoming). A precursor to this work is David Sappington, 'Limited Liability Contracts between Principal and Agent', *Journal of Economic Theory*, 29 (1983), pp. 1–21, which demonstrates the importance of liability limitations in settings of imperfect information.
4. See Oded Galor and Joseph Zeira, 'Income Distribution and Macroeconomics', *Review of Economic Studies* (1993), pp. 35–52; Abhijit Banerjee and Andrew Newman, 'Occupational Choice and the Process of Development', *Journal of Political Economy*, 101 (1993), pp. 274–98; Aghion and Bolton, 'A Theory of Trickle-Down Growth and Development'; Vicky Barham, Robin Boadway, Maurice Marchand and Pierre Pestieau, 'Education and the Poverty Trap', *European Economic Review*, 39, pp. 1257–75; and Roland Bénabou, 'Inequality and Growth', *NBER Macroeconomics Annual* (1996).
5. And so within this model, the statement cited above by the Joint Economic Committee of the US Congress is valid.
6. Kaldor assumes that the marginal rate of savings for low-income persons is low, and on this basis builds his famous model, 'Capital Accumulation and Economic Growth', in Nicholas Kaldor (ed.), *Further Essays in Economic Theory* (New York: Holmes and Meier Publishers, 1978). His hypothesis regarding savings behavior has not been established in empirical studies: see Mark Gersovitz, 'Saving and Development', in Hollis Chenery and T. N. Srinivasan (eds.), *Handbook of Development*

Economics I (Amsterdam: North-Holland, 1988); and Jeffrey Williamson, *Inequality, Poverty, and History: The Kuznets Memorial Lectures*, lecture 3 (Cambridge, Mass: Basil Blackwell, 1991).

7. Two overviews of the economics of information are Kenneth Arrow, 'Limited Knowledge and Economic Analysis', *American Economic Review* (1974), pp. 1–10; and Joseph Stiglitz, 'Information and Economic Analysis: A Perspective', *Economic Journal* (1985), pp. 21–41. They are interesting to read together as the first was written when the new paradigm was just emerging, and the second reviews the achievements of the period 1975–1985.

8. The use of the terms principal and agent in economic theory is due to Stephen Ross, 'The Economic Theory of Agency: The Principal's Problem', *American Economic Review*, 63 (1973), pp. 134–9. Helpful and accessible overviews are Kenneth Arrow, 'Agency and the Market', in K. Arrow and Michael Intriligator (eds.), *Handbook of Mathematical Economics*, vol. III (Amsterdam: North-Holland, 1986), pp. 1183–95; and David Sappington, 'Incentives in Principal–Agent Relationships', *Journal of Economic Perspectives* (1991), pp. 45–66.

9. Legros and Newman, 'Wealth Effects, Distribution, and the Theory of Organization'.

10. The model presented in this section is based on Bernanke and Gertler, 'Financial Fragility', and Hoff and Lyon, 'Non-Leaky Buckets'. The same result – that low-wealth individuals lose access to credit – is derived from quite different information assumptions in Aghion and Bolton, 'A Theory of Trickle Down Growth and Development'.

11. A proof is in Hoff and Lyon, 'Non-Leaky Buckets', p. 373.

12. For simplicity, figure 2 assumes that the opportunity cost of capital in end-of-period dollars (= 1) is the same as the initial fixed capital cost; i.e., the pure time cost of funds is assumed to be zero. Notice also that for $W \geq 1$, an individual does not borrow but instead self-finances. Since he has no agency costs ($L = 0$), his expected gain from preparing a project is S, invariant with respect to his initial wealth.

13. A proof is in Bernanke and Gertler, 'Financial Fragility'. Part of the proof entails showing that the optimal private financial contract is a debt contract. An interpretation of conditions under which debt is the optimal contract is in Karla Hoff, 'Adverse Selection and Institutional Adaptation', University of Maryland, mimeo (1998).

14. A proof is in Hoff and Lyon, 'Non-Leaky Buckets', pp. 381–2. The proof uses the fact that grants, by increasing individuals' stake in the projects they undertake, will tend to discourage those individuals who have the lowest probability of success and thereby raise the average quality of borrowers and *lower* equilibrium interest rates. In contrast, subsidies will tend to draw in borrowers who have the lowest probability of success and so *increase* equilibrium interest rates. This is the idea used in the proof that any government policy of replacing grants by credit subsidies that have an equivalent effect on the government budget will leave individuals with strictly lower expected welfare.

15. For a proof, see Hoff and Lyon, 'Non-Leaky Buckets', pp. 374–9. In the case that grants are financed by taxes on labor, what is required to obtain this result is that the efficiency gains from the collateralizable grant exceed the efficiency costs of the tax. A sufficient, but not necessary, condition is that the labor market be initially undistorted. See ibid., p. 385.

16. A survey of this work is outside the scope of this essay. The reader is referred to Mark Gertler, 'Financial Structure and Aggregate Economic Activity: An overview', *Journal of Money, Credit, and Banking*, 20 (1988), pp. 559–88; and also Mark Gertler and Simon Gilchrist, 'Monetary Policy, Business Cycles, and the Behavior of Small Manufacturing Firms', *Quarterly Journal of Economics*, 109 (1994), pp. 309–40. These studies, like the ones cited in the text below, are based on econometric analysis of data generated by the market. Interest in testing the extent of the barriers that low-wealth individuals face in participating in credit markets and in making productive investments has also motivated the undertaking of randomized experiments. Michael

Kremer is undertaking an experiment in Viet Nam where grants equal to a substantial fraction of average household annual income will be awarded to a random sample of households and their behavior compared to a control group's. If limited access to credit markets is important, then farm productivity, the establishment of small businesses, self-employment, and investment in education should be greater in the households that receive the grants than in the control group. 'Testing the Relationship Between Credit Constraints, Efficiency, and Redistribution Using Randomized Trials', MIT, mimeo (1996).

17. David Blanchflower and Andrew Oswald, 'What Makes a Young Entrepreneur?' *Journal of Labor Economics* (forthcoming).

18. Jane Black, David de Meza and David Jeffreys, 'House Prices, the Supply of Collateral and the Enterprise Economy', *Economic Journal*, 106 (1996), pp. 60–75.

19. Cited in ibid., p. 73.

20. Lawrence Summers, 'Some Skeptical Observations on Real Business Cycle Theory', Minneapolis Federal Reserve, *Bank Quarterly Review* (Fall 1986), pp. 23–7; cited in Gertler, 'Financial Structure and Aggregate Economic Activity'.

21. Bruce Greenwald and Joseph Stiglitz, 'Financial Market Imperfections and Business Cycles', *Quarterly Journal of Economics*, 108 (1993), pp. 77–114.

22. Glenn Hubbard and Anil Kashyap, 'Internal Net Worth and the Investment Process: An Application to US Agriculture', *Journal of Political Economy*, 100 (1989), pp. 506–34.

23. It may be worthwhile presenting this idea formally. With the assumption of a rational, self-interested agent and, for simplicity, risk-neutrality, the agent's effort level is the solution to

$$\text{Max}_e \{\pi w^g + [1 - \pi]w^b - D(e)\}.$$

Under standard conditions, his effort level is implicitly defined by

$$[w^g - w^b]\pi'(e) = D'(e)$$

where the primes (') represent derivatives. The above equality says that the agent chooses his effort by equating the marginal benefit to *him* (the left-hand side of the equality) to *his* marginal cost (the right-hand side). Under an incentive contract, the value $[w^g - w^b]\pi'$ is in effect the *price* (in expected value terms) that he is paid for an additional expenditure of effort; *it determines his incentives to expend effort*. The assumption of risk neutrality is important here because it means that labor contracts have no welfare dimension other than that of the implicit price. Allowing for risk-aversion means that such contracts may also serve as insurance devices.

24. See Sappington, 'Limited Liability Contracts between Principal and Agent', *Journal of Economic Theory*, 29 (1983), pp. 1–21. Two ways to extend this framework of analysis are (1) to consider risk aversion on the part of the agent, which means that stronger incentives come at the expense of reduced insurance, and (2) to widen the set of punishments for bad outcomes that are admissable, as in Michael Chwe, 'Why Were Workers Whipped', *Economic Journal*, 100 (1990), pp. 1109–21. Chwe examines the question, would a principal and agent choose a contract that entailed the administration of pain as an incentive device? Chwe shows that such a contract may indeed be the choice of rational individuals when the agent's wealth is sufficiently low and his reservation utility is low. Physical punishment fills in part the gap created first by failure of the price system in a setting of asymmetric information, and second by the limited scope for incentive payments arising from the agent's limited wealth. But even in Chwe's model the equilibrium contract will not entail the surplus-maximizing level of effort when the agent's reservation utility is sufficiently low.

25. For the same reason, the tenant's access to credit is limited.

26. Jean-Jacques Laffont and Mohamed Salah Matoussi, 'Moral Hazard, Financial Constraints and Sharecropping in El Oulja', *Review of Economic Studies*, 62 (1995),

pp. 381–99. See also Radwan Shaban, 'Testing Between Competing Models of Share-cropping', *Journal of Political Economy*, 95 (1987), pp. 893–920.

Related studies have been undertaken in the US service industry by comparing the performance of owner-operated outlets and outlets run by hired managers. For instance, in a study of restaurants that experienced a shift from franchisee-ownership to company-ownership, or vice versa, J. P. Shelton found that the profit margin under franchisee ownership was 9.5 per cent, compared to 1.8 per cent under company management. See J. P. Shelton, 'Allocative Efficiency vs. "X-Efficiency": Comment,' *American Economic Review*, 57 (1967), pp. 1252–58. A study of agency contracts in the fast food industry is Alan Krueger, 'Ownership, Agency and Wages: An Examination of Franchising in the Fast Food Industry', *Quarterly Journal of Economics*, 106 (1991), pp. 75–101.

27. The idea is expressed, for example, by Anne Robert Jacques Turgot, a minister under Louis XVI, cited in Hans Binswanger and Mark Rosenzweig, 'Contractual Arrangements, Employment, and Wages in Rural Labor Markets', in Hans Binswanger and Mark Rosenzweig (eds.), *Contractual Arrangements, Employment, and Wages in Rural Labor Markets in Asia* (New Haven, CT: Yale University Press, 1984), p. 49.

28. Abhijit Banerjee and Maitreesh Ghatak, 'Empowerment and Efficiency: The Economics of Tenancy Reform', mimeo, MIT and Harvard University (1996), p. 2.

29. Ibid., table 1.

30. The aggregate pattern that the authors seek to explain is as follows: between 1968 and 1981 the annual average rate of growth of production of foodgrains in West Bengal was 0.43 per cent, whereas that of India was 1.94 per cent. However, between 1981 and 1992, the respective growth rates were 5.05 per cent and 3.08 per cent. Ibid., table 2.

31. Ibid., p. 47. Efforts to refine this estimate, based on household data collected by the authors jointly with Paul Gertler, are in progress.

32. A formal statement of this result is Karla Hoff, 'The Second Theorem of the Second Best', *Journal of Public Economics*, 45 (1994), pp. 223–42.

33. Bowles and Gintis, 'Efficient Redistribution'.

34. Legros and Newman, 'Wealth Effects, Distribution, and the Theory of Organization', cited in note 3.

35. For simplicity, the model abstracts from the possibility of a continuum of effort levels.

36. In Legros and Newman's example, the technology takes the following form: $\pi_0 = 0$, $\pi_1 = .1$, $\pi_2 = .6$, $\pi_n = .8$ for $n \geqslant 3$. A firm's success pay-off is 15 and its failure pay-off is zero, the capital costs of a partnership are 1, and the capital costs of a hierarchy are 2. Thus, any single-person firm generates negative profits, and it never pays for there to be more than three individuals who work in a firm.

Average profits per person in a firm are maximized by forming partnerships of size 2. It follows from appendix A that the minimum incentive payment needed to induce effort in a 2-person partnership is $y = 1/[\pi_2 - \pi_1] = 2$ with expected value $\pi_2 y = 1.2$.

37. The equilibrium concept that Legros and Newman use in their proof is that of 'the core', which is a stronger notion of equilibrium than that of a perfectly competitive market. In their model, an outcome is an equilibrium if no finite *subset* of individuals, by trading among themselves, can on their own improve their own lot. The usual definition of competitive equilibrium is one that no *single* individual can deviate from and thereby improve their own lot. Thus the core embodies a notion of unrestricted competition.

38. This is because of the particular assumptions about technology and information made in the example. Recalling note 36, it does not pay to expand firm size beyond three individuals. And poor individuals do not themselves have the initial wealth needed to create a firm.

39. If agents are risk-averse, a further obstacle to the transfer of ownership is that

workers would not wish to concentrate their wealth in a single asset, as Bowles and Gintis emphasize in 'Efficient Redistribution'.

40. Including John Roemer, *A General Theory of Exploitation and Class* (Cambridge, Mass: Harvard University Press, 1982); Pranab Bardhan, 'Determinants of Supply and Demand for Labor in a Poor Agrarian Economy: An Analysis of Household Survey Data for Rural West Bengal', in Hans Binswanger and Mark Rosenzweig (eds.), *Contractual Arrangements, Employment, and Wages in Rural Labor Markets in Asia* (New Haven, CT: Yale University Press pp. 242–62; Samuel Bowles, 'The Production Process in a Competitive Economy: Walrasian, Neo-Hobbesian, and Marxian Models', *American Economic Review*, 75 (1985), pp. 16–36; Samuel Bowles and Herbert Gintis, 'Contested Exchange: Political Economy and Modern Economic Theory', *American Economic Review*, 78 (1988), pp. 145–50; Mukesh Eswaran and Ashok Kotwal, 'Why Are Capitalists the Bosses', *Economic Journal*, 99 (1989), pp. 162–76; and Dilip Mookherjee, 'Informational Rents and Property Rights in Land', in John Roemer, (ed.) *Property Rights, Incentives and Welfare* (MacMillan Press, forthcoming).

41. Enrique Iglesias, 'Income Distribution and Sustainable Growth: A Latin American Perspective, in Vito Tanzi and Keyoung Chu (eds.), *Income Distribution and High-Quality Growth* (Cambridge: Cambridge University Press, forthcoming).

42. The example of section 1 assumes that projects have fixed capital costs, a special case of increasing returns. The example of section 3 assumes, in addition, increasing returns to scale with respect to labor inputs over some initial range.

43. Karla Hoff and Joseph E. Stiglitz, 'Moneylenders and Bankers: Price-Increasing Subsidies with Monopolistic Competition', *Journal of Development Economics*, 55 (1998), pp. 485–518.

44. Joseph Stiglitz, *Whither Socialism?* (Cambridge, MA: MIT Press, 1994), p. 174.

45. The appendix is based on Legros and Newman, 'Wealth Effects, Distribution, and the Theory of Organization'.

PART VI

Reconsiderations

17

Recasting Egalitarianism

Samuel Bowles and Herbert Gintis*

1 Egalitarianism On Its Own

Radical egalitarianism is now the orphan of a defunct socialism. The unruly and abandoned child of the liberal enlightenment had been taken in by socialism in the mid-nineteenth century. Protected and overshadowed by its new foster parent, radical egalitarianism was relieved of the burden of arguing its own case: as socialism's foster child, equality would be the byproduct of an unprecedented post-capitalist order, not something to be defended morally and promoted politically on its own terms in the world as it is.

It thus fell to reformists, be they laborist, social democratic, Euro-communist or New Deal, to make capitalism livable for workers and the less well off, a task they accomplished with remarkable success in the advanced economies. But in the process the egalitarian project was purged of its utopian yearnings for a world of equal freedom and dignity, and narrowed to the pursuit of a more equal distribution of goods. Over the years even this project has encountered increasingly effective resistance and experienced major political reversals.

Is egalitarianism passé? We think not. But recasting the egalitarian project will require a radical reconsideration of both goals and the means for achieving them. An apt beginning for this reconsideration is the Atlantic republicanism of the late eighteenth century, a tradition born of the tension between egalitarianism and emergent liberal democratic thought.[1]

Thomas Jefferson's draft of the Virginia Constitution of 1776 included a radical provision for freeborn male suffrage with the rather

* We would like to thank Ernst Fehr, Elisabeth Wood and Erik Wright for comments, and the MacArthur foundation for financial support. We would especially like to thank each of the authors of the responses to our initial essay appearing in the preceding pages.

minimal property qualification of 25 acres. In the same document we find Jefferson advocating that 'Every person of full age neither owning or having owned 50 acres of land shall be entitled to an appropriation of 50 acres' (Jefferson, 1950, p. 349). The personal autonomy on which a democratic society must be based required, in Jefferson's eyes, an end to economic dependence and hence secure access to the means of one's livelihood.[2]

Jefferson's vision of a yeoman democracy based on a commercial agrarian economy now seems quaint, for the autonomous property-owning farmer has been replaced by the collective work and dispersed property of modern industry. Writing in *Democracy in America* just two generations later, Alexis de Tocqueville (1833/1945) observed that in the great industrial centers 'the workman is generally dependent on the master . . .' and he warned his readers:

> I am of the opinion . . . that the manufacturing aristocracy which is growing up under our eyes is one of the harshest that ever existed in the world . . . the friends of democracy should keep their eyes anxiously fixed in this direction; for if ever a permanent inequality of conditions and aristocracy again penetrates into the world, it may be predicted that this is the gate by which they will enter. (II, pp. 170–1)

As Tocqueville feared, with the waning of the bucolic foundations of yeoman democracy and the emergence of a modern capitalist economy, the Jeffersonian marriage of autonomy and equality would prove increasingly elusive. Tocqueville's warning of the fragility of Jefferson's egalitarianism under modern conditions bore implications for political accountability in a democratic order as well:

> It is indeed difficult to conceive how men who have entirely given up the habit of self-government should succeed in making a proper choice of those by whom they are to be governed; and no one will ever believe that a liberal, wise, and energetic government can spring from the suffrages of a subservient people. (II, p. 339)

Karl Marx echoed the agrarian republican conviction that secure access to one's livelihood is a precondition of freedom, but like Tocqueville recognized the anachronistic nature of the Jeffersonian solution in a world of increasingly collective production. Democratic socialists subsequently elaborated models of common property ownership as the basis of a democratic and egalitarian society. Yet the common ownership of property, whether in nationalized industry,

local environmental commons, or more comprehensive market socialist blueprints, often undermines the effectiveness of markets in
assuring economic accountability, and thus exacerbates the difficulty
of reconciling personal autonomy with effective economic governance.

In *Recasting Egalitarianism* we have sought to revive and update
the Jeffersonian vision, providing a foundation for its egalitarianism
in the realities of modern economic life and addressing the related
problem of the accountability of power. Our 'neo-Jeffersonian' paradigm is based on three constitutional *desiderata* governing the nature
and assignment of property rights and other rights of governance.

First, asset-based policies of redistribution should seek to
implement a sustainable assignment of private property rights that
make economic actors both effective decision-makers and the owners
of the results of their actions.

Second, insurance-based policies of redistribution should seek to
indemnify individuals against risks they cannot avoid and over which
they have no control, including accidents of birth, while maintaining
individual responsibility for the consequences of one's own actions.[3]

Third, state, market, and community should be complementary,
not competing, governance structures. Government policies should
seek not to supplant markets and communities but to ensure their
accountability and enhance their capacity to support equitable and
efficient outcomes. Conversely, market and community should be
organized to promote the accountability of government to the people.[4]

These *desiderata* reflect our understanding of how individuals interact with the rules of the game structuring economic and other social
interactions. Our understanding is far from universally shared among
those who count themselves as egalitarians. Because commonly held
views on the left are at variance with those motivating our proposals,
it may be useful to spell out our position on four points of contention.

First, we see no point in advocating particular social outcomes
unless we can specify the structurally determined individual incentives
and sanctions that allow the implementation of these outcomes and
support their sustainability in the long run. This includes, of course,
having compelling reasons to believe that those entrusted with *applying* the incentives and sanctions have the incentive to do so. Egalitarian projects often founder on the failure to take account of the
incentive structures facing the relevant actors. Instead, such projects
often assume 'oversocialized' decision-makers who fully internalize
the objectives motivating the policy in question.

Second, egalitarian policies must not only be implementable, they
must also be politically and economically sustainable in the long run.

By this we mean that they are capable of securing the support of effective governing coalitions and that they cannot be undone through the private contracting of individuals and groups. We take up the issues of political and economic sustainability respectively in Sections 3 and 4.

Third, many egalitarians overstate the benefits of simply redividing the pie. The gains from what we have termed hard redistribution are limited for the obvious reason that redistributing the wealth of the rich to the less well-off would accomplish relatively little redistribution: unearned income (meaning income from non-human assets) constitutes less than a third of all income in most advanced capitalist economies, and since the wealthy tend to invest a large fraction of their income, consumption from unearned income is considerably less than a third of all consumption.

If economic interactions had the character of zero-sum games, then hard redistribution would be the only option; but most interactions are neither pure conflicts (situations in which one's gains entail another's losses) nor pure coordination problems (situations in which if anyone gains, everyone does). The prisoner's dilemma is an archetypal example of this joint conflict and coordination structure of interaction. Our proposals are based on the conviction that there exist egalitarian policies that allow mutual gains, through what we have termed 'efficiency-enhancing redistributions.'

Fourth, while we advocate new roles for the government in regulatory and insurance activities, we have no predisposition for a large role for government production. We find little reason for the state to engage extensively in productive activities, and we stress the many unavoidable obstacles to citizen accountability over governmental actions. The assumption of oversocialized decision-makers is nowhere more evident and damaging than in the presumption that state managers and functionaries will faithfully carry out what an egalitarian citizenry would have them do.

In this brief reflection we will address the question of the objectives of egalitarian redistribution and then take up the question of means. Along the way we will respond to a few of the critical comments on our initial essay.

2 Ends: What is Wrong with Inequality?

Programs to assure a modicum of economic security for the poor and to guarantee equality of opportunity for all have faltered in recent years. Other egalitarian initiatives have come under attack and suffered defections from erstwhile supporters. Unemployment rates have risen in some countries, and real wages of the poorest workers have fallen in others. Redistributive programs have been cut and dramatic increases in measured inequality of income have taken place in a number of countries. For the most part people have responded with resignation or approval rather than resistance.

Among the reasons for this reversal, we think, is a growing ambiguity in public sentiment concerning the requirements of justice, and skepticism concerning the possibility of achieving a more just distribution of society's rewards. Even Americans, no doubt one of the most conservative of the world's bodies politic, remain deeply committed to equality of opportunity as a goal. But Americans and others are profoundly divided on how to define this objective and bewildered by contradictory claims on how any of the competing conceptions of equality of opportunity might be advanced through social policy. An orphaned egalitarianism, detached from its erstwhile base in popular movements for institutional change has sought to defend itself on moral and empirical grounds that many, even among the less well-off, find weak and uncompelling. Four sources of the demoralization of the egalitarian project are notable.

The first concerns objectives. When applied to national aggregates, both 'equality' and 'income' are depersonalized abstractions unlikely to evoke visceral reactions or to move people to act politically. The standard measures of inequality, the Gini ratio, for example, are abstractions which are only with difficulty related to everyday concerns of fairness and compassion. Knowing that the Gini ratio for real earnings of male workers is 0.42 evokes shrugs, which is not the case for the fact that a white person whose income is below $7,500 is three times as likely to be the victim of a rape, sexual assault or other violent crime as another earning over $50,000.[5] Moreover, except among the very poor, income is surprisingly weakly related to one's reported sense of well-being.[6]

Second, the concept of fairness, in the everyday sense of a level playing field, no longer enjoys a consensus as to its implications. As a result the concept fails to provide much guidance in promoting egalitarian efforts. Even so basic a concept as equality of educational opportunity eludes definition, with proposals ranging from securing the absence of overt discrimination based on race, gender, or family class origins to the far more ambitious goal of eliminating race, gender, and class differences in educational outcomes.

Third, and relatedly, publics appear to focus attention on the process of redistribution rather than on the state of inequality that distributive programs are intended to correct. It may be, as Daniel Kahneman (1993) has suggested, that people tend to evaluate events rather than states in making judgments: people are more affected by *getting* a new shirt or *losing* one than by *having* one or *not having* one. Or it may be that loss aversion is such a powerful predisposition that egalitarian programs are thwarted by a strong *status quo* bias in people's evaluation. Whatever the cause, redistributive processes are closely scrutinized while seemingly (to us) unjust levels of inequality are unblushingly accepted. Moreover, some redistributive programs fail commonly held tests of fairness. Examples include violations of equal treatment and protecting people from their own mistakes, often at great cost to others.

The fourth contributor to the unraveling of the egalitarian project concerns the belief that public policy cannot affect the degree of inequality in a cost-effective manner. Many hold the view that our current levels of inequality, however reprehensible, are simply immune to public policy intervention whether in the form of employment training, tariff protection of goods produced by low-wage labor, or expanded educational opportunity. Thus for example, the much touted hypothesis that cognitive abilities are partially inherited is falsely thought to imply that the knowledge capacities of people are immune to societal influences such as enriched education. Many who believe that deficiencies of 'cultural capital' impede the economic advancement of the poor argue that the scope for public policy in the expansion of economic opportunity is severely limited. Many go beyond the view that the government cannot affect inequality to embrace the conservative position that government action is the *source* of poverty and inequality. In a 1991 US poll, over two thirds agree strongly or somewhat with the statement that 'one of the main reasons for poverty is bad government policy' (Wright, 1994, p. 34).

How might this analysis of the current trials of egalitarianism inform our own project? To some extent, if we are right, egalitarianism has suffered political reversals because it has substituted an abstract and morally ambiguous objective, such as greater equality in the distribution of income, for egalitarian objectives at once more fundamental and more compelling. What offends the public's moral sensibilities is not so much inequality of income *per se*, but severe deprivations, unfairness and social indignities that so often accompany income inequality.

First, people object to severe deprivation, including people's lack of access to an adequate diet, health care, and personal and economic security, particularly when the rectification of these lacks would not be unduly costly to others.

Second, unfair treatment, including discrimination by race, gender, religion and sexual preference, as well as some forms of privilege transmitted from generation to generation, excite widespread condemnation.

Third, socially contrived inequality that deprives people of dignity and the capacity to pursue full lives is generally seen as reprehensible.

Displacing the target of egalitarianism from income to more fundamental determinants of dignity and well-being does not reduce the importance of economics in the pursuit of a more just society.[7] But it does make clear that forms of egalitarianism which provide a basis for personal autonomy and effective voice in shaping one's life trajectory should be given priority. We believe that the asset-based strategy we have outlined does just this.

A second implication of the above is that the necessity to contain costs of pursuing egalitarian strategies is not simply an unfortunate constraint imposed by the veto power of the well-to-do. Costs imposed on others affect the political viability of egalitarian programs in a democratic society because, for wholly defensible reasons, people's concerns are not limited to the well-being of the least well-off. Egalitarian policy must therefore be based on the willingness of non-wealthy citizens to support policies that redistribute in favor of the less well off among themselves.

The poor showing of egalitarian projects in recent years has convinced many that it is naïve to expect support to be forthcoming from a selfish and indifferent electorate. This pessimism is fundamentally misdirected, however. It misunderstands the reasons for opposition to egalitarian programs, and it underestimates the ability of egalitarians to design redistributive programs capable of evoking deeply rooted human commitments to justice. Unlike many who suspect that the basis for an egalitarian movement collapsed with the demise of socialism, we discover a solid foundation for cooperation and sharing at the root of human motivation.

3 Homo Reciprocans: The Motivational Basis of Sustainable Redistribution

The modern welfare state is but a single example of a ubiquitous social form. Sharing institutions, from families, to extended gift giving, to tithing and other religion based charity, to potlatches, to egalitarian division rules for the catch of the hunt, have cropped up in human history with such regularity and under such diverse circumstances that one is tempted to place them among Talcott Parsons' (1964) *evolutionary universals*: social institutions that confer such extensive benefits upon their users that they regularly appear and reappear in the course of history in otherwise diverse societies. The evolutionary viability of sharing institutions and of the motivations which support them counsels against those who have written off egalitarianism as an idea whose time has come and gone.

Consider one of these institutions, the practice that the Peruvian highlanders call *sunay* whereby herders give a llama to a fellow herdsman in need. Economists and biologists might doubt that this practice would be evolutionarily viable, as it appears to confer no benefit on the giver while imposing substantial costs. Yet *sunay* and the associated practice *kuyaq* of confirming ritual status of family membership on needy individuals persisted over centuries. Seeking to solve the mystery of this evolutionarily improbable form of generosity, Kent Flannery, Joyce Marcus and Robert Reynolds (1989) studied the demography of the llama herds and then simulated the evolution of the herds under various sharing rules including the lack of sharing of any kind. They found that:

> the advantages of widespread generosity in *sunay* outweigh the advantages of cheating or ignoring those who are not one's kin ... the *custom* of sunay, once adopted, might have been strongly selected for at the group level. In our models, herd systems that practise it have larger and far more stable herds after 100 years than systems without it ... universal adherence to *sunay* – even if it includes giving good breeding stock to non-kin – can make it possible for one's children to pass on more animals to one's grandchildren. It does that by ensuring that there will be lots of other herds around from which the children and grandchildren can get *sunay* when they need it.

Sunay, aided by the fictive kin generated by *kuyaq*, is practiced on an extended scale: 'in the context of a ritual, *kuyaq* converts non-kin into kin and makes possible the universal extension of *sunay*.' Flannery et al. conclude that unlike other species, humans

> can use culture to create fictive kin towards whom they behave altruistically ... and there may be situations in which such extensions of kinship would be selected for. Note that we do not argue that such extensions result from shrewd decisions based on practical reason; rather, we suggest that, once made, they may be selected for – which is not the same thing.

Thus the motivations supporting sharing rules need be neither explicitly altruistic nor instrumentally self-interested.[8] Moreover over very long periods of time, cultural or genetic group selection may have supported the emergence and proliferation of other-regarding individual traits sharply at variance with the dismal predispositions of *Homo economicus*. We will see that a wide range of motivations apparently influences people's stance towards redistribution in modern societies.

There are two distinct reasons why the non-wealthy might support egalitarian redistributions. The first, stressed by Karl Moene and Michael Wallerstein in this volume, is that many egalitarian programs are forms of social insurance that will be supported for prudential reasons, even by those who may anticipate paying in more than their expected claims over a lifetime. Included among these are unemployment and health insurance, and more broadly the various social programs that soften the blows during the rocky periods that many people experience in the course of their lives.

The insurance motive supporting egalitarian programs is consistent with conventional notions of self interest, once account is taken of risk-aversion. The second reason for support of egalitarian programs, by contrast, is not fundamentally self-regarding: egalitarianism is often based on a commitment to what we will term 'reciprocal fairness'.[9] As we will see presently, people are considerably more generous than the model in economics textbooks allows, and they are equally unselfish in seeking to punish, often at great cost to themselves, those who have done harm to them and others. Programs designed to tap these other-regarding motives may succeed where others that offend underlying motivational structures have been abandoned.

Both historical and contemporary experimental evidence support this position. In his magisterial *Injustice: the Social Bases of Obedience and Revolt*, Barrington Moore (1978) sought to discern if there might be common motivational bases – 'general conceptions of unfair and unjust behavior' – for the moral outrage fueling struggles for justice that have recurred throughout human history. 'There are grounds,' he concludes from his wide-ranging investigation,

for suspecting that the welter of moral codes may conceal a certain unity of original form . . . a general ground plan, a conception of what social relationships ought to be. It is a conception that by no means excludes hierarchy and authority, where exceptional qualities and defects can be the source of enormous admiration and awe. At the same time, it is one where services and favors, trust and affection, in the course of mutual exchanges, are ideally expected to find some rough balancing out.

Moore termed the general ground plan he uncovered 'the concept of reciprocity – or better, mutual obligation, a term that does not imply equality of burdens or obligations . . .'

Recent experimental research has affirmed the centrality of the reciprocity motive. An impressive body of evidence, much of it deployed in the first instance to validate the model of the selfish purveyor of market rationality, *Homo economicus*, in fact has served to bury this model. In its place this body of evidence suggests a new *persona*, whom we may call *Homo reciprocans*. *Homo reciprocans* comes to new social situations with a propensity to cooperate and share, responds to cooperative behavior by maintaining or increasing his level of cooperation, and responds to selfish, free-riding behavior on the part of others by retaliating against the offenders, even at a cost to himself, and even when he could not reasonably expect future personal gains from such retaliation. *Homo reciprocans* is neither the utopian socialist's unconditional altruist nor the hedonistic sociopath of neoclassical economics. Rather, he is a conditional cooperator whose strong instincts for sharing can be elicited, under the proper circumstances, towards achieving socially egalitarian goals.

A convenient starting point in tracing the birth of *Homo reciprocans* is the study of the iterated prisoner's dilemma undertaken two decades ago by Robert Axelrod at the University of Michigan.[10] Axelrod asked a number of behavioral scientists (game theorists, economists, political scientists, sociologists, and psychologists) to submit computer programs giving complete strategies for playing the iterated prisoner's dilemma. Each program was pitted against every other program, as well as itself and a program that randomly chose to cooperate and defect. The winner among the fourteen strategies submitted was the simplest, called 'tit-for-tat' (submitted by game theorist Anatol Rappoport). Tit-for-tat cooperates on the first round, and then does whatever its partner did on the previous round.

Following up on this result, Axelrod held a second tournament in which a larger number of participants, including the original contributors, were told of the success of tit-for-tat and asked to submit another program for playing the iterated prisoner's dilemma. Knowing that tit-for-tat was the strategy to beat did not help the players: once again Rappoport submitted tit-for-tat, and once again, it won.

Speculating on the strong showing of tit-for-tat, Axelrod noted that this strategy for cooperation has three attributes that are essential for successful cooperation. The first is that tit-for-tat is *nice*: it begins by cooperating, and it is never the first to defect. Second, tit-for-tat is *punishing*: it retaliates relentlessly against defection. Finally, tit-for-tat is *forgiving*: as soon as a defecting partner returns to cooperating, tit-for-tat returns to cooperating.

The reader may wonder whether a battle of computer games created by behavioral scientists has a counterpart in dynamic social processes. To explore this issue, we simulated a society composed of two hundred individuals. Each was assumed to follow a 'rule of thumb' represented by a particular strategy in playing an iterated prisoner's dilemma against a randomly chosen partner.[11] Our objective was to determine which, if any, of these rules of thumb would come to predominate in competition with a wide variety of alternative strategies played over thousands of generations.

In each round of the game, we randomly matched individuals and allowed them to play the prisoner's dilemma a varying number of times with each other. We determined the number of repetitions with a given partner by setting a probability of 2 per cent that the encounter would end with each play, so partners played an average of fifty repetitions with each other before the round terminated. We endowed our individuals with a memory of the three previous plays, so an individual strategy consisted of a particular response, cooperate or defect, for each of the eight possible patterns of cooperation and defection of the player's partner in the past three plays of the game. We also included in an individual strategy a predisposition to cooperate or defect upon an initial meeting of a new partner, so that in all there were over two thousand possible strategies, of which fewer than ten had the characteristics of tit-for-tat (nice, punishing, and forgiving). Finally, we randomly assigned a rule of thumb strategy to each player at the start of the simulation.

Our simulation is designed to represent the process of differential replication by either cultural learning or genetic copying. After each hundred rounds, with a certain probability, low-scoring individuals replaced their rules of thumb with those of high-scoring individuals. We also added a small probability that strategies had random mutations, so that new strategies were continuously injected into the game. The results are exhibited in figure 1. In this figure, the solid line is the fraction of all plays by all individuals using their given rules of thumb, playing the 'cooperate' move. The dashed line is the fraction of members of the population currently holding rules of thumb

Figure 1:   The Evolution of Cooperation in a Dynamic Setting

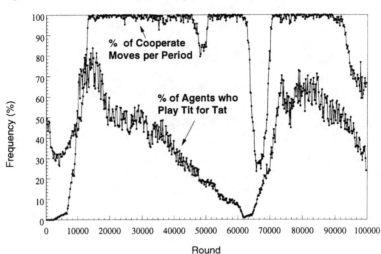

corresponding to the generic tit-for-tat behaviors, namely nice, punishing, forgiving.

In line with the Axelrod experiment, we find that after about
15,000 rounds the rate of cooperation has risen from 30 per cent at
the start to nearly 100 per cent, and the fraction of tit-for-tat strategies
has risen from zero to about 65 per cent. Since the level of cooperation
is so high at this point, however, players rarely meet defectors, and
hence the propensity to punish defectors is rarely exercised. As a
result, random mutations undermine the propensity to retaliate, until
by round 75,000, there are virtually no tit-for-tat'ers left, and the
dominant strategy types cooperate unconditionally. At this point, a
mutant defector can 'invade' the population of cooperators and do
extremely well. This accounts for the precipitous decline in cooperation at round 85,000, to a low of about 18 per cent. At this point the
benefits of tit-for-tat are restored, and there is a fairly rapid return to
cooperation, and the growth of tit-for-tat to almost its earlier peak
level. Once cooperation becomes complete, however, the process of
deterioration of tit-for-tat resumes.

This 'artificial life' experiment suggests that there may be a cyclical
pattern of rise and fall in the frequency of tit-for-tat strategies. In
periods in which levels of defection are high, tit-for-tat spontaneously
emerges as an individually successful strategy that leads to a very high
level of cooperation. In a highly cooperative society, however, the

attractive features of tit-for-tat disappear, and there is a movement towards unconditional cooperation (altruism) that in turn invites high levels of defection and non-cooperative behavior.

What does this have to do with people? There have been many experiments with human subjects involving the iterated prisoner's dilemma. If Axelrod's tournaments showed that nice guys finish first, the experiments reveal that there are lots of nice guys, even among the economics majors who show up for experimental games. Among the most revealing of these experiments use the 'public goods game', designed to illuminate such problems as the voluntary payment of taxes and the restriction of one's use of an endangered environmental resource. The following is a common variant. Ten subjects are told that $1.00 will be deposited in each of their 'private accounts' as a reward for participating in each round of the experiment. For every dollar they move from their 'private account' to a 'public account', the experimenter will deposit half a dollar in the private accounts of *each* of the subjects. This process will be repeated ten times, and at the end, the subjects can take home whatever they have in their private accounts.

In this public goods game, if all ten subjects are perfectly cooperative, each will put their $1.00 in the public account, and having received $10.00 in the public account, the experimenter will put $5.00 in the private account of *each* subject on each round, for a total of $50.00 per subject after ten rounds. But if a subject is perfectly selfish, he will keep all of his money in his private account, so if the other nine subjects remain perfectly cooperative, he will end up with $55.00 at the end of the game, and the other players will end up with $45.00 each. If all players are perfectly selfish, each will end up with $10.00 at the end of the game. It is thus clear that this is indeed an iterated prisoner's dilemma, since whatever anyone else does on a particular round, a player's highest pay-off comes from contributing nothing to the public account, but if all do this, all receive less than they would had all cooperated.

Public goods experiments of this type have been run literally hundreds of times, under varying conditions, since the pioneering work of the sociologist G. Marwell, the psychologist R. Dawes, the political scientist J. Orbell, and the economists R. Isaac and J. Walker in the late 1970s and early 1980s.[12] We may summarize this research as follows. Only a fraction of subjects conform to the *Homo economicus* model, contributing nothing to the public account. Rather, in the early stages of the game, people generally make contributions that average about halfway between the perfectly cooperative and the perfectly selfish levels. In the later stages of the game, contributions decay until at the end, they are close to the *Homo economicus* level.

Proponents of the *Homo economicus* model initially suggested that the reason for decay of public contribution is that participants really do not understand the game at first, and as they begin to learn it, they begin to realize the superiority of the free-riding strategy. However, there is considerable evidence that that interpretation is incorrect. For instance, Andreoni (1988) finds that when the whole process is repeated with the same subjects, the initial levels of cooperation are restored, but once again cooperation decays as the game progresses. Andreoni (1995) suggests a *Homo reciprocans* explanation for the decay of cooperation: public-spirited contributors want to retaliate against free-riders and the only way available to them in the game is by not contributing themselves.

Support for this *Homo reciprocans* interpretation has been supplied by Fehr and Gächter (1998). The experimenters here allow cooperators to retaliate directly against free-riders, at a cost to themselves. In this context, *Homo economicus* will always free-ride, and will never punish other free-riders, because punishing is itself a public good of little personal benefit to the punisher. In fact, however, the authors find that people do retaliate, and expecting this to happen, potential free-riders do not free-ride. The result is that cooperation begins as expected at about one half the total and over successive rounds *rises* to virtually complete cooperation.[13]

This research into public goods sharing shows an uncanny parallelism with Axelrod's computerized tournaments. Much like the tit-for-tat strategy, *Homo reciprocans* is nice, punishing, and forgiving. What is not clear from these experiments is that reciprocity involves a well-developed notion of *fairness*.

The notion of fairness underlying reciprocity is brought out in a series of experiments involving what have come to be known as *ultimatum games* and *dictator games*. In the ultimatum game (Guth *et al.*, 1982), the experimenter chooses two subjects and tells the first: 'I am going to provisionally allocate $10.00 to you. You, the proposer, can offer any amount of this, from nothing to the whole $10.00, to the other player, the respondent. If the respondent accepts your offer, he gets that amount and you get whatever is left over. If the respondent rejects your offer, I take back the $10.00 and you each get nothing.' If both proposer and respondent were *Homo economicus* in this game, the proposer would offer the respondent one cent, and the respondent would accept, the proposer walking away with $9.99. In fact, as dozens of replications of this experiment have documented, under varying conditions and with varying amounts of money, proposers commonly offer the respondent very substantial amounts, and respondents frequently reject offers that are below one-third of the total.[14] Similar results have occurred in experiments with stakes as high as three months' earnings.[15]

When asked why they offer more than one cent, proposers commonly say that they are afraid that respondents will consider low offers unfair and reject them as a way to punish proposer's unfairness. When respondents reject offers, they give virtually the same reasons for their actions. The proposers' actions might be explained by selfish motives but the respondents' cannot, and possibly anticipating the desire of the respondent to punish offers considered to be unfair, the proposer makes a substantial offer. The experimental evidence gives additional support to this interpretation. Thus Roth *et al.* (1991) conducted ultimatum games in four different countries (United States, Yugoslavia, Japan, and Israel), and found that while the level of offers differed in different countries, the probability of an offer being rejected did not. This indicates that both proposers and responders share the same notion of what is considered 'fair' in that society. In fact evidence from dictator games indicates that proposers also may act out of fairness motives. In the dictator game, the proposer offers a split of the money and the respondent has no choice but to accept. While proposers could keep all the money themselves, they typically offer respondents a considerable share of the total (Forsythe *et al.*, 1994, Hoffman *et al.*, 1996b).

A remarkable aspect of these experiments – and one very germane to our concern with redistributive policy – is the degree to which behaviors are affected by the experimentally contrived social relationship between players. Communication among participants prior to the game, or experimental conditions that reduce the subjective 'social distance' among participants, lead to higher and more sustained levels of generosity and cooperation.[16] For example, students facing a prisoner's dilemma pay-off structure tended nonetheless to cooperate rather than defect when they were matched with fraternity brothers, but to defect when they were informed that their partner was a police officer (Kollock, 1997). Eckel and Grossman (1997) found that proposers in a dictator game gave more when told that the respondent was the Red Cross, rather than another (anonymous) experimental subject. Finally, when the right to be proposer in the ultimatum game is 'earned', by being a 'winner' in a trivial knowledge quiz, proposers offered less, and respondents accepted lower offers (Hoffman *et al.*,

1994). It appears that minor manipulations of the social context of interactions may support significant behavioral differences.

In all of the experiments a significant fraction of subjects (about a quarter, typically) conform to the self-interested preferences of *Homo economicus*, and it is often the self-serving behavior of this minority that, when it goes unpunished, unravels initial generosity and cooperation.

These experiments also indicate that reciprocity is linked to a concept of fairness across all the societies studied, but that the content of fairness is somewhat flexible and subject to varying cultural forces. The following generalizations appear to be compatible with the experimental evidence. First, people exhibit significant levels of generosity, even towards strangers, the motivation for which may be compassion, just division, or perhaps other motives. Second, people feel a greater obligation to share that which they acquire through luck rather than through one's own efforts.[17] Third, people consider it fair to contribute to public goods and cooperate to collective endeavors, and unfair to free-ride on the contributions and efforts of others. Fourth, people consider it fair to punish free-riders, and do so even at substantial costs to themselves. Fifth, each of these aspects of reciprocity is more salient, the less is the perceived social distance among the participants.[18]

This model of *Homo reciprocans* supports our optimism concerning the possibility of egalitarian redistribution. Moreover, it may begin to explain widespread public opposition to welfare state policies in the advanced market economies in the past decades. Specifically, in light of the experimental regularities outlined above, we suspect the following to be true as well: redistributive policies that reward people independent of whether and how much they contribute to society are considered unfair and are not supported, even if the intended recipients are otherwise worthy of support, and even if the incidence of non-contribution in the target population is rather low. This would explain the opposition to many welfare measures for the poor, particularly since such measures are thought to have facilitated various social pathologies. At the same time it explains the continuing support for social security and Medicare in the United States, since the public perception is that the recipients are 'deserving' and the policies are incentive compatible. The public goods experiments are also consistent with the notion that tax resistance by the non-wealthy may stem from their perception that the well-to-do are not paying their fair share.

The implication of this analysis concerning our proposal for asset-based redistribution is straightforward. In our essay introducing this volume, we defended asset-based egalitarian redistribution on the grounds that it can be efficiency-enhancing, and by relocating control of productive resources to direct producers, it increases the scope for policies involving egalitarian wealth redistribution. We can now add another, and we think important, attractive feature: because asset-based redistribution makes the recipients residual claimants on the consequences of their actions, their rewards are more likely to be considered fair, and hence approved of by *Homo reciprocans*, thus justifying the social policies leading to these rewards.

We now turn to a reconsideration of the underlying economic logic of our proposals.

4 The Economic Logic of Sustainable Asset Redistribution

Our proposed redistribution of productive assets to direct producers and tenants raises three questions that we will now address. First, how might such a redistribution be implemented? Second, under what conditions would such a redistribution be sustainable in the sense that it would not be overridden by the post-redistribution exchange of titles by the beneficiaries of the redistribution and others? Third, what might be the scope for productivity-enhancing redistributions of this type?[19] We take up the first two questions in this section and the third in the subsequent section.

The distribution of assets in a population is a summary of who holds the right of residual claimancy on the income streams and the right of control over how the asset is used, as well as the right to reassign these rights through gift or sale.[20] As Michael Carter's contribution to this volume makes clear, how this distribution is determined is of critical importance to the possibility of a sustainable egalitarian asset-redistribution, and the question is of course hotly contested.

One view, associated with Marxism and the populist traditions, holds that property rights are acquired by *force*, and transmitted by inheritance. The other, fully developed in neoclassical economics, holds that the distribution of property rights reflects past earning and savings decisions by individuals as well as the imperatives of profitable use of assets imposed by the competitive process. As in the 'force' interpretation, this *choice* interpretation recognizes the role of inheritance as a determinant of the distribution of wealth. If the 'force' interpretation is correct, then the logic of asset redistribution is clear: the state can simply redistribute by *fiat*. On the one hand such a policy is legitimate, since it rectifies the wrong occasioned by the original forceful acquisition of property. On the other hand, it is permanent, since wealth will remain in the hands of the new owners and their heirs. In the force view, then, history matters, and the state through its coercive powers can simply impose a new set of initial conditions supporting a more egalitarian outcome.

But if the second, 'choice', view is correct, it may be that no redistribution of assets, whether egalitarian or otherwise, is sustainable in the long run. The reason according to this view is that individuals will simply adjust their saving and earning behavior to the windfall gain or loss associated with the asset redistribution, the winners saving and working less and the losers saving and working more, so as eventually to restore the initial distribution reflective of the underlying preferences and associated earning and saving behaviors. Moreover the new distribution of residual claimancy and control rights will be rearranged through the process of purchase and sale of titles to restore the initial competitively determined allocation. According to this view, a sustainable redistribution of assets requires an alteration of the incentive structures governing savings and investment or the process of inheritance, or both.

Michael Carter provides a vivid example of the reshuffling that may undo an asset-redistribution: in the Central Valley of Chile three quarters of those families who received individual assignment of land rights under a 1970s land redistribution program eventually sold their assets.[21] Carter's example points to an important distinction, that between the redistribution of wealth and the reassignment of control rights and residual claimancy. Consider this case in more detail. The Central Valley farmers sold both because they lacked sufficient wealth to make the investments necessary to participate in the lucrative fruit export boom and because the boom had raised land prices to very attractive levels (Jarvis, 1989). Selling their land increased the liquid assets of the beneficiaries, but also undid the associated reassignment of residual claimancy and control rights. In this case the wealth distribution may have been sustainable while the rights distribution was not.

There is some truth in both the 'force' and the 'choice' interpretation: as we will see presently, had the Chilean farmers received two hundred hectares each rather than an average of ten, the reassignment of rights might have proven sustainable. To see what is at issue, consider a society composed of a given number of workers and some lesser number of wealthy individuals. Let ω represent the fraction of the wealth owned by all workers and let δ represent the fraction of firms that are worker-owned (we assume the size of all firms has been given). Because the lack of wealth is one of the main impediments to worker-ownership of firms, δ varies with ω: when workers own a larger share of the total wealth of society, more find it possible and advantageous to acquire ownership of their workplace. Correspondingly, worker-owners are more likely to save and accumulate assets, both because their incomes will be higher on average (in joining a worker-owned firm they have chosen an income stream which is more risky but with a higher expected value) and being exposed to greater risk, they will save more from each unit of income.[22] Thus ω varies positively with δ. We picture the interaction of these two underlying causal relationships in figure 2, indicating the equilibrium distribution of wealth ω^* and the distribution of contracts δ^*. The equilibrium may be described as the level of worker-ownership consistent with the wealth-holding of workers, which is itself consistent with the fraction of workers in worker-owned enterprises.

Consider now a government-mandated redistribution of wealth to workers such that $\omega = \omega +$. What will be the long-term consequences? If none of the underlying relationships has changed, a succession of adjustments will lead first to an increased level of worker-ownership, but one insufficient to support the distribution of wealth $\omega+$, prompting dissaving by workers, followed by a gradual return to the equilibrium wealth and contractual distribution (ω^*, δ^*), as indicated by the arrow in figure 2. The initial redistribution $\omega+$ was thus unsustainable. When we refer to sustainable wealth redistributions we mean redistributions consistent with the kind of equilibrium described by (ω^*, δ^*).

How then might a more egalitarian distribution of wealth be sustainable? There are two ways. The first is by changing the incentives to hold and accumulate wealth. Extending credit to worker-owners on terms comparable to that of wealthy borrowers, for example, would make enterprise ownership more attractive to workers and thus would shift the $\delta(\omega)$ function upwards, supporting both a more egalitarian distribution of wealth w^{**} and a larger share δ^{**} of workers in worker-owned firms. The resulting changes are indicated by the dashed lines in figure 2. The new equilibrium $(\delta^{**}, \omega^{**})$ is sustainable as long as the credit subsidies remain in place. It should be noted that provision of adequate insurance to workers considered in isolation would shift δ upwards (the risk entailed by ownership would now be less onerous) and shift ω to the left (there would be a

Figure 2:   Equilibrium Wealth and the Fraction of Worker-owned
Firms

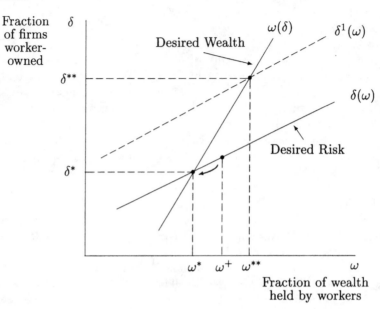

Fraction of wealth
held by workers

correspondingly reduced precautionary incentive to save), with indeterminate effect on the distribution of wealth and extent of worker-
ownership.

The second way that an egalitarian redistribution could be sustained requires that the asset transfer be large enough so that high-
return/high-risk projects that were previously unattractive to risk-
averse individuals with low wealth become attractive by dint of the
effect of their increased wealth in reducing their aversion to risk or
giving them favorable access to capital markets. In these cases, many
very unequal as well as many egalitarian distributions of wealth may
be self-sustaining, and in this case history does matter – see Bardhan
et al. (1999).

To see this, consider the case of an individual worker choosing
between allocating wealth to a low-risk asset (perhaps the family
residence) or putting a substantial fraction of it into a higher expected
return but also higher-risk asset, namely an ownership share in a
workplace. We make the reasonable assumption that the higher the
worker's wealth, the higher the level of risk that will be chosen.
Suppose that $\tilde{\omega}_c$ is the minimum amount of wealth holding that
would induce a worker to purchase the sizable share required for

Figure 3: Self-Sustaining Redistribution of Wealth for an Individual

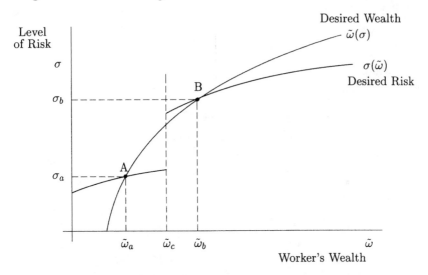

employment in a worker-owned firm. Let $\sigma(\tilde{\omega})$ be the amount of risk the individual would choose to sustain if his wealth were $\tilde{\omega}$. Then this schedule would be upward-sloping, with a discontinuity at $\tilde{\omega}_c$, where the worker shifts over to worker ownership. For levels of wealth below $\tilde{\omega}_c$ the worker chooses a low-risk low-return asset. Levels of wealth above $\tilde{\omega}_c$ induce the worker to hold a higher return but riskier asset, namely workplace ownership. This is depicted by the broken solid line through A and B with a vertical jump at $\tilde{\omega}_c$, labeled $\sigma(\tilde{\omega})$ in figure 3. Now let $\tilde{\omega}(\sigma)$ be the amount of wealth the individual would choose to hold, given a level of risk σ. The individual would adjust to this level of wealth by varying savings and taking more or less leisure.[23] We expect this curve to be upward-sloping, since the individual requires higher wealth as a buffer against the downside losses associated with a high level of risk exposure. This is indicated by the solid line through A and B in figure 3, labelled $\tilde{\omega}(\sigma)$.

To illustrate the case where a government mandated asset redistribution would be sustainable, we position the two curves so they intersect at two points, A and B.[24] The equilibria at A and B are both stable (small movements away from each equilibrium will be self-correcting, as was the initial redistribution to ω^* in figure 2). A and B are both sustainable outcomes. Moreover, if the individual begins at equilibrium A, any wealth distribution that leaves the worker with

Figure 4:   Multiple Equilibria in Wealth and Control of the
Enterprise

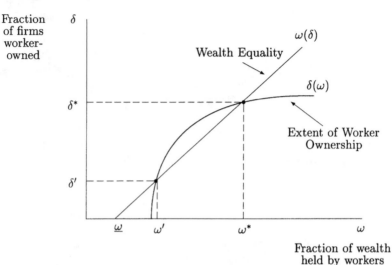

Fraction of wealth
held by workers

total wealth less than $\tilde{\omega}_c$ will induce a reduction in saving and an increase in leisure until wealth returns to $\tilde{\omega}_a$ at equilibrium A. However any wealth redistribution that pushes worker wealth just above $\tilde{\omega}_c$ will lead the individual to shift to worker-ownership, and to increase saving and decrease the amount of leisure taken until the self-sustaining, stable equilibrium at B is attained.

Policies to attenuate the credit and insurance market disabilities of the non-wealthy would reduce (perhaps to zero) the level of mandated redistribution necessary to induce a shift from the lower to the higher equilibrium. The reason is that insurance against market risks (that is, risk facing the worker-owned cooperative but not arising from an action taken by the cooperative) and credit to the worker-owned coop on favorable terms would reduce $\tilde{\omega}_c$, the level of wealth required to induce the worker to shift assets to ownership of the workplace.

The fact that more than one wealth *level* is sustainable for a given individual means that more then one wealth *distribution* is sustainable for the whole society. Suppose there were some minimum level of worker wealth below which no worker-owned firms could be formed, but above which there were many attractive opportunities for worker-owned firms, with successive increases in worker wealth opening up further opportunities, but at a diminishing rate, as is pictured in figure 4. Suppose the wealth function $\omega(\delta)$ is as it was presented in figure 2.

Figure 5:   Effect of Policies to Reduce Credit Market Constraints

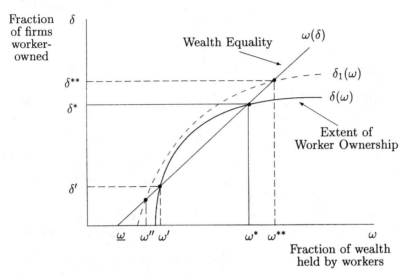

Fraction of wealth
held by workers

Then there are two stable equilibria in this economy: one with wealth $\underline{w}$ and no worker-owned firms, and the other with high levels of both worker wealth and ownership of workplaces (ω^*, δ^*). There is an unstable equilibrium in between (ω', δ'). Any initial distribution of wealth to workers above ω' will lead (by successive adjustments of savings behavior and extension of worker ownership) to the higher equilibrium; an initial distribution in which workers are less wealthy than ω' will lead to the low wealth, no worker ownership equilibrium. History definitely does matter in this case, and by like reasoning a one-time governmental redistribution by *fiat* might have durable effects.

Similarly, policies to overcome the credit market disabilities of wealth-poor workers, subsidized borrowing for example, would both lower the critical wealth hurdle ω' and increase the levels of worker wealth and ownership in equilibrium. These effects are illustrated in figure 5 by the upward shift of the (ω) schedule.

5   Outcomes

But are we correct in claiming that the lack of wealth limits the kinds of productive projects that are open to people? Do those without wealth suffer credit market handicaps sufficiently costly to explain the prevalence of capitalist firms, the considerable extent of residential and agricultural tenancy and the other forms of ownership which we think to be inefficient? Or are we simply wrong about the inefficiency of these forms?

That most people lack the wealth necessary to become residual claimants on the income created by their labor is not controversial. In the US in 1992 the median net worth of families in every occupational group fell well short of the mean capital–labor ratio for the economy as a whole. Few Americans hold wealth sufficient to purchase the tools with which they work. In all occupational groups except for 'professional and managerial', moreover, median wealth was less than half the capital–labor ratio (Kennickell and Starr-McCluer, 1994). The only major sectors of the US economy in which self employment is prevalent are personal services and retail trade. Consistent with our view, the capital–labor ratio in these sectors is less than a third of the average.[25] That residential tenancy is explained in large measure by wealth constraints is suggested by the fact that in the US the median level of net worth among the roughly one third of families who are renters is $3,700 while the median net worth of owners is $108,500 (Kennickell and Starr-McCluer, 1994).

But can those with a productive project not borrow? An informed look at the financial pages of most local newspapers will help answer this question. To compare the capital costs of an established capitalist firm with a new worker-owned firm, consider what each might have to pay on a substantial loan to purchase equipment. A start-up worker-owned firm, like its capitalist competitor, will be seeking to purchase industrial assets that may be highly specific to the project and thus have little salvage value if the project fails. Unlike its competitor, however, the cooperative will have virtually no collateral. While the established capitalist firm will be able to borrow funds at one or two percentage points below the prime rate, the cooperative proposal might be regarded as equivalent to an application for a used car loan, with interest rates (for those successful in securing a loan) typically four points above the prime rate.[26] An interest cost penalty of five or more points is more than enough to spell the difference between survival and extinction in highly competitive industries in which the real after tax profit rate of successful firms may be considerably less than ten per cent.

A few studies have sought to quantify the extent to which wealth constraints inhibit productive investment. Distinguishing cause from effect in evaluating the relationship between wealth and business opportunity is always difficult. A number of studies, however, have explored the changes in economic activity undertaken by individuals following an inheritance.[27] Blanchflower and Oswald (forthcoming), using the British National Child Development Study, found that controlling for many variables, including a broad set of personality characteristics associated with entrepreneurship, an inheritance of 5,000 British pounds renders an individual twice as likely to enter self-employment. Another British study (Holtz-Eakin et al., 1994b) found an elasticity of self-employment with respect to inherited assets of 0.52, and that inheritance leads the self-employed to increase the scale of their operations considerably. Black et al. (1996) found that as the collateral position of British families rises due to rising house prices the number of business startups increase significantly, holding constant other macroeconomic measures likely to affect business startups. Evans and Jovanovic (1989) find that among white males in the US, wealth levels are a barrier to becoming entrepreneurs, and that credit constraints typically limit those starting new businesses to capitalization of not more than 1.5 times their initial assets: 'most individuals who enter self-employment face a binding liquidity constraint and as a result use a suboptimal amount of capital to start up their businesses.'[28]

While we cannot be sure of the precise magnitude of the impediments to productive investment facing the non-wealthy, it appears that such impediments are substantial. A redistribution of wealth might eliminate or at least attenuate these impediments.

Have we exaggerated the productivity gains that asset redistribution might bring? These cannot be estimated with any precision. Nor is this our major concern. Indeed, we would expect egalitarians to favor some egalitarian redistributions even when they are *not* productivity-enhancing. However, in some areas the gains may be considerable. The worker-owned firms most closely approximating our suggested form of property rights and governance – the plywood cooperatives of the US Northwest – exhibit levels of productivity well in excess of the conventional capitalist firms with which they compete. The total factor productivity (measuring the productivity of both capital and labor combined) in the cooperatives was between 6 and 45 per cent higher than in the conventional capitalist firms.[29] The coexistence of the capitalist and worker-owned firms is most likely explained by the cooperatives' productivity advantages being offset by the heightened costs of capital and risk exposure of the worker-owners.

Further evidence comes from share contracting. Share contracts are a halfway house between a fixed-price contract like wage labor, and full residual claimancy associated with full ownership or working under a fixed land-rent contract. Share contracts are widely used in farming in both rich and poor economies, as well as in managerial labor markets. There is compelling evidence that these contracts are inefficient by comparison to full residual claimancy. The most telling evidence comes from a recent investigation of an agricultural community in Tunisia studied by Laffont and Matoussi (1995). Data on wealth levels, farming practices, details of other relevant contracts and other information allowed a particularly rich evaluation of the effects of contractual form on productivity. Farmers lacking wealth tended to farm under share arrangements, while those with more wealth mixed a fixed rent with a share contract, and those with even more wealth simply paid a fixed rent or owned the land outright. Laffont and Matoussi found that changing a contract from the typical share contract to full residual claimancy (with no other changes) increased predicted output by 49 per cent, indicating substantial disincentive effects of the share contracts under which those without wealth are working.[30]

Long-run effects on productivity will depend critically on the effectiveness of insurance and other risk-sharing policies in addressing the tendency of risk-averse owners with limited wealth to adopt overly conservative policies with respect to innovation. Any assessment of the balance of these productivity effects would be highly speculative.

The benefits of home ownership are perhaps less controversial. Our claim that home ownership would give residents more incentive to engage in efforts to improve not only their own residence but the community as well is suggested by a recent study showing that while home ownership does not predict higher levels of *national* political participation, it is highly significant as a predictor of *local* partici- pation, rivaling years in the community (with which it is correlated) and eclipsing the number of school-aged children.[31] Home ownership is also a strong predictor of many forms of beneficial community involvement, including the willingness to sanction the anti-social behaviors of neighbors (Sampson, Raudenbush and Earls 1997).

6 Concerns

We can now address some of the concerns raised in the comments by our colleagues.

First, we do not propose that workers be given the machinery which they now work with, for the simple reason that this would be unlikely to result in a sustainable redistribution of assets. Whatever led these workers not to be owners before the redistribution is likely to reassert itself following the redistribution. Like the farmers in the Central Valley of Chile, they would probably simply sell their assets. A further objection could be raised: the capital stock per worker varies greatly between sectors, the assets a petrochemicals worker deploys being worth more than twenty times that of a clothing worker. Redistributing existing assets to the workers currently using them would be unjust, as it would confer on some workers (for the most part the better paid) major increases in wealth, while conferring little on others, and none on those without jobs.

Rather, our proposals for credit subsidies and insurance to worker-owned firms or favorable terms for the purchase of low-income housing would effect the types of curve-shifting illustrated in figures 2 and 5. This approach has the advantage that it would support redistributions of assets that are sustainable because they contribute to the solution of costly incentive problems associated with concentrated wealth.

Second, we do not favor universal worker-ownership of firms or resident ownership of all housing. Both tenancy and capitalist ownership of firms serve the useful purposes already noted. We expect both forms would persist, though in reduced degree, under the proposals we advocate.

Third, we propose the rectification of market failures impeding investment by those without wealth.[32] But our egalitarianism is not limited to policies necessary to accomplish this: letting the poor borrow at the same rate of interest as the rich would be no small accomplishment, but the poor would for the most part remain poor. Rather, *our asset-based strategy is a means of reducing the cost of redistribution.* As such it is mute on the question of *how much* redistribution ought to be done. But by lowering the costs, it might make more extensive redistribution both morally defensible and politically feasible. To question whether our proposals entail 'enough' redistribution, as do some of the commentators in this book (Wright, Levine, and Hausman come to mind) is beside the point: a well-designed and substantial redistribution of assets would enhance the ability of large numbers of the non-wealthy to be more nearly the authors of their own lives. Remediable injustices would certainly remain. If we are correct, a low-cost way of rectifying some of these remaining injustices would be further policies of asset-based redistribution.

Fourth, by an 'asset' we mean any unconditional claim on a future income stream. Assets may be of two types, those which can be used as collateral and those which cannot. If the relevant government bodies were capable of credible commitments, an unconditional basic income grant promising a fixed real amount over the life of the citizen might be considered an asset, the same could be said of a child's secure claim on the income of her or his parents. But neither could readily be used as collateral.[33]

Breaking the credit market constraints facing the poor requires the redistribution of assets which are usable as collateral, such as land, residences, and productive equipment. However our case for asset-based redistribution is not (as was pointed out by England, Wright, Skott, Moene and Wallerstein and others in this volume) an argument against tax-and-transfer based redistribution *per se*. Our objection to the latter is that both the tax and the transfer are typically conditional on the income status of the recipient and this often shields the individual from the results of his or her actions. Tax-and-transfer systems may be designed to minimize these disincentive effects, and the effectiveness and political viability of social democratic redistribution may be substantially explained by the considerable success of social democratic governments in doing just this.[34]

Fifth, we have no adequate response to Harry Brighouse's thoughtful objection that our design for an egalitarian system of school choice may well not pass the political sustainability test precisely because its egalitarianism would be so transparent.[35] Without diminishing the problems he raises, we are prepared to take our chances with a democratic electorate as long as the policies in question are consistent with fundamental motivations of reciprocal fairness.

Sixth, we find Steven Durlauf's arguments for the benefits of associational redistribution important and we note that a number of our proposals might lead to greater homogeneity (of firms, for example, or schools) than currently exists. There thus may be unavoidable conflicts between gains associated with matching heterogeneous types, as advocated by Durlauf, and the economic benefits of endogenous enforcement in community-like organizations, which we have stressed. We note, however, that the efficiency gains indicated by Durlauf rely critically on presumed high levels of complementarity between different types of individuals in production or in other situations. We know of no evidence for complementarities of a magnitude sufficient to generate large economic gains through associational redistributions. Needless to say, the many other benefits of heterogeneity are not affected by this note of skepticism concerning Durlauf's proposal.

Seventh, John Roemer has criticized the private property basis of our egalitarian proposals, preferring public ownership. We agree with Roemer that restrictions on sale and use of assets along the lines embodied in William Simon's concept of 'social republican property' are often desirable. Indeed, our model of a worker-owned firm would place exactly such requirements in the form of limiting the use of nonowners as workers and limiting the ownership share of the capital stock held by nonmembers. However we believe that Roemer's concern that highly concentrated private wealth will detrimentally influence public policy is overly pessimistic, given precisely the capacity of a continuing process of asset-based redistribution to limit the concentration of wealth and of electoral reform in limiting the political power of moneyed interests.

Finally, a number of comments – including those by McCrate, Wright and Levine – express concerns that our proposals might favor the evolution of objectionable norms. These criticisms cannot be dismissed lightly because, as Elinor Ostrom has stressed, it is important to evaluate governance structures from the standpoint of their ability to foster desirable norms, and particularly to those conducive to solving coordination problems. We are mindful of the possibility that governance structures can sometimes undermine the moral basis of cooperation, thus exacerbating the coordination problems the structures are said to solve. Michael Taylor's (1987) demonstration that the Hobbesian man may be the product of living under a Hobbesian state comes to mind (see also Bowles 1998a).

The study of how institutions shape culture is still in its infancy and little can be said with confidence about the likely effects of the configuration of markets, communities, and states that we advocate. We know of no evidence, for example, that people in market societies are more selfish or more alienated from their fellow human beings than people in societies that rely less on market allocations.[36] By contrast there is some evidence that markets do not extinguish valued norms. Kollock (1997) and Fehr *et al.* (1997a) found that markets with incomplete contracts of the type we have stressed often support high levels of trust and of reciprocity even under perfectly competitive conditions. Third-party enforcement of complete contracts, not competition *per se*, may account for the self-regarding behaviors associated with markets.

In addition, we think that the autonomy *cum* responsibility associated with residual claimancy and control rights in productive assets supports enhanced individual dignity and mutual respect, as Jefferson and the Atlantic Republicans maintained. Home ownership is another example. As we have seen, there is evidence that a redistribution of titles to residential tenants would predictably encourage a norm of contributing to neighborhood social capital.

Another example is provided by school choice. A study of individuals in otherwise similar districts with and without choice options in New Jersey shows higher levels of both school- and non-school-related community involvement among those who had experienced choice over a long period (Schneider, 1997).

However we cannot exclude the possibility that markets might have some of the effects prompting the concerns of our critics. Indeed our current research on this topic suggests a disturbing possibility: where markets create an unfavorable environment for cooperative and generous norms they may do so precisely by enlarging the range of choices that people may take, a valued objective in its own right.[37]

7 Conclusion: Recasting Egalitarianism

In the essay opening this volume, we stressed the importance of developing *economically efficient* egalitarian policies. In the current essay, partially in light of the criticisms of our colleagues and partly through our own intellectual evolution, we have stressed the need to design egalitarian policies that affirm and evoke widely held *moral sentiments*. Asset-based redistribution, we have argued, fulfills both these requirements.

There is an obvious criticism of this new direction in our argument. 'Morality is socially determined,' we hear the reader musing, 'so why not transform morality to fit the needs of egalitarian policy rather than the other way around?' Have not radical egalitarians, from nineteenth-century abolitionists to contemporary feminists and civil libertarians, made consciousness raising a central part of their political practice? Why bow to the puny morality instilled by a society that thrives on greed, when we can look for a model of moral sentiments to the Enlightenment idea of the 'perfectibility of Man' and the socialist ideal of 'from each according to his ability, to each according to his need'? Why, in short, be trapped by the present in designing a future?

Our answer is that we have no choice. Abolitionists, feminists, civil libertarians, and advocates of the welfare state alike have been successful in appealing to the more elevated human motives precisely when they have shown that domination and inequality violate fundamental notions of reciprocal fairness and may be overcome, or at least attenuated, by policies and institutions consistent with these motives. Countless other egalitarian initiatives have failed.

The human mind is not a blank slate that is equally disposed to accept whatever moral rules are presented to it as valid, right and just. Rather human beings are predisposed to accept some moral rules, others can be imposed upon them with some difficulty, and still others cannot be imposed in any stable manner at all. Barrington Moore, Jr., in his comparative study of revolution and revolt, expresses this idea in the following words:

> awareness of social injustice would be impossible if human beings could be made to accept any and all rules. Evidently there are *some* constraints on the making of moral rules and therefore on the possible forms of moral outrage.

What accounts for our moral predispositions? The answer, uncontroversially, is some combination of genes and culture. Neither is immutable, but likewise neither is amenable to reconstruction in an arbitrary and ahistorical manner. The cultural and the genetic structures that frame our lives and affect our propensity to accept or reject particular moral principles are products of social and biological evolution. Moral principles succeed not because they conform to a particular philosophical, political, or religious logic, but because they have aided those individuals who have used them and those groups in which they have been prevalent. The individuals and social groups that have deployed these moral principles have flourished, while others that have not have perished or been assimilated.

The question as to whether genes or culture is more responsible for the inertial character of moral sentiments is not the issue, since genes and culture are evidently jointly responsible, and it is the nature of their interaction that is of importance for social change. Again quoting Barrington Moore,

> To the extent that there are any recurring or constant features in moral outrage, they would have to derive from the interaction between more or less constant aspects of human nature and equally recurring imperatives that stem from the fact that human beings live with each other, that is, in human society.

This is not to say that cultural change is always conservative and slow-moving, for we know that this is not the case. Rather it is to say that cultural change, like technical change, is subject to enduring laws and material constraints. The evidence is that among these regularities is the ease with which people assume the behavior of *Homo reciprocans* and the difficulty of devising egalitarian principles that violate norms of reciprocity. If we are correct, an egalitarian society can be built on the basis of these norms.

Notes

1. On goals, see Roemer (1993), van Parijs (1995), as well as the contributions of John Roemer and David Hausman in this volume.

2. One hardly need add that Jefferson's egalitarian impulse did not extend to women or to his or anyone else's slaves.

3. See Roemer (1996), chapters 5–8, for an elaboration of an egalitarian ethic based on personal responsibility. In some cases this goal may not be completely attainable. For instance, if an 'accident of birth' includes having irresponsible and uncaring parents, then indemnifying this accident rewards, and hence implicitly encourages, irresponsible parenting.

4. Our proposals are thus similar in spirit (if not in particulars) to those advanced recently by Gamble and Kelly (1996) and Przeworski (1995).

5. See Levy and Murnane (1992) for the Gini coefficient statistics and US Bureau of the Census (1993) for victimization rates.

6. Lane (1991), pp. 524–47 surveys the evidence. In one study of the United States (Oswald, 1994) being unemployed (statistically holding income constant) has a larger negative impact on subjective well-being than halving one's income, being divorced, separated or widowed. This is true for both men and women. For additional evidence and interpretation, see Brickman *et al.* (1978), Veenhoven (1984), Lane (1993) Argyle and Martin (1991), Oswald (1997), Clark and Oswald (1996), Easterlin (1974), Easterlin (1995) and Blanchflower *et al.* (1993).

7. See David Gordon's contribution to this volume. Gordon argues from cross-country comparisons that egalitarian objectives have not motivated workers' movements, but rather demands for job security, union or work council representation, and a rising real wage.

8. We have considerable confidence in the conclusions of Flannery *et al.*, in part because their study was replicated in a similar but distinct population. D.A. Weinstein, H.H. Shugart and C.C. Brandt (1983) studied the Quechua indians of the Peruvian highlands, concluding: 'A population without substructures for resource sharing is shown to be unstable in such an unpredictable environment ... Under such potential conditions of intense selection, complex sharing institutions should develop and be maintained' (pp. 201, 222).

9. The term is Ernst Fehr's. See Fehr and Tyran (1996).

10. See Axelrod and Hamilton (1981) and Axelrod (1984) for details and theoretical development. The iterated prisoners' dilemma is simply repeated play of the well-known game with 'winners' being those with high cumulative scores over however many rounds are played.

11. The details of this simulation are available from the authors.

12. For a summary of this research and an extensive bibliography, see Ledyard (1995).

13. These results are reported in Fehr *et al.* (1997b). For a similar outcome in an employer/employee simulation in which 'employers' can pay higher than market-clearing wages in hopes that 'workers' will reciprocate by supplying high levels of effort, see Fehr and Gächter (1998) and Fehr and Tyran (1996).

14. For examples and analyses of ultimatum games, see Forsythe *et al.* (1994), Hoffman *et al.* (1994), Hoffman *et al.* (April, 1996a), Roth *et al.* (1991).

15. See Cameron (1995) on experiments in Indonesia and Fehr and Tougareva (1995) on experiments in Russia.

16. For the communication result, see Isaac and Walker (1988), and for the social distance result, see Kollock (1997).

17. Fong (1998) shows that when people have differing beliefs about the role of effort in determining individual incomes, they are likely to support differing levels of redistribution, those holding the view that effort is important being less egalitarian. See also Piketty (1995).

18. There is an impressive body of experimental literature supporting the notion that human beings possess cognitive capacities specialized for dealing with the detection of defection from norms of cooperation and reciprocity. See Caporael (1987), Cosmides (1989), and Cosmides and Tooby (1992), who discuss the evidence and explain the phenomenon in terms of the fact that throughout most of its evolutionary history, *Homo sapiens* was organized socially in small groups who depended upon cooperation for survival.

19. We address this question in considerably greater detail in Bardhan *et al.* (1999).

20. See John Roemer's and Ugo Pagano's analyses of property rights in this volume. Our initial exposition of the logic of asset-redistribution was incomplete in a number of respects and we will take this opportunity to clarify and extend our position.

21. See Carter *et al.* (1996) as well as his contribution to this volume.

22. A Federal Reserve Bank survey suggests that such 'rainy day' motives for saving predominate. Reasons such as 'saving for reserves against unemployment' and 'saving in case of illness' grouped under the heading of 'liquidity reasons' for savings are far more important than saving for home buying, education or retirement (Kennickell and Starr-McCluer, 1994, p. 864).

23. See Bowles and Gintis (1996) for a complete exposition of this model.

24. We assume a dynamic adjustment process in which the individual adjusts both wealth and risk towards their equilibrium values, according to the equations

$$\frac{d\tilde{\omega}}{dt} = \gamma_{\tilde{\omega}}(\tilde{\omega}(\sigma) - \tilde{\omega}) \tag{1}$$

$$\frac{d\sigma}{dt} = \gamma_{\sigma}(\sigma(\tilde{\omega}) - \sigma) \tag{2}$$

where $\gamma_{\tilde{\omega}}, \gamma_{\sigma} > 0$ are coefficients reflecting the rate of adjustment.

25. See *Statistical Abstract of the United States* (1994) and Bates (1993).

26. The US Federal Reserve System reports that in 1992, interest rates on long-term loans of less than $100,000 to all borrowers averaged four and a half percentage points higher than on loans of a million dollars or more (Board of Governors of the Federal Reserve System, 1992).

27. Hoff's paper in this volume, as well as Malherbe (1996), summarizes these studies.

28. See also Evans and Leighton (1989).

29. See Craig and Pencavel (1995). The wide range of the estimates is based on differing techniques of estimation.

30. Hoff's essay in this volume presents additional evidence of impressive productivity gains associated with increased wealth of more closely aligned incentives of residual claimancy in agriculture.

31. See Verba *et al.* (1995), p. 453. Suggestive evidence that owner-occupiers provide more care for their units is the following: while maintenance costs of rental units for such items as roofing and plumbing are in line with maintenance costs for owner-occupied units, the painting maintenance costs for the tenant held units are almost double. See *Statistical Abstract of the United States* (1994), table 1224.

32. See also Karla Hoff's analysis in this volume, which complements our own.

33. South Africa's effectively unconditional old age pensions do sometimes provide the basis for credit not available to those without pensions (Ardington and Lund, 1995).

34. It is possible that in our original paper we exaggerated the disincentive effects of income-based redistribution. While a number of disincentive effects have been identified econometrically, evidence of large disincentive effects stemming either from taxation or redistributive expenditure has not been forthcoming, at least in the case of the United States (Moffit, 1992; Putterman et al., 1988).

35. See also Daniel Hausman's remarks on the sustainability of school choice.

36. See Lane (1991).

37. See Bowles and Gintis (1997), Bowles and Gintis (1998), Bowles (1998a), and Bowles (1998b).

References

Andreoni, James, 'Why Free Ride? Strategies and Learning in Public Good Experiments', Journal of Public Economics, 37 (1988), pp. 291–304.

——, 'Cooperation in Public Goods Experiments: Kindness or Confusion', American Economic Review, 85,4 (1995), pp. 891–904.

Ardington, Elisabeth and Frances Lund, 'Pensions and Development: Social Security as Complementary to Programs of Reconstruction and Development', Southern Africa, 12, 4 (August 1995), pp. 557–77.

Argyle, Michael and Maryanne Martin, 'The Psychological Causes of Happiness', in Michael Argyle and Norbert Schwartz (eds.), Subjective Well-Being (Oxford: Pergamon Press, 1991).

Axelrod, Robert, The Evolution of Cooperation (New York: Basic Books, 1984).

——, and William D. Hamilton, 'The Evolution of Cooperation', Science, 211 (1981), pp. 1390–6.

Bardhan, Pranab, Samuel Bowles, and Herbert Gintis, 'Wealth Inequality, Credit Contstraints, and Economic Performance', in Anthony Atkinson and François Bourguignon (eds.), Handbook of Income Distribution (North Holland, 1999).

Bates, Timothy, 'Banking on the Black Enterprise: The Potential of Emerging Firms for Revitalizing Urban Economies', Technical Report, Joint Center for Political and Economic Studies, Washington (1993).

Black, Jane, David de Meza, and David Jeffreys, 'House Prices, the Supply of Collateral and the Enterprise Economy', Economic Journal, 106 (January 1996), pp. 60–75.

Blanchflower, David and Andrew Oswald, 'What Makes a Young Entrepreneur?', Journal of Labor Economics (forthcoming).

Blanchflower, David G., Andrew J. Oswald, and Peter B. Warr, 'Well-Being over Time in Britain and the USA', November 1993, preprint.

Board of Governors of the Federal Reserve System, 'Survey of Terms of Bank Lending', Statistical Release E.2 (June 12 1992), reprinted in The State of Small Business: A Report to the President, (1994).

Bowles, Samuel, 'Mandeville's Mistake: The Evolution of Norms in Competitive Environments', University of Massachusetts Discussion Paper (1998a).

——, 'Endogenous Preferences: The Cultural Consequences of Markets and Other Economic Institutions', Journal of Economic Literature, 36 (March 1998b), pp. 75–111.

——, and Herbert Gintis, 'The Distribution of Wealth and the Assignment of Control Rights', University of Massachusetts Working Paper, (July 1996).

——, 'Optimal Parochialism: The Dynamics of Trust and Exclusion in Communities', University of Massachusetts Working Paper, (June 1997).

——, 'The Moral Economy of Community: Structured Populations and the Evolution of Prosocial Norms', *Evolution & Human Behavior*, 19 (January 1998), pp. 3–25.

Brickman, P., D. Coates and R. Janoff-Bulman, 'Lottery Winners and Accident Victims: Is Happiness Relative?', *Journal of Personality and Social Psychology*, 36 (1978), pp. 917–27.

Cameron, Lisa, 'Raising the Stakes in the Ultimatum Game: Experimental Evidence from Indonesia', Discussion Paper 345, Department of Economics, Princeton University, (1995).

Caporael, L. R., 'Homo Sapiens, Homo Faber, Homo Socians: Technology and the Social Animal', in W. Callebaut and R. Pinxten (eds.), *Evolutionary Epistemology: A Multiparadigm Program* (Reidel, 1987).

Carter, Michael, Bradford Barham, and Dina Mesbah, 'Agro Export Booms and the Rural Poor in Chile, Guatamala and Paraguay', *Latin American Research Review*, 31, 1 (1996), pp. 33–66.

Clark, Andrew E. and Andrew J. Oswald, 'Satisfaction and Comparison Income', *Journal of Public Economics*, 61, 3 (September 1996), pp. 359–81.

Cosmides, Leda, 'The Logic of Social Exchange: Has Natural Selection Shaped How Humans Reason? Studies with the Watson Selection Task', *Cognition*, 31 (1989), pp. 187–276.

——, and John Tooby, 'Cognitive Adaptations for Social Exchange', in Jerome H. Barkow, Leda Cosmedes, and John Tooby (eds.), *The Adapted Mind* (New York: Oxford, 1992), pp. 162–228.

Craig, Ben and John Pencavel, 'Participation and Productivity: A Comparison of Worker Cooperatives and Conventional Firms in the Plywood Industry', *Brookings Papers: Microeconomics* (1995), pp. 121–60.

Easterlin, Richard A., 'Does Economic Growth Improve the Human Lot? Some Empirical Evidence', in *Nations and Households in Economic Growth: Essays in Honor of Moses Abramovitz* (New York: Academic Press, 1974).

——, 'Will Raising the Incomes of All Increase the Happiness of All?', *Journal of Economic Behavior and Organization* (June 1995).

Eckel, Catherine and Philip Grossman, 'Chivalry and Solidarity in Ultimatum Games', (Virginia Polytechnic Institute, Working Paper E92–23, February 1997).

Evans, David and Linda Leighton, 'Some Empirical Aspects of Entrepreneurship', *American Economic Review*, 79, 3 (June 1989), pp. 519–35.

Fehr, Ernst and E. Tougareva, 'Do Competitive Markets with High Stakes Remove Reciprocal Fairness? Experimental Evidence from Russia', (Working Paper, Institute for Empirical Economic Research, University of Zürich, 1995).

——, and Jean-Robert Tyran, 'Institutions and Reciprocal Fairness', *Nordic Journal of Political Economy* (1996).

——, and Simon Gächter, 'Cooperation and Punishment', Working Paper, Institute for Empirical Economic Research, University of Zürich, 1998).

——, Erich Kirchler and Andreas Weichbold, 'When Social Norms Overpower Competition – Gift Exchange in Labor Markets', *Journal of Labor Economics* (forthcoming 1997).

——, Simon Gächter and Georg Kirchsteiger, 'Reciprocity as a Contract Enforcement Device', *Econometrica* 65, 4 (July 1997), pp. 833–60.

Flannery, Kent, Joyce Marcus, and Robert Reynolds, *The Flocks of the Wamani: A Study of Llama Herders on the Puntas of Ayacucho, Peru* (San Diego: Academic Press, 1989).

Fong, Christina, 'Economic Experience, Endogenous Beliefs, and Public Generosity' (University of Massachusetts, 1998).

Forsythe, Robert, Joel Horowitz, N. E. Savin, and Martin Sefton, 'Replicability, Fairness and Pay in Experiments with Simple Bargaining Games', *Games and Economic Behavior* 6, 3 (May 1994), pp. 347–69.

Gamble, Andrew and Gavin Kelly, 'The New Politics of Ownership', *New Left Review*, 220 (November–December 1996), pp. 63–97.

Güth, Werner, R. Schmittberger, and B. Schwarz, 'An Experimental Analysis of Ultimatum Bargaining', *Journal of Economic Behavior and Organization*, 3 (May 1982), pp. 367–88.

Hoffman, Elizabeth, Kevin McCabe and Vernon L. Smith, 'Social Distance and Other-Regarding Behavior in Dictator Games', *American Economic Review*, 86, 3 (June 1996), pp. 653–60.

———, 'Behavioral Foundations of Reciprocity: Experimental Economics and Evolutionary Psychology', (April, 1996). Unpublished.

Hoffman, Elizabeth, Keith Shachat and Vernon L. Smith, 'Preferences, Property Rights, and Anonymity in Bargaining Games', *Games and Economic Behavior*, 7 (1994), pp. 346–80.

Holtz-Eakin, Douglas, David Joulfaian and Harvey S. Rosen, 'Entrepreneurial Decisions and Liquidity Constraints', *RAND Journal of Economics*, 25, 2 (Summer 1994), pp. 334–47.

———, 'Sticking it Out: Entrepreneurial Survival and Liquidity Constraints', *Journal of Political Economy*, 102, 1 (1994), pp. 53–75.

Isaac, R. Mark and James M. Walker, 'Group Size Effects in Public Goods Provision: The Voluntary Contribution Mechanism', *Quarterly Journal of Economics*, 103 (1988), pp. 179–200.

Jarvis, Lovell, 'The Unravelling of Chile's Agrarian Reform, 1973–1986', in William Thiesenhusen (ed.), *Searching for Agrarian Reform in Latin America*, (Boston: Unwin–Hyman, 1989), pp. 240–65.

Jefferson, Thomas, *The Papers of Thomas Jefferson, Volume I: 1760–1776*, Julian P. Boyd (ed.), (Princeton, NJ: Princeton University Press, 1950).

Kahneman, Daniel, 'The Cognitive Psychology of Consequences and Moral Intuition', (Princeton University, 1993).

Kennickell, Arthur B. and Martha Starr-McCluer, 'Changes in Family Finances from 1989 to 1992: Evidence from the Survey of Consumer Finances', *Federal Reserve Bulletin*, 80, 10 (October 1994), pp. 861–82.

Kollock, Peter, 'Transforming Social Dilemmas: Group Identity and Cooperation', in Peter Danielson (ed.), *Modeling Rational and Moral Agents* (Oxford: Oxford University Press, 1997).

Laffont, Jean Jacques and Mohamed Salah Matoussi, 'Moral Hazard, Financial Constraints, and Share Cropping in El Oulja', *Review of Economic Studies*, 62 (1995), pp. 381–99.

Lane, Robert, *The Market Experience* (Cambridge: Cambridge University Press, 1991).

Lane, Robert E., 'Does Money Buy Happiness?', *The Public Interest*, 113 (Fall 1993), pp. 56–65.

Ledyard, J.O., 'Public Goods: A Survey of Experimental Research', in J.H. Kagel and A.E. Roth (eds.), *The Handbook of Experimental Economics* (Princeton: Princeton University Press, 1995), pp. 111–94.

Levy, Frank and Richard Murnane, 'US Earnings Levels and Earnings Inequality: A Review of Recent Trends and Proposed Explanations', *Journal of Economic Literature*, 30, 3 (September 1992), pp. 1333–81.

Malherbe, Paul, 'Effects of Wealth Constraints on Self-Employment: A Survey of Empirical Evidence', (University of Massachusetts Working Paper, 1996).

Moene, Karl Ove and Michael Wallerstein, 'Solidaristic Wage Bargaining', *Nordic Journal of Political Economy*, 22 (1995), pp. 79–94.

Moffit, Robert, 'Incentive Effects of the US Welfare System: A Review', *Journal of Economic Literature*, 30, 1 (March 1992), pp. 1–61.

Moore, Jr. Barrington, *Injustice: The Social Bases of Obedience and Revolt* (White Plains: M.E. Sharpe, 1978).

Oswald, Andrew J., 'Four Pieces of the Unemployment Puzzle', (London School of Economics, 1994).

Oswald, Andrew J., 'Happiness and Economic Performance', *Economic Journal*, 107, 445 (November 1997), pp. 1815–31.

Parsons, Talcott, 'Evolutionary Universals in Society', *American Sociological Review*, 29, 3 (June 1964).

Piketty, Thomas, 'Social Mobility and Redistributive Politics', *Quarterly Journal of Economics*, CX, 3 (August 1995), pp. 551–84.

Przeworski, Adam, 'Commentario', in Fundacao Alexandre Gusmao (ed.), *O Brasil e as tendencias economicas e politicas contemporaneas* (Brasialia: Fundacao Alexandre Gusmao, 1995).

Putterman, Louis, John E. Roemer, and Joaquim Silvestre, 'Does Egalitarianism Have a Future?', *Journal of Economic Literature* (1988).

Roemer, John, *A Future for Socialism* (Cambridge: Harvard University Press, 1993).

——, *Theories of Distributive Justice* (Cambridge: Harvard University Press, 1996).

Roth, Alvin E., Vesna Prasnikar, Masahiro Okuno-Fujiwara and Shmuel Zamir, 'Bargaining and Market Behavior in Jerusalem, Ljubljana, Pittsburgh, and Tokyo: An Experimental Study', *American Economic Review*, 81, 5 (December 1991), pp. 1068–95.

Sampson, Robert J., Stephen W. Raudenbush and Felton Earls, 'Neighborhoods and Violent Crime: A Multilevel Study of Collective Efficacy', *Science*, 277 (August 15, 1997), pp. 918–24.

Schneider, Mark, 'Institutional Arrangements and the Creation of Social Capital: The Effects of Public School Choice', *American Political Science Review*, 91, 1 (March 1997), pp. 82–93.

Statistical Abstract of the United States, (Washington, DC: US Department of Commerce, 1994).

Taylor, Michael, *The Possibility of Cooperation* (Cambridge: Cambridge University Press, 1987).

US Bureau of the Census, *National Crime Survey* (Washington: Government Printing Office, 1993).

van Parijs, Philippe, *Real Freedom for All: What (if anything) Can Justify Capitalism?* (Cambridge: Cambridge University Press, 1995).

Veenhoven, R., *Conditions of Happiness* (Dortrecht: Reidel Press, 1984).

Verba, Sidney, Kay Lehman Schlozman, and Henry Brady, *Voice and Equality: Civic Voluntarism in American Politics* (Cambridge, MA: Harvard University Press, 1995).

Weinstein, D.A., H.H. Shugart, and C.C. Brandt, 'Energy Flow and the Persistence of a Human Population: A Simulation Analysis', *Human Ecology*, 11, 2 (1983), pp. 201–23.

Wright, Erik Olin, *Interrogating Inequality* (London: Verso, 1994).